# MAMMAL ANATOMY

## *An Illustrated Guide*

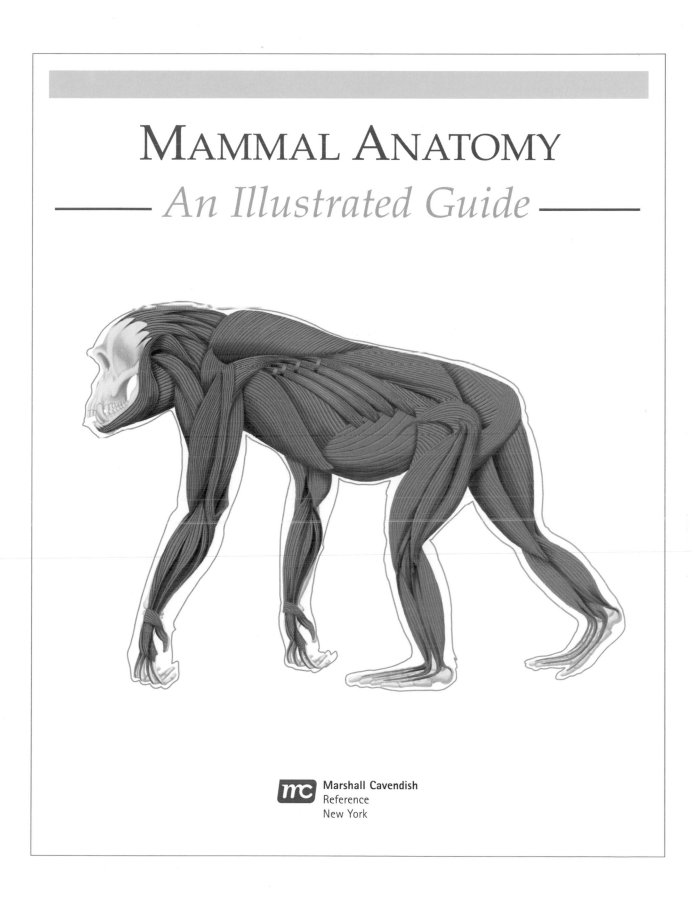

**Marshall Cavendish**
Reference
New York

**Marshall Cavendish**
99 White Plains Road
Tarrytown, NY 10591–9001

www.marshallcavendish.us



**Library of Congress Cataloging-in-Publication Data**

Mammal anatomy : an illustrated guide.
p. cm.
Includes bibliographical references and index.
ISBN 978-0-7614-7882-9 (alk. paper)
1. Mammals--Anatomy. 2. Mammals--Anatomy--Pictorial works. I. Marshall Cavendish Corporation.
QL739.M35 2010
571.3'19--dc22

2009011440

Printed in Malaysia
13 12 11 10 09 1 2 3 4 5

This work is not intended for use as a substitute for advice, consultation, or treatment by licensed practitioners. The reader is advised that no action of a medical or therapeutic nature should be taken without consultation with licensed practitioners, including action that may seem to be indicated by the contents of this work, since individual circumstances vary and medical standards, knowledge, and practices change with time. The publishers, authors, and consultants disclaim all liability and cannot be held responsible for any problems that may arise from use of this work.

MARSHALL CAVENDISH
*Publisher:* Paul Bernabeo
*Production Manager:* Michael Esposito

THE BROWN REFERENCE GROUP PLC
*Managing Editor:* Tim Harris
*Subeditors:* Jolyon Goddard, Paul Thompson
*Designers:* Bob Burroughs
*Picture Researcher:* Laila Torsun
*Indexer:* Kay Ollerenshaw
*Design Manager:* David Poole
*Editorial Director:* Lindsey Lowe

PHOTOGRAPHIC CREDITS
**Cover illustration is a composite of anatomical illustrations found within this work.**

**Ardea:** Francois Gohier 83, Denise Herzing 43; **Corbis:** Tom Brakefield 266, Layne Kennedy 236r, Craig Lovell 260-261, Neil Rabinowitz 99, RF 143; **Digital Stock:** 45, 149, 178, 257, 261; **FLPA:** Frans Lanting 171, S & D & K Maslowski 227, Flip Nicklin 98; **Getty Images:** Chabruken 125; **John Foxx Images:** 71; Nature PL: Doug Allan 205, 206, Hermann Brehm 61, Andrew Cooper 233, Richard Du Toit 258, Jeff Foott 102, Jurgen Freund 198, Tony Heald 49, Jorma Luhta 223b, Vincent Munier 211, Doug Perrine 196, 200, Todd Pusser 101, Anup Shah 9, 15, 20, 23, Lynn M. Stone 240, Jeff Turner 253, Tom Vezo 254, Dave Watts 153, David Welling 251, Doc White 26, 87; **NOAA:** Jan Roletto 86; **Photodisc:** 7, 105, 145, 169, 175, James Gritz 92, Jack Hollingsworth 65; Photolibrary Group: Satoshi Kuribayashi 223t, Stan Osolinski 225, Richard Packwood 217, Gerard Soury 215; **Photos.com:** 25, 28, 48, 52, 53, 63, 69, 79, 81, 121, 128, 131, 163, 165, 180, 183, 247, 248, 271, 275; **Rex Features:** Sunada 135; **Still Pictures:** Fred Bavendam 188, 191, John Cancalosi 231, Mark Carwardine 34, Doug Cheeseman 269, 273, Marco Cristofori 182, Douglas Faulkner 194, Michel Gunther 255, Martin Harvey 12, Robert Henno 185, In the Light 119, 243, Steven Kazlowski 123, 209, Rolf J. Kopfle 219, 245, Luiz C. Marigo 237, Lynn & Donna Rogers 236l, Kevin Schafer 29, Roland Seitre 152, 160, Dave Watts 158, Peter Weimann 235, Norbert Wu 203; Topfoto: 74, Jeff Greenberg 126.

**Artworks:** The Art Agency, Mick Loates, Michael Woods.

# Contents

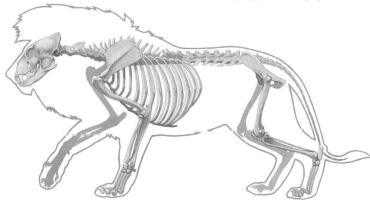

# CONSULTANTS AND CONTRIBUTORS

## CONSULTANTS

- Barbara J. Abraham, PhD, Interim Chair, Department of Biological Sciences, Hampton University, Hampton, VA. • Glen Alm, MSc, Mushroom Research Program, University of Toronto, Ontario, Canada. • Roger Avery, PhD, former Senior Lecturer in Zoology, Bristol University, England. • Amy-Jane Beer, PhD, Director of natural history consultancy Origin Natural Science. • Deborah Bodolus, PhD, Department of Biological Sciences, East Stroudsburg University, PA. • Allan J. Bornstein, PhD, Department of Biology, Southeast Missouri State University, Cape Girardeau, MO. • Erica Bower, PhD, consultant to Royal Botanic Gardens, Kew, England. • John A. Cline, PhD, Assistant Professor in Tree Fruit Physiology, Department of Plant Agriculture, University of Guelph, Ontario, Canada. • Trevor Day, marine scientist and visiting lecturer, University of Bath, England. • John Friel, PhD, Curator of Fishes, Amphibians, and Reptiles, Cornell University Museum of Vertebrates, Research Associate, Department of Ecology and Evolutionary Biology, Cornell University, NY. • Valerius Geist, PhD, Professor Emeritus of Environmental Science, University of Calgary, Alberta, Canada. • John L. Gittleman, PhD, Scientific Fellow of The Zoological Society of London and Professor of Biology, University of Virginia, Charlottesville, VA. • Tom Jenner, PhD, teacher, Academia Britanica Cuscatleca, El Salvador. • Bill Kleindl, MSc, aquatic ecologist. • Thomas H. Kunz, PhD, Director, Center for Ecoology and Conservation Biology, Boston University, MA. • Alan C. Leonard, PhD, Professor of Biological Sciences, Florida Institute of Technology, Melbourne, FL. • Sally-Anne Mahoney, PhD, neuroscience researcher, Bristol University, England. • Chris Mattison, herpetologist and author, Sheffield, England. • Andrew S. Methven, PhD, Professor and Chair, Department of Biological Sciences, Eastern Illinois University, Charleston, IL. • Graham Mitchell, PhD, Malaria Laboratory, GKT School of Medicine, Guy's Hospital, London, England. • Richard J. Mooi, PhD, Curator of Echinoderms, California Academy of Sciences, San Francisco, CA. • Ray Perrins, PhD, former neuroscience researcher, Mount Sinai Medical Center, New York. • David Spooner, PhD, Professor of Horticulture, University of Wisconsin, Madison, WI. • Adrian Seymour, PhD. Senior Forest Scientist, Operation Wallacea Indonesia Program. • John Stewart, BSc, researcher, Natural History Museum, London, England. • Erik Terdal, PhD, Associate Professor of Biology, Northeastern State University, Broken Arrow, OK. • Philip J. Whitfield, PhD, Professor, School of Health and Life Sciences, Kings College, University of London.

## CONTRIBUTORS

- Amy-Jane Beer, PhD, Director of natural history consultancy Origin Natural Science. • Trevor Day, PhD, marine scientist and visiting lecturer, University of Bath, England. • Robert Houston, PhD, natural history writer, London, England. • Tom Jackson, BSc, natural history writer, Bristol, England. • Adrian Seymour, PhD, zoological researcher and natural history writer, Bristol, England. • Steven Swaby, Natural History Museum, London, England. • John Woodward, natural history writer, Sussex, England.

# Foreword

**I**t took evolution millions of years to sculpt the world around us, but fully one quarter (and maybe as many as one third) of the 5,487 mammal species known are now endangered, which means we can expect to see hundreds of them going extinct within just a few decades if there are no concerted efforts to save them.

The staggering magnitude of that potential loss is hard to comprehend—until you encounter the diversity of mammal species whose anatomy, adaptations, and taxonomy are so wonderfully summarized in *Mammal Anatomy: An Illustrated Guide*. The 14 species and groups featured herein receive copious illustration, calling attention to salient aspects of mammal external appearance and skeletal, muscular, nervous, circulatory-respiratory, digestive-excretory, and reproductive systems, clearly explained in a way that shows what makes each one of them special, and what unites them as mammals. Besides *Homo sapiens*, the selection includes denizens of the oceans (gray whales, manatees, dolphins, and seals), favorites of the African savannah (elephants, giraffes, zebras, and lions), those you are apt to see in some American national parks (grizzly bears, wolves, and squirrels), and our closest living non-human relatives, chimpanzees, with whom humans share nearly 99 percent of our DNA.

Ultimately, what makes any species special is the mode of life to which it became adapted. What makes this selection of mammals special is that collectively it illustrates the astonishing diversity of adaptations that give mammals the ability to thrive in nearly every corner of Earth, on land and in the sea. Contrast, for example, the anatomy of a gray whale, making its way from the balmy seas of Mexico to frigid Arctic waters much more easily than a submarine can, with the form of a kangaroo bounding across the hot, dry Australian outback so effortlessly it puts a dirt biker to shame. Then the immensity of what evolution has accomplished in the way of building mammal biodiversity becomes immediately apparent.

Building that kind of diversity is not an overnight project. The range of anatomy exemplified by whales, kangaroos, and people is the end result of at least 225 million years of evolution's work, which traces back to the earliest mammal we know about, a small shrewlike thing dodging around the feet of dinosaurs. That it took so long for mammalian diversity to build makes it particularly important to know that the survival of most of the mammals selected for this book is threatened.

This series of articles, therefore, is more than a beautifully illustrated guide to an exceptionally interesting set of mammals. It is that, for sure, and for that reason alone it is a superb resource for anyone interested in mammals, including students who simply want a fast go-to for essential facts, as well as specialists who need more comprehensive, topically wide-ranging information that is nicely organized and easy to use. But, in its comparative approach and astute selection of species, this book is also a testament to the intricate ways that nature is built, and what we stand to lose if we allow these species to disappear.

**Anthony D. Barnosky**

*Anthony D. Barnosky is Professor of Integrative Biology and Curator of Fossil Mammals in the Museum of Paleontology, and Research Paleoecologist in the Museum of Vertebrate Zoology, both at the University of California, Berkeley*

The articles on mammal anatomy included in this work are also available by subscription online from Marshall Cavendish Digital at www.marshallcavendishdigital.com as part of a larger encyclopedic work, *Animal and Plant Anatomy*, which also contains more than 80 additional articles on the anatomy of other organisms.

# Chimpanzee

ORDER: Primates  FAMILY: Hominidae  GENUS: *Pan*

The common chimpanzee is the closest living relative of human beings. Chimpanzees are intelligent and adaptable and live in complex social groups in African forests. They are good climbers, sleeping and feeding mostly in the trees. On the ground they walk on four legs or on two, leaving the hands free to carry food, young, or simple tools.

## Anatomy and taxonomy

Scientists group all organisms into taxonomic groups based largely on anatomical features. Chimpanzees belong to the great ape family, in the mammalian order Primates. As well as monkeys and apes, this order also includes the prosimians (species such as bush babies and lemurs).

● **Animals** Animals are multicellular organisms that feed on organic matter from other organisms. They are able to move at least some parts of their body, using muscles, and they are able to sense their environment and respond rapidly to stimuli.

● **Chordates** Chordates are a large group of animals that at some point in their life cycle have a stiff rod called a notochord running along the back and providing support for the body.

● **Vertebrates** The majority of chordates are vertebrates—animals in which the supportive function of the notochord is gradually substituted by a spine, or backbone, made up of separate units called vertebrae. Vertebrate animals are bilaterally symmetrical, with muscles in a paired arrangement on either side of the body, and a distinct head at the front (anterior) end.

● **Mammals** Mammals are warm-blooded vertebrates with a body at least partially covered by hair or fur. Females usually give birth to live young and suckle them on milk from mammary glands. Mammalian red blood cells lack nuclei. The lower jaw (mandible) of mammals hinges directly with the upper part of the skull, the cranium.

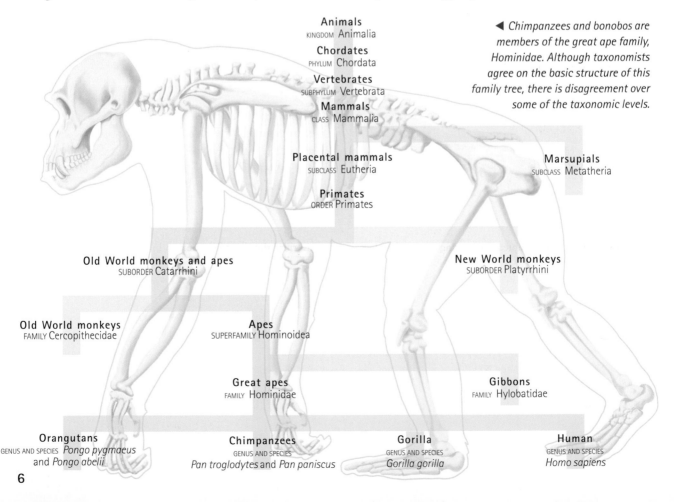

◄ *Chimpanzees and bonobos are members of the great ape family, Hominidae. Although taxonomists agree on the basic structure of this family tree, there is disagreement over some of the taxonomic levels.*

**Animals**
KINGDOM Animalia

**Chordates**
PHYLUM Chordata

**Vertebrates**
SUBPHYLUM Vertebrata

**Mammals**
CLASS Mammalia

**Placental mammals**
SUBCLASS Eutheria

**Marsupials**
SUBCLASS Metatheria

**Primates**
ORDER Primates

**Old World monkeys and apes**
SUBORDER Catarrhini

**New World monkeys**
SUBORDER Platyrrhini

**Old World monkeys**
FAMILY Cercopithecidae

**Apes**
SUPERFAMILY Hominoidea

**Great apes**
FAMILY Hominidae

**Gibbons**
FAMILY Hylobatidae

**Orangutans**
GENUS AND SPECIES *Pongo pygmaeus* and *Pongo abelii*

**Chimpanzees**
GENUS AND SPECIES *Pan troglodytes* and *Pan paniscus*

**Gorilla**
GENUS AND SPECIES *Gorilla gorilla*

**Human**
GENUS AND SPECIES *Homo sapiens*

● **Placental mammals** Eutherian, or placental, mammals give birth to live young in a relatively advanced state of development. While in the uterus, a fetus is sustained by nutrients from the mother's blood, which are transferred to the fetus's bloodstream via a complex temporary organ (the placenta) and an umbilical cord.

● **Primates** Primates are mammals with a long back, a short neck, and grasping hands and feet. Most species have five digits on the hands and feet. Their forearms are linked to the chest by clavicles (collarbones) and move freely in three dimensions. The head is rounded with forward-facing eyes. All primates have hairless finger and toe pads, and hairless palms and soles. Most species have flat nails rather than claws.

● **Old World monkeys and apes** These primates are called catarrhines, from a Greek word meaning hook-nosed, and are named for their small nose, in which the nostrils are separated by a narrow septum. The other major primate group at this taxonomic level, the platyrrhines, New World monkeys, have a flat nose with widely spaced nostrils.

● **Apes** The ape superfamily includes both the gibbons, or lesser apes (family Hylobatidae), and the great apes (family Hominidae). There are 11 living species of gibbons, all of which—in common with great apes—lack a tail. Their arms are very long and their lifestyle is highly arboreal (living in trees). The great apes are large primates with a compact barrel-shaped body, long forearms, a large round head with a big brain, and highly dexterous hands. The great apes include just six living species: orangutans, gorillas, the two species of chimpanzees (common and bonobo), and humans. Orangutans have flowing orange or maroon hair, immensely powerful arms and handlike feet. The two species of orangutans in southeast Asia are the most

▲ *Chimpanzees and bonobos are humans' closest living relatives. They share 99 percent of DNA with humans.*

arboreal of the great apes. Gorillas are the largest of the great apes, and they spend most of the time on the ground, moving on four legs. The three subspecies of gorillas (the mountain gorilla and the eastern and western lowland gorillas) all live in central Africa. Humans are by far the most common and widespread of all primate species, and the only species to walk habitually on two legs.

● **Chimpanzees** There are two species of chimpanzees. Despite its name, the pygmy chimpanzee, or bonobo, is about the same height as the common chimpanzee and only slightly smaller in build. Both species' mobile lips enable a wide range of facial expressions, similar in meaning to those of humans.

**EXTERNAL ANATOMY** Chimpanzees are agile, with a stout, tailless body adapted for moving fast on four legs or on two. The head is small and round with a short, expressive face. *See pages 8–9.*

**SKELETAL SYSTEM** The skeleton is distinguished by a broad, barrel-shaped rib cage; a slouching upright posture; and arms significantly longer than the legs. The skull lacks a forehead, chin, and pronounced sagittal crest but has a prognathic (protruding) jaw. *See pages 10–12.*

**MUSCULAR SYSTEM** The chimpanzee's musculature is very similar to that of other large primates. Specialized muscles exist both for great strength (as in the arms and shoulders) and for fine, subtle movements (as in the hands and face). *See pages 13–15.*

**NERVOUS SYSTEM** The brain is large but only about one-third the size of the human brain. *See pages 16–17.*

**CIRCULATORY AND RESPIRATORY SYSTEMS** These body systems are very similar to those of other great apes, including humans, with which chimpanzees share the same major ABO blood groups. *See page 18.*

**DIGESTIVE AND EXCRETORY SYSTEMS** Large teeth, a simple stomach, and a short intestine process a highly diverse diet containing large quantities of ripe fruit, other plant material, and meat. *See pages 19–20.*

**REPRODUCTIVE SYSTEM** Single young or twins are born at intervals of several years. The young require years of devoted parental care, during which skills are learned and complex social bonds are formed. *See pages 21–23.*

# External anatomy

**COMPARE** the bipedal posture of the chimpanzee with the four-legged stance of the *MANDRILL*.

**COMPARE** the opposable thumb of a chimpanzee with the nonopposable digits of a *LION*.

CONNECTIONS

Chimpanzees are the closest living cousins of modern humans, and chimpanzees are more closely related to us than they are to other great apes. Chimpanzees and humans share almost 99 percent of their DNA.

The close relationship between chimpanzees and humans is apparent in their very similar anatomy. Like humans, chimpanzees have a rounded head on a short neck, forward-facing eyes, a short barrel-shaped torso, and the ability to walk upright on two legs. Bipedalism is especially well developed in the bonobo. In both chimpanzee species, the arms are longer than the legs. When a chimpanzee is standing upright, the arms dangle to just below the knees. They are shorter than the arms of gorillas but longer than those of humans, which reach only partway down the thigh. Chimpanzees have four grasping fingers and an opposable thumb on each hand, and a thumblike big toe that opposes the four toes on each foot. This arrangement allows them to grasp branches and other objects firmly with hands and feet, enabling them to climb trees easily.

▶ **Common chimpanzee**
*Chimpanzees are mostly quadrupedal—they walk on four limbs—although they can walk upright on their hind limbs. Except for the face, hands, and feet, and the region around the genitals, their body is covered with hair.*

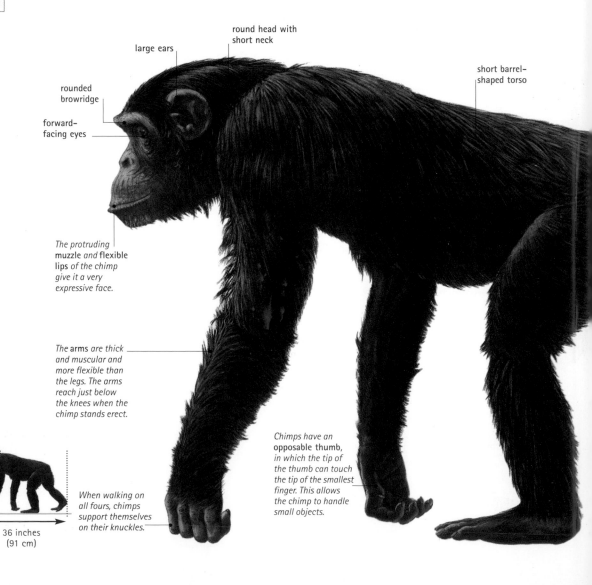

large ears

round head with short neck

short barrel-shaped torso

rounded browridge

forward-facing eyes

*The protruding* **muzzle** *and* **flexible lips** *of the chimp give it a very expressive face.*

*The* **arms** *are thick and muscular and more flexible than the legs. The arms reach just below the knees when the chimp stands erect.*

*Chimps have an* **opposable thumb,** *in which the tip of the thumb can touch the tip of the smallest finger. This allows the chimp to handle small objects.*

30 inches (76 cm)

36 inches (91 cm)

*When walking on all fours, chimps support themselves on their knuckles.*

▲ *All chimpanzees have unique facial characteristics and can be recognized as individuals just as easily as humans.*

*Chimps are covered in **hair** except for the face, palms, soles, and genital area.*

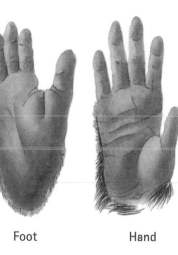

Foot         Hand

▲ *In walking on all fours, the fingers on the hands are bent inward and the chimpanzee supports itself on its knuckles. The digits on the feet, however, are placed flat upon the ground.*

*Slender **toes** help make the chimp a strong tree climber.*

## GENETICS

### The mystery chimpanzee

**About 100 years ago**, a Belgium army officer serving in Africa collected two ape skulls from the jungle near Bondo in what is now the Democratic Republic of Congo. The skulls have the usual proportions of a chimpanzee, but they also had a pronounced sagittal crest, like that found on a gorilla (although there are no gorillas anywhere nearby). Local hunters talk of two types of apes in the area: regular tree-dwelling chimpanzees and large, black animals that look like oversize chimpanzees but behave like gorillas, nesting on the ground. None of these animals has ever been seen alive by a scientist, but samples of hair and feces allegedly collected from nests have been used for DNA analysis. The results suggest they do indeed come from a kind of chimpanzee. In addition, a photograph taken by a remotely triggered camera shows a large ape that looks like a chimpanzee. The clues are intriguing, but until a colony of these animals is subject to proper scientific study, the details of their unusual lifestyle, and indeed their true identity, will remain a mystery.

Chimpanzees have a short face with rounded browridges, more prominent than those of a human but not the heavy, frowning brows of the gorilla. The face is highly mobile, and chimpanzees have a large repertoire of facial expressions, which are rich in meaning. Chimpanzees and their relatives lack a rhinarium, the area of glandular tissue that gives many other mammals a characteristically damp nose.

Chimpanzees are considerably hairier than humans, but the skin of the face, palms, and soles, and around the genitals is naked. In the common chimpanzee the skin is generally pink or brown, often darkening with age; in the bonobo the facial skin is black.

Chimpanzees' fur, especially that around the muzzle and chin, often grays as the animal ages. Chimps are also prone to baldness in later years; unlike in humans, this trend is more common in females than in males.

# Skeletal system

*The chimpanzee's
skeleton provides great
flexibility in the hands
and feet. The ulna and
radius twist around
each other, allowing the
hands and feet to be
turned laterally. The
bones in the hands and
feet are also highly
dexterous, and the
opposable thumbs
and big toes allow
chimpanzees to hold
onto and manipulate
objects with a high
degree of precision.*

In common with other vertebrates, a chimpanzee has a skeleton that supports and protects the body's organs and provides a stiff, jointed structure against which muscles can flex, thus enabling movement.

## Skull

The skull of a chimpanzee usually lacks the large sagittal crest (ridge of bone running along the midline of the top of the skull) seen in gorillas, but it is not as smoothly rounded as that of a human. (The sagittal crest serves to increase the area of bone available as an attachment point for large jaw muscles.) The jaws of chimpanzees and humans are comparable in strength, despite the differences in skull structure. The similar, moderate strength reflects similar dietary preferences in the two species: both chimpanzees and humans like fruit, tender leaves, and soft animal tissues rather than the tough plant material consumed by gorillas, which have a more powerful munching mechanism. Chimpanzees also lack a bony chin; in humans, this structure reinforces the connection between the left and right mandibles (lower jawbones).

The browridges seen in chimpanzees and gorillas are quite pronounced, and the skull slopes back from the brows without much of a forehead. In contrast, the comparatively large, high forehead of a human skull accommodates the enlarged frontal lobes of the brain.

## Axial skeleton

Chimpanzees have a flexible but short neck. The head is carried low, with the jawline level with the shoulders. The same is true for all other apes except humans, who have a longer neck so that, in standing erect, the head is carried well clear of the shoulders.

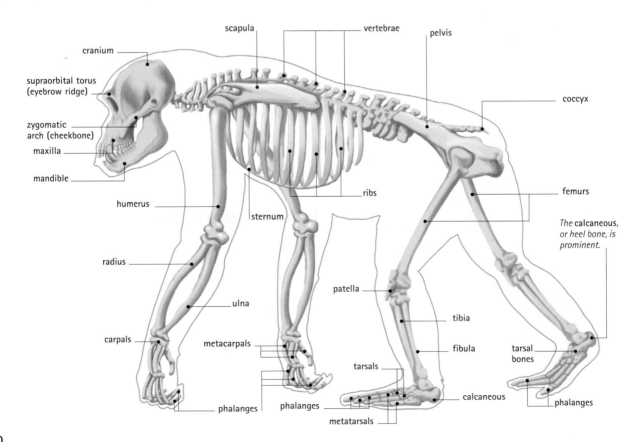

scapula

cranium

vertebrae

pelvis

supraorbital torus
(eyebrow ridge)

coccyx

zygomatic
arch (cheekbone)

maxilla

mandible

humerus

ribs

femurs

sternum

*The calcaneous,
or heel bone, is
prominent.*

radius

patella

ulna

tibia

carpals

fibula

tarsal
bones

metacarpals

tarsals

phalanges

phalanges

phalanges

calcaneous

metatarsals

▶ SKULL
Common
chimpanzee
*A chimpanzee's skull
shows pronounced
eyebrow ridges, a
sloping face, and deep
eye sockets. The large
canine teeth are used
by adult males for
fighting and display.*

supraorbital torus
(eyebrow ridge)

canine tooth

zygomatic arch
(cheek bone)

mandible

**CONNECTIONS**

COMPARE the
sloping face and
large eyebrow
ridges of a
chimpanzee's skull
with the flat face
and large forehead
of a *HUMAN*.

COMPARE the
humerus and
femur of a
chimpanzee with
those of a *HUMAN*.
In a chimpanzee
the humerus is the
longest bone in the
body, but in a
human the longest
bone is the femur.

There are 32 vertebrae in the chimpanzee backbone, one fewer than in humans. These include 7 cervical (neck) vertebrae, 13 thoracic (upper back) vertebrae, 4 lumbar (lower back) vertebrae, 5 sacral vertebrae supporting the pelvic girdle, and 3 vestigial caudal (tail) vertebrae fused into a coccyx. The vertebrae are separated by cartilaginous disks that allow very slight movement. Bony projections on either side of each vertebra protect the spinal nerve cord, and a knobbly structure called the processus spinalis projects backward from the midline of each vertebra, providing an attachment point for the major muscles of the back and trunk.

Attached to the thoracic vertebrae are 13 pairs of ribs (one more than in humans). The rib cage is broad, the shape of a slightly flattened barrel, giving the animals a flattened back and chest—a body shape not seen on non-hominid primates. There is a broad sternum, or breastbone.

## Appendicular skeleton

Like all other primates, chimpanzees and their relatives have a clavicle, or collarbone. The clavicle is vital in allowing rotation of the shoulder joint. Without it, an animal is unable to move its arms out to the side of its body. Animals such as dogs and horses, which lack a clavicle, can move their forelegs only in one plane—forward and backward. Primates, on the other hand, can reach forward, backward,

and from side to side through a wide range of angles. The collarbone effectively turns a forelimb into an arm. The shoulder blades, or scapulae, of chimpanzees and other great apes are mounted on the back of the rib cage, rather than at the sides. This arrangement realigns the whole pectoral girdle and gives great apes their distinctive broad shoulders.

The longest bone in the chimpanzee's body is the humerus, or upper arm bone, closely followed by the radius and ulna. The femur, or thighbone, which is the longest bone in a human skeleton, is only the fourth largest in the common chimpanzee. The long bones of the hands and feet—the metacarpals and metatarsals—are relatively long, as are the

## EVOLUTION

### From tail to coccyx

**The main distinguishing feature** of the great apes is the absence of an obvious tail. The caudal vertebrae that make up the tail in other primates are still present in chimpanzees and other apes, but they are greatly reduced and fused to form a short, bony protrusion at the base of the spine called the coccyx. A person will be painfully aware of his or her own coccyx if he or she falls backward or sits down suddenly and misses the soft landing of his or her buttocks!

▲ *The skeleton of a bonobo enables this animal to adopt a slightly more upright stance than a chimpanzee.*

dexterity in the feet and ankles for improved stability when moving on two legs.

Compared with the pectoral girdle, which is held together mainly by muscle, the pelvic girdle provides a more substantial connection between the axial skeleton (the bones of the trunk and head) and the appendicular skeleton (limb bones). The pelvis itself is connected to the sacrum—a long, rigid section of the backbone formed from the five fused sacral vertebrae. The pelvis of the chimpanzee is comparable in shape, if not in size, to that of the gorilla. It is longer than that of a human and sits at an angle that makes it impossible for the chimpanzee to stand fully upright.

finger and toe bones, or phalanges. The exception is the thumb, which is much shorter relative to the other fingers in chimpanzees than in human hands.

## Flexible limbs

The separate bones of the lower limbs allow the forearms and lower legs to be rotated. For example, the radius and ulna of the forearm twist around each other, allowing chimpanzees, humans, and other apes to make the kind of movements required to turn a doorknob or bring food to the mouth. Animals that have fused lower limb bones have much less rotation. A dog, for example, cannot easily put its paw in its mouth, whereas an ape can do this in any number of ways. Chimpanzees have retained a similar degree of flexibility in the lower leg, ankles, and feet. Humans have traded

## COMPARATIVE ANATOMY

### Standing up

**When standing on two legs**, common chimpanzees adopt a definite slouch. The spine and the long bones of the legs are curved, making it almost impossible for them to stand fully erect like a human. The bonobo is able to get rather more upright, but it still lacks the ability to align its legs vertically below the pelvis.

▼ *An upright stance causes too much strain on a chimpanzee's spine and leg muscles and so cannot be maintained. Chimpanzees walk mostly using all four limbs.*

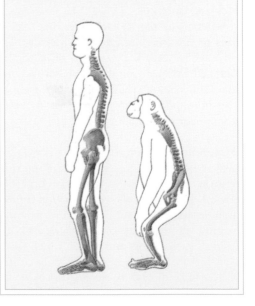

# Muscular system

The musculature of most primates is very similar. Most differences are a matter of relative scale, related to the main method of locomotion—the process of moving from place to place.

### Five forms of movement

Few mammalian groups exhibit such a diverse array of locomotive adaptations as the primates. Within this order are five main categories of locomotion. First, there are the primates that move on four legs through the trees, either fast—like the nimble cercopithicine monkeys—or slowly and carefully, like the lorises. These animals usually have four legs of more or less equal length.

Second are the leapers—animals such as lemurs that spring on four or two legs from branch to branch. Their hind legs are better developed than the forelimbs in order to provide sufficient spring. Third, there are the brachiators, or primates that swing from branch to branch. The gibbons are masters of the art of brachiation, and their arms are much longer and stronger than their legs. A fourth locomotory category covers ground-dwelling apes such as gorillas, which move around on all fours, walking on the soles of the feet and the knuckles of the hands. Finally, there is bipedalism. All great apes are able to adopt a bipedal gait for short periods, but no primates have committed as fully to moving on two legs as humans, in whom the legs are by far the longest and strongest limbs. Most primates can also swim.

### Chimp locomotion

Chimpanzees use a mixture of locomotive styles. They are excellent climbers, and they forage and sleep in the trees. They are able to

▼ **Common chimpanzee**
*Chimpanzees have powerful deltoid muscles in their shoulders, which provide these primates with the strength necessary to swing, or brachiate, from branch to branch.*

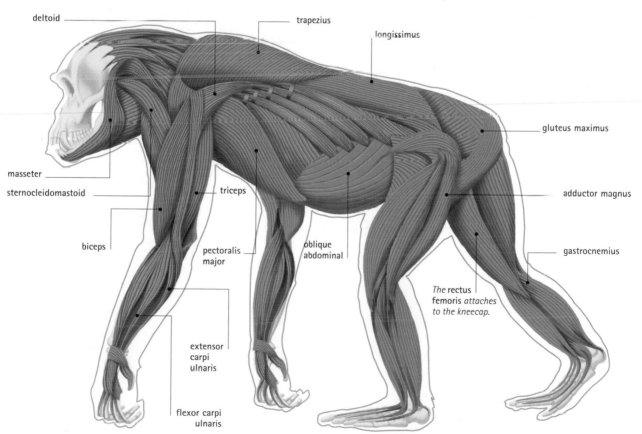

deltoid · trapezius · longissimus · gluteus maximus · masseter · sternocleidomastoid · triceps · adductor magnus · biceps · pectoralis major · oblique abdominal · gastrocnemius · The **rectus femoris** *attaches to the kneecap.* · extensor carpi ulnaris · flexor carpi ulnaris brachiate—that is, to swing suspended from branches—and this ability is reflected in their anatomy: the upper arm bone (humerus) of chimpanzees has a prominent deltoid process for attaching the powerful deltoid shoulder muscles used in brachiating. Chimpanzees are at home off the ground but have not specialized in this lifestyle to the same extent as gibbons, which can hang around all day on very long arms. The tendons in a gibbon's arm are structured so that when the arm is extended (as it is when the gibbon is hanging from a branch), the fingers are automatically curled into hooks. A gibbon cannot open its hand out flat without bending its arm to loosen the tendons, but simply hanging from a branch requires no muscular effort at all. Just as bats can relax dangling from their toes, and horses sleep standing up, a gibbon can doze as it dangles from a tree.

## IN FOCUS

### Making faces

**Great apes do not have the membranous connection** between the upper lip and the gums seen in most mammals. This leaves the upper lip free to form a wide range of expressions. There is no doubt that facial expressions in chimpanzees are just as meaningful as those in humans; indeed, many of them are startlingly similar. The chimpanzee "play face" is virtually identical to human laughter; a frightened chimpanzee and a startled human show the same toothy grimace; and there is no mistaking anger in the face of either species.

◀ A chimpanzee expresses anger by drawing back its lips and baring its large upper and lower canine teeth.

◀ When excited, a chimpanzee pouts its lips by pushing them forward, making a shape like a trumpet.

▶ A happy chimp grins in much the same way as a human. This grin is accompanied by "oh-oh" sounds and barks.

▶ When feeling calm and tranquil, a chimp expresses this with pursed lips.

On the ground, chimpanzees can amble and gallop on all fours using the knuckles of the hands instead of the digits (fingers) to bear weight. As in humans and other great apes, the fingers of the hand are delicate and adapted for dexterity and manipulation rather than bearing weight, so they are kept curled safely out of harm's way in moving on all fours. The backs of the top two joints of a chimpanzee's fingers, like those of gorillas, are covered in calloused skin rather than fur. The short thumb is not used for knuckle walking.

## Bipedalism

Chimpanzees can also walk on two legs. This is a feat that members of certain other mammal groups have also acquired (meerkats stand upright on sentry duty; gerenuk antelopes walk nimbly on their hind legs to feed from acacia trees). However, in great apes, bipedalism is combined with manual dexterity, so that walking on two legs frees the hands for other purposes. Most important, chimpanzees and their relatives are able to hold onto objects such as food, tools, or young as they move around. Many of the most important traits associated with the great apes' intellect and social evolution can be linked to bipedalism. Free hands permit the creation and use of tools; hand gestures can be used to communicate; and hand actions have a host of other important social functions. These include cradling young for comfort, cuddling, stroking, grooming, hitting, and throwing sticks and stones—all of which have much the same meaning for chimpanzees as they do for humans.

### COMPARATIVE ANATOMY

## Strength of 10

**Chimpanzees**, like other nonhuman great apes, are immensely powerful. The arms of a gorilla are at least 10 times as strong as those of a trained human. If a chimpanzee and a human were to arm-wrestle, there would be no question as to who would win. However, it would not be an entirely fair contest. In humans, the arms are not the strongest limbs: it is the legs, rather than the arms, that have evolved to support the body weight.

### CLOSE-UP

## Opposable thumbs and toes

**The first digit on an ape's hand** is the thumb, or pollex. Most primates have an opposable thumb—one which is separated from the other digits of the hand at its base, and which can be brought together with these digits in order to grasp an object such as a branch, or to make a pinching movement to manipulate small objects, such as berries or a pen. It is almost impossible to overstate the usefulness of the opposable thumb: it turns a paw into that most adaptable of tools, a hand.

Chimpanzees also have an opposable big toe, or hallux, which enables them to grasp branches or other objects with their feet. In orangutans, the opposable hallux is almost as well developed as the thumb, making them effectively four-handed.

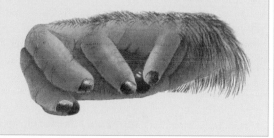

▶ A chimpanzee's opposable thumb can be used to manipulate small objects, such as a berry, with great precision.

◀ This young chimp's opposable thumbs and big toes enable it to hold firmly onto the tree as it climbs.

# Nervous system

COMPARE the forward-facing eyes of a hunting animal such as a chimpanzee with the sideways-pointing eyes of a grazing animal such as a **HARE**. Having eyes placed more toward the side of the head permits greater all-around vision and enables the animal to detect predators.

Chimpanzees are alert, perceptive, and intelligent. They demonstrate several aspects of behavior that were once considered exclusively human, including reasoned thought and a concept of self. They also exhibit a broad range of emotions, from fear and anger to happiness and despair.

As with most other mammals, the brain of a chimpanzee is divided into five structural components: the cerebrum, diencephalon and mesencephalon (making up the forebrain), and the cerebellum and medulla oblongata, which together make up the hindbrain. The medulla oblongata forms the base of the brain and connects directly to the spinal cord. It is responsible for controlling fundamental involuntary processes such as breathing, and is also the source of the vagus nerve, which meanders though the upper body connecting many of the principle organs. The brain and the spinal cord together make up the central nervous system. The cerebellum is concerned with coordination, movement, and muscle control, and it processes certain sensory information gathered by the eyes, ears, and body surfaces. Sensory information is also processed by the forebrain, which regulates drives such as pain, hunger, sleep, and sexual activity through the action of hormone-producing glands such as the hypothalamus and pineal organ. The forebrain is also the seat of "higher" thought.

To a large extent, the brain of a chimpanzee is like a scaled-down version of a human brain. However, there are some significant structural differences, most notably in the relative sizes of the parts of the brain concerned with communication and creativity. The power of speech is considered one of the most important characteristics that set humans apart from other apes.

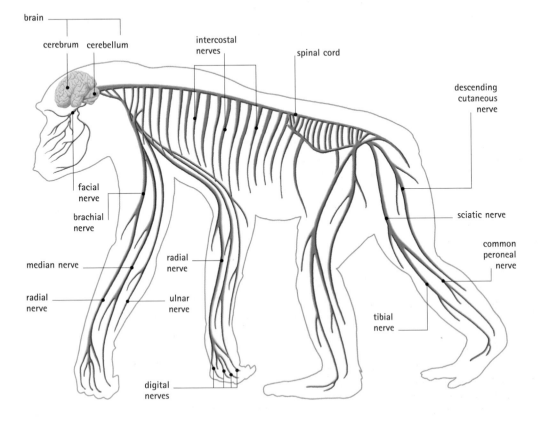

◄ **Common chimpanzee**
*The nervous system of chimpanzee is similar to that of a human but the chimpanzee has a smaller brain. The nervous system is divided into two main parts—the central nervous system, which comprises the brain and spinal cord, and the peripheral nervous system, which is made up of the nerves that connect to the spinal cord and brain.*

## If only chimps could talk

**Chimpanzees have shown** a surprising aptitude for language skills. They lack the anatomical and physiological adaptations needed to produce the complex sounds of vocal speech, but under controlled conditions, a few individual animals in captivity have demonstrated a remarkable understanding of language and willingness to communicate using forms of sign language. They have used signs to convey wants, needs, and emotions such as fear and contentment. Some can even understand simple sentences. With training, a chimpanzee can demonstrate language skills comparable to those of a human toddler. However, while their vocabulary skills are impressive, chimpanzees—unlike human children—do not seem able to progress beyond this stage to mastering a full-fledged language.

### Sounds and sights

Chimpanzees and other great apes lack the extensive area of scent-sensitive tissues seen in many other mammals: there is no damp rhinarium, and the smelling sensors are all inside the nostrils. Chimpanzees' sense of smell is poor in comparison with that of many other mammals, but scent still plays an important role in chimpanzee society. Chimpanzees do not have specially developed scent glands, but each animal undoubtedly has its own personal body smell, recognizable to others.

A chimpanzee's eyes are usually golden brown with a brown sclera (the area around the iris that is white in humans). Chimpanzees see in color—a characteristic shared by most primates. This visual ability is thought to have developed in our common ancestor as an adaptation to a mainly fruit-eating arboreal lifestyle: the ability to distinguish red from green, for example, allows ripe fruits to be spotted quickly amid foliage. The primate retina contains two types of light receptors, called rods and cones. Rods are sensitive to low level light, whereas cones are sensitive to color and work best in bright light. Chimpanzees, like humans, see better in

daylight. There are far more cones than rods in the central part of the retina, forming a highly sensitive area called the macula lutea. Like other apes, chimpanzees have stereoscopic vision. This is essential for judging distance, but it does result in a relatively narrow field of vision, which is compensated for by flexibility of the neck.

The nerves that carry visual information from the retina to the brain are split, so information from each eye is carried to both sides of the brain. This is the typical placental mammal arrangement, differing from that seen in reptiles and marsupials, where the optic nerves from each retina carry information only to the opposite side of the brain.

## Big brains

**As the diagram below shows**, large animals tend to have large brains, but this in itself is not really a fair measure of intellectual ability. Relative brain size—that is, brain mass as a proportion of body mass—is only slightly better: not many people would credit a rabbit with greater intelligence than a gorilla, or a newborn baby with being smarter than an adult. A better guide is the relative size of the forebrain. This is the area that controls reasoned thought and creativity. Not surprisingly, this area is larger in great apes than in most other animals, and it is especially well developed in humans.

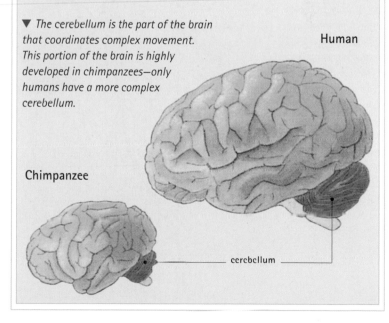

▼ *The cerebellum is the part of the brain that coordinates complex movement. This portion of the brain is highly developed in chimpanzees—only humans have a more complex cerebellum.*

Human

Chimpanzee

cerebellum

# Circulatory and respiratory systems

**COMPARE** the heart rate of a chimpanzee with the very rapid heart rate of a *HUMMINGBIRD*.

**COMPARE** the vocalizations of a chimpanzee with those of a marine mammal such as a *DOLPHIN*.

**CONNECTIONS**

A relaxed chimpanzee takes about 30 breaths a minute and has an average heart rate of about 120 beats per minute. This is significantly faster than that of an average human. The body is maintained at an average temperature of 98 to 100°F (36.7 to 37.8°C) and blood pressure averages at around 127/96 mmHg. In the wild, chimpanzees rarely suffer from heart disease, but studies of captive animals have shown that, just as in humans, bad diet and a sedentary lifestyle in chimpanzees can lead to thickening of arteries and high blood pressure.

### Blood groups

Chimpanzee blood is remarkably similar to that of humans. Chimpanzees are the only other apes known to have all the major ABO blood groups A, B, O, and AB. In humans, the relative proportions of each blood group vary between races; in chimpanzees, the proportions are different again. Gorillas, in contrast, all have blood type B.

IN FOCUS

### Vocalizations

**Many structures used in human breathing** are also used in speech production, but chimpanzees lack the basic apparatus for producing complex vocalizations. The larynx is located lower in the throat in humans than in chimpanzees, creating the voice box—an area of the throat in which movements of the tongue and vocal cords can create a great diversity of precise sounds. Chimpanzee vocalizations are all made using simple exhalations of varying intensity, from soft "hoo" sounds signifying distress or anxiety to a wheezy laugh, excited pant-hoots, or wild screams of anger. More than 30 calls have been recorded, conveying a variety of meanings concerning mood, status, danger, threat, sexual excitement, food, and social interactions.

▶ **Common chimpanzee**
*The circulatory and respiratory systems of a chimpanzee are typical of those of many mammals. Blood is pumped around a closed system by a four-chamber heart. As the blood passes through the lungs, oxygen and carbon dioxide are exchanged across the lungs' surface.*

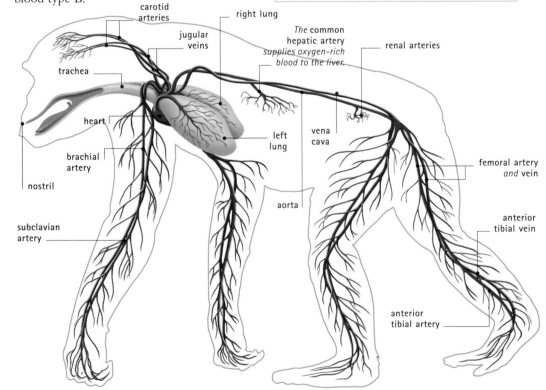

carotid arteries

right lung

jugular veins

trachea

*The* common hepatic artery *supplies oxygen-rich blood to the liver.*

renal arteries

heart

left lung

vena cava

brachial artery

nostril

aorta

femoral artery *and* vein

subclavian artery

anterior tibial vein

anterior tibial artery

# Digestive and excretory systems

Chimpanzees are omnivores: they have been recorded consuming more than 300 different types of food, including fruit, leaves, bark, stems, flowers, insects, and vertebrates—even killing and eating other chimpanzees. On average, fruit makes up about half the chimpanzee's intake of food. The precise composition of the diet varies considerably from place to place and season to season.

## Teeth

Chimpanzees have four types of teeth: incisors, canines, premolars, and molars. Each jaw has two pairs of flat, spatula-shaped incisors used for nipping, a single pair of pointed canines or eyeteeth, two robust premolars, and three large molars. The premolars and molars have cusped grinding surfaces. This is the same arrangement as in an adult human, but the teeth of chimpanzees are notably larger, especially the canines of males, which are used for fighting and display. There is a gap (the diastema) in the upper tooth row between the second incisor

### Ancestral diets

**The fossilized teeth of the ancestors of all primates** suggest that they were mainly insectivorous. Many modern primates still eat insects and other invertebrates. The primate ancestors graduated to other easily digested foods such as soft, ripe fruit and small vertebrates, which they caught with their hands. Then, different lineages began to specialize in hard fruits, resin, flowers, nectar, buds, tender young leaves, and finally mature leaves, which are most difficult to digest but very abundant. Modern chimpanzees have reverted somewhat to a more generalist diet, but have retained the ability to digest low-grade vegetation if necessary.

and the canine, into which the lower canine fits when the mouth is closed. In a chimpanzee, as in other large apes, the cheek teeth are arranged in parallel rows and the incisors are set well in from of the canines, so the bite mark is rather like a flat-bottomed "U"—instead of the semicircular shape of a

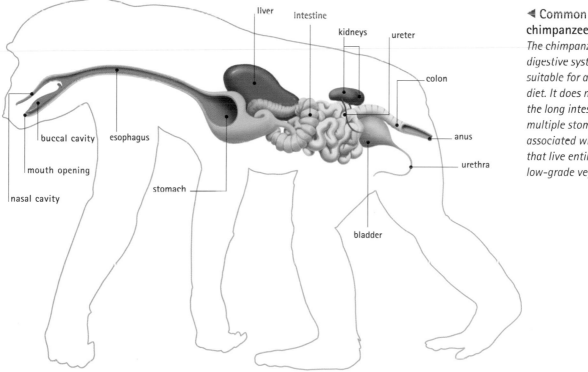

liver   Intestine   kidneys   ureter   colon   anus   urethra

buccal cavity   esophagus   mouth opening   stomach   nasal cavity   bladder

◀ **Common chimpanzee**
*The chimpanzee's digestive system is suitable for a generalist diet. It does not have the long intestine or multiple stomachs associated with animals that live entirely on low-grade vegetation.*

▲ MOUTH
**Common chimpanzee**
*Chimpanzees' large canines are used by males in display and fighting. The molars are smaller than those of a gorilla, reflecting chimpanzees' largely fruit-based diet.*

▲ *Chimpanzees' digestive system has evolved to process a wide range of foods, including soft vegetation, fruit, insects, and meat.*

human bite. This matches the more elongated shape of the chimpanzee face, which is referred to as progranthic, while the flat face of a human is orthognathic.

## Digestion

In the chimpanzee's mouth, food is chewed well and mixed with saliva, which begins the process of digestion. On reaching the simple, baglike stomach, food begins to be broken down by highly acidic stomach juices. The large intestine and rectum are short compared with those of "lower" primates such as leaf-eating monkeys.

At the junction between the small and large intestine, there is a pronounced offshoot from the gut called the cecum. The cecum is something of an evolutionary relic: in some true herbivores, such as rabbits, it plays a vital role in microbial digestion of cellulose. In great apes, there is a further branch off the cecum, known as the true appendix. The true appendix contains lymphatic tissue, but its precise function is not clearly understood. The acutely painful and potentially dangerous condition known as appendicitis results from sudden inflammation of the true appendix.

### Meat eaters

**The chimpanzee's desire for meat** stems from a basic need for protein—one of the most essential building materials of life. Plant material also contains protein, but in lower concentrations. Animal protein is easier to digest, and eating meat is a much more convenient way of meeting the dietary requirement for protein. However, eating meat usually implies first catching an animal, and chimpanzees have a variety of hunting techniques. Acting alone, they hunt termites and other insects, or they might raid the nests of birds or small mammals. Larger prey require a more cooperative effort, and chimpanzee troops have been recorded hunting bush pigs, small antelope, and other primates, which are usually killed by being beaten to death or hurled from a tree. Most hunts involve only male chimpanzees. Females are just as willing to eat meat, but the demands of motherhood give them little liberty to engage in a hunt.

# Reproductive system

Female common chimpanzees reach puberty at around the age of 7, but do not usually breed until the age of 12 or 13, by which time they have already been engaging in mock sexual behavior for several years. Likewise, males may begin to simulate sexual activity at about 5 years of age but do not usually breed until they are fully mature at around 15 years old.

Gestation periods among the great apes are remarkably similar considering the variation in size. In the common chimpanzee, gestation takes an average of 33 weeks but can be up to 37 weeks, approaching the human gestation period. In bonobos it is slightly shorter, 32 to 33 weeks. Orangutans and gorillas are pregnant for about 37 weeks. However, predicting gestation periods is difficult to do with much precision, and—like humans—chimpanzee babies are frequently born two weeks or more before the expected date.

### Ready to breed

It is easy to tell when a female chimpanzee (unlike a female human) is ready to conceive. The skin surrounding the anal and genital region becomes swollen and brightly colored. Mothers with babies do not come into estrus, and they adopt an almost reclusive lifestyle, avoiding contact with males and keeping their offspring out of harm's way. The females

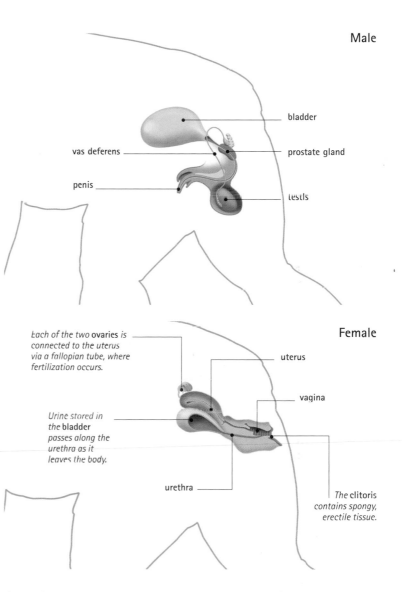

**Male**

bladder

vas deferens

prostate gland

penis

testis

**Female**

Each of the two **ovaries** is connected to the uterus via a fallopian tube, where fertilization occurs.

uterus

vagina

Urine stored in the **bladder** passes along the urethra as it leaves the body.

urethra

The **clitoris** contains spongy, erectile tissue.

themselves are not usually at risk, although sometimes they are attacked. However, their young may be attacked by males of neighboring groups. There is a logic in this behavior: a mother will not come into breeding condition again unless her young is ready to be weaned or has died, so killing a baby may hasten the female's return to fertility. Females that are ready to breed enter estrus every 30 days. They remain receptive for about a week at a time.

▲ **Common chimpanzee**
*During copulation, the male chimpanzee transfers sperm to the female by inserting his erect penis into the female's vagina. Usually only one egg is fertilized, and this takes place in the fallopian tubes.*

## Tool use

**Another advantage of a big brain**, a long childhood, and close social bonds is that chimpanzees are able to learn from one another. Mothers and family members teach young chimpanzees many important life skills, including the location of feeding areas, how to respond to higher-ranking animals, and how to make and use tools. Different populations of chimpanzees have distinctly different specialities when it comes to using tools. Some are expert at fishing out termites from their nests with a long grass stem; others know how to crack nuts open with a stone. Most of these skills take a long time to learn, and so the spread of skills takes place very slowly. Captive chimpanzees can be encouraged to use more complex tools by repeated demonstration.

### Dependent babies

All great ape babies are born in a highly dependent, or altricial, state: they need prolonged care and attention from parent animals in order to survive. At birth they are small and utterly helpless, unable to feed themselves, move about, or even stay warm without being continually cuddled. Compared with the young of other large animals such as horses and elephants, which are born alert and lively and can walk within minutes of birth, great ape babies seem premature, underdeveloped, and dangerously vulnerable. The reason for this apparently premature departure from the womb is the large brain that confers such a great advantage in later life, and which require large heads. Staying any longer in the womb would allow the baby's head to grow so large that it could not pass through the pelvic opening at birth.

Indeed, many human babies fail to be born naturally: many mothers and babies died in childbirth before cesarean sections became routine practice. The problem is not quite so acute in chimpanzees, whose brains and therefore skulls are considerably smaller than our own—but so too is the opening in the pelvis through which the young are born. The size and shape of the opening in the pelvis closely matches those of a newborn ape's head, and childbirth appears to be much more of an ordeal for great apes than for other, smaller-brained mammals.

The extended childhood of chimpanzees plays a large part in their social development.

▶ A chimpanzee baby is dependent on its mother for survival. Like all mammals, the mother provides the baby with nourishing milk from mammary glands. By the age of three the young chimp will have been weaned; but it will not become completely independent until it is around seven or eight years old.

**GENETICS**

## Social structure

**Chimpanzee society is complex.** The animals in a given area form a distinct local community, but it is very rare for them all to gather together in one place. More usually, they move about in small groups of three or four, often mothers with young or small bands of males. The community is dominated by high-ranking males, but lower-ranking individuals can better their position by forming alliances with their superiors, currying favor with submissive behavior and attentive grooming. Rank is passed on from mother to offspring, but size and strength also play an important part.

The bond between mothers and their offspring is very strong and enduring. Young females may eventually leave to join another troop, but young males tend to remain in the group where they were born. Female chimps are usually more tolerant and benevolent toward their older sons than toward their daughters. The gap between births is usually about five years, but older offspring take great interest in their younger siblings, sometimes becoming jealous.

AMY-JANE BEER

**FURTHER READING AND RESEARCH**

Goodall, Jane. 1996. *My Life with the Chimpanzees.* Aladdin Paperbacks: New York.

Macdonald, David. 2006. *The Encyclopedia of Mammals.* Facts On File: New York.

JGI Center for Primate Studies: www.discoverchimpanzees.org

▲ *After a baby is born, it clings to its mother's belly fur, but when it is about five months old it begins to ride on its mother's back.*

# Dolphin

ORDER: Cetacea  SUBORDER: Odontoceti
FAMILY: Delphinidae  GENUS: *Delphinus*

There are two species of common dolphins—a widely distributed short-beaked species that occurs in saltwaters from open ocean to inland seas, and a long-beaked species that favors coastal waters. Both have adapted to life in the warm surface waters. With sleek, streamlined bodies, they are fast-moving predators of fish and squid.

## Anatomy and taxonomy
Scientists categorize all organisms into taxonomic groups based partly on anatomical features. The two species of common dolphins belong to the family of oceangoing dolphins and blackfish, the Delphinidae, which includes about 36 species in all. Oceanic dolphins, in turn, belong to the suborder Odontoceti, which includes river dolphins,

porpoises, beaked whales, and sperm whales. There are about 73 species of toothed whales, although experts still occasionally discover new species.

The distinction between whales, dolphins, and porpoises is based on size and on anatomy. Strictly, all cetaceans are whales—whatever their size—but most people use the term *whale* for larger species only. The term *dolphin* refers to one family of small- to medium-sized oceangoing cetaceans, the Delphinidae; and four freshwater families, the river dolphins. Dolphins have cone-shaped teeth. The word *porpoise* refers to small cetaceans of the family Phocoenidae that have chisel- or spade-shaped teeth.

● **Animals**  These organisms are multicellular and depend on other organisms for food. Animals differ from other multicellular life-forms in their ability to move from one place to another (in most cases, using muscles). They generally react rapidly to touch, light, and other stimuli.

● **Chordates**  At some time in its life cycle a chordate has a stiff, dorsal (back) supporting rod called the notochord. It runs along most of the length of the body.

▶ *The common dolphin has only recently been split by biologists into two species, but short- and long-beaked versions are very difficult to tell apart. In waters around Australia both forms appear to be present. However, DNA analysis of this population has shown that all are actually short-beaked common dolphins. However, they are much more variable in size and shape than elsewhere in the world and some look just like the long-beaked form.*

**Animals**
KINGDOM Animalia

**Chordates**
PHYLUM Chordata

**Vertebrates**
SUBPHYLUM Vertebrata

**Mammals**
CLASS Mammalia

**Placental mammals**
SUBCLASS Eutheria

**Cetaceans**
**(whales, dolphins, and porpoises)**
ORDER Cetacea

**Baleen whales**
SUBORDER Mysticeti

**Toothed whales**
SUBORDER Odontoceti

**Beaked whales**
FAMILY Ziphiidae

**Sperm whales**
FAMILIES Physeteridae and Kogiidae

**Narwhal and beluga**
FAMILY Monodontidae

**Oceanic dolphins and blackfish**
FAMILY Delphinidae

**Porpoises**
FAMILY Phocoenidae

**River dolphins**
FAMILIES Iniidae, Lipotidae, Pontoporidae, Platanistidae

**Long-beaked common dolphin**
GENUS AND SPECIES *Delphinus capensis*

**Short-beaked common dolphin**
GENUS AND SPECIES *Delphinus delphis*

● **Vertebrates** The vertebrate notochord develops into a backbone made up of units called vertebrae. Vertebrate muscle blocks are generally bilaterally symmetrical about the skeletal axis—those one one side of the backbone are the mirror image of those on the other side.

● **Mammals** Mammals are warm-blooded vertebrates with hair. Females have mammary glands that produce milk to feed their young. Mammals have a single lower jawbone that hinges directly to the skull, and their red blood cells do not contain nuclei.

● **Placental mammals** Placental mammals nourish their unborn young through a placenta, a temporary organ that forms in the mother's uterus during pregnancy.

● **Cetaceans** These mammals are supremely adapted for life in water, where they spend their entire lives. Cetaceans have bodies that are streamlined to minimize drag as they swim through the water. Cetacean nostrils have moved over millions of years of evolution from the front of the head to the top. This enables breathing at the sea surface; the nostrils end at one or two blowholes. Cetaceans have paddlelike tails. Their forelimbs form flippers and lack visible digits. Cetaceans do not have functional hind limbs. Most have a dorsal (back) fin that aids steering and provides stability against rolling from side to side when swimming.

● **Baleen whales** There are 12 species of baleen whales, including most of the larger whales. Instead of teeth, baleen whales have fringes called baleen plates, which hang from the upper jaws and strain small fish or shrimplike crustaceans from the water. All baleen whales have two blowholes, side by side.

▲ *Dolphins have beaklike snouts containing pointed, conelike teeth that are ideal for holding slippery fish.*

● **Toothed whales** These whales have teeth rather than baleen. In most of the 73 or so species, the jaws are extended into a beaklike snout. The forehead bulges upward, enclosing a "melon," a fatty structure that focuses sound waves to enable the whale to echolocate (create an image of the surroundings using sound). All toothed whales have a single blowhole.

● **Sperm whales** The three species of sperm whales have a huge, square head. These deep divers have a wax-filled structure in the head called the spermaceti organ. This focuses echolocation sounds and helps adjust buoyancy.

---

**FEATURED SYSTEMS**

**EXTERNAL ANATOMY** Dolphins are toothed whales with a sleek, streamlined body, flippers, and a powerful, horizontally flattened tail for swimming. *See pages 27–29.*

**SKELETAL SYSTEM** The backbone acts as an anchor for muscles that flex the body and fins and that raise the tail up and down. *See pages 30–32.*

**MUSCULAR SYSTEM** Large muscles power vertical movements of the tail; a system of fibers, acting as springs, stores and releases energy, making tail movement an efficient process. *See pages 33–34.*

**NERVOUS SYSTEM** The dolphin brain is relatively complex, with a large and highly folded cerebral cortex. This reflects the animal's social behavior, its life in a complex, three-dimensional habitat; and the high processing power needed to interpret sounds created for echolocation. It is also a sign of intelligence. *See pages 35–37.*

**CIRCULATORY AND RESPIRATORY SYSTEMS** These systems ensure that oxygen reaches vital organs during long dives, while minimizing the dangers of dissolved nitrogen at high pressures. *See pages 38–39.*

**DIGESTIVE AND EXCRETORY SYSTEMS** Dolphins and other toothed whales swallow their prey whole or in large chunks. The first part of the complex stomach breaks down food mechanically. *See pages 40–41.*

**REPRODUCTIVE SYSTEM** Reproductive adaptations for life underwater include internal male sex organs, hidden mammary glands, and giving birth tail first. *See pages 42–43.*

▲ *As with most oceanic dolphins, this bottle-nosed dolphin is countershaded—dark above, lighter below. This camouflages the animal against prey and predators from both above and below.*

● **Narwhal and beluga** These two species are medium-sized whales that live in arctic and subarctic waters and feed on fish, squid, and crustaceans such as crabs and shrimp. The beluga is white or pale yellow. The narwhal has a dark mottled back and a pale underside. Male narwhals sport an impressive unicorn-like tusk. Both species have a flexible neck. They are the only whales that can dramatically alter their facial expressions. Belugas and narwhals gather in large numbers at breeding time.

● **Beaked whales** The 21 or so species of deep-diving beaked whales have pointed snouts that contain few teeth. These animals feed on squid. The males of most beaked whales have two or four teeth in the lower jaw and none in the upper. The teeth probably serve as weapons in fights between males. Most females have no erupted teeth at all.

● **Porpoises** The six species of blunt-headed porpoises are mainly coastal but may occur in rivers or the open sea. They have spade- or chisel-shaped teeth for grasping prey.

● **River dolphins** Four of the five species of river dolphins live in large, muddy rivers of South America or Asia; the fifth species lives in South American coastal waters. River dolphins have a long narrow beak, a highly domed forehead, and tiny eyes. In the cloudy waters in which they live, eyesight is almost useless. They rely on sophisticated echolocation to find their way about and to detect prey.

● **Killer whales and pilot whales** Six species of whales are called blackfish because of their dark color. They belong to the Delphinidae, the same family as the oceanic dolphins, but blackfish are larger than dolphins and have large flippers, a blunt head lacking a beak, and fewer teeth. Blackfish are hunters that often work together to catch fish and squid. Killer whales regularly kill and eat other cetaceans, and may even attack giants such as blue whales.

● **Oceanic dolphins** Of the 30 or so species of oceanic dolphins, about half (including the common and bottle-nosed dolphins) have a prominent beak. Almost all oceanic dolphins have more than 100 small, conical teeth for grasping fish and squid.

● **Common dolphins** The long-beaked common dolphin has a pronounced beak and a slightly longer body and head than the short-beaked form, and it is less boldly colored. Both species are social, often traveling in groups of more than 100. Long-beaked dolphins live around coasts; short-beaked dolphins live in deeper waters.

## COMPARATIVE ANATOMY

### Dorsal fins

**Killer whales have very tall dorsal fins.** Most dolphins have more moderately sized ones, while the sperm whale has an irregular ridge or hump and the narwhal, beluga, and finless porpoise have no dorsal fin at all. In many cases, the dorsal fin serves as a keel that helps prevent the whale from rolling (rotating to one side) as it swims. In some species this fin may also serve as a temperature regulation device; by holding the dorsal fin above the water, the animal can lose or absorb heat. Male killer whales have larger dorsal fins than the females, and this feature may help individuals identify the sex and status of others.

# External anatomy

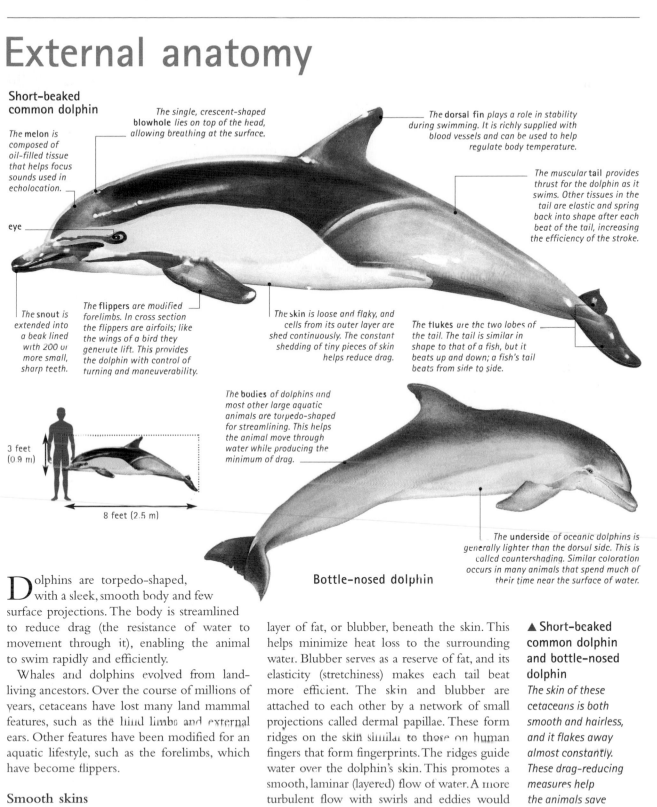

**Short-beaked common dolphin**

The **melon** is composed of oil-filled tissue that helps focus sounds used in echolocation.

The single, crescent-shaped **blowhole** lies on top of the head, allowing breathing at the surface.

The **dorsal fin** plays a role in stability during swimming. It is richly supplied with blood vessels and can be used to help regulate body temperature.

The muscular **tail** provides thrust for the dolphin as it swims. Other tissues in the tail are elastic and spring back into shape after each beat of the tail, increasing the efficiency of the stroke.

eye

The **snout** is extended into a beak lined with 200 or more small, sharp teeth.

The **flippers** are modified forelimbs. In cross section the flippers are airfoils; like the wings of a bird they generate lift. This provides the dolphin with control of turning and maneuverability.

The **skin** is loose and flaky, and cells from its outer layer are shed continuously. The constant shedding of tiny pieces of skin helps reduce drag.

The **flukes** are the two lobes of the tail. The tail is similar in shape to that of a fish, but it beats up and down; a fish's tail beats from side to side.

The **bodies** of dolphins and most other large aquatic animals are torpedo-shaped for streamlining. This helps the animal move through water while producing the minimum of drag.

3 feet (0.9 m)

8 feet (2.5 m)

**Bottle-nosed dolphin**

The **underside** of oceanic dolphins is generally lighter than the dorsal side. This is called countershading. Similar coloration occurs in many animals that spend much of their time near the surface of water.

Dolphins are torpedo-shaped, with a sleek, smooth body and few surface projections. The body is streamlined to reduce drag (the resistance of water to movement through it), enabling the animal to swim rapidly and efficiently.

Whales and dolphins evolved from land-living ancestors. Over the course of millions of years, cetaceans have lost many land mammal features, such as the hind limbs and external ears. Other features have been modified for an aquatic lifestyle, such as the forelimbs, which have become flippers.

## Smooth skins

Cetacean skin is smooth and almost hairless. Instead of relying on hair to provide heat insulation, whales and dolphins have a thick layer of fat, or blubber, beneath the skin. This helps minimize heat loss to the surrounding water. Blubber serves as a reserve of fat, and its elasticity (stretchiness) makes each tail beat more efficient. The skin and blubber are attached to each other by a network of small projections called dermal papillae. These form ridges on the skin similar to those on human fingers that form fingerprints. The ridges guide water over the dolphin's skin. This promotes a smooth, laminar (layered) flow of water. A more turbulent flow with swirls and eddies would cause increased drag. The skin lacks sweat glands but releases an oily substance that helps the animal slide effortlessly through the water.

▲ **Short-beaked common dolphin and bottle-nosed dolphin**
*The skin of these cetaceans is both smooth and hairless, and it flakes away almost constantly. These drag-reducing measures help the animals save energy as they swim swiftly through the ocean.*

## Blubber

**Like many other warm-blooded** marine animals, such as seals, sea lions, walruses, and sea cows, whales have a thick layer of fat called blubber beneath the skin. Apart from insulating the animal against the cold, blubber is a food store and provides buoyancy.

▼ *A cross section through dolphin skin.*

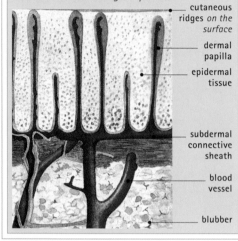

cutaneous ridges *on the surface*

dermal papilla

epidermal tissue

subdermal connective sheath

blood vessel

blubber

### Limb morphology

Cetacean front limbs form flippers used for steering. The hind limb bones are now absent, and the connecting pelvic bones are vestigial (greatly reduced in size and no longer serving their original purpose). The tail is broadened horizontally into two blades, or flukes. Up-and-down movement of the tail powers swimming; it enables most species to leap clear of the water, during porpoising in dolphins or breaching in whales.

Toothed whales breathe through a single blowhole on top of the head. Compared with the heads of other mammals, a dolphin's head is elongated and grades into the trunk with no visible neck or shoulders. Most types of dolphins, including common and bottle-nosed dolphins, have a prominent snout, or beak.

▲ *When swimming at top speed, dolphins leap from the water. This is called porpoising. It allows them to take a breath without needing to slow down at the water's surface.*

## Ancient forerunners of the whales

**Whales and dolphins descend from condylarths,** an ancient group of ungulates (hoofed mammals). Modern artiodactyl (even-toed) ungulates are whales' closest relatives. They include animals like hippopotamuses and antelope. The oldest fossil cetacean discovered to date is the 52-million-year-old *Pakicetus*, which belonged to a group called the Archaeoceti, or ancient whales. *Pakicetus* is known only from its skull; features associated with hearing show that this wolf-sized animal lived at least partly on land. Within a few million years the archaeocete whales were fully aquatic.

*Rodhocetus*, for example, had well-developed hind limbs but its pelvic vertebrae (unlike those of land mammals), were not fused to form a rigid sacrum. Over the next 10 million years, the archaeocetes diversified to include some true giants, such as *Basilosaurus*, which measured up to 60 feet (18 m) long. This beast still had complete hind limbs, including knee joints and toes. By this stage, though, these tiny limbs were useless for propulsion through the water. Around 33 million years ago, the Archaeoceti split into the two main modern whale groups: toothed and baleen whales.

## Whale facial expressions

**Of the cetaceans,** only the beluga whale and narwhal can alter their facial expressions. The beluga's neck and mouth are highly flexible. It also has a very large melon, the forehead bulge containing tissues that focus echolocation signals.

Belugas communicate by sound, producing a wide range of clicks, cheeps, and bell-like tones. By altering the shape of the mouth, lips, and melon, beluga whales appear to smile, frown, and whistle. The meaning of these expressions is unknown.

*Smiling, pursed lips (left) and a grumpy frown (right) have specific but unknown meanings in beluga communication.*

pattern on their flanks that is created by combinations of yellow, white, gray, and black. Bold coloration serves a number of functions.

Cetaceans echolocate and communicate with each other using sound, but visual identification is important at close range. Individuals can probably recognize the age, sex, and status of of other individuals by sight as well as sound. Patches of color may also act as movement and orientation signals. As a common dolphin banks to change direction, new colors and shapes are brought into sharper view. Other individuals respond, helping a school of dolphins turn as one and move in a tight formation when hunting prey or avoiding predators. Contrasting colors also help break up the body outline, which can confuse attacking predators or fleeing prey.

▼ *A beluga whale has a very large melon, which plays a vital focusing role during echolocation and is also used to convey visual signals to other belugas.*

Dolphins and whales do not have external ears as most other mammals do. Two tiny openings lead from the outside directly to the hearing organs, but they are largely non-functional. Instead, toothed whales hear by channeling sound waves through the jaw to the inner ears. Most dolphins have forward-looking eyes and can see well both above and below the water. River dolphins' eyes are not so good. These dolphins rely on echolocation to find their way around in murky waters.

The dolphin's external reproductive organs are tucked away inside the body. In this way, streamlining of the body is not compromised. The male's penis is hidden behind muscular folds and emerges only when the male is aroused and ready for copulation. The teats of the female's mammary glands are housed within slits and appear only for suckling.

### Body color

Most whales are drab combinations of gray, black, brown, or white. However, some dolphins, particularly oceanic dolphins that congregate in large numbers, are more boldly marked. Long-beaked common dolphins, for example, have a characteristic "hourglass"

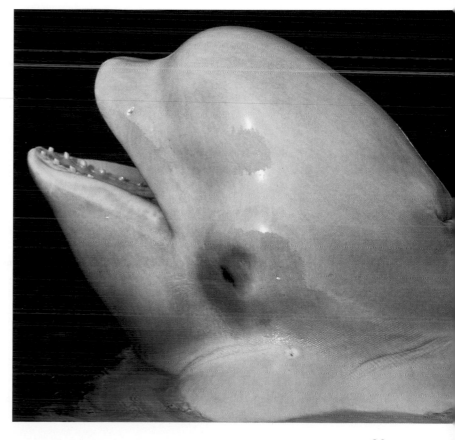

# Skeletal system

The cervical vertebrae are small and compressed.

thoracic vertebrae

lumbar vertebrae

The first and second cervical vertebrae are fused into one.

skull

scapula

maxilla

The dorsal processes are large to serve as attachments for the powerful tail muscles.

rib

sternum

humerus

radius

ulna

metacarpal

phalanges

The digits are extended and form a flipper.

dentary (or mandible)

▲ **Short-beaked common dolphin**
*The bones of a short-beaked common dolphin. The remnants of the pelvic bones (not shown) lie below the junction of lumbar and caudal vertebrae.*

In all vertebrates, the skeleton has four principal functions: it shapes and supports the animal's body; it protects vital internal organs such as the brain, heart, and lungs; it allows movement of body parts such as the head and limbs; and it enables locomotion, the movement of the whole animal.

A dolphin's skeleton is very different from that of a land mammal. Air does not provide physical support for an animal. Water is a relatively thick fluid that provides support to a swimming creature. Land-living mammals have a strong skeleton with limbs that raise the body off the ground. The legs act as vertical compression struts, rather like the piles that support a bridge. Mammals that spend their entire lives in water do not need this kind of support. In fact, a dolphin with its lungs full of air is effectively weightless in water. However, a cetacean's skeleton and muscles cannot support the animal out of water. If a large whale gets stranded on the shore, it lies helpless and eventually suffocates under its own weight.

## Skull and jaws

In any vertebrate, the skull's primary function is to protect the brain. The mammalian skull, however, is much larger than required for this function alone. It also contains large air spaces that connect to the nasal passages. When air is breathed in through the nose, its winding route through the skull ensures that the air is warmed and moistened before it reaches the lungs. This keeps heat loss in the lungs to a minimum and helps stop the membranes of the trachea (windpipe) from drying out.

### Light bones

**The bones of whales** are astonishingly light. Unlike those of land mammals, they do not need to be strong enough to support the animal in air. A whale's long bones consist of a thin outer shell of hard, compact bone, while the inside contains thin bony bars with large spaces in between. This is called spongy bone.

Whale skeletons contain far more spongy bone than those of land mammals. In adult whales, spongy bone is filled with fatty, yellow marrow. It also contains red bone marrow, which produces red and white blood cells, and platelets. In whales, the marrow-filled spongy bone also contributes to the animal's buoyancy.

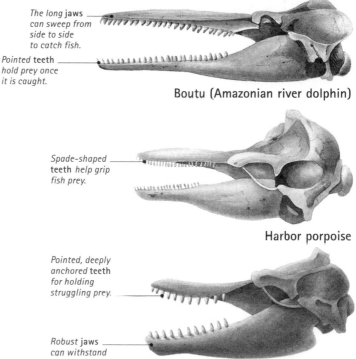

The long jaws can sweep from side to side to catch fish.

Pointed teeth hold prey once it is caught.

**Boutu (Amazonian river dolphin)**

Spade-shaped teeth help grip fish prey.

**Harbor porpoise**

Pointed, deeply anchored teeth for holding struggling prey.

Robust jaws can withstand the impact of large prey.

**Killer whale**

As in other mammals, the sacral vertebrae lie between the lumbar and caudal vertebrae and fuse with the pelvis. In dolphins, the sacral vertebrae are indistinguishable from the lumbar vertebrae and are usually counted as lumbar vertebrae.

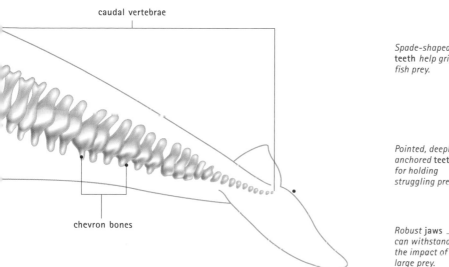

caudal vertebrae

chevron bones

In comparison with that of a zebra, the skull of a toothed whale is elongated (stretched lengthwise). This produces a jaw arrangement suitable for grasping narrow prey such as fish. The beak of most dolphins is streamlined, enabling it to cut through the water when swimming. A depression at the front and top of the skull accommodates the fat-containing melon, which is important for echolocation. The dolphin breathes through a blowhole at the top of the skull, so only a small part of the body needs to break the water's surface.

### The backbone

In land mammals, the backbone acts as a firm girder that supports the animal's weight. In whales, water supports the animal's weight. The backbone of a whale has become more important for the attachment of muscles that propel the animal through water. In most toothed whales, muscles account for about 40 percent of the animal's weight.

The trunk region of a whale is fairly rigid. The head and neck region can bend up and down to some extent, and the caudal (tail) region is very flexible. The varying degrees of movement are reflected in the number of vertebrae in different regions of the spine—more vertebrae generally allow for greater flexibility. The extent of firm or flexible connecting tissues between the vertebrae is also of importance.

Common dolphins have 75 vertebrae—more than most other mammals. Extra vertebrae in the tail provide the muscle attachments and flexibility required for swimming. Whales do have a neck, but in most species it is short and rigid. Dolphins can nod their head, but not swivel it or turn it to look backward. The limited movement of the neck is caused by the fusion of the first and second cervical vertebrae (the atlas and axis). The bottle-nosed dolphin is an exception, since its

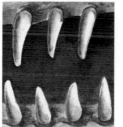

**Dolphin**

**Porpoise**

▲ **SKULLS**
Boutu and harbor porpoise are specialist fish eaters, while the killer whale eats much larger (often mammalian) prey. These skulls are not shown to scale.

◄ **TEETH**
Dolphins and porpoises have very different teeth. Those of dolphins are long and pointed, while porpoise teeth are shovel shaped. Both groups, however, feed mainly on fish and squid. Some porpoises have horny bumps on the gums between the teeth. These help grip slippery prey, although they are worn down in older porpoises.

31

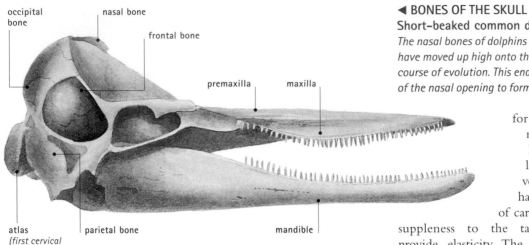

occipital bone
nasal bone
frontal bone
premaxilla
maxilla
atlas *(first cervical vertebra)*
parietal bone
mandible

## Short-beaked common dolphin
*The nasal bones of dolphins and other cetaceans have moved up high onto the forehead over the course of evolution. This enabled the movement of the nasal opening to form the blowhole.*

▲ WHALE TOOTH
*This is a cross section through a killer whale's tooth. Each line represents a year's growth. By cross-sectioning the teeth of a stranded cetacean, biologists can get a good idea of how long the animal lived.*

neck can bend up or down by 45 degrees. The five other neck vertebrae are compacted together in most whales, including all the oceanic dolphins. The short, rigid neck helps keep the head from wobbling from side to side when the animal is swimming. Head wobbling would cause drag and a sideways movement called yaw.

Most of the 13 or 14 thoracic vertebrae of common dolphins are fairly rigid. In whales only the first few are shaped to allow much flexibility and movement. Most vertebrae have flat faces that lie against each other and therefore allow little movement.

The lumbar (lower back) region of the spine is extraordinarily long in whales. The individual lumbar vertebrae are large, with broad surfaces and large extensions

for the powerful tail muscles to attach to. Dolphins have at least 30 caudal (tail) vertebrae. These bones have cushioning pads of cartilage that give great suppleness to the tail. The pads also provide elasticity. The joints between the vertebrae cushion the compressive (squeezing) forces that occur when the tail muscles contract. Most of the caudal vertebrae have bony extensions on top and below for muscle attachment. The last few caudal vertebrae are simple, flattened bones. They provide the central support for the broad tail flukes.

## Limbs and their supports
In land-living mammals, forelimbs and hind limbs are connected to the spine by the limb girdles. The fore, or pectoral, girdle contains two scapulae (shoulder blades) that allow most land mammals to move their forelimbs flexibly through wide arcs.

The hind, or pelvic, girdle is more robust than the pectoral girdle, and is anchored to the backbone through sacral vertebrae that are themselves fused together. Over millions of years, the front legs of whales' increasingly aquatic ancestors evolved to become flippers. The humerus (upper forelimb bone) of a typical whale flipper connects via a joint (the "elbow" in humans) to the ulna and radius— these are the lower forelimb bones. The basic setup is similar to a human arm. However, a dolphin's upper and lower forelimb bones are much shorter than a human's, while the digits are considerably longer. The second and third digits are very long, with extra phalanges providing support. The whole arrangement is enclosed by skin and connective tissue so the outline of the limb is smooth and streamlined. Cetacean hind limbs have disappeared. Of the pelvic girdle, just a few tiny bones remain. Biologists refer to these as vestigial structures.

### CLOSE-UP

## Losing legs

**During the evolutionary transition** from life on land to an aquatic existence, whales' hind limbs shrunk in size; today's whales have entirely lost their hind limb bones. Without hind limbs to support, the pelvic bones have also become greatly reduced. Modern whales have a small bone that represent the remnants of the pelvis. This is usually functionless, although it is used to anchor the muscles of the penis in the males of some species.

# Muscular system

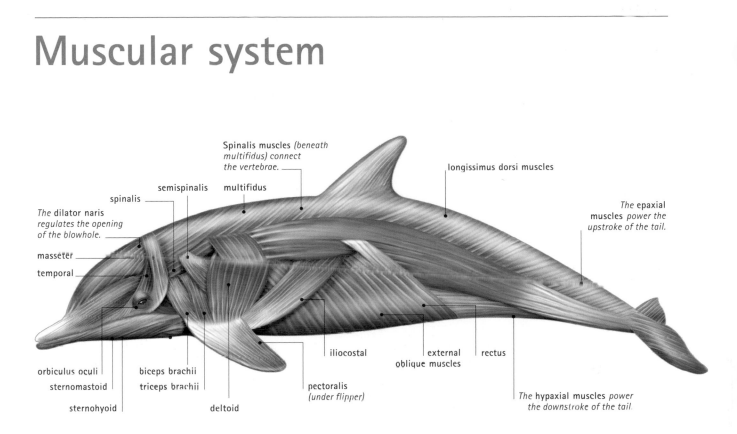

Spinalis muscles *(beneath multifidus)* connect the vertebrae.

longissimus dorsi muscles

semispinalis

multifidus

spinalis

The dilator naris *regulates the opening of the blowhole.*

The epaxial muscles *power the upstroke of the tail.*

masseter

temporal

orbiculus oculi

sternomastoid

sternohyoid

biceps brachii

triceps brachii

deltoid

pectoralis *(under flipper)*

iliocostal

external oblique muscles

rectus

The hypaxial muscles *power the downstroke of the tail.*

▲ **Short-beaked common dolphin**
*The musculature of a short-beaked common dolphin.*

As in other vertebrates, the movement of the bones of the skeleton is brought about by antagonistic pairs of muscles—sets of muscles that work against each other. The contraction of one set moves a bone in one direction, and the contraction of another set moves it in the opposite direction.

The flippers of a dolphin are supported by bones within, but the dorsal fin and the tail flukes are not. In the case of the dolphin's tail, muscles running from the lumbar (lower back) and caudal regions of the backbone connect through tendons to systems of tough fibers in the flukes. Contraction of the muscles not only bends the tail as a whole, but also changes the orientation of the flukes. At certain stages of the power and recovery strokes of the swimming cycle, the tail flukes move through the water with ease; at other stages, they push against the water to propel the animal forward.

## CLOSE-UP

## Muscular oxygen stores

**Working muscles have a high demand** for oxygen. To gain energy to contract, they need oxygen to release energy through a series of chemical reactions—this is called aerobic respiration. Deep-diving sperm whales can stay underwater for up to two hours. How can the whale's muscles gain the oxygen they need when the whale is cut off from the supply of air at the surface?

The answer lies in the muscles themselves. They have their own stores of oxygen bound to a pigment protein called myoglobin. The myoglobin gradually releases its oxygen store during the whale's dive. Weight for weight, sperm whale muscle can store twice as much oxygen as that of any land mammal. Sperm whale muscle is dark in color because of the large quantities of myoglobin it contains.

▲ *A common dolphin leaps from the ocean surface. All the power required to propel the animal into the air is generated by the tail.*

The beating of the whale's tail is brought about by two main sets of muscles. One set, the epaxial muscles, lies above the backbone. The other set, the hypaxial muscles, lies below it. The epaxial muscles are much larger than the hypaxial muscles. Contraction of the epaxial muscles raises the tail. This is called the power stroke, since it provides most of a dolphin's thrust. Large epaxial muscles enable a strong power stroke.

## Connecting muscles

A spiral of connective tissue called the subdermal sheath winds around the epaxial and hypaxial muscles. When the epaxial muscles contract to power the tail's upstroke, the hypaxial sheath stores energy like a coiled spring. The energy is released to help power the downstroke. This makes the dolphin's tail more powerful and energy-efficient than the size of its muscles would suggest. When the hypaxial muscles contract for the tail's downstroke, the epaxial sheath stretches in readiness for the upstroke.

Blubber helps, too. The blubber above and below the tail muscles is arranged in wedges that contain springlike collagen fibers. When the tail rises, the topmost wedge compresses, storing energy, which is released when the tail descends. Then the lower wedge compresses, storing energy for the upward rebound. Together with the dolphin's skin properties, this helps explain why dolphins can swim so fast—at 20 mph (32 km/h) or more.

### CLOSE-UP

# Dolphin flukes and vortices

**If a dolphin's tail** simply beat up and down in the water, the animal could not move forward through the water. The flukes in the dolphin's tail must bend and alter their angle of attack at different points of the swimming stroke. Water leaves the trailing edge of the flukes in the form of swirls called vortices. Stages in the power and recovery stroke of a dolphin's tail include these:
**1.** Epaxial muscles contract, and the tail moves upward. This power stroke creates a vortex and a point of high pressure beneath the tail.

**2.** The dolphin moves forward and down.
**3.** At the top of the power stroke, the vortex leaves the trailing edge of the flukes.
**4.** The dolphin glides through the water with the tail contracted to offer minimum resistance.
**5.** The hypaxial muscles contract and slowly lower the tail in readiness for the next power stroke. This is called the recovery stroke; it is partly powered by elastic recoil of the tissues.
**6.** At the end of the recovery stroke the fluke is extended, ready for a new stroke cycle.

# Nervous system

**CONNECTIONS**

**COMPARE** the echolocation system of a dolphin, which operates in water, with that of a **FRUIT BAT**, which functions in air.

**COMPARE** the size and shape of a dolphin's brain with those of other intelligent mammals, such as the **HUMAN** and the **CHIMPANZEE**.

▼ **Short-beaked common dolphin**
*Important parts of the dolphin nervous system. Relative to body size, the dolphin brain is among the largest in the animal kingdom.*

Dolphins and other toothed whales have a nervous system that is responsible for rapidly coordinating activities within the body and for responding to environmental changes outside the body. Coordination is brought about by electrical impulses that travel along nerve cells called neurons. They are bundled together to form nerves.

A vertebrate's nervous system is divided into the central nervous system (CNS), which consists of the brain and spinal cord, and the peripheral nervous system, or PNS. The PNS contains the nerves that connect the CNS with the sensory organs, such as the eyes and ears, and also with responding structures (effectors), such as muscles and glands.

Stimuli from the external environment, such as light waves or sound vibrations, stimulate receptors in sensory organs such as the eyes or inner ears. Sensory neurons deliver nervous impulses from these organs through the PNS to the CNS, where the brain or spinal cord processes them. The CNS then executes an appropriate response by sending nerve impulses along motor neurons to muscles—for example, to change behavior in response to the environmental stimuli.

## The structure of the brain

Toothed whales, like mammals in general, have a brain with three main regions: the forebrain, the midbrain, and the hindbrain. The hindbrain contains the medulla and cerebellum. The medulla regulates automatic activities; it is involved in the control of physiological features such as body temperature, heartbeat, and breathing, for example. The cerebellum automatically controls body movements, making them smooth and coordinated. This structure is large in dolphins; it needs to be large to help control the animal's rapid, highly coordinated swimming. The midbrain, which contains the thalamus, is a relay center for directing nerve impulses from sensory organs to different parts of the forebrain.

The forebrain contains the cerebrum. This has an outer layer, the cerebral cortex, that is made up of gray brain matter. Gray matter contains numerous connections between nerve cells. The cerebral cortex is folded so it looks like the surface of a walnut. Folding increases the surface area and hence the number of connections. As a rule, the greater the degree of folding, the greater the

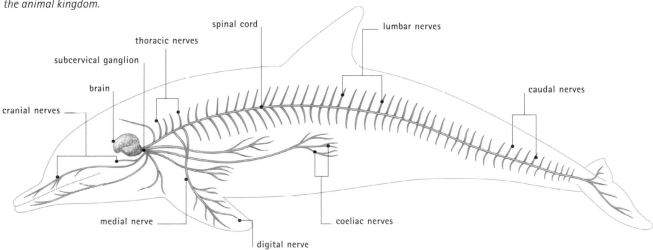

spinal cord

thoracic nerves

lumbar nerves

subcervical ganglion

brain

caudal nerves

cranial nerves

medial nerve

coeliac nerves

digital nerve

## IN FOCUS

### Stunning with sound?

**Scientists have recorded** wild dolphins hunting using loud, narrow beams of sound as they focus tightly on individual fish. These beams of sound may serve to stun or disorientate the dolphin's prey. This hypothesis is difficult for biologists to confirm because dolphins do not make such sounds in captivity. Some other cetaceans, such as group-feeding humpback whales, use loud sounds to confuse and terrify schools of fish. Humpbacks also blow out curtains of air bubbles to herd the fish into one place.

▶ **Sound hunters**
*This pair of spotted dolphins may use beams of sound to stun their fish prey.*

intelligence of the animal. In humans and toothed whales the cerebral cortex is highly folded. The cerebrum is responsible for memory, learning, and reasoning, and for processing complex sensory information, such as that relayed from the eyes and ears.

### Touch, taste, and smell

Toothed whales such as dolphins have all the senses generally found in land-living mammals, although the sense of smell (olfaction) may be limited. Researchers have found taste receptors on the tongue of various species of toothed whales, and these may help the animals select food items. Toothed whales might also be able to taste chemicals released by other individuals that give clues to their availability for mating. Tasting the chemical signature of a current might also help whales navigate the oceans.

The skin of toothed whales is sensitive, especially the region around the blowhole. Touch is important in the social life of toothed whales. Stroking and touching are part of the courtship rituals in many species, and mothers and their calves touch regularly. This helps maintain their close bond.

### Sight

Dolphins see well in both air and water. When hunting for flying fish, bottle-nosed dolphins are able to track their quarry as they glide through the air. Killer whales often spyhop when they are hunting; they raise their heads up out of the water and look

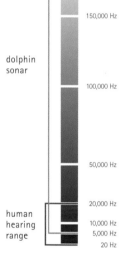

dolphin sonar

200,000 Hz

150,000 Hz

100,000 Hz

50,000 Hz

20,000 Hz

10,000 Hz
5,000 Hz
20 Hz

human hearing range

◀ *Dolphins produce high-frequency sounds to echolocate. Some overlap with the range of human hearing but most are many times higher.*

▼ *How dolphins make and receive echolocation signals.*

around for seals resting on ice floes. Light is more strongly refracted (bent) by the eye in air than it is in water. An eye that can see well in air cannot focus as sharply underwater. Whales get around this problem by using different parts of the eye for focusing in air and in water.

In most toothed whales, the field of vision of one eye overlaps that of the other. So, there is a large area toward the front where the vision is binocular (both eyes can focus on an object). This allows the animal to see well in three dimensions and to accurately judge the distance to prey and other objects. The eyes of toothed whales with large blunt heads, such as sperm whales, are set far back, and the animal has little or no binocular vision. Sperm whales do much of their hunting in or beyond the twilight zone, at depths beyond 3,300 feet (1,000 m). Sperm whales have less need for good vision

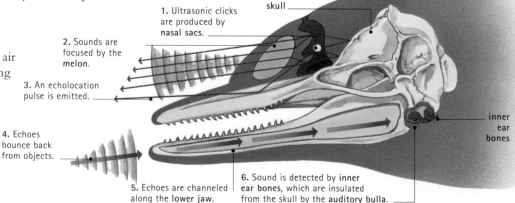

1. Ultrasonic clicks are produced by nasal sacs.

skull

2. Sounds are focused by the melon.

3. An echolocation pulse is emitted.

4. Echoes bounce back from objects.

5. Echoes are channeled along the **lower jaw**.

6. Sound is detected by **inner ear bones**, which are insulated from the skull by the **auditory bulla**.

inner ear bones

since little light reaches this part of the ocean. Vision is also less important for dolphins that live in murky water, such as river dolphins.

### Hearing and echolocation

Sound travels much farther and faster in water than in air, and all toothed whales have good hearing. They can detect sounds that are higher pitched (ultrasonic) and lower pitched (infrasonic) than humans can hear. Several features make dolphin hearing very different to that of land mammals.

In toothed whales, a sound-conducting channel of fat in the lower jaw carries sound waves from the surrounding water to the bones of the middle ear; they pass the vibrations to the inner ear, where they are converted into nervous impulses that travel on to the brain. Only the lowest-pitched sounds travel through the dolphin's external ear—the channel normally used in land mammals. It is tiny in dolphins. Dolphins' hearing is extremely sensitive. It is aided by foam-filled spaces that cushion the inner ear from the skull, ensuring that other sounds do not interfere with those channeled out through the melon and those returning through the jaw. Toothed whales communicate with a wide range of sounds, including croaks, whistles, and squeaks. The beluga is sometimes called the "sea canary" for its melodious calls. Orcas, or killer whales, living in different localities have distinctive "dialects."

Toothed whales can hunt for food at night, or in deep or murky waters where there is little or no light. They create a mental image of their surroundings using sound, a strategy called echolocation. Dolphins make high-frequency clicks by vibrating air in the nasal passages beneath the blowhole. The skull reflects the sounds as a beam. The melon in the dolphin's forehead focuses this beam. The dolphin listens for the echoes reflected back. The echoes are channeled through the lower jaw. The time delay between the sound being sent and its return, and the way it is distorted, tells the dolphin how far away an object is, whether it is moving, and what it is made of. The sound beam is like an X ray, able to penetrate through sand and living tissue. Air spaces, such as a fish's swim bladder, produce a particularly strong echo that the dolphin can home in on.

## IN FOCUS

### Dolphin intelligence

**In captivity,** animal trainers can teach dolphins to perform a wide range of tricks and to carry out complex tasks, such as retrieving specific objects when told to. In the wild, dolphin behavior is flexible, and individuals can learn quickly from each other: for example, to pick up and use a natural sponge as a "tool" to protect the snout when digging for food. Dolphins and most toothed whales have a large brain relative to their body size. A bottle-nosed dolphin has a brain that is, relatively, just a little smaller than a human's (and twice the size of a chimp's). Dolphin brains have a high degree of cerebral folding. This reflects the fact that their brain must process a fast stream of sound and visual information about their surroundings. Also, dolphins lead rich social lives and have to interpret each other's communications and behavior. Cerebral size and folding are good indicators of intelligence.

▶ Captive dolphins can learn a range of tricks. These are leaping in unison.

# Digestive and excretory systems

Most toothed whales are fish eaters, although they are quite opportunistic and will take other available prey, such as squid and crustaceans. All toothed whales can use echolocation to home in on their prey. The arrangement of teeth reflects the whale's main food. Orcas have large, backward-curving, interlocking teeth that can snatch wriggling fish and bite chunks out of medium-sized whales.

Most dolphins have many small, pointed teeth to grasp slippery fish, which are swallowed whole. Risso's dolphin has a few teeth in the lower jaw only, which help it suck in and swallow squid. Sperm whales have a row of large, rounded teeth in the lower jaw that allow them to capture giant squid up to 50 feet (15 m) long. Porpoises have chisel-shaped teeth that work together like scissors to slice through their fish prey, which are large in proportion to their mouth.

## Digestion

Toothed whales swallow their prey whole or in large chunks. After swallowing, the food travels down the esophagus to arrive at the stomach, a muscular sac where digestion (the process of breaking down food) starts in earnest. A whale's stomach has three compartments; it is more complex than that of other meat-eating mammals, such as humans, cats, and dogs. These types of animals have only one stomach chamber.

Muscular churning in the first part of the whale's stomach, the forestomach, grinds up the food. This process is called mechanical digestion. The resulting mush, called chyme, is squirted into the second chamber, the main stomach, where chemical digestion begins. The walls of the main stomach secrete hydrochloric acid to reduce the pH (increase the relative acidity) and protein-digesting enzymes to chemically break down the food. The walls of the third stomach compartment, the pyloric stomach, secrete fat-digesting enzymes, more protein-digesting enzymes, and an alkaline fluid that neutralizes the acidity of the main stomach juices.

## Liver and pancreatic secretions

The partly digested food now enters a short tube called the duodenum, the first part of the small intestine. The pancreatic duct (leading from the pancreas) and the bile duct (from the liver) empty their contents into this organ. Pancreatic juices contain a mixture of digestive enzymes for different food types—proteins, fats, and carbohydrates. Bile is a liquid that contains bile salts. They emulsify (break up) globules of fat, making them smaller and easier to digest.

▼ **Short-beaked common dolphin**
*The gut and excretory system (female). The kidney produces urine, which leaves the body at the urogenital opening. This opening also has other functions. In females, sperm is introduced there by a male, and young are born through it.*

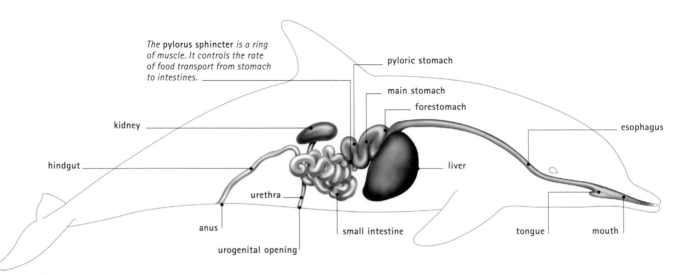

The **pylorus sphincter** *is a ring of muscle. It controls the rate of food transport from stomach to intestines.*

pyloric stomach

main stomach

forestomach

kidney

esophagus

hindgut

liver

urethra

anus

small intestine

tongue

mouth

urogenital opening

## Valuable vomit

**Ambergris is a waxy substance** that accumulates in the intestines of sperm whales. Tough bits of prey, such as squid beaks, collect in the whale's digestive tract. A thick, dark gray liquid is released by the intestine walls that coats this irritating material. The liquid hardens to form ambergris. Sometimes a whale vomits a lump of ambergris, which floats on the water surface.

Despite its strange origins, ambergris has a fragrant smell and was once highly prized by whalers. They sold it to perfume makers, who used it as a fixative in cosmetics.

PREDATOR AND PREY

## Hunting as a team

**Many toothed whales cooperate when** hunting. Bottle-nosed dolphins often work together to drive a shoal of fish into shallow water. Boutu river dolphins may even drive the fish onto the shore before grabbing individual morsels and wriggling back into the water.

*A pod of killer whales, or orcas, corrals a school of herring into a small area. The whales may emit high-pitched sounds to help them herd the terrified fish.*

*Members of the killer whale pod then take turns to drive through the tightly packed school of herring, snatching fish as they go.*

### Absorption and expulsion

Further chemical digestion takes place in the final section of the small intestine, the ileum, the walls of which release more digestive enzymes. Water and digested food are absorbed in the ileum and in the large intestine, which follows the small intestine. Indigestible waste is stored temporarily in the last part of the large intestine, the rectum, before being expelled through the anus.

Small and large intestines together form an immensely long tube, up to 500 feet (150 m) long in an adult sperm whale. The walls are highly folded and rich in blood vessels. This tube creates a very large surface area across which water and digested food substances can be absorbed efficiently, so little is wasted.

### Expelling salts

Toothed whales, like other mammals, have a concentration of salts in their blood that is lower than the saltiness of seawater. Whales must take in water to keep their blood diluted, but at the same time they must get rid of excess salts; otherwise, their blood and tissues would become too salt-rich. Whales gain most of their water from the food they eat.

The kidneys remove excess salts from the bloodstream along with the by-products of cellular activity and other wastes. The kidneys filter the blood, reabsorb what is useful, and allow the rest to pass out of the body in urine. The bladder temporarily stores the urine until it is expelled to the outside through the urethra.

Whale kidneys are only moderately efficient at expelling salts. Thus whales have to excrete large quantities of water along with the salts. They have to replace the lost water through feeding rather than drinking.

# Reproductive system

**▶ Short-beaked common dolphin**
*Details of the male reproductive system.*

*Tiny channels exit the rear of the testes. These merge to form the* **epididymis,** *a coiled duct inside which sperm matures.*

*Sperm is produced in the* **testes,** *a pair of organs kept cool by blood routed from the dorsal fin. Sperm production increases during the breeding season.*

*The* **vas deferens** *channels sperm from testes to the penis.*

**pelvic bone**

**anus**

*The* **penis** *is kept inside the body but it can quickly be everted.*

*The* **penis retractor muscle.** *Muscular control gives the penis a degree of flexibility.*

*The* **genital slit,** *through which the penis protrudes during copulation and also some social interactions.*

**fallopian tubes**

**fundus**

**cervix** *(neck of uterus)*

**uterus**

**vagina**

*The* **ovary** *is suspended from the abdominal wall by ligaments.*

*The* **genital slit,** *through which the calf is born.*

**▲ Short-beaked common dolphin**
*The female reproductive system. Usually only one egg is released at a time.*

Toothed whales have a similar reproductive system to that of placental land mammals, although adaptations have evolved that allow mating, birth of the calf, and suckling to take place underwater. To keep the body streamlined, male cetaceans have an internal penis and testes.

The penis normally lies coiled inside the abdomen and is extended through a genital slit before mating. Muscles attached to the vestigial pelvis make the penis quite mobile, and it is used as a sensory organ, not just for mating but in other social encounters as well.

*▶ Before mating, male and female dolphins stroke each other with their flippers. Copulation takes place as the dolphins swim together belly to belly.*

In most toothed whale species, including dolphins, pairs practice considerable touching and rubbing before mating. Copulation, the process whereby the male's penis is inserted into the female's genital slit and sperm is released, is short-lived in dolphins. It typically lasts about one minute, but it may be repeated many times. Toothed whales are either promiscuous (males and females having many partners, as is the case in most dolphins) or polygynous (males mate with several females, as in sperm whales and narwhals).

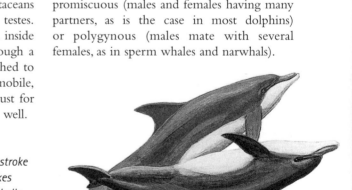

Some adult male bottle-nosed dolphins form friendship alliances to gain access to mates and to keep other males at bay. The males within the alliance all mate with each female they successfully court; sperm from the different males compete inside the female to reach the ovum (egg cell) first. Male narwhals use their tusks to joust with each other for access to a particular female. Female toothed

## GENETICS

### Who are the parents?

**Scientists can discover** who the father of a dolphin calf is by taking tissue samples from the calf and matching its DNA with that of the local males. Researchers collect tissue samples using a small dart to remove a plug of skin. In some toothed whales, such as sperm whales, individuals slough off fragments of skin when they dive, and researchers collect these for DNA study.

## Suckling young

**A female dolphin's mammary glands** are located on either side of the genital slit. They are normally hidden, but when the area is nuzzled by the calf, muscles contract to force a nipple to emerge from one of the mammary glands. Milk is then squirted directly into the calf's mouth. The calf does not need to suck, so it can drink underwater. Whale milk is much richer in fat than human or cow's milk. This helps the calf lay down a thick layer of insulating blubber within a matter of weeks.

whales often exercise their right to choose a mate by signaling to a male that they are receptive. Females signal behaviorally or by releasing chemical attractants in their urine.

### Pregnancy and birth

Typically, a female dolphin's ovaries (egg-producing organs) release only one ovum at at a time. So if the female mates successfully only one calf is normally born. The gestation period (time from fertilization to birth) is 10–12 months in most toothed whales, but can be between 16 and 18 months in sperm whales.

A whale calf is born tail-first, so the young whale is supplied with oxygen through the placenta until the very last moment. Then the calf's blowhole emerges from the mother's genital slit, and the newborn is guided swiftly to the surface by its mother to take its first breath. This arrangement reduces the chances of the calf's drowning during birth. Calf and mother are linked by a short umbilical cord, connected to the placenta, but this severs naturally at a weak spot shortly after birth. The mother expels the placenta an hour or so later.

Several months before giving birth to her calf, a dolphin chooses another experienced female to act as a "midwife." The midwife looks after the expectant mother and helps her through the birth. The two adult dolphins move away from the rest of the school at this time. A strong bond often develops between the two female dolphins.

### Growing up

Feeding a calf is energetically demanding. Also, a long time is needed to teach the calf the hunting and social skills it must have before it can fend for itself. For these reasons, a female usually produces a calf only every two to three years. Bottle-nosed dolphin calves begin to take solid food after about six months but are not fully weaned off milk until they are 18 to 20 months old.

The age of sexual maturity varies depending on species and gender. In dolphins, it is 5 to 14 years for females and 9 to 14 years for males. Female sperm whales typically mature at about 9 years old; males at 15 to 20.

TREVOR DAY

**FURTHER READING AND RESEARCH**

Mead, James G., and Joy P. Gold. 2002. *Whales and Dolphins in Question: The Smithsonian Answer Book.* Smithsonian Books: Washington, DC.

▲ *Dolphins are unusual in that they enjoy play throughout their lives. Most animals play only when they are young. Play helps reinforce social bonds within the dolphin school.*

▼ *Attended by a helpful midwife dolphin, a female gives birth tail-first to her calf.*

# Elephant

ORDER: **Proboscidea** FAMILY: **Elephantidae**
GENERA: *Loxodonta* and *Elephas*

The three species of elephants—the Asian elephant, African savanna elephant, and African forest elephant—are the sole remnants of the order Proboscidea. Until a few thousand years ago, however, there were many more species of proboscideans, including the mastodons, gomphotheres, and mammoths. Not all these beasts were giants: pygmy elephants lived on some Mediterranean islands until as recently as 4,400 years ago.

## Anatomy and taxonomy
Proboscideans, the group that includes both elephants and extinct animals such as mammoths, share a number of unusual characteristics, such as a trunk and tusks, and are only distantly related to other mammals.

- **Animals** All animals are multicellular and depend on other organisms for food. Unlike other multicellular organisms such as plants and fungi, most animals are able to move about and react quickly to stimuli.

- **Chordates** At some time in their life cycle, all chordates have a stiff supporting rod called a notochord running along the back of their body.

- **Vertebrates** The notochord of vertebrates is in the form of a spinal cord. This is encased by the spine, composed of bones called vertebrae. Most vertebrates are bilaterally symmetrical—the body shape is roughly the same on either side of the backbone. All vertebrates have a skull made of either bone or cartilage surrounding a brain.

- **Mammals** Mammals are unique among vertebrates in having mammary glands. Females nourish their young with milk secreted from these glands. Unlike all other vertebrates, most mammals have fur covering their body, a single lower jawbone that hinges directly with the skull, and red blood cells that lack nuclei.

▶ *This family tree shows the major groups to which elephants belong, as well as some close relatives. After recent DNA analyses, the African elephants have been separated into two species. Note that the order Proboscidea contains many species that are extinct, including groups such as the mammoths and mastodons.*

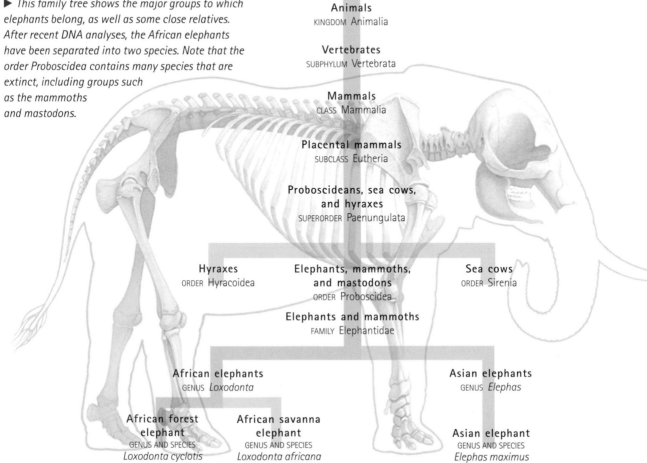

**Animals**
KINGDOM Animalia

**Vertebrates**
SUBPHYLUM Vertebrata

**Mammals**
CLASS Mammalia

**Placental mammals**
SUBCLASS Eutheria

**Proboscideans, sea cows, and hyraxes**
SUPERORDER Paenungulata

**Hyraxes**
ORDER Hyracoidea

**Elephants, mammoths, and mastodons**
ORDER Proboscidea

**Sea cows**
ORDER Sirenia

**Elephants and mammoths**
FAMILY Elephantidae

**African elephants**
GENUS *Loxodonta*

**Asian elephants**
GENUS *Elephas*

**African forest elephant**
GENUS AND SPECIES
*Loxodonta cyclotis*

**African savanna elephant**
GENUS AND SPECIES
*Loxodonta africana*

**Asian elephant**
GENUS AND SPECIES
*Elephas maximus*

● **Placental mammals** These mammals develop inside the mother's uterus. There, they receive nourishment and oxygen through an organ called the placenta, which develops during pregnancy. The other major mammal groups are the egg-laying monotremes and the marsupials. They give birth to very small young that develop in a pouch on the surface of the mother's body.

● **Elephants, sea cows, and hyraxes** The orders that contain the elephants (Proboscidea) and the sea cows (Sirenia) are more closely related to each other than to other mammals. Sea cows are completely aquatic. Their front limbs have evolved into fins, and the rear limbs have disappeared altogether. They swim using large tail flukes. Dugong flukes resemble those of a whale, but manatees have a flat, round paddle. Hyraxes are also distant relatives of elephants. These small, rodentlike mammals live in rocky habitats or in trees in the Middle East and Africa.

● **Elephants and mammoths** Both living and extinct proboscideans have an elongated nose that forms a trunk and have a very large body. Like modern elephants, most extinct proboscideans bore tusks that protruded through the upper lip. Although modern elephants are the largest living land animals, some mammoths weighed more than twice the maximum recorded weight of an African savanna elephant. All living elephants are plant eaters, and so were their ancestors.

● **African elephants** The African savanna elephant is the biggest modern species, with large ears and a back that slopes down from the shoulders. Until recently, the African forest elephant was considered a subspecies (local form) of savanna elephant, but studies of forest elephant DNA have shown that it is genetically distinct. The forest elephant is

▲ *An African savanna elephant uses its trunk to pull vegetation from the ground and pass it to the mouth for chewing.*

smaller and darker than its savanna cousin and lives in the rain forests of west and central Africa. The savanna elephant lives on the grasslands of eastern and southern Africa. Both species have two fingerlike processes at the tip of the trunk.

● **Asian elephant** The Asian elephant has a humped back and relatively small ears, and the females lack tusks. The Asian elephant has just one fingerlike trunk process.

**FEATURED SYSTEMS**

**EXTERNAL ANATOMY** Elephants are massive, four-legged mammals. They have a large, short head with a trunk, large ears, and sometimes long tusks. *See pages 46–49.*

**SKELETAL SYSTEM** An elephant's skeleton is adapted for bearing great weight, with thick limb bones arranged like vertical pillars, so the weight passes along the length of the bones, reducing the need for muscular exertion and minimizing risk of injury to joints. *See pages 50–53.*

**MUSCULAR SYSTEM** Powerful leg muscles help the elephant maintain its posture when walking. The head, trunk, and neck are served by large muscles that support the trunk and tusks. *See pages 54–55.*

**NERVOUS SYSTEM** Elephants have the largest brain of any species of land animal and show a variety of complex behavioral adaptations, including use of tools. *See pages 56–57.*

**CIRCULATORY AND RESPIRATORY SYSTEMS** An elephant's oxygen requirement is less per unit of body weight than that of smaller mammals, and its heart rate is much slower. *See pages 58–59.*

**DIGESTIVE SYSTEM** Elephants eat large amounts of low-quality food. This is digested with the help of bacteria that live in the elephant's enlarged cecum at the junction of the small and large intestines. *See pages 60–61.*

**REPRODUCTIVE SYSTEM** Male elephants regularly enter a period of heightened aggression and sexual activity called musth. At such times, they seek out receptive females and fight off rivals. *See pages 62–63.*

# External anatomy

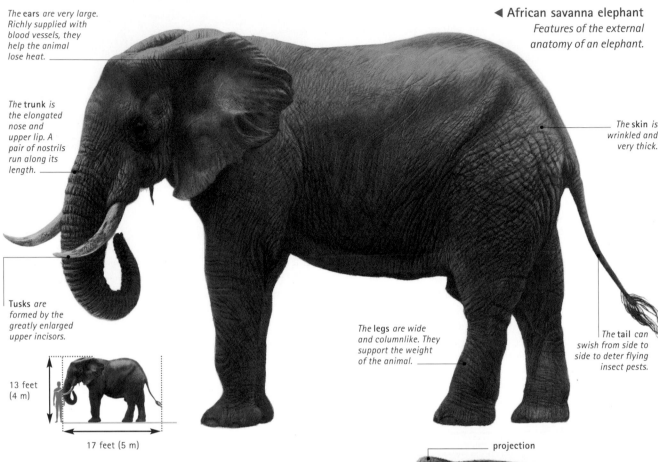

The **ears** *are very large. Richly supplied with blood vessels, they help the animal lose heat.*

The **trunk** *is the elongated nose and upper lip. A pair of nostrils run along its length.*

**Tusks** *are formed by the greatly enlarged upper incisors.*

◀ **African savanna elephant**
*Features of the external anatomy of an elephant.*

The **skin** *is wrinkled and very thick.*

The **legs** *are wide and columnlike. They support the weight of the animal.*

The **tail** *can swish from side to side to deter flying insect pests.*

13 feet (4 m)

17 feet (5 m)

**CONNECTIONS**

**COMPARE** the elephant's tusks with the incisors of a *LION*, a *ZEBRA*, and a *HUMAN*.

**COMPARE** the posture of an elephant with that of a *RHINOCEROS* and a *HIPPOPOTAMUS*.

Elephants have a huge but relatively short head, and a massive body supported by long, powerful, columnlike legs. Elephants have the longest nose, largest ears, and the longest teeth of any living mammal. In both African and Asian elephants, males weigh nearly twice as much as females. A large male Asian elephant weighs about 10,000 pounds (4,500 kg), and a good-sized male African savanna elephant weighs about 14,000 pounds (6,300 kg) and occasionally up to 16,500 pounds (7,500 kg).

African and Asian elephants have different body shapes. The middle of the back is the highest point of an Asian elephant, reaching up to 11 feet (3.3 m) high. The highest point of African savanna and forest elephants is the shoulders, rising up to 13 feet (4 m) in savanna males. Forest elephants are much smaller; the tallest are around 7 feet (2.2 m) tall.

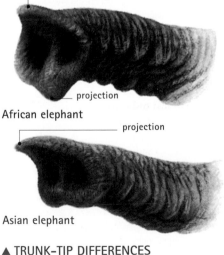

projection

projection

**African elephant**

projection

**Asian elephant**

▲ **TRUNK-TIP DIFFERENCES**
*Asian elephant trunks bear a single fingerlike projection at the tip. African elephant trunks have two of these projections.*

## The elephant's trunk

The most striking feature of an elephant is its trunk, which is a flexible, muscular, elongated nose. The trunk may be more than 6 feet (1.8 m) long in African savanna elephants. There are two nostrils at the tip of the trunk. Elephants also have fingerlike projections at the end of the trunk that they use to pick up small objects. African elephants have two projections, while Asian elephants have one.

Elephants use their trunk for both eating and drinking. The trunk is used to grasp hard-to-reach twigs or grasses close to the ground. Elephants also use their trunk to suck up water, which they squirt into their mouth for drinking or spray over their body to cool down. When walking through deep water or swimming, elephants can use their trunk as a snorkel to breathe even if submerged. Elephants are intelligent animals and can use their trunk to make tools, such as fly switches made from branches. Elephants even use their trunk to throw stones and other objects at animals that may be bothering them.

## Giant incisors

All male elephants and female African elephants bear tusks—greatly elongated upper incisor teeth. Female Asian elephants have

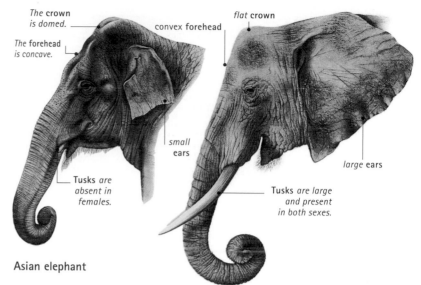

The **crown** is domed.

The **forehead** is concave.

convex **forehead**

flat **crown**

small ears

large ears

**Tusks** are absent in females.

**Tusks** are large and present in both sexes.

**Asian elephant**

tusks only rarely. The largest tusk ever recorded came from a male African savanna elephant; it was nearly 11.5 feet (3.5 m) long and weighed 236 pounds (107 kg). By contrast, the largest recorded tusk from a female African elephant weighed only 40 pounds (18 kg). Large tusk size in male elephants is an adaptation for combat. Males sometimes use their tusks to fight each other for the right to mate with females. Rivals can inflict severe injuries, and occasionally

## ▲ TRUNK AND HEAD

*Head anatomy provides a number of clues for figuring out to which species an elephant belongs.*

---

**EVOLUTION**

## Ancient elephants

**In the distant past** there were many species of proboscideans quite different from modern elephants. For example, deinotheres had tusks that curved downward from the lower jaw, and *Gomphotherium* had tusks protruding from the upper and lower jaws. *Platybelodon* had shovel-shaped lower incisors, a flattened trunk, and small, downward curving upper tusks. The mammoths became extinct relatively recently, about 10,000 years ago. They included the largest known probiscidean, the steppe mammoth. This beast stood up to 15 feet (4.5 m) high and weighed more than 44,000 pounds (20,000 kg).

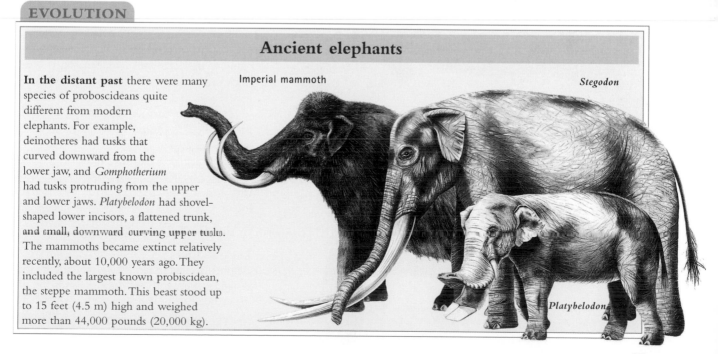

Imperial mammoth

*Stegodon*

*Platybelodon*

▶ *Elephant hide is wrinkled, thick, and very tough, and is resistant to all but the most specialized parasites. Nonetheless, it can be damaged by intense sunlight. Elephants seek out shade in which to rest during the hottest part of the day.*

## COMPARATIVE ANATOMY

# Manatees and dugongs

**A group of mammals** called tethytheres lived about 50 million years ago. The tethytheres gave rise to both the Probiscidea and the Sirenia, the group that contains manatees and dugongs. Only four species of sirenians remain, though they were much more abundant and diverse in the past. All sirenians are completely aquatic; they have a large, spindle-shape body, weighing up to 2,000 pounds (900 kg). Sirenians have paddle-shape front limbs and a flat lobed or fluke-shape tail for swimming.

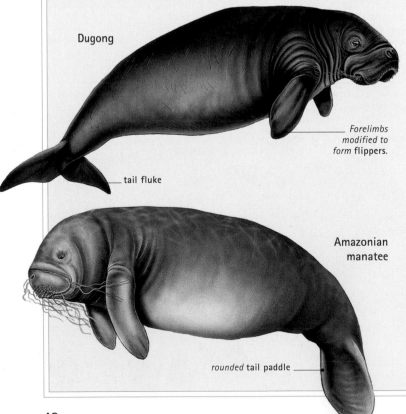

Dugong

*Forelimbs modified to form **flippers**.*

— tail fluke

Amazonian manatee

*rounded **tail** paddle* —

individuals may die after receiving tusk wounds in battle. Elephants also use their tusks for digging up tasty roots and for stripping bark from trees. Domesticated elephants can be trained to use their tusks to carry heavy objects such as logs.

## Big ears

African savanna elephants have huge ears that can measure nearly 4 feet (1.2 m) from top to bottom. On average they are three times larger then the ears of Asian elephants. Because of their large bulky body shape, elephants sometimes have problems keeping cool in the sweltering midday heat of the tropics. Having large flapping ears helps them lose body heat, thus preventing overheating.

When elephants flap their ears, air currents cool the warm blood passing through the dense network of blood vessels lying close to the surface on the underside of the elephant's ears. They can lose enough heat through the blood vessels in their ears to lower their body temperature to comfortable levels. Elephants also use their ears to signal anger; they spread their ears wide during aggressive encounters.

## Elephant skin

The skin of an elephant is wrinkled and usually gray or dull brown, although very rarely white albino elephants occur. Most of the time it is hard to see the true color of elephants because they cover themselves in mud or dust that makes them appear the same color as the local soil. Elephant skin is very thick in places, up to 1.2 inches (3 cm) on the legs, back, and trunk. Elephants sometimes suffer from sunburn. A covering of dirt helps protect the skin from the sun's rays; it may also keep biting insects at bay.

Asian elephants are born with a sparse covering of hair over their body, mostly on the top of their head and back. Most of this hair is lost after their first year. African elephants have some hair but less than their Asian relatives.

## Legs and feet

Elephants sometimes have to travel long distances between feeding grounds or the water holes in which they wallow and drink. If food and water are scarce, elephants may journey across hundreds of miles to find better

## Hyraxes

**Although they look very different,** hyraxes (below) are among the closest relatives of elephants. Hyraxes resemble rabbits with short, rounded ears, but unlike rabbits hyraxes have toes with hooflike nails. Leathery footpads lubricated with glandular secretions give hyraxes amazing traction for bounding around the steep rocky slopes where they live. Hyraxes weigh up to 10 pounds (4.5 kg).

conditions. Elephants need very strong legs to move their great weight over long distances. The legs are long and powerful, and are able to support heavy loads with little effort; they direct the animals' weight through the leg bones rather than through muscles, which would quickly tire. Since they are long, the legs give the elephants an extended gait, allowing them to amble along at a steady 10 mph (16 km/h) for long periods, or at up to 25 mph (40 km/h) when charging.

Both African and Asian elephants have wide, flat feet with soft elastic soles. African elephants have five nails or "hooves" on each of their front feet and three nails on each of the hind feet. Asian elephants have five nails on each front foot and usually four nails on the back foot. Elephants have very broad feet, measuring 5 feet (1.5 m) or more in circumference. Interestingly, the shoulder height of an elephant is approximately twice the circumference of its feet, allowing trackers to estimate an elephant's size from its footprints.

▲ *The trunk has many uses besides picking up food and other objects. Water can be drawn up into the nostrils. It can then be passed into the mouth or sprayed over the body to cool the elephant down.*

# Skeletal system

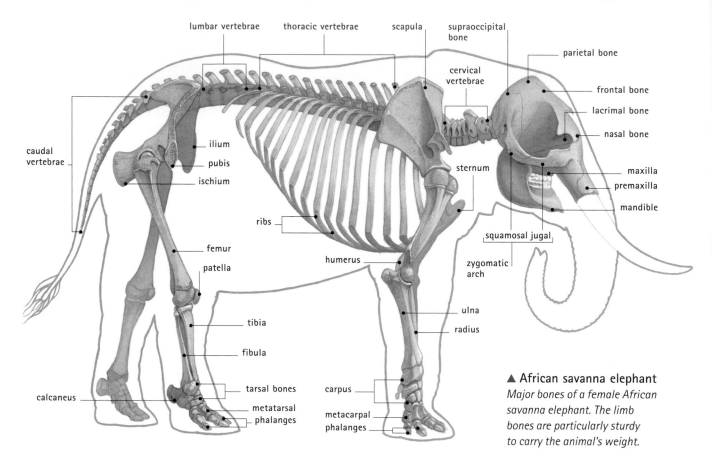

lumbar vertebrae · thoracic vertebrae · scapula · supraoccipital bone · parietal bone · cervical vertebrae · frontal bone · lacrimal bone · nasal bone · caudal vertebrae · ilium · pubis · ischium · sternum · maxilla · premaxilla · mandible · ribs · squamosal jugal · zygomatic arch · femur · patella · humerus · tibia · ulna · radius · fibula · calcaneus · tarsal bones · carpus · metatarsal · phalanges · metacarpal · phalanges

▲ **African savanna elephant**
*Major bones of a female African savanna elephant. The limb bones are particularly sturdy to carry the animal's weight.*

**CONNECTIONS**

**COMPARE** the limb posture and bone structure of an elephant with that of lighter four-legged mammals such as the *RED DEER* and *WILDEBEEST*.

**COMPARE** the structure of an elephant's backbone with that of fast-running land mammals such as the *ZEBRA*.

Like all mammals, an elephant has a skeleton that can be divided into three major sections: the skull, the backbone and ribs, and the limb bones. The total number of bones in an elephant skeleton varies slightly between individuals and species. The skeleton as a whole is massive, accounting for between 12 and 15 percent of an elephant's body weight. The skeleton must support the elephant's great weight as efficiently as possible.

Heavy animals such as elephants have thicker, more bulky bones than lighter species. However, elephant bones are not as thick as scientists would predict on the basis of their weight, because of their unusual construction. Elephant leg bones do not have marrow-filled spaces like the bones of most other land mammals. Instead, they are filled with spongy bone tissue, which makes them stronger while keeping their weight down.

Manatees and dugongs are relatives of elephants. They have particularly heavy skeletons composed of solid bones. These animals are aquatic, and their bodies are supported by water, so the extra bone mass is not necessary for strength. The additional weight helps keep them submerged and allows them to maintain their position in the water.

## The skull

An elephant's skull is very large but relatively short compared with the skulls of other mammals. With the skull bones plus the tusks, and a long muscular trunk, an elephant's head can weigh up to 660 pounds (300 kg). It takes less muscle power to hold up a short skull than a longer one, owing to reduced leverage. The main part of the skull is composed of very thick bone filled with air cavities. This makes the skull strong but relatively light.

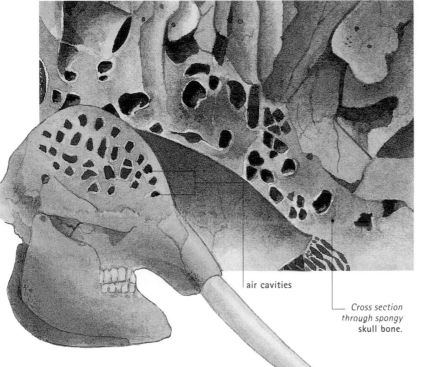

air cavities

*Cross section through spongy skull bone.*

## ▲ REDUCING WEIGHT

*Much of the skull contains hollow cavities formed by spongy bone. These are strong yet light compared with the denser bones of the legs. The skull is supported by ligaments and muscles attached to the thoracic vertebrae.*

In the center of the large mass of skull bones is a relatively small brain chamber. The large surface area of the back of the skull provides ample attachment space for the large muscles that run to the shoulders. These muscles support the head.

The elephant's lower jaw, or mandible, is also very large. Unlike the skull it is made of solid bone. The front parts of the upper jawbone, the premaxillary bones, form sheaths for the tusks, a feature unique to elephants.

## The backbone

Like all vertebrates, mammals have a backbone made up of units called vertebrae. The vertebral column can be divided into five sections: the cervical (neck), thoracic (upper back), lumbar (lower back), sacral (above the pelvis), and caudal (tail) sections. Most

of the variation in the total number of bones between elephants comes from differences in the number of vertebrae between individual animals. The caudal section alone can contain between 18 and 33 vertebrae in the African savanna elephant and 24 to 34 vertebrae in the Asiatic elephant. The thoracic and lumbar sections of the backbone support the considerable weight of the digestive system and other internal organs, as well as the surrounding musculature. As in other types of large mammals, these sections of the backbone form a gentle arch, like a bridge. This shape provides extra strength.

Compared with backbones of smaller mammals, an elephant's backbone is relatively stiff and allows little flexibility. The stiffness maintains the backbone's arched shape and also helps reduce excessive movements of the body during locomotion, which could endanger the load-bearing bones and joints in the limbs. The thoracic vertebrae closest to the shoulder have particularly long dorsal (upper-side) processes, or projections. These are most notable in African savanna elephants; they act as anchorage points for ligaments that extend to the skull and help support the head.

## Comparing skulls

**Both African and Asian elephants** have skulls that contain between 53 and 55 bones, depending on the individual. Although the skulls of both species have a similar structure, they have a slightly different shape. When viewed sideways, the Asiatic elephant has a concave (curving inward) forehead, while the African elephant has a convex forehead (curving outward). The skull of the African elephant is broader than that of its Asiatic cousin. Owing to their much larger tusks, African elephants have larger tusk tubes, formed by the premaxillae, on their upper jaws.

convex bone

concave bone

premaxilla

tusk

◀ **Elephant skulls**
*Comparison of the skulls of an African savanna (left) and Asian (right) elephant. Note the differences in premaxilla and tusk size.*

## The limbs

An elephant's leg bones are massive, relatively thicker than the leg bones of smaller mammals. As with any column-shape object, the bone of a leg is better at withstanding the compressive forces that run along the length of the bone than the bending forces operating across it. Since elephant bones have straight shafts and are aligned vertically, the weight

of the animal passes through the length of the bones. To prevent shearing (tearing) forces at bone junctions, all the joint surfaces are in line with the bone shafts.

Elephant limb bones have a number of features that help the animals maintain their vertical alignment. As in all mammals, an elephant's principal limb bones are the humerus (upper forelimb), the radius and ulna (lower forelimb), the femur (thighbone), and the fibula and tibia (lower hindlimb). Unlike humans, the elephant has a scapula (shoulder blade) positioned directly above the humerus and not held in place by a clavicle or collarbone—this is absent in elephants. The heads of the humerus and femur point nearly straight upward, so they transfer weight directly down the length of the leg bone. Compare this with the head of the femur in the human skeleton, which sticks out sideways and connects with the hipbones (pelvis).

## Wrists and ankles

In the skeletons of mammals that specialize in running, such as horses and cheetahs, the wrist bones, or carpals, and ankle bones (the tarsals) may be as long as, or longer than, the other limb bones. This allows them to provide enormous leverage. By contrast, the carpal and tarsal bones of elephants are small and blocklike. Elephants never actually run,

▲ *Elephants do not run. Running would place too great a strain on their limbs and joints. Instead, when speed is required they use a fast walk or jog.*

▶ FOOT
**African savanna elephant**
*Surprisingly, elephants walk on their toes. An elastic pad supports and cushions the rear of the foot against impact.*

tarsal bones

metatarsal

Phalanges. *Each foot bears five toes, though the side ones are often much reduced.*

nails

tibia

calcaneus

*The **pad** is made of fatty, elastic tissues.*

*The **sole** of the foot is covered by a thick layer of skin. Skin is replaced as soon as it is sloughed.*

although they can move surprisingly fast when necessary, adopting a kind of bustling jog. The heavy jolting that occurs in running would cause injury to the animal's joints, bones, and muscles.

## The feet

An elephant has five toes on each foot, although the outer pair of toes may be very small in some individuals. Unlike humans, who walk with their heels on the ground, an elephant stands on what corresponds to the ball of the foot. This kind of stance is called digitigrade (from Latin, meaning "finger walking"). Most of an elephant's weight rests on a broad pad of elastic tissue behind the toes. This acts as a shock absorber and prevents the skeleton from jolting too much when the elephant walks. It also allows elephants to move surprisingly quietly despite their size.

▼ Elephants are social animals. Several anatomical adaptations, from the structure and location of the hyoids to a resonating pouch in the throat, allow them to produce a range of sounds for communication.

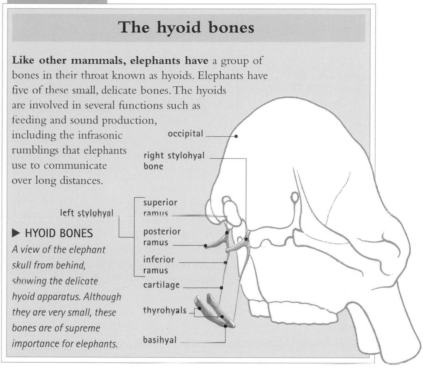

**CLOSE-UP**

# The hyoid bones

**Like other mammals, elephants have** a group of bones in their throat known as hyoids. Elephants have five of these small, delicate bones. The hyoids are involved in several functions such as feeding and sound production, including the infrasonic rumblings that elephants use to communicate over long distances.

▶ HYOID BONES
*A view of the elephant skull from behind, showing the delicate hyoid apparatus. Although they are very small, these bones are of supreme importance for elephants.*

occipital
right stylohyal bone
left stylohyal
superior ramus
posterior ramus
inferior ramus
cartilage
thyrohyals
basihyal

# Muscular system

Elephants, like other vertebrates, have three main types of muscles: skeletal or striated muscle, smooth muscle, and cardiac muscle. Skeletal muscles are the large muscles attached to the skeleton; they are mostly used for locomotion and other body movements and to maintain posture. When viewed under a microscope, skeletal muscle fibers are seen to have distinctive dark and light bands, or striations. Smooth muscles are present in many internal organs, such as the esophagus, stomach, and intestines, and in blood vessels. These muscles are composed of relatively short cells and are responsible for moving food down the throat during swallowing and moving food through the intestines. Cardiac muscle occurs only in the walls of the heart. It is responsible for pumping blood around the circulatory system.

**▼ African savanna elephant**
*Powerful muscles in the limbs and neck are vital for locomotion and for moving the head.*

**▶ HEAD AND NECK**
*An elephant uses the auriculo-occipitalis to flap its ears.*

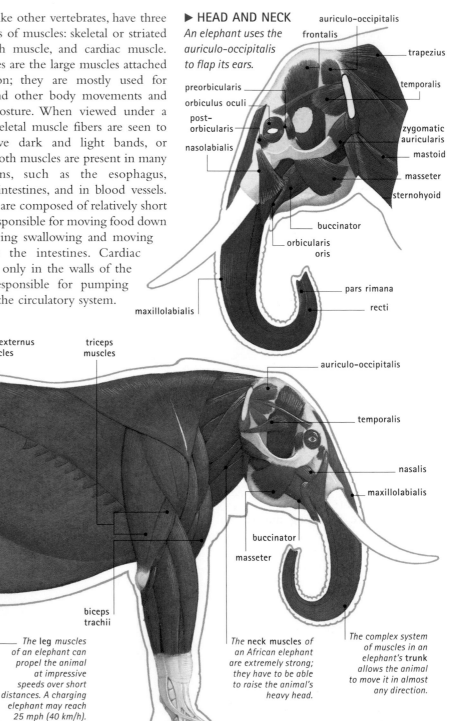

auriculo-occipitalis
frontalis
trapezius
temporalis
preorbicularis
orbiculus oculi
post-orbicularis
zygomatic auricularis
nasolabialis
mastoid
masseter
sternohyoid
buccinator
orbicularis oris
pars rimana
recti
maxillolabialis

obliquus externus muscles
triceps muscles
auriculo-occipitalis
temporalis
nasalis
maxillolabialis
biceps femoralis
buccinator
masseter
biceps trachii

*The leg muscles of an elephant can propel the animal at impressive speeds over short distances. A charging elephant may reach 25 mph (40 km/h).*

*The neck muscles of an African elephant are extremely strong; they have to be able to raise the animal's heavy head.*

*The complex system of muscles in an elephant's trunk allows the animal to move it in almost any direction.*

## A lack of rotation

The muscular systems of African and Asian elephants are virtually identical, and they are structurally similar to those of most other mammals. For example, there are 41 muscles in an elephant's foreleg; most of these occur in a human arm, although their relative proportions may differ. However, unlike humans and most other mammals, elephants are unable to rotate their forelimbs. The inability to rotate the forelimbs is one of the features that define the order Proboscidea and is probably an adaptation for reducing the risk of injury to heavy weight-bearing leg joints. Two of the forelimb muscles used by mammals to rotate the foot, the pronator quadratus and the pronator radii teres, are small or absent in elephants. The other forelimb muscles—such as the biceps and brachialis, which flex the front leg; and the triceps muscles, which extend the front leg—are also found in the human arm. Many skeletal muscles, such as the triceps and biceps, act in antagonistic pairs; they work against each other in opposite directions.

## Size and shape

Since elephants have a different posture from humans, the relative sizes and shapes of their muscles are different from those of their human equivalents. For example, the foreleg extensor muscles, or triceps, which help maintain the elephant's upright posture during walking, are relatively powerful. Elephants also have particularly large neck muscles to maintain their heavy head in an upright position. There are 48 muscles in the elephant's hind legs, the largest being the principle hamstring muscle, the biceps femoris. The hamstring muscles flex the back legs and are used to provide much of the forward thrust of a walking elephant.

Excluding the trunk, elephants have 140 muscles in the head. These muscles determine head position and control the movement of the jaws, lips, and eyes. Unlike humans, elephants are able to use well-developed muscles (the auriculo-occipitalis) for flapping their large ears. There are only 16 main muscles around the body wall, including some of the largest in the elephant's body. The body-wall muscles maintain posture and help hold in the intestines and other internal organs.

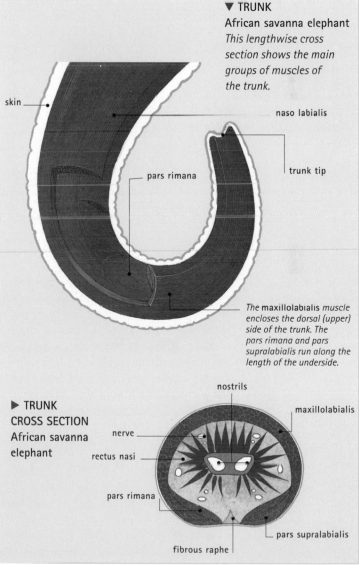

# Muscles of the trunk

**An elephant's trunk contains** no bone or cartilage and is made up mostly of muscle. Elephants can move their trunk in almost any direction and hold it in a variety of positions. The trunk is strong enough to pick up a large log yet has enough dexterity to manipulate small stones. To be able to accomplish such contrasting tasks, the trunk needs a complex muscular structure. French anatomist Georges Cuvier (1769–1832) estimated that there were about 40,000 muscles in an elephant's trunk. Modern anatomists, however, believe that many of these are subunits, or fascicles, from seven major muscle groups.

▼ TRUNK
African savanna elephant
*This lengthwise cross section shows the main groups of muscles of the trunk.*

skin

naso labialis

trunk tip

pars rimana

*The maxillolabialis muscle encloses the dorsal (upper) side of the trunk. The pars rimana and pars supralabialis run along the length of the underside.*

► TRUNK
CROSS SECTION
African savanna elephant

nostrils

maxillolabialis

nerve

rectus nasi

pars rimana

pars supralabialis

fibrous raphe

# Nervous system

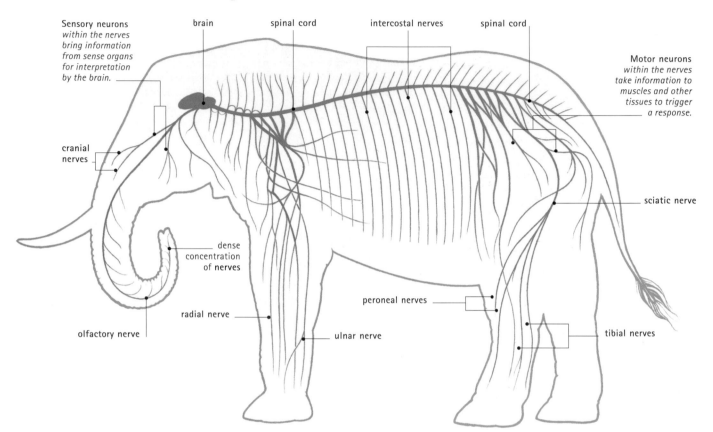

Sensory neurons *within the nerves bring information from sense organs for interpretation by the brain.*

brain

spinal cord

intercostal nerves

spinal cord

Motor neurons *within the nerves take information to muscles and other tissues to trigger a response.*

cranial nerves

sciatic nerve

dense concentration of nerves

olfactory nerve

radial nerve

ulnar nerve

peroneal nerves

tibial nerves

**▲ African savanna elephant**
*Nerves near the tip of the trunk connect with the olfactory nerve. This arrangement gives the trunk its extreme sensitivity.*

CONNECTIONS

COMPARE the shape and relative size of an elephant's cerebrum with that of a *HUMAN*.

COMPARE the sound-based communication of an elephant with that of a *DOLPHIN*.

Like all mammalian nervous systems, an elephant's nervous system can be divided into two main parts: the central nervous system (CNS) and the peripheral nervous system (PNS). The CNS includes the brain and the spinal cord. The PNS includes all the other nerves that lead to and from the CNS. Both the brain and the spinal cord have a hollow cavity at the center, though the elephant's spinal cord cavity is notably reduced compared with that of some other mammals. The spinal cord of all vertebrates passes through the middle of the vertebral column.

## Types of cells
The nervous system is made up of specialized cells called neurons, which are able to transmit electrical signals. There are three main types of neurons. Sensory neurons conduct nervous impulses from sense organs such as the eyes, ears, and skin to the central nervous system.

Motor neurons carry signals to the muscles and initiate muscle contraction. Finally, interneurons connect the sensory and motor neurons. Nerves are bundles of neurons along with small blood vessels that bring nutrients and oxygen to the neurons. Like all other vertebrates, elephants have pairs of large nerves leaving each side of the spinal cord at regular intervals. These nerves divide into many branches, leading to specific parts of the body. For example, the nerves leaving the thoracic region of the spine carry sensory and motor neurons to and from organs such as the heart, lungs, stomach, liver, pancreas, and kidneys, as well as many of the muscles of the neck and chest region.

## The brain
Elephants have the largest brain of any land mammal, although it is not especially large relative to the size of the body. An

African savanna elephant's brain weighs up to 14 pounds (6.5 kg). It is slightly larger than that of the Asian elephant, which weighs up to 12 pounds (5.5 kg). An elephant's brain can be divided into five distinct parts. The largest is the cerebrum, which in turn is divided into two halves called cerebral hemispheres. In relatively intelligent animals, such as elephants, the cerebrum is the largest part of the brain.

The outer layer of the cerebrum (the cerebral cortex) is highly folded in elephants, resulting in an increased surface area and many more neurons. The cerebral cortex gives the brain its characteristic appearance. It is made up of gray matter comprising billions of neurons. The cerebral cortex of the human brain has 100 billion neurons, and the figure for elephants is probably similar. The cerebral cortex determines how sensory information is interpreted, controls voluntary movements, and is the seat of consciousness, memory, and learning. Another notable feature of an elephant's brain is the large cerebellum, which is located behind the cerebrum. In mammals, the cerebellum is important for coordinating movement and balance.

## The sense organs

Elephants gather information from the world around them using their senses of sight, hearing, smell, touch, and taste. For elephants, the sense of hearing is particularly important, and they are able to communicate over distances of several miles using low-frequency

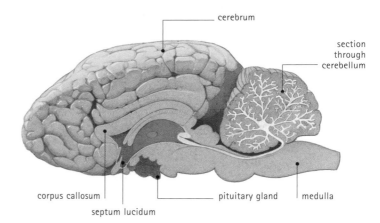

cerebrum

section through cerebellum

corpus callosum

septum lucidum

pituitary gland

medulla

sound, or infrasound. Infrasound is significant for African forest elephants, because unlike higher-frequency sounds, infrasound can travel relatively long distances through forest vegetation. Elephants are also capable of detecting ground vibrations through their feet. This allows them to keep in contact with herds up to 10 miles (16 km) away.

Elephants have a very keen sense of smell and can detect chemical signals called pheromones left by other elephants. Elephants are also able to smell approaching predators. When elephants catch the scent of an enemy, they raise their trunk to sniff the air. If the danger is close they form a protective circle around their young. Elephants are particularly sensitive to touch, especially on the tip of their trunk, the skin of which has a very high density of touch receptors.

▲ BRAIN
**African savanna elephant**
*The brain is very heavy, weighing up to 12 pounds (5.4 kg) in males and 9.5 pounds (4.3 kg) in females. Also, the active surface area of the brain is large, suggesting intelligence.*

▼ SENSITIVE TRUNK
**African savanna elephant**
*The tip of the trunk is highly sensitive. Fine hairs are able to feel even tiny objects.*

## Tool-using tuskers

**The ability to make and use tools** is considered to be one of the most important signs of intelligence in animals. Many animals use tools, but elephants are unusual because they also modify objects to make them more effective as tools. A study of Asian elephants in India showed that many captive and wild elephants used switches made of branches to keep flies away. Some of these elephants modified branches by stripping some of the leaves and shortening the stem to make them into more effective fly switches. Using their trunk, elephants sometimes pick up stones and other material to throw at enemies. In one case, a female African savanna elephant was observed throwing mud and sticks at a white rhinoceros that was bothering her.

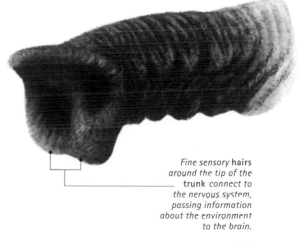

*Fine sensory hairs around the tip of the trunk connect to the nervous system, passing information about the environment to the brain.*

# Circulatory and respiratory systems

Elephants have the same basic plan for their circulatory and respiratory systems as other mammals, but because of their large size these systems include some unusual features.

### The circulatory system

In common with other mammals, elephants have a four-chamber heart, consisting of two ventricles and two atria. Arteries carry blood away from the heart, while veins carry blood toward the heart. Deoxygenated blood from the elephant's body passes into the right atrium via a pair of thick veins, the vena cavae. Contractions of the right atrium force blood through a one-way valve into a larger, more powerful, chamber, the right ventricle.

The right ventricle then squeezes the blood via the pulmonary artery through the small blood vessels, or capillaries, of the lungs. There, red blood cells release waste carbon dioxide and pick up oxygen. Oxygenated blood returning from the lungs passes into the left atrium, which pushes the blood through another one-way valve into the most powerful chamber of the heart, the left ventricle. The left ventricle needs to be powerful to pump the oxygenated blood through the main artery, the aorta, and onward around the rest of the elephant's body.

A peculiar feature of the elephant's heart is that the two ventricles are separated near the top of the heart, giving it the appearance of a "double heart." The only other mammals to share this characteristic are the sirenians, elephants' closest relatives. The heart of a large bull African elephant can weigh up to 60 pounds (27 kg). This might seem very large, but it is not excessively heavy compared with an elephant's body size.

### Cells and vessels

An African savanna elephant can have up to 200 gallons (750 l) of blood, accounting for 10 percent of its body weight. Like almost all

▼ **CIRCULATORY SYSTEM**
**African savanna elephant**
*Despite their large size, elephants display similarities with other mammals in their respiratory and circulatory systems.*

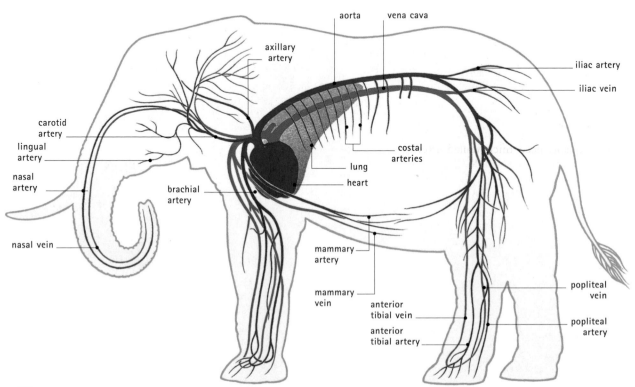

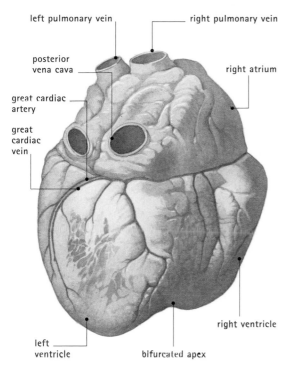

left pulmonary vein

right pulmonary vein

posterior vena cava

right atrium

great cardiac artery

great cardiac vein

right ventricle

left ventricle

bifurcated apex

▲ *Just as in smaller mammals, the heart accounts for about 0.5 percent of the body weight. However, in elephants, unlike most other mammals, the two ventricles are divided near the top of the heart.*

vertebrates, elephants have red blood cells containing the red pigment hemoglobin. Hemoglobin binds to oxygen so it can be transported around the body. Elephant hemoglobin has a higher affinity for oxygen than that of humans.

Elephant arteries are large and heavy, and are supported by ridges of connective tissue or muscles. Elephants need thick-walled arteries so they can withstand a high blood pressure, nearly 50 percent higher than that of humans. Elephant veins are also thick-walled; this keeps these wide blood vessels from collapsing. Some blood vessels in an elephant reach up to 11 feet (3.5 m) long.

## Lymphatic system

The elephant circulatory system also includes the lymphatic system. The lymphatic system is a network of vessels transporting fluid and plasma proteins that leak from blood capillaries into surrounding body tissues. The lymphatic system takes these materials back to the main circulatory system. Lymph nodes occur in places where small lymphatic vessels come together. The lymph nodes are important sites for the production of white blood cells, which combat invading microorganisms and other objects in the body.

## The respiratory system

Elephants can breathe through their mouth or their trunk. This ability enables them to breathe when their mouth is full or when they are using their trunk to suck up water or dust. Air passes down the trachea (windpipe) and into two lungs via the bronchial tubes. Elephants inhale around 80 gallons (310 l) of air each minute.

Elephants and most other mammals have a space between the lungs and the chest wall called the pleural cavity. Raising the ribs and lowering a membrane called the diaphragm will increase the volume of the pleural cavity, creating a negative pressure that causes the lungs to inflate. An elephant's pleural cavity is filled with a stretchy network of collagen fibers that connects the lungs to the chest wall and the diaphragm. Elephants rely more on the diaphragm and less on the muscles raising the rib cage than other mammals. Elephant lungs have a network of thick elastic tissues that prevents the alveoli (air sacs) from being squashed by the mass of surrounding tissues. These unusual features help the animals overcome being heavy and allow them to snorkel (using their trunk for breathing) in deep water.

### IN FOCUS

## Heart rate and energy efficiency

**The heart rate of an elephant** is about 30 beats per minute, which is considerably slower than that of smaller mammals. For example, an average human has a resting heart rate of 70 beats per minute, and a mouse has a heart rate of 500 beats per minute. An elephant can afford to have a comparatively slow heart rate, and hence a relatively slow rate of oxygen delivery to the body, because pound for pound it needs less energy than smaller mammals. This is because the large bodies of elephants conserve heat well, so they do not need to generate as much heat as small mammals do. Elephants are also able to tolerate a fairly wide range of body temperatures. In addition, elephants use relatively little energy in moving around because of the efficiency of their skeleton and musculature.

# Digestive and excretory systems

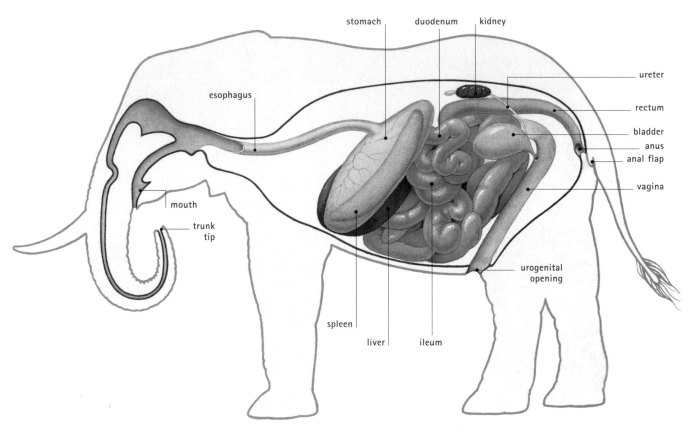

stomach  duodenum  kidney

esophagus

ureter

rectum

bladder

anus

anal flap

vagina

mouth

trunk
tip

urogenital
opening

spleen

liver  ileum

▲ **Female African savanna elephant**
*The very long intestine is necessary for the digestion and absorption of nutrients from woody vegetation.*

**CONNECTIONS**

**COMPARE** the structure of an elephant's stomach with that of ruminants such as a **WILDEBEEST** or a **RED DEER,** which have a complex multichamber stomach for the breakdown of tough cellulose.

Elephants eat a range of vegetation that includes grass, leaves, fruit, and woody material such as twigs, roots, and even bark. Asian elephants sometimes raid crops such as sugarcane and bananas. Considering that Asian elephants can eat about 330 pounds (150 kg) of food each day, it is not surprising that crop-raiding elephants are unpopular with farmers.

## The advantage of size

In dry habitats, much of an elephant's diet is made up of tough fibrous plant material, particularly twigs. Even though this food is not very nutritious and is difficult to digest, elephants are able to live on it because of their very large size and relatively low energy requirements. Being large, an elephant can have the long and voluminous digestive system needed to digest and absorb woody vegetation. An elephant's intestines can measure up to 115 feet (35 m) long.

The digestion process starts in the mouth, where vegetation is chewed and mixed with saliva. Elephants chew with great molars that can weigh up to 11 pounds (5 kg) each. The surfaces of these teeth bear enamel ridges that help grind vegetation. Unlike the teeth of

**IN FOCUS**

### A gargantuan thirst

Elephants prefer to drink every day, although they can go for several days without drinking water if necessary. A large male will drink about 58 gallons (220 l) of water in a day—and can take up to 26 gallons (100 l) in one go. Elephants obtain water from rivers and pools, or from groundwater, which they get at by digging pits with their tusks and trunk.

other mammals, which are replaced with new teeth erupting from below, new elephant teeth come from behind the old ones as if on a conveyor belt. An elephant can have six sets of teeth throughout its 50- to 70-year lifetime.

Elephants have well-developed salivary glands and also mucus glands in the esophagus that moisten dry vegetation, allowing it to move easily down to the stomach. The elephant digestive system is simple compared with those of other plant-eating mammals. Elephants have a vertical, cylinder-shape stomach that acts as a food-storage chamber.

## Micro-partners

Cellulose is a tough chemical found in the walls of plant cells. Some plant-eating animals, such as ruminants (antelopes, deer, and their relatives) have a multichamber stomach where the cellulose is broken down by micro-organisms. Elephants also need the help of symbiotic microorganisms to digest cellulose. Rather than taking place in the stomach, this process occurs in a chamber called the cecum. The cecum lies at the junction of the small and large intestines. Nutrients released by cellulose breakdown are absorbed directly through the cecum wall, which contains many blood vessels to transport the nutrients around the body.

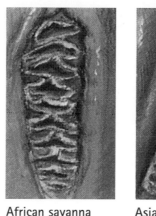

African savanna          Asian

◀ A molar tooth of an African savanna elephant and an Asian elephant. Key differences allow the teeth to be told apart. The African elephant's molars are lozengelike, while the Asian elephant's are more rectangular. There are also differences in the pattern of enamel ridges on the teeth.

### Elephant dung

The indigestible remainder of food passes from the cecum into the large intestine, from where water is reabsorbed. Then food passes to the rectum. There, feces are stored until they are ejected as droppings. Elephants can produce 240 pounds (110 kg) of dung per day.

Except for their large size, the other organs involved in digestion and excretion in elephants, such as the liver, kidneys, and pancreas, are typically mammalian. Elephants do not have a gallbladder, but instead have an enlarged hepatic duct that pipes bile from the liver to the intestines.

## IN FOCUS

# A keystone species

**Partly because of their size,** elephants play an important role in the ecosystems in which they live. Elephants effectively shape the plant communities around them by selectively browsing certain plants and by killing trees. They do this by pushing trees over to get at leaves high in the canopy, or by stripping bark. Elephants also act as seed and nutrient dispersers. Because of elephants' relatively inefficient digestive system, their dung is full of nutrients and often contains seeds. Elephant dung is an important resource for insects such as flies and dung beetles; the young insects feed on the droppings.

▶ Nutrient-rich elephant dung provides a food source for a wide range of animals, plants, and fungi.

# Reproductive system

Both African and Asian elephants are slow breeders. Female, or cow, Asian elephants do not become sexually mature until eight years old, and maturity does not occur until the age of 11 in female African savanna elephants. In all elephant species, males reach sexual maturity even later. They do not usually have the opportunity to mate until they are much older when they have a higher social position. Female elephants usually give birth to a single calf every five years or so, depending on conditions.

## The estrus cycle

Like all placental mammals, female elephants produce and release eggs at regular intervals in response to changing hormone concentrations in the blood. When the eggs are released from the ovaries, they pass down the fallopian tubes into the uterus ready to be fertilized. At this time females become much more sexually receptive. The time between periods of sexual

▶ **FEMALE REPRODUCTIVE ORGANS African savanna elephant**
*The vaginal tract opens between the female's hind legs.*

▼ **MALE REPRODUCTIVE ORGANS African savanna elephant**
*The elephant's penis is S-shaped and is the largest of any land mammal.*

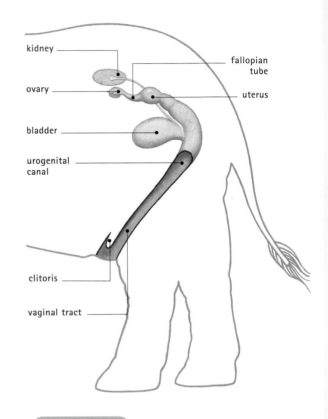

kidney
ovary
bladder
urogenital canal
clitoris
vaginal tract
fallopian tube
uterus

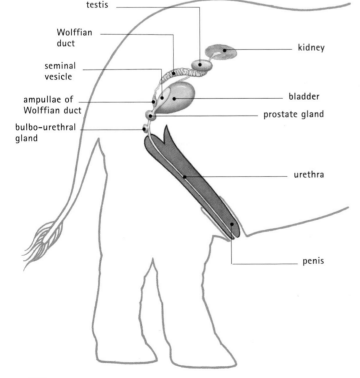

testis
Wolffian duct
seminal vesicle
ampullae of Wolffian duct
bulbo-urethral gland
kidney
bladder
prostate gland
urethra
penis

## IN FOCUS

### Meeting mates

**Elephants live in family groups** made up of several related adult female elephants and their young. Each family group is led by a dominant female. Adult bulls spend much of their time away from these family groups, and usually join a group only to mate. Adult females in breeding condition, or estrus, make low-frequency calls inaudible to humans to attract males from up to several miles away. Sometimes the older bull elephants become very aggressive and actively seek out females in estrus. This period, which can last from a few days to a few months in more mature bulls, is called musth.

receptivity is called the estrus cycle. In Asian elephants, this period is around 22 days, and in African savanna elephants it is about 60 days.

## Female reproductive organs

Apart from their large size, the reproductive organs of female elephants are typical for a mammal. The embryo develops in the uterus, which is located under the pelvis. The time from egg fertilization to birth (the gestation period) is around 22 months. At birth, the baby elephant, which weighs around 265 pounds (120 kg), passes through the vaginal opening. This lies between the elephant's hind legs; the vaginal openings of most other large quadrupedal (four-legged) mammals, such as cattle and deer, is under the tail.

Females have a pair of milk-producing mammary glands. Unlike the mammary glands of other quadrupedal mammals, those of elephants are located between the front legs. Mother and calf can maintain trunk contact during feeding, helping strengthen their bond.

## Male reproductive anatomy

Like other male mammals elephants have two testes and a penis. During mating with a female, sperm passes from the testes along the genital ducts to the penis, from where it passes into the female's vagina. The testes of male elephants are located inside the elephant's

body, close to the kidneys. This is unusual in mammals, though the elephant's relatives, the sirenians—dugongs and manatees—also have internal testes.

A male elephant's penis is controlled by powerful muscles and can, when erect, reach more than 3 feet (1 m) long in mature males. When not erect, the penis is retracted within the elephant's body.

ADRIAN SEYMOUR

FURTHER READING AND RESEARCH

Hare, T. and M. Lambert. 1997. *The Encyclopedia of Mammals.* Marshall Cavendish: New York.
MacDonald, David. 2006. *The Encyclopedia of Mammals.* Facts on File: Tarrytown, NY.

▼ *A newborn elephant calf may consume 24 pints (11.4 l) of its mother's milk every day.*

---

**CLOSE-UP**

## Male musth

**At around the age of 20**, bull elephants experience a phase called musth, which lasts two or three months every year. Bull elephants in musth produce large amounts of fluid from the temporal glands, which are located behind each eye. Cow elephants in estrus usually choose a large bull in musth and ignore the smaller males. Males in musth are chosen over other bulls, even those larger than themselves. Bull African savanna elephants can be particularly aggressive during musth periods, and occasionally they inflict fatal tusk wounds on their opponents.

---

**CLOSE-UP**

## Elephant pheromones

**Like many mammals, elephants** communicate their sexual condition to potential mates and competitors using pheromones. Pheromones are volatile chemicals in body secretions such as urine or sweat. Elephants detect pheromones using their powerful sense of smell. Bull elephants in musth pass large amounts of urine with strong pheromones. While these pheromones may serve to attract dominant females in estrus, subordinate females or females with calves will back away from these secretions or even display defensive behavior.

# Giraffe

ORDER: Artiodactyla FAMILY: Giraffidae GENUS: *Giraffa*

The giraffe is the tallest animal in the world, reaching a height of 18 feet (5.5 m). It lives in savannas and open woodland areas across much of Africa south of the Sahara, but its range has become heavily fragmented over the last hundred years or so. The animal's name derives from *zirafah,* which means "fast walker" in Arabic. Adult giraffes can run at up to 35 miles per hour (56 km/h).

## Anatomy and taxonomy

Scientists group all organisms into taxonomic groups based largely on anatomical features. Giraffes belong to the order Artiodactyla, the even-toed ungulates, one of the largest mammal groups. The artiodactyl families closest to the Giraffidae are the Moschidae (musk deer), Antilocapridae (pronghorn antelopes), Cervidae (deer), and Bovidae (antelopes and relatives).

- **Animals** Animals are multicellular (many-celled) organisms that feed off other organisms. They differ from other multicellular life-forms in their ability to move around (generally using muscles) and their ability to respond rapidly to stimuli.

- **Chordates** Chordates have a dorsal nerve cord—a bundle of nerves running down the back—and a stiff rod called a notochord running along their dorsal (top) side during at least part of their life cycle.

- **Vertebrates** The notochord of a vertebrate transforms into a backbone, or vertebral column, during the development of the embryo. The backbone is made up of a chain of smaller bones called vertebrae, which are made of either cartilage or bone.

- **Mammals** Mammals are warmblooded vertebrates with mammary glands, which secrete nutritious milk to feed their growing young. All mammals have hairs covering their body, and their lower jaw consists of a single bone. The hinge between the lower jaw and the skull is farther forward than the equivalent jaw hinge of their reptilian ancestors, allowing mammals to chew sideways.

- **Placental mammals** Placental mammals (eutherians) nourish their developing young for an extended period inside the uterus, by means of a temporary organ called a placenta. The placenta joins the developing young to the mother and is formed jointly by the tissue of the embryo and the tissue of the mother's uterus.

▼ *This tree shows the major animal groups to which giraffids belong. Note that some biologists include the cetaceans—whales and dolphins—with the artiodactyls.*

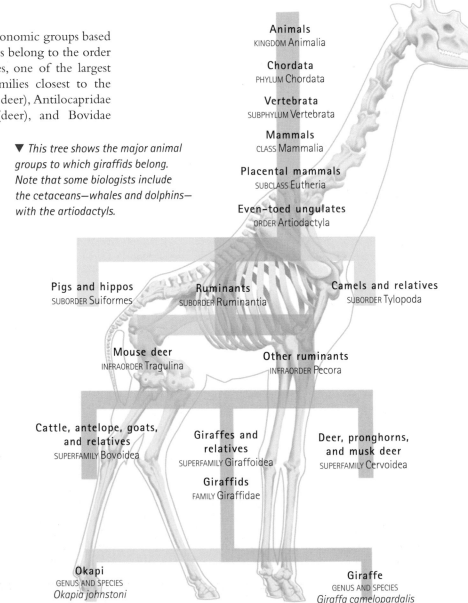

**Animals**
KINGDOM Animalia

**Chordata**
PHYLUM Chordata

**Vertebrata**
SUBPHYLUM Vertebrata

**Mammals**
CLASS Mammalia

**Placental mammals**
SUBCLASS Eutheria

**Even-toed ungulates**
ORDER Artiodactyla

**Pigs and hippos**
SUBORDER Suiformes

**Ruminants**
SUBORDER Ruminantia

**Camels and relatives**
SUBORDER Tylopoda

**Mouse deer**
INFRAORDER Tragulina

**Other ruminants**
INFRAORDER Pecora

**Cattle, antelope, goats, and relatives**
SUPERFAMILY Bovoidea

**Giraffes and relatives**
SUPERFAMILY Giraffoidea

**Deer, pronghorns, and musk deer**
SUPERFAMILY Cervoidea

**Giraffids**
FAMILY Giraffidae

**Okapi**
GENUS AND SPECIES
*Okapia johnstoni*

**Giraffe**
GENUS AND SPECIES
*Giraffa camelopardalis*

● **Even-toed ungulates** These mammals form the order Artiodactyla. They have an even number of well-developed toes on each foot. The second and fifth toes are usually thinner than the third and fourth toes, and are sometimes tiny or even absent. The animal's body weight is supported along the central axis running between the third and fourth toes. Many species have horns or antlers, and some have enlarged tusklike canine teeth. Artiodactyls range from the tiny mouse deer to the towering giraffe and the 5-ton (4.5-metric ton) common hippopotamus.

● **Deer** These long-legged artiodactyls form one of the larger artiodactyl families. The males of most deer species have antlers, which are usually cast off and regrown each year. Deer skulls have bony platforms that support the antlers. Worldwide, there are at least 41 species of deer, with varying degrees of side-toe reduction.

● **Antelopes and relatives** This diverse family is the largest artiodactyl group, comprising 140 species of antelopes, cattle, goats, and sheep. Most species have horns. All are hoofed, long-legged ruminants, with their weight evenly distributed on two toes on each foot. The third and fourth metapodial bones (metacarpals in the forelimbs and metatarsals in the hind limbs) in each foot are fused to form a single, longer bone called the cannon bone. All bovids have a four-chamber stomach, inside which plant material is digested.

● **Giraffids** There are just two living species of giraffids— the giraffe and the okapi. Both are tall animals that browse on vegetation; today giraffes occur only in Africa south of the Sahara, although they formerly lived in North Africa, too. Giraffes have a long, narrow head; thin lips; and a long, flexible tongue for browsing. Okapis are smaller and shorter-necked than giraffes, but both species have long,

▲ *The skin pattern of giraffes varies between subspecies, but the markings of all giraffes darken with age.*

narrow legs and feet without lateral toes; also, their third and fourth metapodial bones are fused to form cannon bones. Giraffes exist in a number of local forms, or subspecies, which have different skin patterns and geographic ranges.

**FEATURED SYSTEMS**

**EXTERNAL ANATOMY** Giraffes are large, hoofed mammals with long legs and a very long neck. Their skin is distinctively patterned, and there are between two and five small horns above the eyes. *See pages 66–69.*

**SKELETAL SYSTEM** The giraffe's skeleton supports its great size and the animal's high-rise browsing lifestyle. *See pages 70–71.*

**MUSCULAR SYSTEM** Muscles power the giraffe's movements, producing bursts of speed when the animal needs to escape danger. Ligaments extend from the base of the neck to support the massive neck. *See pages 72–73.*

**NERVOUS SYSTEM** The giraffe has the longest single nerve in the animal kingdom. It runs from the brain to

the heart and back again—a distance of around 15 feet (4.5 m). *See pages 74–75.*

**CIRCULATORY AND RESPIRATORY SYSTEMS** Pressure-reducing vessels offset sudden buildups in blood pressure as the animal bends its long neck. *See pages 76–77.*

**DIGESTIVE AND EXCRETORY SYSTEMS** Giraffes are ruminants, with a digestive system that enables them to extract the maximum nutrition from their tough food. *See pages 78–79.*

**REPRODUCTIVE SYSTEM** Male giraffes can determine whether or not a female is ready to mate by tasting chemicals in her urine. *See pages 80–81.*

# External anatomy

**CONNECTIONS**

**COMPARE** the horns of a giraffe with those of a *RED DEER*.

**COMPARE** the coat patterns of a giraffe with those of other large grassland ungulates, such as the *WILDEBEEST* or *ZEBRA*.

With its extraordinarily long neck and high shoulders that slope steeply to its hindquarters, a giraffe resembles a crane on a construction site. In addition to its great height, it is also one of the heaviest land animals: large males can weigh up to 4,200 pounds (1,900 kg). Females are smaller, usually less than half that weight. Compared with other hoofed mammals the giraffe has a relatively short body, but its legs are disproportionately long. The front legs are marginally longer than the hind legs, a feature that contributes to the animal's steeply sloping back. Mature giraffes have hooves as large as dinner plates.

The giraffe and okapi have short **horns** that are fused to the skull. The horns are unique among mammals, consisting of bony cores (called ossicones) covered by skin and fur.

The large **eyes** are protected by thick eyelashes and are set wide on the head, giving the giraffe maximum field of vision.

The **body** appears disproportionately small compared to the neck and legs, with high shoulders sloping steeply down to the tail. The deep chest contains the very large lungs and heart. Enlarged groups of muscles bunched above the shoulders make the front of the animal appear even bulkier.

▶ **Reticulated giraffe**
*With its long legs, towering neck, and patterned hide, the giraffe is unique and unmistakable.*

The giraffe's **tongue** is 18 to 20 inches (46 to 50 cm) long and blue-black. It is extendible and flexible enough to curl around the most nutritious foliage high in trees when the giraffe is browsing. The tongue is also used for grooming.

The giraffe's **markings** vary from one geographical region to another and provide a means of identifying the eight different subspecies. The markings break up the outline of the giraffe and may provide camouflage.

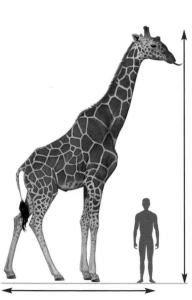

18 feet (5.5 m)

15 feet (4.7 m)

Despite appearances, the hind **legs** are almost as long as the front.

The **foot** is very large—6 inches (15 cm) high in males. Giraffe hooves lack the scent glands that occur in okapi hooves.

The giraffe's long neck helps it eat leaves that are beyond the reach of other animals. A giraffe can extend its tongue 18 inches (45 cm), curling it around leaves and pulling them toward the mouth. The canine teeth have deep grooves that enable the animal to strip the foliage. The tongue and lips are covered by hard growths called papillae, which are a vital adaptation for feeding on thorny trees. Giraffes have a good sense of smell, their eyes are large, and their vision is excellent. With their unique high-rise vantage point, giraffes have a panoramic view of their surroundings and the best range of vision of any land animal.

### Perfect patterns

Giraffes have short, thick fur with intricate patterns of colored patches, which vary from sandy yellow and pale tan to chestnut and almost black, depending on the area in which the giraffe lives and the dominant food types there. Giraffes' striking coloration breaks up their outline, helping conceal them among the trees and bushes of the savanna landscape.

Although no two giraffes' skin patterns are identical, some regional trends are apparent. These provide the basis for the division of the giraffe into a number of subspecies. Eight subspecies are currently recognized, although there may be 12 or more. Among the most striking subspecies are the reticulated giraffe, which has a bold pattern of squares separated by thin white lines that looks like broken paving stones. The Masai giraffe, which sports jagged patterns resembling leaves, is equally striking. Each animal also has its own unique pattern, which enables scientists to study the lives of individual giraffes closely.

### A horny head

Both sexes have two to five distinct, bony horns on their head called ossicones. They are covered in skin and, in females, are slender and

▼ *A giraffe's tongue and lips are covered with hard growths called papillae. They enable the giraffe to eat leaves from thorny trees, such as acacias, without being cut by the thorns.*

---

## COMPARATIVE ANATOMY

### Skin patterns

**Giraffes are patterned** with brown patches against a light background. These unusual markings may act as camouflage. In reticulated giraffes, the skin has dark, evenly spaced, boxlike patterns. White spaces between the patches form narrow lines that further break up the animal's shape. This complex pattern may provide excellent camouflage in dry, sunny bush country. In Nubian giraffes the dark patches are darkish-red to chestnut-colored; Masai giraffes have irregular dark patches on a buff-colored background. The exact pattern on a particular giraffe's skin is unique; this may help individuals identify each other. The body of the okapi is much darker than that of the giraffe. The okapi has zebralike stripes on its legs and hindquarters.

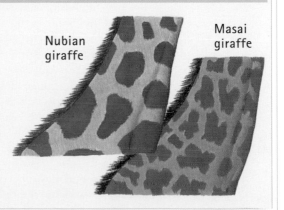

Nubian giraffe

Masai giraffe

## Beasts of myth and mystery

### Okapi

*The distinctive striped rump of the okapi led zoologists to think this animal was a type of zebra, but its anatomy showed it to be a relative of the giraffes.*

**Owing to the remoteness** of their central African rain forest habitat, okapis were not discovered by Western scientists until the start of the 20th century. Toward the end of the 19th century, colonial authorities in the region received reports suggesting the existence of a curious leaf-eating donkey in the Congo forests. Local peoples had hunted okapi for thousands of years, and they supplied skin fragments to biologists, who duly proclaimed the discovery of a new type of zebra.

It was not until 1901, when a team of British explorers and their local guides found tracks, droppings, and, eventually, a skeleton, that the okapi's true anatomical affinities were revealed. Amazingly, another large forest ungulate was discovered by Western science as recently as 1992. Again, this animal, from northwestern Vietnam, had been hunted by local people for many years. The first specimens were horns bought from a hunter. With the later acquisition of a skin, biologists announced the discovery of the Vu Quang ox, a bizarre animal that shows characteristics of both cattle and antelopes.

tufted with black hair. Males have larger, thicker horns that are bald on top; they grow up to 10 inches (25 cm) long. Males use their horns to spar with one another during fights to establish dominance in the breeding season. The ossicones start off as bumps of cartilage on the forehead, with the cartilage being replaced by bone as the animal ages. This process of bone replacement is called ossification. Eventually the ossicones fuse with the bones of the skull. They remain covered by skin throughout the giraffe's life and continue to grow bigger and thicker in males. Some giraffes also develop a central knob between the eyes, making them five-horned.

A deposition of bony layers onto the skull of males occurs as the animals get older. The head becomes progressively heavier, more clublike, and more angular throughout the animal's life—a trait found in no other mammals.

### Long legs and big feet

A giraffe's legs are very long, but despite appearances to the contrary, there is little difference in length between the forelegs and hind legs. The limbs appear inflexible, giving the animal a stiff-legged appearance when walking. The hooves are huge, measuring up to 6 inches (15 cm) across in large males and up to 4 inches (10 cm) across in females. In okapi, the hooves contain scent-secreting glands. These are absent in giraffes.

Legs and hooves are used as formidable weapons when a would-be predator, such as a lion, threatens. The hind legs can give a powerful and direct kick to the rear. The front legs may be employed to deliver either a "chop kick" with the hooves or a bludgeon with the whole straight leg. Either defensive maneuver is effective. One well-placed kick can easily cripple or kill a predator.

## EVOLUTION

# A shrinking family

**Scientists think that giraffids evolved** from small, deerlike ancestors around 20 million years ago. Early giraffids were among the first artiodactyls to evolve into large animals and move from dense forests into more open habitats. The expansion of Africa's plains during the Pliocene epoch (2 million to 5 million years ago) triggered a rise in the number of giraffid species, such as *Samotherium boissieri*, a type of grazing okapi. By the start of the Pleistocene, around 2 million years ago, at least seven species of giraffids browsed on the plains of Africa and Asia. They included *Giraffa jumae*, an animal even taller and heavier than the modern giraffe.

However, over time the family dwindled. Just two species of giraffids survive, but some relatives disappeared quite recently. *Sivatherium* was a genus of stocky giraffes with two large ossicones on the head and a smaller pair on the muzzle. The last of the genus, *Sivatherium giganteum*, may have become extinct as recently as 8,000 years ago; a Sumerian bronze statuette, which looks very like a *Sivatherium*, suggests that this species may have survived even later in parts of Asia.

▼ *Modern giraffes have a relatively longer neck than their extinct Sivatherium cousins, which looked more like okapis.*

# Muscular system

A giraffe's muscular system provides the pulling power needed to move its huge body around. The muscular system consists of three different types of muscle tissues: skeletal, cardiac, and smooth. Each can contract to allow body movement and functions. Some muscles are voluntary; the giraffe controls voluntary muscles when it requires a specific action or movement, such as moving its legs or neck. Involuntary muscles are those that contract automatically, such as the heart muscles and intestinal muscles.

## Muscle power

Giraffes, along with other ruminants, have no clavicle (collarbone). Instead, the shoulder blades are deeply embedded in thick muscle. Several enormous muscles support the front end of a giraffe's torso: the cephalo-humerals, deltoids, triceps, and latisimus dorsi muscles. Between these muscles and the leg bones is an area of tough, elastic cartilage that helps the animal run efficiently.

### IN FOCUS

#### Tests of neck strength

**A giraffe's neck is held upright** by a strong, elastic tissue called the ligamentum nuchae. This extends from as far back as the lumbar vertebrae and connects regularly all along the spine before running up the neck in two tightly bound halves to join the back of the skull. Young bull giraffes take part in "necking" contests, ritualized fights in which both males slowly entwine their necks, push backward and forward against each other, and butt heads. These wrestling matches may last for 30 minutes or more and provide the young males with an opportunity to develop and test their neck muscles. These contests, however, become more serious in adults, when they determine which males get to mate with the local females.

### IN FOCUS

#### Squeezing power

**The tongue is useful** for grabbing food. The tongue is also vital in the process of rumination: the rechewing of food to help maximize digestion. A bolus of food is regurgitated from the rumen (front part of the stomach) into the mouth, where it is chewed. The tongue's muscular strength is used to apply pressure on the bolus, squeezing the moisture out of the food parcel. Then the giraffe swallows it for a second time, and it is further digested.

The leg muscles are concentrated in the upper leg; the lower leg mainly contains long tendons that facilitate movement of the hooves. This structure acts as another energy-saving device: at high speed, only a little effort is needed to move the muscles near the leg's pivot. This small movement is translated into a wide arc of movement of the hoof.

A giraffe has two modes of movement, or gaits—an ambling walk and a gallop. As it walks, the legs on one side of the body move together, followed by their partners on the opposite side. Body weight is therefore supported alternately on the left and right sides. In the galloping gait, forelegs and hind legs work in pairs: the front pair first, then the back. The hind hooves swing up like a pendulum and are placed in front of the fore hooves. This gait enables the giraffe to reach speeds of up to 38 miles per hour (60 km/h). A giraffe maintains its balance because the neck moves back and forth simultaneously with the legs.

## Lips and tongue

A giraffe's long, black, muscular tongue reaches up to 18 inches (46 cm) in length. It is also prehensile, acting like a grasping hand as it wraps around branches and leaves. The tongue

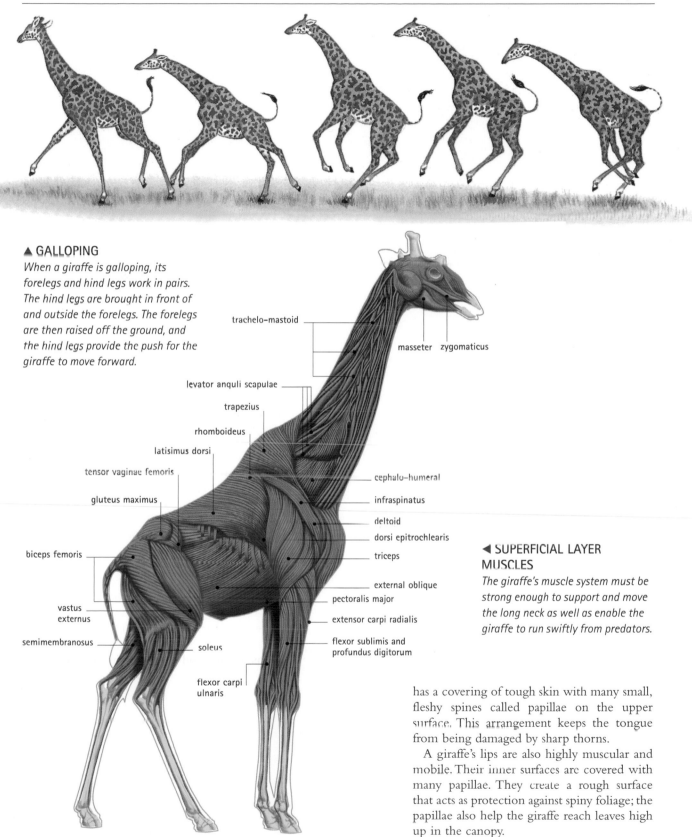

## ▲ GALLOPING

*When a giraffe is galloping, its forelegs and hind legs work in pairs. The hind legs are brought in front of and outside the forelegs. The forelegs are then raised off the ground, and the hind legs provide the push for the giraffe to move forward.*

trachelo-mastoid

masseter   zygomaticus

levator anquli scapulae

trapezius

rhomboideus

latisimus dorsi

tensor vaginae femoris

gluteus maximus

cephalo-humeral

infraspinatus

deltoid

dorsi epitrochlearis

biceps femoris

triceps

external oblique

pectoralis major

extensor carpi radialis

vastus externus

semimembranosus

soleus

flexor sublimis and profundus digitorum

flexor carpi ulnaris

## ◄ SUPERFICIAL LAYER MUSCLES

*The giraffe's muscle system must be strong enough to support and move the long neck as well as enable the giraffe to run swiftly from predators.*

has a covering of tough skin with many small, fleshy spines called papillae on the upper surface. This arrangement keeps the tongue from being damaged by sharp thorns.

A giraffe's lips are also highly muscular and mobile. Their inner surfaces are covered with many papillae. They create a rough surface that acts as protection against spiny foliage; the papillae also help the giraffe reach leaves high up in the canopy.

73

# Nervous system

◀ *A giraffe's highly movable lips are covered with sensitive hairs. Giraffes also have a good sense of smell, good hearing, and keen eyesight.*

The nervous system is a vast network of cells carrying information through the body by means of chemical and electrical signals. The nervous system is divided into two main sections: the central nervous system (CNS) and the peripheral nervous system (PNS). The CNS comprises the brain and the spinal cord; the PNS includes nerves that transmit signals from the sense organs to the CNS and vice versa.

The nervous system is made up of specialized cells called neurons. They bear long processes, or dendrites. Many neurons have one or more extra-long processes called axons that allow long-distance communication. These neurons are the longest cells in an animal's body, and giraffes have some of the longest nerve cells in the animal kingdom.

There are three main types of neurons: sensory neurons, motor neurons, and interneurons. Sensory neurons connect sense organs such as the eyes and ears to the CNS. Motor neurons carry signals from the CNS to muscles. Interneurons, which occur only in the CNS, connect sensory and motor neurons together.

## Voluntary and involuntary

The PNS is divided into two distinct systems: the somatic nervous system and the autonomic nervous system. The somatic system controls voluntary actions, such as walking. The autonomic system controls involuntary body processes over which the animal has no conscious control, such as the heartbeat. The autonomic nervous system also triggers output from certain glands around the body.

## Neck and throat

A giraffe's neck has eight pairs of nerves along its length. Most notable of these is the giraffe's laryngeal nerve—the longest nerve in the animal kingdom—which measures around 15

## IN FOCUS

### Communicating over distance

**Giraffes and okapis were once** thought to be virtually silent. However, they can communicate vocally over enormous distances. They make long-distance calls using infrasound. A giraffe typically lowers its chin, then quickly raises it to produce the sounds. Infrasonic signals are sound waves produced at such a low frequency that they cannot be heard by the human ear. Infrasound provides a good way to warn other giraffes of danger while remaining hidden. Infrasonic signals are very difficult to pinpoint, so any predators that could hear infrasound would find it hard to locate their source.

feet (4.5 m) long. It begins at the brain and runs down the length of the neck. It crosses over a blood vessel at the top of the heart before looping back up the neck to the larynx.

## Vision

Giraffes depend on vision. They have excellent eyesight, enabling them to locate both food and distant predators from their lofty position above the savanna. A giraffe's eyes are proportionally larger than those of other ruminants, such as deer and cattle. The positioning of the eyes on the sides of the head also gives the giraffe superior peripheral (sideways) vision. A giraffe has good color vision. This helps giraffes recognize each other and remain in visual contact with other giraffes over long distances.

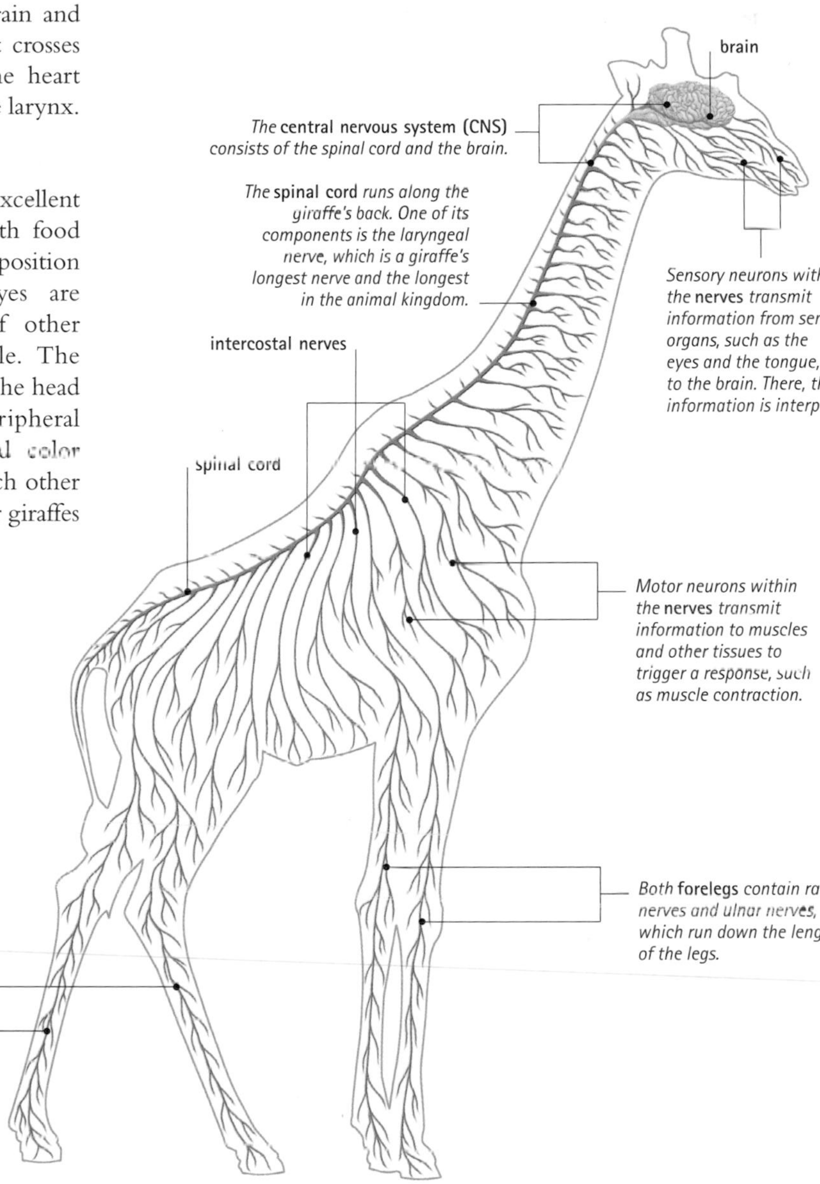

▶ A giraffe's nervous system is similar to that of other mammals, with nerves of the peripheral nervous system (PNS) branching in pairs from the spinal cord.

The **central nervous system (CNS)** consists of the spinal cord and the brain.

The **spinal cord** runs along the giraffe's back. One of its components is the laryngeal nerve, which is a giraffe's longest nerve and the longest in the animal kingdom.

brain

Sensory neurons within the **nerves** transmit information from sense organs, such as the eyes and the tongue, to the brain. There, the information is interpreted.

intercostal nerves

spinal cord

Motor neurons within the **nerves** transmit information to muscles and other tissues to trigger a response, such as muscle contraction.

Both **forelegs** contain radial nerves and ulnar nerves, which run down the length of the legs.

Both **hind legs** have peroneal nerves and tibial nerves, which run along their entire length.

## COMPARATIVE ANATOMY

# The brain

**Giraffes have a small brain,** weighing just 1.5 pounds (680 g). This represents 0.05 percent of the animal's body weight, a little less than that of a cow. By contrast, a dolphin's brain makes up 0.8 percent of its total weight, and a human's brain accounts for 2 percent. The giraffe's brain is actually smaller than expected for an animal of its size. This disproportion may be related to the length of a giraffe's neck. Much more energy would be used to supply enough oxygen to a larger brain at the end of such a long neck.

# Circulatory and respiratory systems

Like all vertebrates, giraffes have a closed circulatory system—blood is pumped through a system of arteries, veins, and capillaries. As oxygen and nutrients diffuse from the blood into the tissues, waste materials move into the blood to be taken away.

## Pressure regulation

Giraffes have a four-chamber heart with two atria and two ventricles. Oxygenated blood from the lungs and deoxygenated blood returning from the body are kept separate; the four chambers ensure efficient transport of oxygenated blood to the body's organs. The giraffe's large heart weighs more than 24 pounds (10 kg) and is among the strongest in the animal kingdom. That is because almost double the normal amount of pressure is needed to pump blood 10 feet (3 m) up the neck to the brain.

The heart beats around 150 times per minute. This rate is unusually high for an animal of such a size; usually, the larger the animal, the slower its heartbeat. Scientists have calculated that blood leaves the giraffe's heart at a pressure of up to 6 pounds per square inch (40 kilopascals), which is the highest blood pressure of any living animal. The red blood cells are small, but there are twice as many of them per unit of volume as in human blood. This combination of small size and very high density allows the cells to absorb oxygen quickly and efficiently.

▶ ARTERIAL SYSTEM
*The most important arteries are shown on the diagram. Arteries carry oxygenated blood to all parts of the body, while veins (not shown) carry deoxygenated blood back to the heart.*

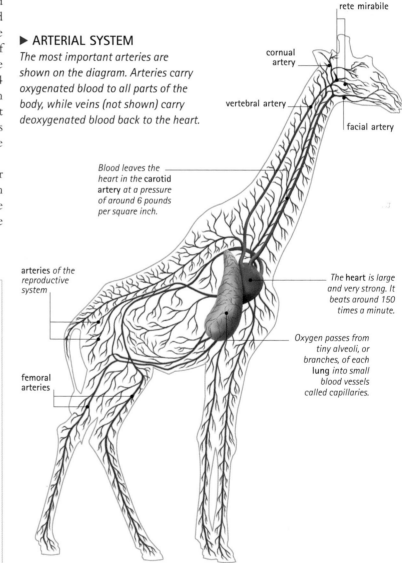

rete mirabile

cornual artery

vertebral artery

facial artery

*Blood leaves the heart in the **carotid artery** at a pressure of around 6 pounds per square inch.*

arteries *of the reproductive system*

femoral arteries

*The **heart** is large and very strong. It beats around 150 times a minute.*

*Oxygen passes from tiny alveoli, or branches, of each **lung** into small blood vessels called capillaries.*

Another unusual feature of a giraffe's circulatory system is its ability to maintain a far lower pressure at the brain of around 1.7 pounds per square inch (12 kilopascals), which is no higher than in other large mammals. This regulation is essential when a giraffe lowers its head to eat or drink. Without it, blood would rush down the long neck into the brain, causing the blood vessels to burst.

## The rete mirabile

Blood pressure in the brain is controlled by a web of tiny blood vessels located at the base of the brain. This is called rete mirabile and is formed by many subdivisions of the carotid arteries. This web is crucial for maintaining blood flow to a giraffe's brain at the right pressure. The walls of the rete mirabile blood vessels are elastic and can expand to cope with the increase in blood pressure when the giraffe lowers its head. The walls can also contract again when the head is raised.

The carotid artery is a single strand along most of the neck but divides into an internal and an external branch near the head; the external branch forms the rete mirabile. The carotid artery is also linked by a small branch to another artery, the vertebral. This runs down the neck, with many branches supplying

the muscles. The vertebral artery acts as a further safeguard, draining off much of the blood before it even reaches the rete mirabile when the giraffe's head is lowered. Retia mirabilia occur in the carotid arteries of many other artiodactyl mammals. They may have an important role in dissipating heat.

## How giraffes breathe

**A giraffe's unusually long neck** poses a great challenge to efficient breathing. A giraffe's windpipe is more than 5 feet (1.5 m) long, yet it is only around 2 inches (5 cm) in diameter. The tube usually contains around 0.8 gallon (3 l) of air. A giraffe inhales a lot of air that is never used for respiration, so the windpipe is always filled with a mix of inhaled and exhaled air, and oxygen levels are correspondingly low. To overcome this problem, a giraffe has to breathe much more regularly than would be expected for an animal of its size. A giraffe takes more than 20 breaths a minute when resting, compared with around 12 in humans and 10 in elephants.

▼ PRESSURE CONTROL
*When a giraffe drinks, it has to lower its head far below its heart, so one would expect the blood pressure to increase. A network of elastic blood vessels called the rete mirabile expands to lower the pressure of blood entering the brain. Without this elasticity the blood vessels in the giraffe's head would burst.*

# Digestive and excretory systems

Giraffes are highly selective when it comes to diet. They browse on trees, especially acacias, and eat their leaves, buds, and young shoots. Acacias are well-protected, with sharp thorns, and ants live inside the branches that protect their homes with staggering ferocity. With their tough mouthparts, reinforced tongue, and thick skin, giraffes can overcome these defenses. As well as essential fatty acids, acacia also contains a high percentage of water, providing giraffes with much of their required daily liquid intake, so they have to seek out water holes only occasionally. The giraffe's esophagus is very long and muscular, and connects to the large stomach. The esophagal muscles are used not only to swallow food but also to push it back up the throat when it is regurgitated for further chewing.

## ▶ FOUR STOMACHS

*The giraffe's stomach is divided into four parts: reticulum, omasum, abomasum, and rumen. This arrangement enables the giraffe to extract the maximum nutrition from its leaf diet. In the diagram most of the intestines are hidden by the stomachs.*

## Up and down

A giraffe's stomach has four chambers, as is typical of many ruminants. After being swallowed, a giraffe's briefly chewed food is passed into the first stomach chamber, the rumen. The food is softened there, then regurgitated back into the mouth as a ball of chewed-up food called a bolus. There it is

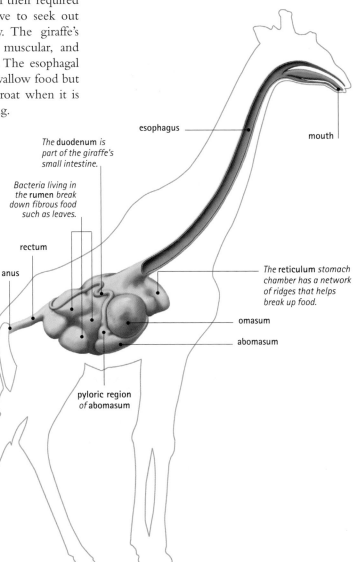

The **duodenum** *is part of the giraffe's small intestine.*

*Bacteria living in the* **rumen** *break down fibrous food such as leaves.*

rectum

anus

esophagus

mouth

*The* **reticulum** *stomach chamber has a network of ridges that helps break up food.*

omasum

abomasum

pyloric region *of* abomasum

## IN FOCUS

### A lost organ

**Giraffes have kidneys, a pancreas**, and a spleen that are similar to those of other ruminants, but the liver is surprisingly small and compact. Giraffes lack a gallbladder, an organ that stores and releases bile; deer and some other ruminants also lack this organ. Bile helps emulsify fats in other organisms, permitting their digestion. The ancestors of these ruminants had a gallbladder, but lost it as they evolved. A tiny gallbladder is present in an unborn giraffe while it is developing in the uterus, but this has disappeared by the time of birth.

subjected to further chewing. The food is swallowed again and forced into the reticulum. This second chamber contains a network of ridges that forms a honeycomb-like pattern. Digestion takes place in the third and fourth stomach chambers, the omasum and the abomasum.

### Digestion in the stomach

During digestion, solid food flows slowly through the rumen while water extracted from the plant materials flows through rapidly. This flow of water helps flush the solid food downstream. Bacteria begin to act on the plant matter in the rumen, and fermentation begins. The food is broken down and reduced to ever smaller sizes. The rumen's contractions constantly flush lighter solids back upward, while the smaller, thicker materials are pushed into the reticulum. From there food particles are ejected, floating in a liquid thick with bacteria, into the omasum. Some fatty acids may be absorbed through the walls of this chamber before the food passes into the abomasum—the giraffe's true stomach. This fourth chamber functions in much the same way as a nonruminant mammal's stomach, secreting acids to break down food. Unlike nonruminant stomachs, the abomasum secretes an enzyme called lysozyme, which breaks down bacteria, which is essential, considering the large numbers that collect there.

### The intestines

Digested food is absorbed through the walls of the intestines. A giraffe's intestines are longer than those of other ruminants and may be as long as 280 feet (85 m). The small intestine is tightly coiled and cushioned by a mass of elastic tissue to prevent it from pressing against the surrounding organs. A sheet of muscle called a diaphragm further separates the intestines from the heart and lungs.

▲ *A giraffe pulls leaves from a tree. The food will pass to the stomach along the esophagus. In a process called peristalsis, muscles in the esophagus force the food down. Peristalsis also forces food back up for rechewing.*

# Reproductive system

Male, or bull, giraffes produce sperm in organs called testes, which largely consist of twisted spaghetti-like tubes called seminiferous tubules. The female produces eggs in her ovaries. These become mature during estrus, the period when mating takes place. There is little courtship between the sexes. Bulls, however, battle for access to females in estrus. Bulls stand side by side and swing their necks, striking each other with their heads.

Mating is brief. After testing the female's receptivity by tasting her urine, the bull may nudge her gently or attempt to rest his neck across her back. The giraffes circle each other before the bull mounts the female, sliding his forelegs along the female's flanks and propping himself against her.

## Fertilization and development

Fertilization of the egg by sperm occurs in the reproductive tract of the female. Female giraffes and okapi have a bicornate uterus. This consists of two "horns," which extend from the cervix (neck of the birth canal) to each of the fallopian tubes.

The fertilized egg develops into an embryo. Giraffes are placental mammals; unborn young receive nourishment from the female through a structure called the placenta, which connects to the young by the umbilical cord. This arrangement allows nutrition and oxygen to enter the developing calf, and waste to move in the opposite direction. It also allows the female to pass on antibodies, which will help the calf fight disease.

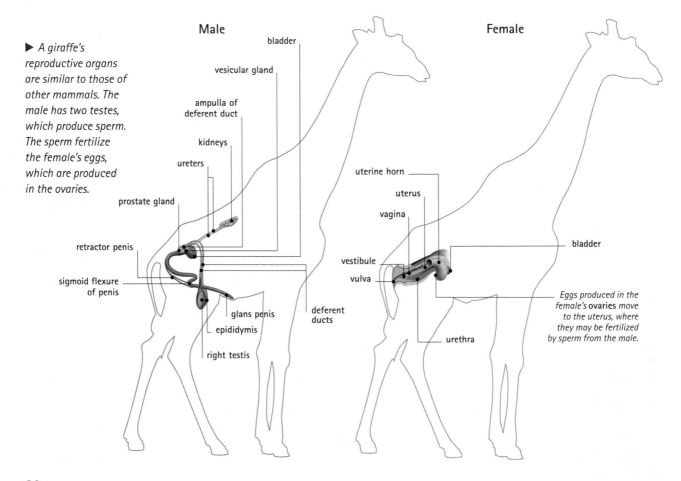

▶ *A giraffe's reproductive organs are similar to those of other mammals. The male has two testes, which produce sperm. The sperm fertilize the female's eggs, which are produced in the ovaries.*

Male

bladder
vesicular gland
ampulla of deferent duct
kidneys
ureters
prostate gland
retractor penis
sigmoid flexure of penis
glans penis
epididymis
right testis
deferent ducts

Female

uterine horn
uterus
vagina
vestibule
vulva
bladder
urethra

*Eggs produced in the female's **ovaries** move to the uterus, where they may be fertilized by sperm from the male.*

## Surviving the fall

**The long neck of a baby giraffe** is fragile. If the calf emerged from the female headfirst, as occurs in humans and other mammals, the neck would risk being broken as the rest of the body fell on top of it. For that reason, giraffes are born feet first. The feet help break the animal's fall. Newborn giraffes need to be tough to survive this fall. This partly explains why they are precocious (well developed at birth). Precocious young are also better able to escape predators and other hazards during the dangerous first few days of life.

## The hazards of birth

Gestation, or pregnancy, is long in giraffes, lasting around 14.5 months—one of the longest in the animal kingdom. The female gives birth to one calf, which she delivers while standing, since she is unable to squat. The newborn calf drops to the ground from a height of 5 feet (1.5 m); it must be robust to survive such a fall. Within two months of giving birth, the female is in estrus again and is able to mate once more. Giraffes usually give birth at intervals of 20 to 23 months.

## Mother's milk

A female giraffe has two or four teats. The milk is concentrated and highly nutritious, around five times richer in proteins than cow's milk. However, after a few weeks the protein level in the milk drops by 50 percent, and the fat content is reduced by two-thirds. In contrast, the sugar content (in the form of lactose) doubles at this time. Giraffe calves suckle for between 10 and 16 months, but the young giraffes are able to ruminate solid food after four months.

STEVEN SWABY

FURTHER READING AND RESEARCH

Nowak, Ronald M. 1999. *Walker's Mammals of the World.* Johns Hopkins University Press: Baltimore, MD.

Vaughan, Terry A. 1999. *Mammalogy.* Brooks/Cole: Belmont, CA.

## Dangerous days

**The first few months** of a giraffe's life are by far the most dangerous. Between 50 and 75 percent of calves fall prey to lions or hyenas during this time, despite rigorous protection from their mothers. Young giraffes rely on their patterned coat to camouflage them; they usually keep a low profile by crouching out of sight in tall grass. Their rich diet helps them quickly develop the muscular power to outrun predators such as lions. However, until they are much older giraffes cannot sustain the speed necessary to outpace more persistent predators such as hyenas over longer distances.

▲ *Newborn giraffes are around 6 feet (1.8 m) tall and are often on their feet within 20 minutes of birth. The young giraffe grows swiftly, reaching adulthood in just four years. During this time the neck grows from being one-sixth to one-third of the giraffe's total height. After four years the females are ready to breed, but bulls do not usually breed until they are around seven years old.*

# Gray whale

ORDER: Cetacea  SUBORDER: Mysticeti
FAMILY: Eschrichtiidae  SPECIES: *Eschrichtius robustus*

The gray whale is a slow-swimming marine mammal that lives in coastal waters of the North Pacific. It migrates between its winter breeding grounds in tropical waters and its summer feeding grounds in polar waters. Gray whales and others of their suborder have a filtering device in the mouth called baleen. They use it to sieve crustaceans and other invertebrates from the seabed.

## Anatomy and taxonomy

Biologists categorize all organisms into groups based partly on anatomical features. The gray whale differs enough from other whales to merit placement in a family of its own, the Eschrichtiidae. This family is part of the suborder Mysticeti, the baleen whales, which includes 13 other species.

- **Animals** Animals, are multicellular (many-celled) and gain their food supplies by consuming other organisms. Animals are able to move from one place to another (in most cases, using muscles).

- **Chordates** At some time in its life cycle a chordate has a stiff, dorsal (back) supporting rod called the notochord that runs along most of the length of its body.

- **Vertebrates** The vertebrate notochord develops into a backbone made up of units called vertebrae. The vertebrate muscular system that moves the head, trunk, and limbs consists primarily of muscles that are arranged in a mirror image on either side of the backbone.

- **Mammals** Mammals are warm-blooded vertebrates that have hair made of keratin. Females have mammary glands that produce milk to feed their young. The mammalian lower jaw is a single bone that hinges directly to the skull, and the middle ear contains three tiny bones.

- **Placental mammals** Placental mammals, or eutherians, nourish their unborn young through a placenta, a structure that forms in the mother's uterus during pregnancy.

- **Cetaceans** Members of this group are supremely adapted for life in water, where they spend their entire life. Cetaceans are streamlined like fish. This helps minimize drag as the animal swims. Cetaceans differ from the other

▶ This tree shows all the major groups to which baleen whales belong. The number of known rorqual species has recently increased from seven to nine (not all shown). DNA analysis showed that Bryde's whale is, in fact, two species; and a new species, Balaenoptera omurai, was discovered by Japanese biologists in 2003.

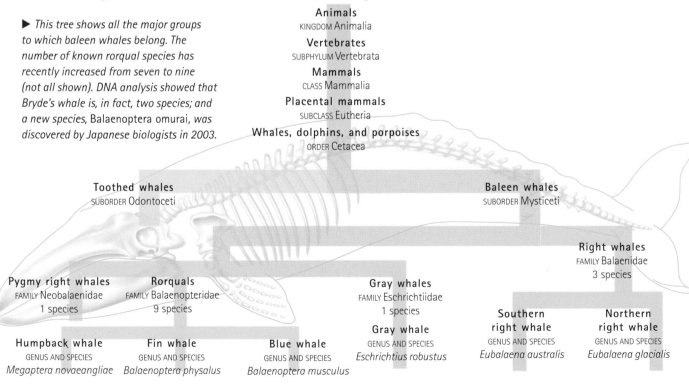

**Animals**
KINGDOM Animalia

**Vertebrates**
SUBPHYLUM Vertebrata

**Mammals**
CLASS Mammalia

**Placental mammals**
SUBCLASS Eutheria

**Whales, dolphins, and porpoises**
ORDER Cetacea

**Toothed whales**
SUBORDER Odontoceti

**Baleen whales**
SUBORDER Mysticeti

**Right whales**
FAMILY Balaenidae
3 species

**Pygmy right whales**
FAMILY Neobalaenidae
1 species

**Rorquals**
FAMILY Balaenopteridae
9 species

**Gray whales**
FAMILY Eschrichtiidae
1 species

**Gray whale**
GENUS AND SPECIES
*Eschrichtius robustus*

**Southern right whale**
GENUS AND SPECIES
*Eubalaena australis*

**Northern right whale**
GENUS AND SPECIES
*Eubalaena glacialis*

**Humpback whale**
GENUS AND SPECIES
*Megaptera novaeangliae*

**Fin whale**
GENUS AND SPECIES
*Balaenoptera physalus*

**Blue whale**
GENUS AND SPECIES
*Balaenoptera musculus*

major marine mammal groups—sea cows, seals, and sea lions—in many ways. For example, cetacean nostrils have moved from the front of the head to the top. This enables easy breathing at the sea surface. The nostrils exit through one or two blowholes. Like sea cows, cetaceans have paddlelike tails, their forelimbs form flippers that lack visible digits, and they have no functional hind limbs.

● **Toothed whales** In most of the 73 or so species of toothed whales, the jaws extend into a beaklike snout armed with teeth. The forehead bulges upward, enclosing the melon, a fat-containing structure that focuses sound waves. This enables the whale to use sound to visualize its surroundings, a process called echolocation. Toothed whales breathe through a single blowhole.

● **Baleen whales** There are 14 species of baleen whales. They include most of the larger whales and the largest whales of all, the fin and blue whales. Instead of teeth, baleen whales have thin, flexible plates of baleen hanging from their upper jaw. Whales strain fish or shrimplike crustaceans from the water with their baleen. All baleen whales have two blowholes lying side by side.

● **Rorquals** Rorquals are named for a Norwegian phrase meaning "furrow whale," referring to the pleats or grooves on the throat. Rorquals are gulpers; they take in large quantities of water when they feed. The pleats allow the throat to expand massively. The water is squeezed through the baleen, filtering out small fish or planktonic organisms.

● **Right whales** The three right whales—the bowhead, southern right whale, and northern right whale—form the family Balaenidae. They were named "right" by medieval whalers who considered them the best whales to catch; right whales swim slowly, migrate along regular

▲ *A breaching gray whale. The loud splash provides one of the ways that these whales communicate over short distances.*

coastal routes, and (because of their thick layer of blubber) float when dead. They have a very large head, with an upcurved upper jaw from which hang long baleen plates. Southern and northern right whales have bumps of rough skin, called callosities, on their heads. The bumps encourage the growth of barnacles.

● **Gray whale** The gray whale is extinct in the North Atlantic and lives only in the North Pacific and Arctic. An adult has a mottled body. Rather than a dorsal fin, it has a series of humps, or crenulations, running along the lower back. The barnacle-encrusted head has two or four throat grooves. The upper jaw of the gray whale is shorter and thicker than that of other baleen whales; it is used to dig up food-rich sediment from the seabed. The baleen has stiff bristles for straining invertebrates from the water.

---

**FEATURED SYSTEMS**

**EXTERNAL ANATOMY** Gray whales are baleen whales with moderately streamlined bodies, flippers shaped like hydrofoils, and a powerful, horizontally flattened tail for swimming. *See pages 84–87.*

**SKELETAL SYSTEM** The backbone acts as an anchor for muscles that flex the body and flippers, and raise the tail up and down. Hind limb bones are still present, though tiny and largely without function. *See pages 88–90.*

**MUSCULAR SYSTEM** Large muscles above and below the vertebral column power vertical movements of the tail for locomotion. *See pages 91–92.*

**NERVOUS SYSTEM** The brain of a baleen whale has a large and highly folded cerebrum. The cerebrum's extensive surface area provides room for the vast number of nerve cell interconnections needed to process and interpret substantial amounts of sensory information. *See pages 93–96.*

**CIRCULATORY AND RESPIRATORY SYSTEMS** Both systems ensure that oxygen reaches vital organs during dives. *See pages 97–99.*

**DIGESTIVE AND EXCRETORY SYSTEMS** Gray whales and other baleen whales swallow small prey whole and in large quantities. Their three-chamber stomach digests food mechanically and then chemically. *See pages 100–101.*

**REPRODUCTIVE SYSTEM** Internal male sex organs and hidden mammary glands assist streamlining and ease of movement through water. *See pages 102–103.*

# External anatomy

Whales use their flipper-shaped forelimbs for steering but have no hind limbs. Instead, the boneless tail flukes propel these animals through the water. The flippers and tail flukes act as hydrofoils. In cross section they are shaped like the wings of an aircraft. This shape generates a force by causing the pressure of water above the fluke to be lower than the pressure below. Over the course of a tail beat, the net effect of this force acts forward. The force, called thrust, drives the whale through the water. Unlike flying birds, which require considerable upthrust to remain aloft, whales are nearly weightless in water and usually need little upthrust to keep them swimming level.

## The importance of streamlining

For a swimming animal, drag (the resistance to motion when an object passes through a fluid) is a major physical force to overcome. A streamlined body shape, like a torpedo, helps reduce drag. That is why baleen whales do not have external ears. Similarly, a baleen whale's external reproductive organs, when not in use, are tucked inside the abdomen, so improving streamlining. A whale's skin is smooth and almost hairless; baleen whale skin releases an oily substance that reduces drag further. Keeping the leading edge of appendages like flukes and flippers as narrow as possible also helps minimize drag. By swimming beneath the water rather than at the surface (where disturbance creates waves), whales can save a great deal of energy. A baleen whale's two blowholes, positioned on top of the head, allow the animal to breathe while barely breaking the surface.

Unlike most toothed whales, which are predators of fast-swimming prey, most baleen whales feed on slow-moving crustaceans and other small invertebrates. Baleen whales can easily maintain moderate speeds. Blue whales and fin whales can swim at 19 mph (30 km/h) when threatened; even the slow-swimming gray whale reaches 13 mph (21 km/h).

49 feet (15 m)

Gray whales have a shallow **dorsal hump** followed by a series of **knuckles**.

The two **blowholes** are the whale's nostrils. They release a spout of condensed water vapor when the animal surfaces.

Different parts of the **eye** are specialized for vision above and below water.

The **rostrum**, or upper jaw, has many small dimples, each containing a stiff touch-sensitive hair.

The **mouth** contains the fringe of baleen plates that the whale uses to sieve food from the water.

Clusters of barnacles grow on patches of rough skin called **callosities**.

The forelimbs are modified into short **flippers**. They are used for maneuvering and stability when swimming.

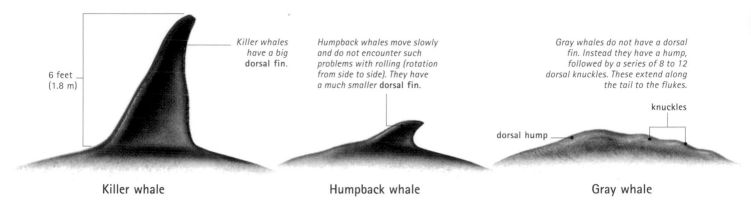

*Killer whales have a big dorsal fin.*

6 feet (1.8 m)

*Humpback whales move slowly and do not encounter such problems with rolling (rotation from side to side). They have a much smaller dorsal fin.*

*Gray whales do not have a dorsal fin. Instead they have a hump, followed by a series of 8 to 12 dorsal knuckles. These extend along the tail to the flukes.*

knuckles

dorsal hump

Killer whale

Humpback whale

Gray whale

## Large size

Most baleen whales are very large animals. The blue whale may be the largest animal that has ever lived. It reaches lengths of up to 110 feet (33 m) and weighs up to 200 tons (180 metric tons). This is equivalent to the weight of more than 30 male African elephants, the largest living land animals, and is at least twice the size of the biggest known dinosaurs. Land animals cannot reach the sizes of these marine giants, since their limbs would need to be enormous to support their weight in air. Such limbs would not be strong enough for the job.

In cooler environments large size gives animals an advantage. Whales are warm-blooded, or endothermic: they control their body temperature physiologically rather than by relying on environmental or behavioral control. Because baleen whales have a core body temperature of 97–99°F (36–37°C), and because most of them live in water at temperatures at least 27°F (15°C) cooler than this for part of the year, reducing heat loss is of great survival value. For this reason, whales have thick layers of insulating blubber.

Large whales also have physics on their side. A small animal has a much higher surface-area-to-volume ratio than a large one. Therefore, large animals lose or gain heat from their surroundings more slowly, and need to use less energy to maintain their body temperature at a near-constant level.

### ▲ DORSAL FINS
### Cetaceans

*The dorsal fins of cetaceans help the animal stabilize as it swims. This is more important for faster-swimming species. Slower species usually have smaller fins, and gray whales have dispensed with them altogether. They instead have a row of smaller humps that run along the lower back.*

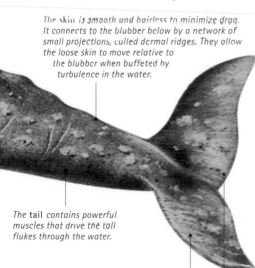

*The skin is smooth and hairless to minimize drag. It connects to the blubber below by a network of small projections, called dermal ridges. They allow the loose skin to move relative to the blubber when buffeted by turbulence in the water.*

*The tail contains powerful muscles that drive the tail flukes through the water.*

*The tail flukes measure more than 10 feet (3 m) from tip to tip. Their shape and angle are altered by muscles attached to tendons. They are driven through the water to provide a forward-acting force.*

### EVOLUTION

## Relatives of baleen whales

**Baleen whales split from the toothed whales** around 33 million years ago. The distribution of early mysticete fossils—along with abundant zooplankton fossils—suggests that the baleen whales evolved in the South Pacific and Antarctic before swiftly spreading throughout tropical and more northerly oceans. Baleen whales' toothed ancestry is betrayed by the presence of tooth buds in their developing embryos. These structures develop into teeth in toothed whales, such as sperm whales and dolphins. In baleen whales the tooth buds do not develop further, but baleen forms instead.

Studies of whale DNA (genetic makeup) and blood composition, together with anatomical evidence from living and fossil species, show that whales' closest relatives are the artiodactyl (even-toed) ungulates. Artiodactyls are hoofed mammals that include groups such as camels, sheep, and antelope. The closest living relatives of whales are probably hippopotamuses.

▲ *Whale lice shelter among barnacles on a gray whale. Swimming barnacle larvae are encouraged to settle on rough patches of skin around the whale's head called callosities. The barnacles then transform into sessile (attached) adults.*

### Baleen

Baleen plates are made of keratin—the same tough, flexible protein that hair and fingernails are made of. Baleen plates have a consistency and springiness similar to that of human fingernails. Depending on the species, between 140 and 430 baleen plates hang in two rows from both sides of the upper jaw. The plates are arranged like rows of kitchen dishes stacked in a drying rack. As the tip of a baleen plate wears down, new keratin is added at the base of the plate where it is embedded in the gum.

Seen from the front, a baleen plate is triangular, with its inner edge a fringe of fibers rather like the splayed-out bristles of a broom. The size, flexibility, and number of baleen plates govern the foods that the whale eats.

### Unwanted passengers

Patches of roughened skin on the body of gray, humpback, and right whales attract barnacles. The barnacles gain a safe home from which they can feed freely on small plankton floating in the water. Whale researchers use the pattern of barnacle growths as identification markers.

The purpose of these barnacle clumps, or callosities, is unclear. They reduce the whale's streamlining and seem to serve no obvious benefit. However, male right whales sometimes use their callosities as weapons in fights for females, raking their opponents with the abrasive patches. Patterns of callosities may also help whales identify one another.

Gray and right whales carry thousands of parasitic crustaceans called cyamids, or whale lice. They feed on flecks of discarded skin, finding a refuge around the barnacles. Some researchers have suggested that the callosities encourage barnacles and lice to concentrate only on certain parts of the body, so the rest is less affected and therefore maintains its streamlining. Whales are sometimes host to larger hitchhikers. Remora fish use suckers on their heads to attach to passing whales, which unwittingly give them a free ride.

### Body coloration

The body of a baleen whale is typically a combination of gray, black, brown, or white. Humpbacks have distinctive patches of black and white on their flippers and the underside of their flukes. Scientists use the fluke markings to identify individuals. Fin whales have a pale patch on the right side of the head.

### Blubber

**Like other marine mammals,** whales have a thick fat-rich layer called blubber beneath the skin. Whale blubber is a mixture of fibrous connective tissue interspersed with oil-filled cells. Blubber insulates the whale against the cold, acts as a food store, and, being less dense than water, provides buoyancy. With the exception of Bryde's whale, all baleen whales inhabit cool temperate, subpolar, or polar waters for at least part of the year. The blubber layer of large baleen whales is at least 5 inches (12 cm) thick. The bowhead whale, which spends all year in subpolar or polar waters, has a blubber layer up to 20 inches (50 cm) thick.

The giant liver of baleen whales is also an important fat store, providing energy reserves during winter when food is scarce. The blubber of gray whales, together with fat stores in the bones and liver, sustains the adults during their seven-month round trip migration between polar and tropical waters.

Scientists think the whales use this patch to scare fish into a tight school at the water's surface. Fin whales typically turn on their right side when feeding, and sometimes they cooperate in a group to encircle their prey.

A baleen whale's upper surface is typically darker than its under surface. That is called countershading. The pale underside makes the silhouette of the body much less visible against the background of sunlight streaming through the surface water. This coloration may act as camouflage against predators attacking from below. The dark upper surface makes the whale less visible from above against the dark, inky depths of the sea. Countershading may be a legacy of the ancient past, when whales were hunted by a wider range of predators than they are now. Nowadays, adult baleen whales have few predators—only killer whales working as a team can kill an adult whale. Human whalers, however, are hunters against which the mightiest whales have no defense.

## COMPARATIVE ANATOMY

### Swimming underwater

**Fish, whales, penguins, and ichthyosaurs** (a group of extinct marine reptiles) are only distantly related to one another, but over millions of years of evolution all have adapted to swim through water. The development of a shape that allows optimal streamlining and the development of appendages such as flippers or fins are examples of convergent evolution. This occurs when distantly related organisms develop similar anatomical solutions to similar environmental demands. However, the propulsive tails of fish and ichthyosaurs move (or moved) from side to side, whereas those of whales move up and down. Penguins generate all the thrust they need to swim by flapping their flipperlike wings.

▼ A blue whale at its breeding grounds off Mexico. Note the pleats on the throat. These allow enormous expansion, enabling the whale to take a massive amount of water into its mouth.

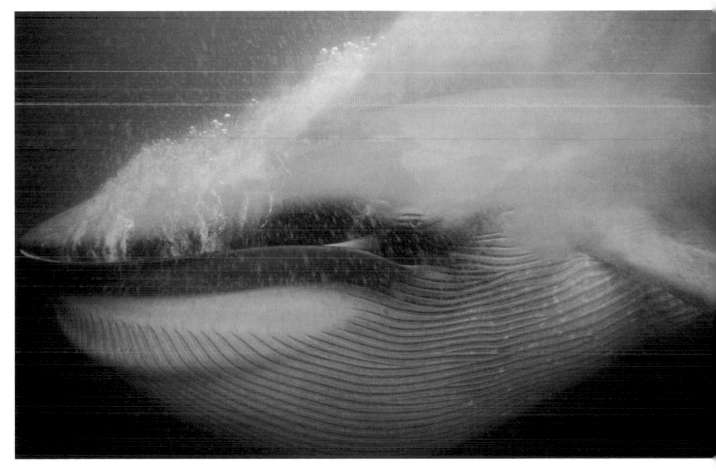

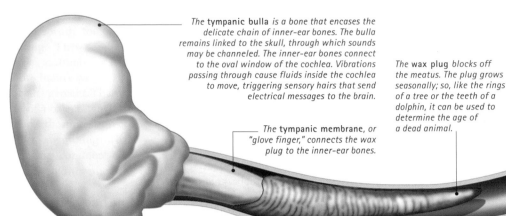

The **tympanic bulla** *is a bone that encases the delicate chain of inner-ear bones. The bulla remains linked to the skull, through which sounds may be channeled. The inner-ear bones connect to the oval window of the cochlea. Vibrations passing through cause fluids inside the cochlea to move, triggering sensory hairs that send electrical messages to the brain.*

*The* **wax plug** *blocks off the meatus. The plug grows seasonally; so, like the rings of a tree or the teeth of a dolphin, it can be used to determine the age of a dead animal.*

*The* **tympanic membrane,** *or "glove finger," connects the wax plug to the inner-ear bones.*

*This tube, the* **external auditory meatus,** *connects the bulla to the outside world. The path of sound to the inner-ear bones is not well understood in baleen whales; this canal may be vestigial and serve no purpose.*

▲ EAR STRUCTURE
**Fin whale**
*A cross section through the head to show the bulla and meatus. How sound gets to the bulla is unknown. The auditory meatus may be important for airborne sounds, but biologists do not know for sure.*

## How whales hear

Sound travels farther and faster in water than in air, and baleen whales have good hearing. Sounds are detected and transmitted to the brain by means of a structure called the cochlea. Just how sound waves reach this structure is not clear. Sounds do not pass through the lower jaw, as in toothed whales. The outer ear opening in a baleen whale is tiny; it lies just behind the eye. The tube into which the ear opening leads, the external auditory meatus, is partly blocked by connective tissue and fully blocked by a waxy ear plug. This connects to a thick tympanic membrane, or eardrum. As in toothed whales, the bones of the inner ear are housed in a bony capsule called a tympanic bulla. Baleen whale bullae are not completely detached from the skull, suggesting that vibrations passing through bone and other tissues may be important. Air spaces in the skull called sinuses may help reflect vibrations through the skull bones toward the cochlea.

Regardless of how the vibrations get there, sounds cause vibrations of part of the cochlea called the oval window. These vibrations generate movements of fluids inside the cochlea. The fluids move sensory hairs, which send electrical signals to the brain.

## Sound production

Baleen whales hear best at frequencies similar to the sounds they produce. Most make deep infrasonic sounds that lie outside the range of human hearing, as well as a range of moans, groans, whistles, and clicks that humans can hear. Bowhead and humpback whales are the most vocal, with male humpbacks producing complex songs that last for 10 minutes or more. Like toothed whales, humpbacks are also sensitive to high-frequency ultrasound, and other baleen whales probably are, too.

Hearing and sound production are vital for communication over both short and long distances. Baleen whales also use hearing to detect the sounds of their prey or of other predators, such as seals or seabirds, that make loud splashes as they hunt. Gray whales listen closely for the vocalizations of killer whales and swim swiftly to the safety of seaweed beds to escape these deadly enemies.

### IN FOCUS

## Do whales echolocate?

**Baleen whales lack** the oil-filled focusing melon present in other cetaceans, plus the blowhole's sound-producing "monkey lips," and the sound-conducting channel of the lower jaw that enables toothed whales to use sophisticated echolocation (the use of sound echoes to generate an "image" of the surroundings). However, minke and gray whales produce clicks that may enable them to echolocate by an unknown mechanism. The bowhead whale, which lives in Arctic waters, probably listens for echoes bouncing off the ice to navigate as it swims.

# Circulatory and respiratory systems

**CONNECTIONS**

**COMPARE** the arrangement of respiratory and digestive system passages in the head of a gray whale with those of a land mammal like a *ZEBRA* or a *HUMAN*.

**COMPARE** the diving adaptations of a gray whale with those of a *PENGUIN* and a *SEAL*.

Like other mammals, a baleen whale has a four-chamber heart that pumps blood through a double circulation (the main and pulmonary circulations). Arteries with thick, muscular walls carry blood under high pressure away from the heart to supply other organs. Thin-walled veins take blood back to the heart under lower pressure. In the pulmonary circulation, waste carbon dioxide gas is released at the lungs as the red blood cells recharge with oxygen.

The heart and major blood vessels of an adult blue whale are astonishingly large. The heart weighs more than 1 ton (0.9 metric ton), with the largest artery (the aorta) and veins (the venae cavae) large enough for a person to swim inside. However, a whale's heart and vessels are no larger than would be expected for an animal of such enormous size.

Whales inhale through their nasal passages, warming the air before it travels down the trachea to the lungs. In the lungs, oxygen is exchanged for carbon dioxide, and stale air is exhaled when the whale surfaces. The respiratory system of a whale is far more efficient than that of most terrestrial mammals.

## Diving

Baleen whales dive to 330 feet (100 m) or more to feed, although gray whales often make much shallower dives to the

**IN FOCUS**

### Breaking the ice

**Bowhead whales are right whales** adapted for life in the high Arctic. They have the thickest blubber of any whale of their size, an amazingly arched upper jaw, and a powerful stocky body. The sturdy body allows them to break through sea ice up to 12 inches (30 cm) thick when they need to surface to breathe. This extends their range into frozen waters that are not accessible to other whales. Belugas benefit from the bowhead's labors and sometimes follow them to the surface. They then breathe through the newly created hole in the ice.

coastal seafloor. Typically, a whale breathes 10 to 15 times at the surface over three minutes or so before diving for around eight minutes. When threatened, a baleen whale can remain underwater for more than 30 minutes.

When a baleen whale dives, its lungs collapse as the surrounding pressure increases. Relative to size, a whale's lungs occupy about half the volume of those of a land mammal. Whale lungs are superefficient at extracting oxygen from air. They remove more than 80 percent of oxygen from inhaled air, as opposed to less than 20 percent in the case of humans.

▼ **Gray whale**

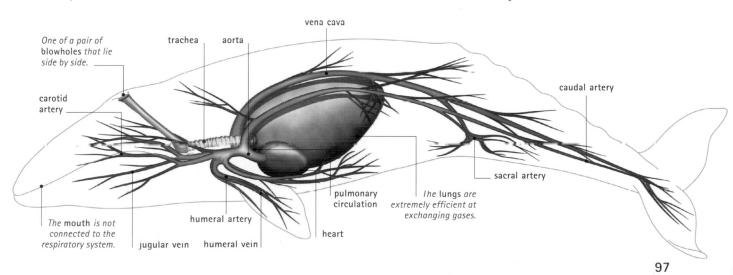

*One of a pair of blowholes that lie side by side.*

carotid artery

trachea    aorta

vena cava

caudal artery

sacral artery

*The mouth is not connected to the respiratory system.*

pulmonary circulation

*The lungs are extremely efficient at exchanging gases.*

jugular vein    humeral vein

humeral artery

heart

▲ To breathe, this gray whale can breach the surface with only the top of its head. That is because cetacean nostrils have moved from the front of the skull to the top over the course of their evolution.

Whales' blood also has many more red blood cells per unit volume of blood. Their red blood cells are larger, and overall the blood contains much more hemoglobin (the pigment that carries oxygen within the red blood cells).

When a baleen whale dives, its heart rate drops. The heart's contractions become smaller, and their frequency slows. Blood is diverted from nonessential organs to those that most need it—particularly the brain and the heart itself. Whale muscle is rich in an oxygen-trapping pigment called myoglobin. Like hemoglobin, myoglobin gradually releases its store of oxygen during the whale's dive.

## CLOSE-UP

### Blowholes and breathing tubes

**Baleen whales have two blowholes**, which are equivalent to the nostrils of land mammals. However, in cetaceans, unlike land mammals, the trachea and the esophagus (the tube leading to the stomach and intestines) are completely separate. Because of this separation, a whale can breathe only through its blowholes, not its mouth.

## The bends

When a person dives deep, nitrogen gas in inhaled air gradually dissolves into the bloodstream under pressure. Then, when the diver returns to the surface, the nitrogen could bubble out of the blood. This causes a condition called decompression sickness, or the bends. The gas bubbles can block small blood vessels or gather in the gaps between bone joints to cause excruciating pain. Whales avoid decompression sickness by having compressible lungs. A whale's rib cage is flexible, and the diaphragm runs at an oblique angle. This allows the lungs to collapse readily under pressure, forcing air inside back up the trachea and into the nasal passages. These have thick, impermeable walls that prevent any gas exchange from taking place, so nitrogen cannot enter the blood when the pressure rises. When the whale moves toward the surface, the pressure lessens and the lungs reinflate.

When a baleen whale surfaces, it breathes out a foul-smelling cloud of air. This is visible above the sea surface as a spout of water, which betrays the presence of the whale. The spout is a fine spray containing seawater trapped in the blowhole and condensing water droplets from inside the whale.

### Keeping warm

At 97–99°F (36–37°C), the body temperature of a baleen whale is always higher than the surrounding seawater. Whales have dense networks of blood vessels called retia mirabilia that help prevent heat wastage. Heat loss is greatest from projections that have a large surface area, such as the flippers, dorsal fin, and tail. Arteries supplying blood to these extremities are surrounded by, and run alongside, veins that carry blood back to the core. The arterial blood warms the blood traveling along the veins. This arrangement is called a countercurrent heat exchange. The extremities remain cool, while the blood returning to the core of the body stays warm.

When whales are active in warm waters there is a real danger of overheating. They avoid this by shutting down the countercurrent systems and routing blood through pathways close to the skin. This enables them to release heat into the surroundings.

### The importance of the mouth

A baleen whale's tongue represents a massive surface area for heat loss. Worse, there is no insulating layer of blubber. Countercurrent heat exchange systems keep the tongue's temperature far lower than the rest of the body. In this way little heat is lost.

▼ *Whales such as this gray whale need blubber and countercurrent heat exchange mechanisms to survive in cold polar waters. Migration into warmer waters necessitates other mechanisms that keep the animal from overheating.*

## IN FOCUS

### Reversing the path of heat

**The countercurrent heat exchangers** inside a whale's body keep the temperature constant and high. However, some parts of the body need to be cooler than others. Whales keep the temperature of these regions low by ferrying in cooler blood from other parts of the body. For example, right whales have a rete mirabile in their upper jaw. Warm blood moves in, loses its heat to the water, and then passes close to the brain. This helps keep the brain from overheating.

As in other mammals, the production and storage of sperm in whales are best at temperatures lower than the rest of the body. Whales cool their testes differently. Most adult mammals' testes lie outside the body as a result. Whale testes are inside the body; they would badly affect streamlining otherwise. In a reverse countercurrent heat exchange system, cool blood is brought from the fins to supply the testes. Female whales have similar problems. Young developing in the uterus run the risk of overheating, which would affect development. Again, cool blood from the fins passes to the uterus. It moves through the placenta, where it comes into close contact with the blood of the calf. Heat is drawn away, warming the mother's blood and cooling the calf's significantly.

# Digestive and excretory systems

Baleen whales are named for their feeding structure, the baleen, which filters small organisms from the water. The size and shape of the skull and baleen plates determine the type of prey taken and the method of capture. Right whales have a very large head that approaches one-third the total length of the body. The narrow upper jaw or rostrum is curved upward and supports long baleen plates, up to 10 feet (3 m) long in northern and southern right whales, and more than 13 feet (4 m) long in bowheads. These whales feed at or near the surface, swimming along with their mouth open. The gap between the bristles is narrow; the whales sieve the water for copepod crustaceans that are less than 0.5 inch (1.25 cm) long. Occasionally, the whales feed on larger crustaceans called krill or on schools of small fish. At intervals, the whale closes its mouth and scrapes the trapped animals off its baleen with its tongue, then swallows the prey.

## Rorquals' feeding

Rorquals have a broader, less curved rostrum, and their baleen is shorter and bushier than that of right whales. Rorquals feed by expanding the mouth and throat cavity and engulfing a large volume of water in one go. Pleats on the underside help the throat stretch to accommodate the massive mouthful. The

▶ FEEDING
**Blue whale**
*Cross sections through the head of a blue whale, showing how these giant mammals use their tongue to force water through their baleen plates.*

*1. The whale opens its mouth, taking in a huge gulp of water containing plankton.*

*2. The mouth closes, and the tongue forces water through the baleen, straining out the plankton.*

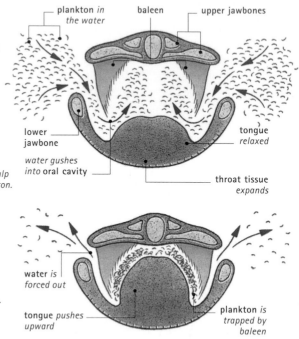

plankton *in the water*  baleen  upper jawbones

lower jawbone

tongue *relaxed*

*water gushes into* oral cavity

throat tissue *expands*

water *is forced out*

tongue *pushes upward*

plankton *is trapped by baleen*

whale then closes its mouth and raises its tongue, forcing water through the baleen and out of the sides of the mouth. Small prey items are trapped on the inside of the baleen plates, scraped off with the tongue, and swallowed.

Rorquals' main prey items vary from species to species, depending on feeding method, locality, and the fineness of the bristles on the

▼ Gray whale

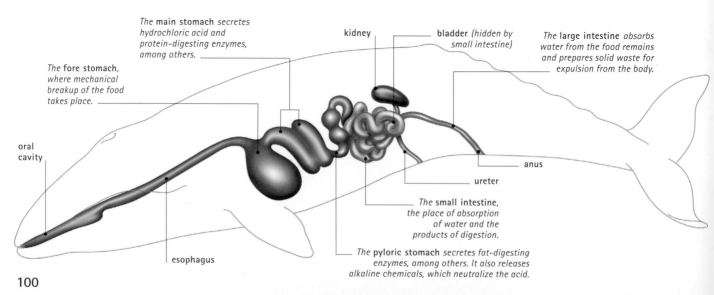

The **main stomach** *secretes hydrochloric acid and protein-digesting enzymes, among others.*

The **fore stomach,** *where mechanical breakup of the food takes place.*

kidney

bladder *(hidden by small intestine)*

The **large intestine** *absorbs water from the food remains and prepares solid waste for expulsion from the body.*

oral cavity

anus

ureter

esophagus

The **small intestine,** *the place of absorption of water and the products of digestion.*

The **pyloric stomach** *secretes fat-digesting enzymes, among others. It also releases alkaline chemicals, which neutralize the acid.*

baleen plates. Sei whales have fine-bristled baleen that captures planktonic crustaceans, especially copepods. The blue whales' baleen is medium-bristled; its preferred diet is krill. Fin and humpback whales have coarser baleen plates, and they often feed on shoals of herring and capelin fish.

## Plowing the seabed

Uniquely among baleen whales, gray whales feed at the seabed. They have stout jaws with short, stiff baleen up to 10 inches (25 cm) long. In their northern feeding grounds, gray whales plow the seabed with their baleen, sieving out amphipod crustaceans and a variety of other invertebrates including clams and worms. They also sieve the water for disturbed invertebrates after most of the sediment has settled. The gray whale's tongue is unusually large. It aids in scooping up sediment and manipulating the mouthful to help separate food from mud.

On migration, gray whales occasionally feed in a manner similar to other baleen whales. They capture small fish at near the surface and take shrimplike mysid crustaceans that thrive in beds of kelp (large brown seaweeds).

## Digestion and absorption

Swallowed food travels down the esophagus to the stomach, where digestion begins. Whale stomachs have three compartments. The first is the fore stomach, where food is ground up into a soup. This is squirted into the second stomach chamber, the main stomach. The walls of this chamber secrete hydrochloric acid, and protein-digesting enzymes that chemically break down the food. The walls of the third stomach compartment, the pyloric

▲ This gray whale is feeding on krill at the ocean surface, a behavior these whales exhibit during their migration from feeding to breeding grounds. Note the wispy edges of the baleen plates that are visible in the animal's mouth.

stomach, secrete fat-digesting enzymes, more protein-digesting enzymes, and an alkaline fluid that neutralizes the acidity of the juice from the main stomach. From the stomach, the food enters the first part of the small intestine. The intestine walls absorb the products of digestion, which enter the bloodstream before circulating to the tissues that need them. The small intestine walls are highly folded and rich in blood vessels. This provides a very large surface area across which digested food and water can be absorbed.

## Gaining water and losing salt

The salt concentration of baleen whale blood is considerably lower than that of seawater. Whales must take in water to keep their blood diluted; they gain much of their water from food. Fish have a salt concentration similar to a whale's own tissues, but invertebrates, such as krill and copepods, have tissues with a salt concentration similar to that of seawater. To get the water they need, whales take on unwanted salts that they must excrete.

Whale kidneys remove excess salts from the bloodstream, along with other wastes. Water, salts, and the other wastes collect in the urine. This travels from kidneys to bladder before being expelled through the urethra. Perhaps surprisingly, whale kidneys are not very efficient. They produce urine that is more concentrated than seawater, but they waste large amounts of water that must be replaced by feeding and drinking.

### CLOSE-UP

## Big appetites

**The fore stomach** of a blue whale can contain about 1.1 tons (1 metric ton) of krill. At the height of the summer feeding season, the whale consumes about 4.4 tons (4 metric tons) of food each day. That is equivalent to the weight of a small truck.

COMPARE the feeding strategy of a gray whale with that of a toothed whale such as a *DOLPHIN*.

COMPARE the three-chamber stomach of a whale with the four-chamber stomach of a ruminant such as a *GIRAFFE*.

CONNECTIONS

# Reproductive system

In many ways, the baleen whale reproductive system is very similar to that of any other placental mammal. However, there are some major differences caused by the need for streamlining, and because mating, giving birth, and suckling must take place underwater.

Male cetaceans have an internal penis and testes to aid streamlining. The penis normally lies inside the abdomen. Before mating, it fills with blood then emerges through the genital slit. Unusually, a muscle attached to the penis makes it relatively mobile, and retracts it back into the abdomen after mating.

## Mating whales

In humpback whales, more than one male will usually compete to mate with a single female. Males advertise their presence by singing mating songs that also serve as challenges to other males. Male and female gray whales caress each other in a courtship ritual before mating (copulation) begins. The male's penis is flexible and about 6 feet (2 m) long. It releases sperm into the female's vagina; copulation may last only 20 to 30 seconds, but it may be repeated on several occasions.

Most baleen whales are probably polygamous—males and females each have several partners. Often, males compete with one another over a female, using their physical bulk to get between the receptive female and rival males. Except in species where several males coerce a female, such as right whales and the gray whale, female whales are not submissive but actively select a mate.

## Pregnancy and birth

In baleen whales, the gestation period (the time from copulation to birth) is between 10 and 13 months, which is no longer than that of the much smaller toothed whales. Adult female gray whales breed only once every two or three years and typically bear one calf at a time. Early whalers nicknamed gray whales "devilfish," after experiencing the wrath of mother whales. They would attack boats when they or their calves were threatened.

Rarely observed, the birth of a baleen whale usually takes place at or near the surface, with the mother helping the calf to the surface to take its first breath. Baleen whale calves are usually born headfirst. However, baleen whales, including gray whales, have been observed giving birth tailfirst, as is generally the case in toothed whales.

## Becoming independent

All traces of the mother's milk-producing mammary glands are usually hidden, but when nuzzled by a calf, a nipple emerges. Whale calves lack the mouth shape and musculature to be able to suck. Instead, they squeeze the mother's nipple between their tongue and the roof of their mouth. In response, muscles

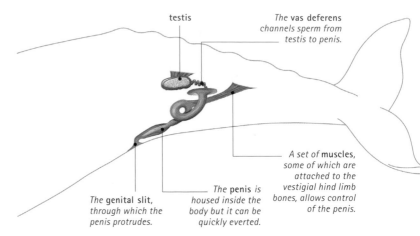

testis

The **vas deferens** channels sperm from testis to penis.

The **genital slit,** through which the penis protrudes.

The **penis** is housed inside the body but it can be quickly everted.

A set of **muscles,** some of which are attached to the vestigial hind limb bones, allows control of the penis.

▲ MALE REPRODUCTIVE SYSTEM
**Gray whale**
*The flexible penis allows great maneuverability during copulation and in other social interactions.*

▼ *Mating gray whales. The long, pink organ is a male's penis. Several males attend to a female when she is in estrus.*

surrounding the mammary glands contract and squeeze, squirting milk directly into the calf's mouth. A calf stays close to its mother during the first few weeks of its life and suckles regularly. It puts on weight at an incredible rate—faster than the young of any other mammal. A blue whale calf is about 23 feet (7 m) long at birth and weighs about 2 tons (1.8 metric tons). It grows at a rate of about 180 pounds (85 kg) each day, reaching 25 tons (23 metric tons) and 48 feet (15 m) long by the age of eight months. Whale milk is 40 percent fat or more. By comparison, cow's milk is between 3 and 5 percent fat. A high fat intake enables a whale calf to develop a thick layer of blubber within weeks.

The calves of rorqual whales begin to eat solid food within six or seven months. All baleen whale calves are fully weaned within 12 months. Gray whales become sexually mature at about eight years old, when males are about 36 feet (11 m) long and females about 38 feet (11.5 m). Gray whales can live to 40 years or more, and some bowhead whales can reach an astonishing 150 years old.

## Migration

Gray whales and almost all the larger rorquals make long-distance migrations between summer feeding grounds in polar or subpolar waters and their winter breeding grounds in

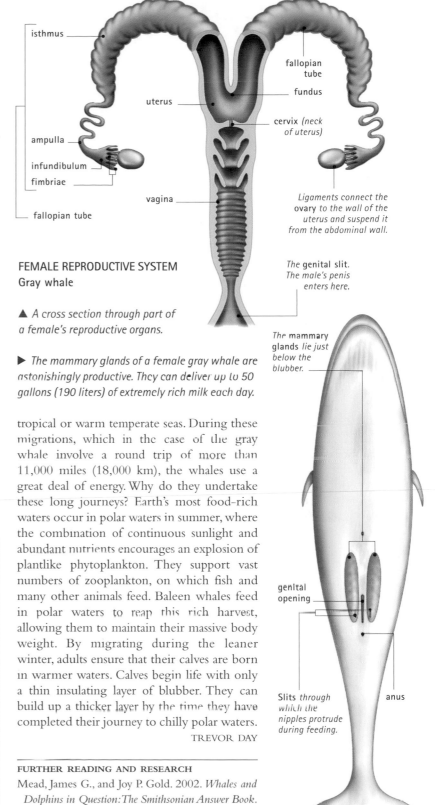

**FEMALE REPRODUCTIVE SYSTEM
Gray whale**

▲ *A cross section through part of a female's reproductive organs.*

▶ *The mammary glands of a female gray whale are astonishingly productive. They can deliver up to 50 gallons (190 liters) of extremely rich milk each day.*

tropical or warm temperate seas. During these migrations, which in the case of the gray whale involve a round trip of more than 11,000 miles (18,000 km), the whales use a great deal of energy. Why do they undertake these long journeys? Earth's most food-rich waters occur in polar waters in summer, where the combination of continuous sunlight and abundant nutrients encourages an explosion of plantlike phytoplankton. They support vast numbers of zooplankton, on which fish and many other animals feed. Baleen whales feed in polar waters to reap this rich harvest, allowing them to maintain their massive body weight. By migrating during the leaner winter, adults ensure that their calves are born in warmer waters. Calves begin life with only a thin insulating layer of blubber. They can build up a thicker layer by the time they have completed their journey to chilly polar waters.

TREVOR DAY

FURTHER READING AND RESEARCH

Mead, James G., and Joy P. Gold. 2002. *Whales and Dolphins in Question: The Smithsonian Answer Book.* Smithsonian Books: Washington, DC.

## IN FOCUS

### Competing sperm

**Male northern and southern right whales** have the largest sperm-producing organs, or testes, in the animal kingdom. Each pair weighs about 1 ton (0.9 metric ton). They release tens of gallons of sperm during mating. In these species, and in gray whales, which have similarly massive pairs of testes, males do not compete for the attentions of a female. Instead, they actively help each other out. Several males mate with any one female. Rather than the whales actively competing, their sperm do battle inside the female instead, in the race to fertilize her ovum (egg). This is called sperm competition.

# Grizzly bear

ORDER: *Carnivora* FAMILY: *Ursidae*
SPECIES: *Ursus arctos* SUBSPECIES *horribilis*

Grizzly bears are a subspecies of the brown bear, *Ursus arctos*. Grizzlies live in the cold forests of the Rocky Mountains and across western Canada and Alaska. Other brown bear subspecies live throughout the Northern Hemisphere.

## Anatomy and taxonomy

Scientists classify all organisms into taxonomic groups based largely on anatomical features. Grizzlies and other brown bears belong to the Ursidae or bear family, which also includes black, sun, sloth, spectacled, and polar bears.

● **Animals**   All animals are multicellular (many-celled). They get the energy and materials they need to survive by consuming other organisms. Unlike plants, fungi, and the members of other kingdoms, animals are able to move around for at least one phase of their lives.

● **Chordates**   For at least some of their lives, all members of the Chordata have a stiff, internal rod called a notochord running along their back.

● **Vertebrates**   In vertebrates, the notochord develops into a backbone, or spine, made up of small units called vertebrae. As well as a backbone, a vertebrate's body is also supported by an internal skeleton made from bone and cartilage. Paired sets of muscles enable the body to move.

● **Mammals**   Mammals are a large group of warm-blooded animals. Unique features include hairs covering the body, milk glands in females to feed young, and a lower jaw formed by a single bone that hinges directly to the skull.

● **Placental mammals**   Unlike marsupials, the other main mammal group, placental mammals nourish their developing young while they are still inside the mother via an organ called the placenta. The placenta is a temporary structure inside the uterus that connects unborn young to the mother's blood supply.

● **Carnivores**   The word *carnivore* is often used to mean any animal that eats meat, but it is also the correct taxonomic name of a large group of placental mammals. As their name

▶ *Land carnivores are divided into two great lineages: the doglike Canoidea and the catlike Feloidea (not shown). Bears are doglike carnivores. The position of the giant panda is uncertain; some biologists place it with the bears (as in this article), but others disagree and classify this species among the procyonids (raccoons and relatives) or in a separate group.*

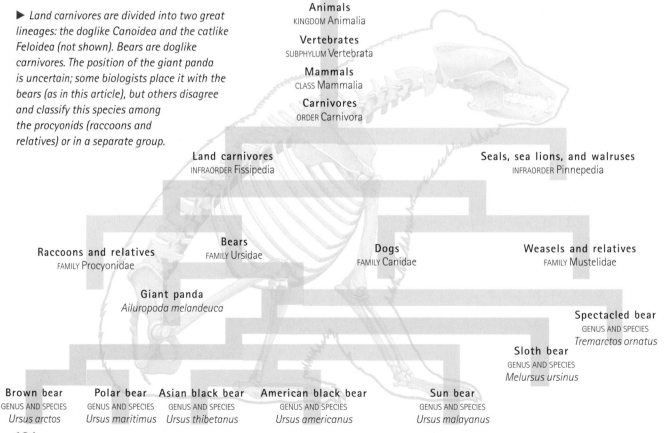

**Animals**
KINGDOM Animalia

**Vertebrates**
SUBPHYLUM Vertebrata

**Mammals**
CLASS Mammalia

**Carnivores**
ORDER Carnivora

**Land carnivores**
INFRAORDER Fissipedia

**Seals, sea lions, and walruses**
INFRAORDER Pinnepedia

**Raccoons and relatives**
FAMILY Procyonidae

**Bears**
FAMILY Ursidae

**Dogs**
FAMILY Canidae

**Weasels and relatives**
FAMILY Mustelidae

**Giant panda**
*Ailuropoda melandeuca*

**Spectacled bear**
GENUS AND SPECIES
*Tremarctos ornatus*

**Sloth bear**
GENUS AND SPECIES
*Melursus ursinus*

**Brown bear**
GENUS AND SPECIES
*Ursus arctos*

**Polar bear**
GENUS AND SPECIES
*Ursus maritimus*

**Asian black bear**
GENUS AND SPECIES
*Ursus thibetanus*

**American black bear**
GENUS AND SPECIES
*Ursus americanus*

**Sun bear**
GENUS AND SPECIES
*Ursus malayanus*

suggests, most are meat eaters and are equipped with sharp teeth and claws. A unique carnivore characteristic is that two pairs of cheek teeth, the carnassials, are shaped to cut up flesh with a scissorlike action. Carnivores include large hunters such as cats, seals, dogs, and hyenas, and smaller animals such as civets, mongooses, and weasels.

● **Bears** These are the largest carnivores, although they do not hunt as often as most other members of the order. There are eight species of bears. All have a large head with a long snout and powerful jaws. Bears have a sturdy and barrel-shaped body, and their legs are short but powerful. Bears have large, flat paws armed with long nonretractable claws. The varied diet of bears is reflected in their teeth. Their carnassials are flattened so they do not slice food but grind it up. This is useful for animals that eat a lot of plants.

● **Giant panda** The giant panda is an unusual bear (and is thought by some biologists to belong to a different group altogether). It has distinctive black and white fur, with black ears and oval spectacles around its eyes. Pandas have a unique sixth digit on their forepaws. This bony extension sticks out from the wrist. It acts like a thumb, allowing a panda to hold bamboo shoots, its main food.

● **Black bears** There are two species of black bears, the American black bear and the Asian black bear. Both are small bears that collect much of their food from trees. They rip off bark and gouge out grubs with their short claws. They also have flexible lips that help them pluck fruits. Black bears have very strong hind legs. This makes them the most adept of all bears at walking on two legs.

● **Polar bear** These are among the largest living land carnivores. They have a pale cream coat that helps them blend into icy Arctic landscapes. Their thick fur helps them

▲ *A foraging grizzly bear. Note the massive hump over the animal's shoulders, a characteristic unique to brown bears.*

stay warm, and a layer of blubber under the skin also keeps out the cold. A polar bear's outer guard hairs are hollow and translucent. These hairs trap heat from the sun and carry it down to the bear's black skin, where it is absorbed. Hairs on the paw pads help reduce the loss of precious body heat through the feet.

● **Brown bears** There are several subspecies of brown bears around the world, generally distinguished by their fur color and body size. The grizzly is the main subspecies in North America, although it is now rare outside Canada and Alaska. Its brown coat is flecked with silver hairs. Kodiak bears, the largest of all the subspecies, live along the southern coast of Alaska. Eurasian brown bears are much smaller. Several Eurasian subspecies are close to extinction, such as the mazaalai from the Gobi Desert of Central Asia.

**FEATURED SYSTEMS**

**EXTERNAL ANATOMY** Grizzly bears are large carnivores with a muscular hump behind the shoulder. They have a dense brown coat which is flecked, or grizzled, with silver and gray hairs. *See pages 106–109.*

**SKELETAL SYSTEM** The grizzly bear's skeleton is sturdy since it must support a large and very powerful body. *See pages 110–113.*

**MUSCULAR SYSTEM** A grizzly's muscles are positioned to produce immense strength rather than speed of movement. *See pages 114–115.*

**NERVOUS SYSTEM** Grizzly bears need to have a good memory so they can remember where food sources are located. They have an excellent sense of smell,

although they cannot see or hear particularly well. *See pages 116–117.*

**CIRCULATORY AND RESPIRATORY SYSTEMS** Although they are generally slow-moving, grizzlies are capable of sudden bursts of speed, with the large heart and lungs supplying oxygen to the muscles. *See pages 118–119.*

**DIGESTIVE AND EXCRETORY SYSTEMS** Being carnivores, bears have a short digestive system suited to breaking down meat. Therefore grizzlies have difficulty digesting the plant material they often eat. *See pages 120–121.*

**REPRODUCTIVE SYSTEM** Grizzlies are born after about eight months of gestation. They are blind, almost hairless, and completely helpless at birth. *See pages 122–123.*

# External anatomy

Grizzly bears are among the largest land carnivores. Everything about them is big. They have a broad, massive head and a stocky body. Male grizzlies can reach more than 7 feet (2 m) long and weigh 1,200 pounds (0.5 metric tons) or more. Females are about the same length but are generally about half the weight of the males.

### Silvertips

Grizzly bears have a thick coat of hair, which helps them keep warm in their cold habitat. The coat, or pelage, is made up of different hair types. Longer guard hairs form a shaggy protective covering. A thicker growth of fine fur grows beneath the guard hairs. The fur and the guard hairs trap a layer of air close to the skin. Since air is a poor conductor of heat, this layer prevents the bear's body heat from escaping to the surroundings. Grizzly bears are named for the color of their guard hairs. The guard hairs of other brown bear

*Adult grizzlies can be huge, reaching 9 feet (2.8 m) when standing on their back legs. Kodiak bears, a separate brown bear subspecies from coastal Alaska, are even larger.*

9 feet (2.8 m)

*The **fur** varies greatly in color from near-white through brown and black. The tips of most hairs are lighter, giving them a silver-flecked (or grizzled) appearance. The coat is long and shaggy in winter, keeping the bears warm as they hibernate. It is molted in spring to reveal a shorter summer coat.*

*The **body** is barrel-shaped and immensely powerful. Coastal brown bears tend to be larger than inland grizzlies. This is because they have regular access to rich supplies of protein in the form of fish.*

*The **tail** (not visible) is very short and serves little function.*

*The powerful and muscular **hind legs** provide a bear with surprising speed; bears can outrun humans and most other animals over short distances.*

*The **soles** are covered by tough, relatively hairless pads of wrinkled skin.*

---

**CLOSE-UP**

## Bear hair

**The long guard hairs** that form a grizzly's outer coat are tipped with silver and gray, but the shorter fur beneath is unusual for another reason. Most mammal hair has an "agouti" pattern. This is a series of light and dark rings, which together give the hair its overall color. The hairs in bear fur, however, are unusual because they have just a single color throughout. The color varies from brown and red to pale yellow. Humans are one of the few other types of mammals to have single-color hairs. Hair color is produced by proteins called melanins. The agouti pattern is produced by two different types of melanins. Eumelanins are very dark and pheomelanins are light. Agouti-type hairs contain both types of melanin, whereas bear fur contains just a single type.

The large **dorsal hump** distinguishes brown bears from other species. The hump contains muscles that add power to the forelimbs.

Grizzlies have good hearing, but the **external ears** are small and furry. This helps minimize heat loss.

The **head** is wide, containing powerful muscles that drive the jaw muscles.

◄ *A grizzly bear's external anatomy. A grizzly's mass varies greatly over the course of a year; fat is deposited throughout summer and fall but is used up as the animal hibernates.*

Bear **eyes** are small relative to the rest of the head. Their visual powers are broadly similar to those of humans. Unlike some other carnivores, bears have color vision. This helps them identify ripe fruits and nuts.

Bears have an excellent sense of smell. This helps them find buried food and detect carrion over long distances.

**CONNECTIONS**

**COMPARE** the claws of a sloth bear with those of other specialist social insect-eaters, such as a *GIANT ANTEATER*.

**COMPARE** the paws of a climbing bear, such as a black bear, with those of other expert climbers such as a *CHIMPANZEE*.

The **lips** are separate from the gums and are tremendously flexible.

At more than 4 inches (10 cm) long, the **front claws** are longer than those of any other bear. The grizzly uses them for digging out dens, scratching at bark, or slashing at prey or rival bears. Unlike black bears, grizzlies do not use their claws for climbing.

The **front paws** are vital food-gathering tools. They are used for fishing, digging up roots or small rodents, or lashing out at prey.

subspecies do not change color along their length. Many of a grizzly's guard hairs, however, are tipped with silver or gray. This has the effect of making the coat look flecked, or grizzled, with silver. Grizzlies are also called silvertips for this reason.

## Big head

In proportion to its body, a grizzly bear's head is very large when compared with that of most other animals. Unlike most other bears, grizzlies have a distinctive concave face, which curves up from their long snout into a wide forehead. Their eyes are small when compared with the wide, rounded head. They sit in the middle of the face on either side of the snout.

The bear's ears are small and heavily furred. Small ears help the animal retain its body heat. Larger ears would radiate more heat into the air. Grizzly bears' ears are often obscured by the long, shaggy coat, especially during the winter months. The animal's hair is longer at this time to help it conserve heat.

CLOSE-UP

## Grizzly feet

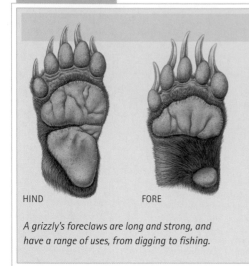

HIND     FORE

*A grizzly's foreclaws are long and strong, and have a range of uses, from digging to fishing.*

**Grizzlies' feet are equipped** with huge claws, longer than those of any other bear. The claws on the forefeet measure around 4 inches (10 cm) long, longer than those on the hind feet. The feet themselves may be up to 16 inches (41 cm) in length.

Unlike most cats, bears cannot retract their claws into a protective sheath when not in use. The claws are therefore subject to a great deal of wear and tear. An older bear with several worn or broken claws may struggle to dig up food during lean periods or to make a den for hibernation in the fall.

Although grizzlies' forefeet are very dexterous and capable of plucking fruits and leaves, the long claws make it harder for them to grip trunks and climb trees. The claws of American black bears are much shorter than those of grizzlies. These smaller bears are expert climbers that spend a lot of time resting or foraging in trees.

Like other bears, grizzlies have a long snout with a pair of large, hairless nostrils. Uniquely among carnivores, bears do not have whiskers—touch-sensitive hairs that project from the snout. They do, however, have an extremely good sense of smell. Hair does grow on the thin upper lip between the nose and mouth. A grizzly's lips are mobile and not attached to the gums. This makes them ideal for scooping up small berries or insects.

CLOSE-UP

## A large hump

**One distinguishing feature** of grizzly bears is the pronounced hump between the shoulders. This is a huge mass of muscles, which helps make the bear's forelimbs enormously strong. The strong limbs are used to club prey or rival bears, to dig out a den, and to dig up roots and other buried foods.

*Silhouettes of a grizzly bear (left) and an American black bear (right).*

### ▼ PAWS OF SMALLER BEARS

*Paw shape and structure give some clues about the lifestyle and feeding habits of some of the smaller species of bears.*

### Sloth bear

*Sloth bears feed extensively on termites. Their front claws are long and the forelimbs powerful to help them rip into the insects' nests. Sloth bears also have protrusible lips, and their front incisor teeth are missing. Thus the lips can form a tube through which the termites can be sucked.*

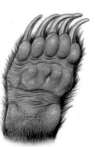

FORE     HIND

### Sun bear

*Sun bears eat a range of foods, such as small mammals, the growing tips of palm trees, and termites. The claws help the bears climb. They often clamber up trees in search of bees' nests, which they break into with their front claws to get at the honey inside.*

FORE     HIND

### Asian black bear

*Black bears eat a lot of plant material, especially in the fall when berries and nuts are available. They use their claws to overturn logs in search of tasty grubs. Fish, small mammals, and the young of larger animals are also eaten by black bears. Black bears spend much of their time in the trees.*

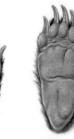

FORE     HIND

### American black bear
*Black bears have a good sense of smell, which helps them find birds' nests and carrion, but it is less important than in other bears, since much of their food is plant material. Their muzzle is relatively short for a bear.*

### Brown bear
*Brown bears have a very good sense of smell and a longer muzzle than a black bear. They eat a wide range of foods and will feed on carrion when they can find it. Smell helps them find hidden foods such as buried roots and tubers.*

### Polar bear
*Polar bears have a long muzzle. This provides for an extremely sensitive sense of smell, essential in a barren habitat where food is always scarce. A polar bear can smell a carcass from as far as 20 miles (32 km) away.*

### A strong body

Although grizzlies can stand on their hind legs, they are generally quadrapedal (they usually move on four legs). The legs are short but very thick, ending with wide, paddlelike paws. Unlike most other bears, grizzly paws have little hair on the soles. Grizzly bears have a distinctive hump between their shoulders, where the huge sets of muscles that power the forelegs and neck are anchored. However, the dorsal hump is not the tallest point on the bear's body. The lumbar region of the spine, just in front of the pelvis, curves up to form the tallest point along the back.

Unlike most other carnivores, bears have only a short tail. The tail appears to be vestigial, a structure left over from a long-tailed bear ancestor that no longer has a function. The lack of a tail is unusual for an animal that often climbs trees, as do most bears apart from grizzles; in climbing, a long tail might help the animal with balance.

**▲ MUZZLE SHAPE**
*The size and shape of a bear's muzzle relate to its feeding habits, habitat, and lifestyle.*

## From small beginnings

**The first bears appeared** around 20 million years ago. The earliest known specimen, the dawn bear *Ursavus*, dates from around this time. Unlike modern bears, the dawn bear had a long bushy tail and a small, agile body similar to that of a raccoon. Modern bears separated into three main groups around 10 million to 12 million years ago. One group is represented today by the giant panda; another, the running or tremarctine bears, by the spectacled bear from South America. The third and largest group, the ursines, includes grizzlies and all other living bears.

Grizzlies and polar bears are the largest modern land carnivores, but they would be dwarfed by an ancient tremarctine called *Arctodus*, the giant short-faced bear. This massive beast lived in North and South America until as recently as 12,000 years ago. It weighed more than 1,800 pounds (820 kg) and could reach 11 feet (3,4 m) tall on its hind legs. Running bears like *Arctodus* had longer legs than grizzlies; they could chase down quick prey including bison, horses, and camels.

*The giant short-faced bear was a powerful pursuit predator. Note how long its legs were compared with those of a grizzly bear.*

# Skeletal system

**CONNECTIONS**

**COMPARE** the plantigrade stance of a bear with the digitigrade stance of other carnivores, such as a *WOLF*.

**COMPARE** the grinding carnassial teeth of a brown bear, which is largely omnivorous, with the shearing carnassials of a carnivore that eats mostly meat, such as a *LION* or *PUMA*.

Grizzly bears have the same basic skeleton as other types of carnivores, but one that is adapted for supporting their huge, powerful body. Other carnivores have a lighter skeleton built for speed at the expense of strength.

## Short and sturdy

While faster-running and more agile types of carnivores have long legs with thin bones, grizzlies and other bears have relatively short legs for their overall body size. The bones inside the legs are able to support the great weight of a grizzly's body because they are extremely thick. Large bears, such as grizzlies and polar bears, are much heavier than other large terrestrial carnivores. For example, tigers, the largest of the cats, may grow to the same length as a grizzly—or occasionally even longer—but they weigh only about half as much. Bears' bones, therefore, have to be much thicker to support the extra weight.

Bears' limbs are also straighter than those of most carnivores. Animals that need to run fast or make long leaps to catch prey tend to have limbs that are held in a bent position at the knee and elbow. This allows the legs to act like springs. The joints are flexed as the animal lands after a bound. They then spring back, releasing energy that is used to propel the animal into the next bound. A bear's legs are not kept bent in this way, since they would collapse under its weight. One effect is that, although capable of bursts of speed, modern bears are not efficient runners and soon tire. As a result, bears tend to rely on ambush when hunting larger mammals.

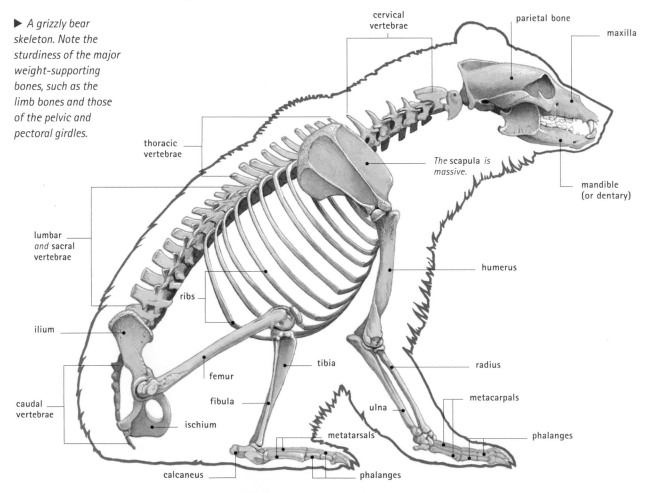

▶ *A grizzly bear skeleton. Note the sturdiness of the major weight-supporting bones, such as the limb bones and those of the pelvic and pectoral girdles.*

cervical vertebrae

parietal bone

maxilla

thoracic vertebrae

The scapula is massive.

mandible (or dentary)

lumbar *and* sacral vertebrae

humerus

ribs

ilium

caudal vertebrae

tibia

radius

femur

fibula

metacarpals

ulna

ischium

metatarsals

phalanges

calcaneus

phalanges

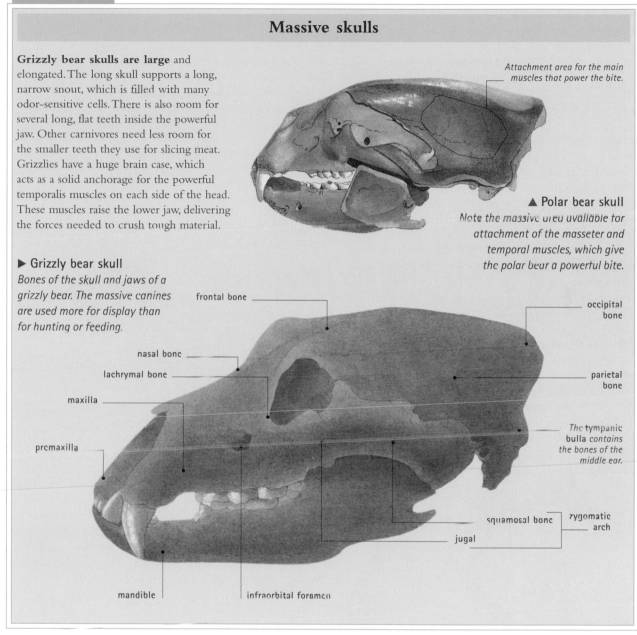

# Massive skulls

**Grizzly bear skulls are large** and elongated. The long skull supports a long, narrow snout, which is filled with many odor-sensitive cells. There is also room for several long, flat teeth inside the powerful jaw. Other carnivores need less room for the smaller teeth they use for slicing meat. Grizzlies have a huge brain case, which acts as a solid anchorage for the powerful temporalis muscles on each side of the head. These muscles raise the lower jaw, delivering the forces needed to crush tough material.

Attachment area for the main muscles that power the bite.

▲ **Polar bear skull**
Note the massive area available for attachment of the masseter and temporal muscles, which give the polar bear a powerful bite.

▶ **Grizzly bear skull**
Bones of the skull and jaws of a grizzly bear. The massive canines are used more for display than for hunting or feeding.

frontal bone

occipital bone

nasal bone

lachrymal bone

parietal bone

maxilla

The tympanic bulla contains the bones of the middle ear.

premaxilla

squamosal bone

zygomatic arch

jugal

mandible

infraorbital foramen

## A small collar

Like other carnivores, grizzly bears have a short, very slender collarbone, or clavicle. This bone connects the scapulae (shoulder blades) to the sternum (breastbone). The clavicle is joined to these bones by long, flexible ligaments. In other mammals, including humans, the clavicles are much longer and more robust. They also have more sturdy connections with the other bones. In humans and other primates, for example, the clavicles are used to keep the scapulae in a fixed position, and they also provide an anchorage for the muscles that are used to swing the arms out to the sides. Bears and other carnivores do not need to move their forelimbs in this way. In fact, movements out to the sides would weaken their limbs and prevent them from running quickly without injuring themselves. Since the clavicle is not needed to give any structural or muscular support, it has been reduced to just a sliver of bone with little real function at all.

Most carnivores are digitigrade—they walk on their toes. Bears are different. Bears are flat-footed. When they walk, the whole length of each foot—from heel to toe—touches the ground. This arrangement is called a plantigrade stance. This is an adaptation that helps support the great weight of the animal.

Bears share with other carnivores an unusual bone in their feet. Most mammals have several bones in the wrist or ankle, but in carnivores three of these are fused, forming the scapholunate bone. It was once thought that this bone was used for running and acted as a shock absorber. It seems more likely that the bone serves as a firm anchorage for the muscles that bend the paw at the wrist, helping the animal climb or grapple with prey.

## Grizzly teeth

Grizzlies have 42 teeth. They grow a full set by the time they are about two and a half years old. Like most other types of mammals, grizzly bears have four types of teeth: incisors, canines, premolars, and molars. An adult grizzly bear has 12 incisors at the front of the jaw: 6 in the

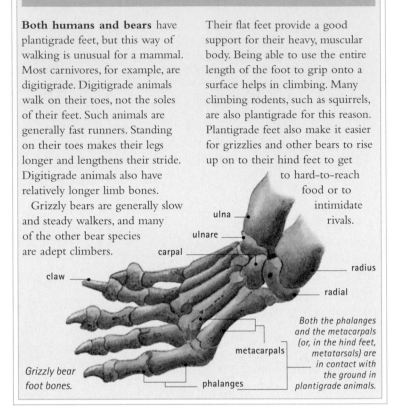

COMPARATIVE ANATOMY

### Flat feet

**Both humans and bears** have plantigrade feet, but this way of walking is unusual for a mammal. Most carnivores, for example, are digitigrade. Digitigrade animals walk on their toes, not the soles of their feet. Such animals are generally fast runners. Standing on their toes makes their legs longer and lengthens their stride. Digitigrade animals also have relatively longer limb bones.

Grizzly bears are generally slow and steady walkers, and many of the other bear species are adept climbers.

Their flat feet provide a good support for their heavy, muscular body. Being able to use the entire length of the foot to grip onto a surface helps in climbing. Many climbing rodents, such as squirrels, are also plantigrade for this reason. Plantigrade feet also make it easier for grizzlies and other bears to rise up on to their hind feet to get to hard-to-reach food or to intimidate rivals.

ulna

ulnare

carpal

claw

radius

radial

*Both the phalanges and the metacarpals (or, in the hind feet, metatarsals) are in contact with the ground in plantigrade animals.*

metacarpals

*Grizzly bear foot bones.*

phalanges

*The pectoral girdle is very sturdy.*

Polar bear

*The hind limb bones are thick to support the animal's weight. Sustained pursuit of prey is not possible; these bears are ambush predators.*

*The forelimb bones are massive.*

*Polar and other bears use the paws to kill prey, rather than the teeth as in other carnivores.*

*The pectoral girdle is smaller, since it bears relatively less muscle.*

*The forelimb bones are slender.*

Spectacled bear

Hind limb bones *are slender and relatively longer than those of the polar bear. This is an adaptation for running. The spectacled bear's ancestors were pursuit predators that chased down their prey.*

upper jaw, and 6 in the lower. They are small but sharp and are used as slicing teeth. Behind the incisors, there are four canines, one on each side of the mouth in both the upper and the lower jaw. Canines are long, pointed fangs. Most carnivores use their canines to bite prey and to rip away chunks of flesh. Although grizzlies do use them occasionally to kill prey, their canines are unsuitably large for their

◀ THE LAST OF THE RUNNING BEARS
*The spectacled bear is a running, or tremarctine, bear. In this illustration, a spectacled bear skeleton has been scaled up to the size of a polar bear. Polar bears belong to the other bear group, the ursines. Although spectacled bears feed mainly on plant material, their skeletons show that their ancestors were more active predators. There were many other tremarctines in the past, some of which pursued and killed large mammal prey.*

## Wolverines

**A wolverine** looks as if it might be related to bears or dogs, but it is in fact a type of mustelid—a relative of the weasels, otters, and skunks. However, it shares many anatomical features with bears.

A grizzly bear is much bigger than a wolverine, being about 10 times as heavy and twice as long. However, both animals have a thick, sturdy skeleton with short muscular legs. The legs end in wide, plantigrade paws. This configuration makes both animals good diggers. A wolverine's wide paws are especially useful in the winter, when deep snow makes moving around hard for larger animals, including grizzlies. A wolverine's feet act like snowshoes, preventing the animal from sinking into the snow. What wolverines lack in size, they make up for in aggression. During the winter, these creatures are remarkably fierce. Wolverines have been known to drive adult grizzlies from their prey.

Another reason why wolverines are often mistaken for dogs or small bears is their robust head and large snout. Wolverines also share with bears an acute sense of smell and extremely powerful jaws. They use their jaws to gnaw meat that has frozen solid or to drag carcasses over long distances.

▶ **SKULL**
**Sloth bear**
*The skull viewed from below with the lower jaw removed, showing the bones of the palate and base of the skull. Note the sloth bear's unique dental adaptations. Several foramina are shown. The word* foramen *means "window." A* foramen *is a hole in bone through which blood vessels or nerves pass.*

▼ **LOWER JAW**
**Grizzly bear**
*Bones and teeth of the lower jaw. Processes and condyles are extensions of bones.*

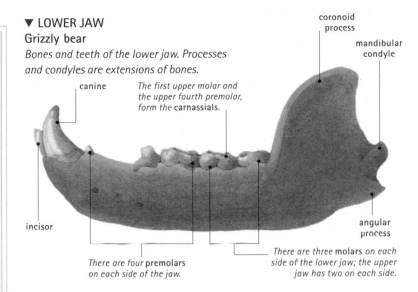

canine

*The first upper molar and the upper fourth premolar, form the* carnassials.

coronoid process

mandibular condyle

incisor

angular process

*There are four* premolars *on each side of the jaw.*

*There are three* molars *on each side of the lower jaw; the upper jaw has two on each side.*

*The inner pair of* upper incisors *are absent. This allows termites to be sucked into the mouth.*

premaxilla

palatine fissure

maxilla

palatine foramen

palatine

*The* jugal bone. *This forms part of the zygomatic arch.*

vomer

presphenoid

alisphenoid

basisphenoid

squamosal

carotid foramen

tympanic bulla

basioccipital

paroccipital process

occipital condyle

mastoid process

hypoglossal foramen

general diet. However, bears display their large canines as a warning of their fighting skills when threatened by a rival.

Grizzlies have two types of cheek teeth. They have eight premolars in each jaw, and four molars in the upper jaw and six in the lower one. The lower first molars and the upper fourth premolars are sometimes called carnassials. Originally adapted for shearing through flesh and hide, they are found only in members of the Carnivora; even the giant panda, which feeds almost exclusively on bamboo leaves and shoots, has two pairs of carnassial teeth. Unlike in most other carnivores, the cheek teeth of bears, including the carnassials, are flat, like millstones, making them suitable for grinding up fibrous plant material. These grinding teeth are bunodont; that is, they have four low cusps, giving them a rough surface that is ideal for crushing up food. A cusp is a point on the surface of a tooth. By comparison, dogs have just a single cusp on their molars.

# Muscular system

**COMPARE** the forelimb muscles of a grizzly bear with those of other carnivores. A *WEASEL*'s forelimb muscles are relatively much smaller than a bear's, since weasels use their teeth to kill prey. A *LION*'s are larger than a weasel's; a lion may use its forelimbs to hold or trip fleeing prey, but again uses its jaws to make the kill.

The phrase "as strong as a bear" is an apt one. No other animal of its size has strength comparable to that of a grizzly bear. The animal's strength comes in part from the rigid anchorage that the thick skeleton provides, and the position and size of powerful blocks of muscles.

## Muscle systems

The muscles are attached by tendons to processes, or outgrowths, on the bones. Tendons are inelastic cords. When a muscle contracts, it shortens in length and pulls back on the tendon. The tendon transmits the force to the bone, causing it to move.

Muscles are generally arranged in pairs, one pulling in the opposite direction from the other. Muscle fibers are made of two types of proteins, which lie side by side in long

### Super strength

**Bears use their tremendous strength** in a number of ways. For example, they use their powerful forelegs to locate and catch prey. The forepaws are used to dig out burrowing mammals, to roll away rocks or logs to expose insects, and to club larger prey. Over short distances, grizzlies can outrun galloping horses, running at up to 30 miles per hour (48 km/h); they are also strong swimmers.

filaments. When the muscle receives a signal from the central nervous system, the two filaments slide past each other, making the fiber

▶ *Important features of a grizzly bear's musculature. Bears are among the strongest and most powerful of all animals.*

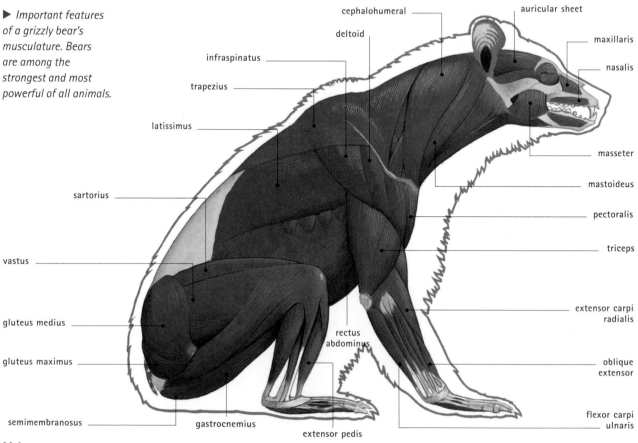

cephalohumeral

auricular sheet

deltoid

maxillaris

infraspinatus

nasalis

trapezius

latissimus

masseter

sartorius

mastoideus

pectoralis

triceps

vastus

extensor carpi radialis

gluteus medius

oblique extensor

gluteus maximus

rectus abdominus

flexor carpi ulnaris

semimembranosus

gastrocnemius

extensor pedis

shorten. A large muscle may contain hundreds of millions of individual filaments. Together, the filaments can create a considerable force.

## Muscle positions

The bones in a limb are connected at joints. Muscles attached at each joint move the bones back and forth like a lever. The positions of the muscles affect the angle through which the bone can move, the speed at which it moves, and the power of the movement. Muscles that attach to bones very close to the joints produce a large range of movement and can make the bone move quickly. However the bone and the limb around it will not move with any great power. Therefore, the limb cannot exert a large force on another object. Fast-running animals, such as gazelles and deer, have muscle systems arranged in this fashion. The muscles of these animals deliver speed but not strength.

Muscles that attach farther away from the pivoting joint produce slower but more powerful movements. Bears' muscles are arranged this way. The processes to which they attach are also longer than in weaker but faster-moving animals. These longer bone processes increase the leverage of the muscles

as they contract. Since their muscles do not attach close to joints, bears have a more limited range of movements. This inflexibility is also a result of bears being so muscle-bound.

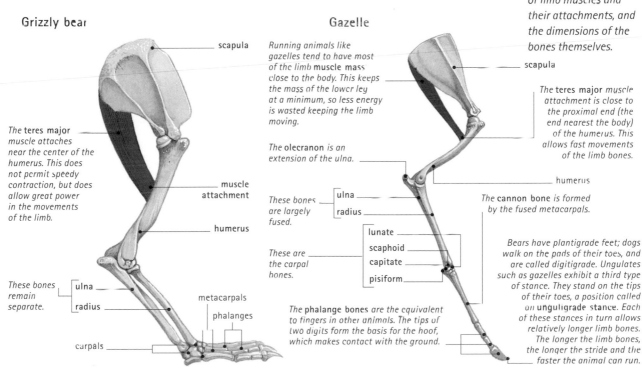

**▼ FORELIMB ATTACHMENTS**
*How adaptations for strength and speed are reflected in the location of limb muscles and their attachments, and the dimensions of the bones themselves.*

**Grizzly bear**

scapula

The **teres major** muscle attaches near the center of the humerus. This does not permit speedy contraction, but does allow great power in the movements of the limb.

muscle attachment

humerus

These bones remain separate.
- ulna
- radius

metacarpals

phalanges

carpals

**Gazelle**

*Running animals like gazelles tend to have most of the limb muscle mass close to the body. This keeps the mass of the lower leg at a minimum, so less energy is wasted keeping the limb moving.*

The **olecranon** is an extension of the ulna.

These bones are largely fused.
- ulna
- radius

These are the carpal bones.
- lunate
- scaphoid
- capitate
- pisiform

The **phalange** bones are the equivalent to fingers in other animals. The tips of two digits form the basis for the hoof, which makes contact with the ground.

scapula

The **teres major** muscle attachment is close to the proximal end (the end nearest the body) of the humerus. This allows fast movements of the limb bones.

humerus

The **cannon bone** is formed by the fused metacarpals.

Bears have plantigrade feet; dogs walk on the pads of their toes, and are called digitigrade. Ungulates such as gazelles exhibit a third type of stance. They stand on the tips of their toes, a position called an **unguligrade stance**. Each of these stances in turn allows relatively longer limb bones. The longer the limb bones, the longer the stride and the faster the animal can run.

# Nervous system

**CONNECTIONS**

**COMPARE** the memory of a bear with that of an *ELEPHANT* or *CHIMPANZEE*. All animals need to remember where they can find food through the year.

**COMPARE** how a grizzly bear smells its surroundings with the methods used by a *LOBSTER*. Both animals have an excellent sense of smell, but they achieve this in different ways.

The nervous system is a grizzly bear's link with the outside world. Information about the environment is collected by the animal's sense organs. The nervous system carries information from one part of the body to another in the form of electrical impulses. The central nervous system (CNS) is made up of the brain and the spinal cord. The spinal cord is a dense mass of nerve tissue that is protected by the vertebrae. Sensory inform-ation is carried to the CNS by a network of sensory neurons (nerve cells). The information is processed and signals are sent to the muscles in response. These signals travel along a separate set of nerve cells called motor neurons.

## Bear senses

There are five main senses—vision, hearing, smell, taste, and touch. However, bears must also be sensitive to other environmental factors, such as temperature, light levels, and day length. A grizzly bear has an extremely acute sense of smell. The bear's long snout is lined with millions of odor-sensitive cells that can detect chemicals in the air. They form a layer called the nasal epithelia. The inner surfaces of the nose are kept moist. Chemicals dissolve into the fluid, allowing their detection. The surfaces are separated from the outside by a thick, moist pad around the nostrils. A grizzly bear relies on its·nose to find food, avoid rival bears, locate mates, and identify its cubs. Male bears advertise their presence to rivals and potential mates by wiping their saliva on rocks and tree trunks.

Grizzlies can smell food, such as a rotting carcass, from several miles away. Their sense of smell is as good as that of any other mammal. Bears rely on smell more than their other senses. Like dogs, another group of carnivores

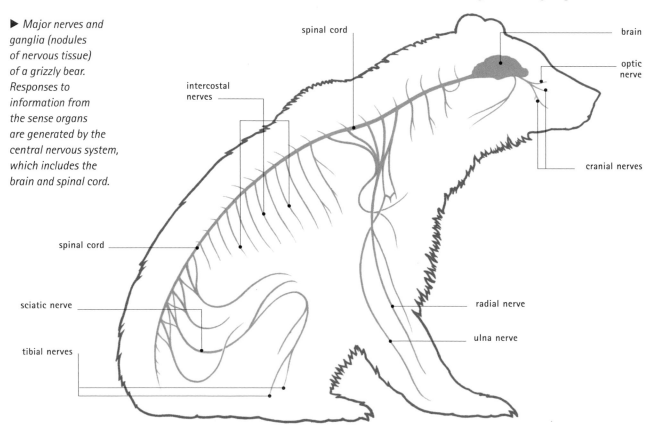

▶ *Major nerves and ganglia (nodules of nervous tissue) of a grizzly bear. Responses to information from the sense organs are generated by the central nervous system, which includes the brain and spinal cord.*

spinal cord

brain

intercostal nerves

optic nerve

spinal cord

cranial nerves

sciatic nerve

radial nerve

ulna nerve

tibial nerves

with an acute sense of smell, bears have a large olfactory lobe at the front of their brain. The olfactory lobe processes information on chemicals in the air sent by the nasal epithelial cells.

### Eyes and ears

Grizzly bears have smaller eyes than humans do. They can see in color, using three types of color-detecting cone cells in the retina, which is the light-sensitive surface at the back of the eyeball. Although they do not have exceptional vision, they are able to see well in dim light, and so they can forage at dawn and dusk. They do this using a different set of

retinal cells called rods. Rods are not sensitive to color, but are much more sensitive to light than cones are. The idea that bears have poor eyesight may come from the fact that they often get very close to an object before they react to it. This may not necessarily be because they cannot see the object. Rather, it may be because they prefer to smell things before acting.

A grizzly's hearing is about as acute as a human's, although grizzlies can probably hear slightly higher frequencies than most people. Hearing is especially useful for tracking small prey animals in dense forest undergrowth and for locating the position of burrows and tunnels where prey may be living.

**▼ BRAIN AND NOSTRIL**
*A powerful sense of smell is essential for a grizzly bear. Millions of sensory cells line the inner walls of the nostrils.*

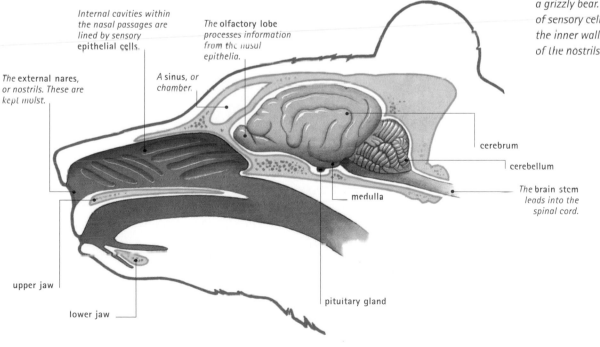

Internal cavities within the nasal passages are lined by sensory epithelial cells.

The olfactory lobe processes information from the nasal epithelia.

The external nares, or nostrils. These are kept moist.

A sinus, or chamber.

cerebrum

cerebellum

The brain stem leads into the spinal cord.

medulla

upper jaw

lower jaw

pituitary gland

117

# Circulatory and respiratory systems

Animals need to take in oxygen to survive. The gas is absorbed into the body from the air through baglike organs called lungs. Once inside the body, the oxygen is carried around the body by the circulatory system to places where it is necessary. The circulatory system consists of tubes that carry blood—a mixture of cells and liquid. Oxygen is carried by red blood cells, which give blood its characteristic color. Oxygen is used by body cells to obtain energy from food. A by-product of this process is carbon dioxide. This waste gas is also carried by the blood until it can be removed at the lungs.

## Breathing

A grizzly has large lungs, enabling it to take in the large quantities of oxygen necessary to power its big, muscular body. Air is inhaled through the nose or mouth and travels into the lungs through the windpipe, or trachea. A grizzly bear takes between 6 and 10 breaths every minute, but this may rise to 45 breaths per minute when the bear is running.

The trachea connects to a branching network of pipes that fills both lungs. The air travels into this network and fills tiny sacs called alveoli. They lie at the tips of the smallest tubes. There, the oxygen dissolves into the moisture that lines the lungs.

The alveoli are surrounded by tiny blood vessels called capillaries. The dissolved oxygen travels across the capillary walls and into the blood. There, it combines with a chemical in the red blood cells called hemoglobin. Hemoglobin also carries away some of the

**CONNECTIONS**

**COMPARE** the grizzly bear's heart and breathing rates with those of a *HUMAN.*

**COMPARE** the ways that a bear regulates its temperature with those used by a *GRAY WHALE* and a *WOLF.*

▶ CIRCULATORY SYSTEM

*Note the very large heart, which is able to pump blood around the body quickly—and so allow lots of oxygen to be passed swiftly to the tissues of the grizzly bear.*

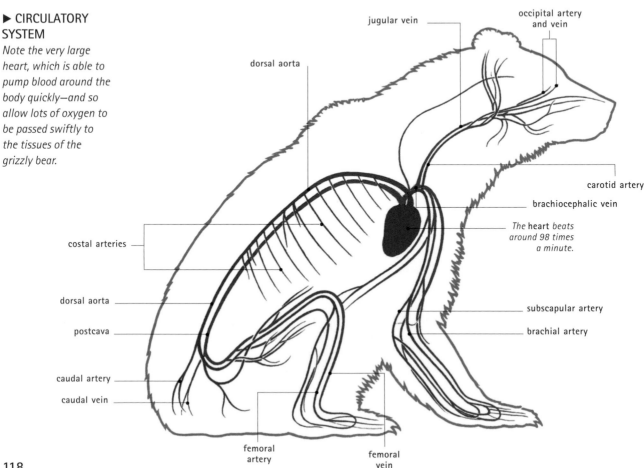

jugular vein

occipital artery and vein

dorsal aorta

carotid artery

brachiocephalic vein

*The* heart *beats around 98 times a minute.*

costal arteries

dorsal aorta

postcava

subscapular artery

brachial artery

caudal artery

caudal vein

femoral artery

femoral vein

## Hibernation

**Grizzly bears rely** on a lot of fruits and other plant foods to survive. However, in winter there is very little of this food around, and the bears are forced to become dormant, or hibernate. By the fall, a grizzly bear has put on a lot of fat, enabling the animal to survive through the winter. This need to store fat is one reason why grizzlies and some other bears are so large. In some places, grizzlies hibernate for six months of the year. The bears use their powerful forepaws to dig dens in which to

hibernate. During hibernation, the bears enter a sleeplike state. Their heart rate drops to about 10 beats a minute, and they breathe only 3 or 4 times a minute.

Unlike other hibernating animals, which may experience a hibernating temperature close to 35°F (2°C), the bear's body temperature falls only to around 93°F (34°C). For this reason, some zoologists do not consider this to be true hibernation of the type practiced by animals such as marmots, bats, and dormice.

carbon dioxide that is released at the lungs. The carbon dioxide passes in the opposite direction from the oxygen, and is breathed out.

### The blood system

As well as oxygen, blood carries everything else that the body needs, such as food, messenger chemicals called hormones, and white blood cells to fight invading organisms.

## Regulating temperature

**Bears control their body temperature**, or thermoregulate, in a number of ways. Normally a bear's body temperature is about 100°F (38°C). Fur and a fat layer keep these animals warm in cold periods, but grizzlies may become too hot during warmer weather or after periods of exertion. Bears do not sweat, but they are able to pant like dogs to lose heat. Panting helps water evaporate from the mouth, taking heat with it.

Grizzlies may also bathe in water or snow to keep cool. They often dig shallow pits in which to rest during the hottest part of the day. Their characteristic dorsal hump also comes in useful as a radiator. The muscles in the hump are full of blood vessels. Heat from the blood is radiated into the air around the hump, keeping the bear cool.

Blood is pumped by the heart. Like all mammals, grizzly bears have a single heart close to the center of the chest. The heart is a muscular pump. With each contraction, the heart forces blood along. A grizzly's heart beats around 98 times a minute when it is awake. This rate halves when the animal is asleep.

Oxygen-depleted blood from the body arrives at the right side of the heart. One of the heart chambers, the right ventricle, pumps this blood to the lungs. There it becomes enriched with oxygen before returning to the left side. This contains a more muscular pump, the left ventricle, which forces the oxygen-rich blood around the body.

▼ This female polar bear has recently left her den in the snow. Her cubs were born as she hibernated. Male and non-nursing polar bears do not hibernate.

# Digestive and excretory systems

Grizzly bears eat a wide range of foods, often feeding on different food types at different times of the year. In spring, for example, bears eat grasses, roots, and mosses, but as the year progresses they eat more fungi, bulbs, and tubers. Whenever possible, grizzly bears catch and eat animals, anything from ants to moose. They also feed on carrion. Grizzlies often use their strong paws to dig out marmots and other burrowing rodents, and to catch salmon that are migrating up rivers from the ocean. Grizzlies are more carnivorous than other types of brown bears, although they still eat more plant material than meat.

## Short guts

Even though grizzly bears eat a lot of plant food, their digestive system is more suited to dealing with meat. Just like their carnivore relatives that eat flesh exclusively, bears have a short digestive tract. Consequently, their food passes through the body quickly. This is not a problem when bears are digesting meals containing meat and other proteins that can be broken down easily by enzymes. Plant material, however, is much harder to digest and needs to be processed for far longer than meat. Plant-eating

animals such as cattle have very long, large guts. Food may take days to digest inside these types of animals. The most easily digested plant foods are ripe fruits; grizzlies target these above all other foodstuffs.

---

**CLOSE-UP**

### Scats

**Bear feces are called scats.** Biologists who study feces are called scatologists. Scatologists can tell a lot about how a bear lives from its scats. Since much of the food is only partially digested, they can tell what the bear has been eating. This lets them know where the bear was feeding and when it might have passed a particular location.

To disperse their seeds, many plants rely on bears and other animals to eat their fruits, such as berries. Since grizzlies can only partially digest much of their food, the seeds pass safely through the gut. They then emerge along with the scats. A fresh scat provides the germinating seeds with fertilizer, giving the seedlings a good start in life.

---

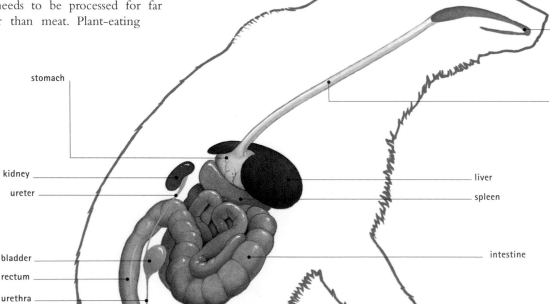

▼ *The digestive system of a grizzly bear. Note how short the gut is compared with that of a ruminant such as a giraffe.*

mouth

esophagus

stomach

kidney

ureter

liver

spleen

bladder

rectum

urethra

intestine

anus

▲ The gap between the large canines and the premolars is called a diastema. Bears pull plant stems through the diastema, ripping away leaves and buds.

COMPARE the grizzly bear's digestive system with that of a ruminant such as a GIRAFFE. A giraffe's digestive system is much more efficient for drawing nutrients from plant leaves.

that live in their gut to produce enzymes that attack cellulose. The gut microorganisms ferment the plant material, breaking it into sugars that can be used both by themselves and by the animal they live in. Grizzly bears do not do this on the scale of animals that eat only plant material. However, bears do have an extended colon, part of the large intestine, where some fermentation takes place. The large colon gives the bear its barrel-shaped body.

## Excretion

Excretion is the removal of waste materials from inside the body. Most waste leaves a grizzly's body in urine. This is a liquid that contains mainly urea. Urea is a nitrogen-containing compound produced by the breakdown of proteins. It is toxic in large quantities, so it must be removed. This task is done by the kidneys.

Like all mammals, grizzly bears have two kidneys. The kidneys filter the blood to remove urea and any excess water, salts, or sugars the blood might contain. The liquid portion of the blood passes through seivelike structures around the outside of the kidney and into fine tubes. The kidney then reabsorbs things the body needs from the filtered liquid. They pass back into the blood. The remaining liquid dribbles into the bladder and is passed from the body as urine.

## Wasting food

Since bears have a meat-eater's short digestive system but a mixed diet, they have difficulty extracting all the nutrients they need from their food. Fruits and other plant materials will sometimes pass right through the bear and remain almost completely intact.

Most digested food is absorbed into the blood through the walls of part of the small intestine, the ileum. Grizzlies and other bears have a longer ileum than other carnivores, so they can absorb more of the digested materials that pass through.

## Fermentation

Tough plant fibers are made of cellulose, a carbohydrate composed of chains of sugar molecules linked together. This composition makes cellulose extremely tough to break down. Many animals rely on microorganisms

IN FOCUS

### Recycling materials

**Grizzly bears may hibernate** for a period of up to six months, and while doing so they do not eat, drink, urinate, or defecate. In place of food, the bears get energy from their stores of fat. If they have laid down enough fat before winter begins, they will not lose much muscle during hibernation. Instead, the proteins the bears need to maintain their body functions are made by recycling the waste urea, which is usually excreted in urine. Fluids are also recycled from the bladder. This system keeps the bear's bones and muscles healthy through many months of inactivity each year.

CONNECTIONS

# Reproductive system

Like most carnivores, male grizzly bears have a baculum, or penis bone. The function of this bone is not fully understood. It may be that the bone hooks onto the female during mating. This prevents the female from breaking away from the male easily and makes copulation last longer. Longer copulation not only makes it easier for the male to deposit plenty of sperm inside the female but may also have the effect of causing her to produce eggs, or to ovulate. A short copulation might not be enough to ensure that this happens.

### The mating season

Mating takes place in summer. Male and female grizzly bears seek each other out, principally by scent. A male guards his mate aggressively for around three weeks after copulation. This prevents other males from attempting to mate with her. After this time, the female bear is sure to have ovulated, so it will be the guarding male's sperm that has fertilized her eggs, not that of a rival. In many placental mammals, the fertilized eggs, or blastocysts, implant into the wall of the uterus within a few weeks. However, grizzly bear eggs are not implanted until the fall. This delayed implantation is necessary to prevent the cubs from being born too early.

### Sleeping mothers

Grizzly bears give birth between January and March, producing up to four cubs. During this period, adult grizzly bears are hibernating in underground dens. Females give birth to their cubs while in this state of dozy dormancy. Grizzly bear cubs are born undeveloped and helpless. Their eyes are closed, and they have only a fine covering of fur. They generally weigh between 12 and 24 ounces

▶ Females delay implantation of fertilized eggs into the wall of the uterus from spring, when they mate, to fall. This ensures that cubs are born at just the right time, during the winter.

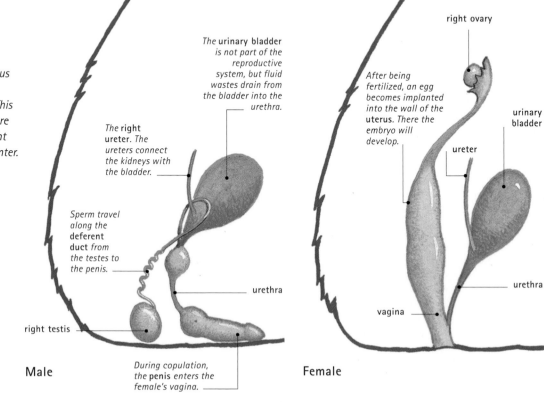

The **urinary bladder** is not part of the reproductive system, but fluid wastes drain from the bladder into the urethra.

The **right ureter**. The ureters connect the kidneys with the bladder.

Sperm travel along the **deferent duct** from the testes to the penis.

urethra

right testis

During copulation, the **penis** enters the female's vagina.

Male

right ovary

After being fertilized, an egg becomes implanted into the wall of the uterus. There the embryo will develop.

urinary bladder

ureter

urethra

vagina

Female

▶ *Having spent the first three months of their lives in their mother's den, bear cubs are playful and inquisitive. The cubs grow rapidly during their first year. This is due to the rich nature of bear milk, which contains more than 20 percent fat.*

(340–860 g), less than 1 percent of their mother's weight. When compared with the size they will become as adults, newborn grizzly bear cubs are smaller than the young of any other placental mammal.

### A fat supply

Why are the cubs born so helpless in the middle of winter, when their mother is fast asleep? The answer lies in their need to put on as much weight as possible so they, too, can hibernate when the next winter comes. Mammal fetuses cannot receive much fat through the placenta. Only when they have been born do the bear cubs get the fats they need from their mother's milk. The female grizzly produces the milk from her store of fat. A nursing mother generally uses up to twice as much of her fat reserves during winter than a male or non-nursing mother. She will typically lose up to 40 percent of her body weight by the time spring arrives.

Unlike most hibernating mammals, grizzly bears do not lower their body temperature much while they are dormant. This may be because they need to be ready to defend themselves if attacked by wolves or another bear and cannot wait to warm up first. However, the main reason is probably to provide a heat source for newborn cubs.

Grizzly cubs begin to eat solid food at the age of 5 months, but they will stay with their mother for between 18 months and 3 years. They become sexually mature between the ages of 4 and 6, but may continue to grow until they are 11 years old. Adult males will mate with several females each year if possible. Females, on the other hand, produce litters only once every two years.

TOM JACKSON

**FURTHER READING AND RESEARCH**
Russell, C., and M. Enns. 2003. *Grizzly Seasons: Life with the Brown Bears of Kamchatka.* Firefly Books: Richmond Hill, Ontario, Canada.
Schneider, B. 2003. *Where the Grizzly Walks: The Future of the Great Bear.* Falcon: Guilford, CT.

## GENETICS

### Breeding problems

**In some parts of their range**, grizzly bears are now very rare. This is because much of their habitat has been destroyed by loggers or developers. Many are shot on sight by people who think they are dangerous or a threat to livestock—although the dangers posed by grizzlies are vastly exaggerated. The population of grizzlies in the lower 48 states of the United States was estimated at around 100,000 in the early 20th century. Just 100 years later it was closer to 1,000.

This reduction in numbers causes a problem called inbreeding depression. If a bear is lucky enough to find a mate, there is a high chance that its mate will be a close relative. Breeding with close relatives is called inbreeding. Close relatives share many genes, and inbred offspring are less able to survive than those produced by more distantly related parents. A breeding program might help increase genetic diversity, but achieving this with wild grizzly bears is an almost impossible task.

# Human

ORDER: **Primates** SUBORDER: **Catarrhini** FAMILY: **Hominidae**
GENUS: *Homo*

The modern human, *Homo sapiens*, is the only surviving member of the genus *Homo*. There have been several other species in the genus *Homo*; they walked upright and had a relatively large brain. The earliest member of the genus, *Homo habilis*, evolved from another hominid (humanlike ancestor), *Australopithecus*, around 2.4 million years ago. Modern humans did not appear until around 100,000 years ago. They shared the world with one or more other types of humans, including the Neanderthal people of Europe and western Asia.

## Anatomy and taxonomy

Human classification is riddled with controversy. Anatomical studies have been relatively ineffective for determining human relationships with other hominids, but genetic research has proved a valuable tool.

● **Animals** All animals are multicellular. They get the energy and materials they need to survive by consuming other organisms. Unlike other multicellular organisms such as plants and fungi, animals are able to move around for at least one phase of their lives.

● **Chordates** At some time in their life cycle, all chordates have a stiff supporting rod called a notochord running along the back of their body.

● **Vertebrates** In vertebrates the notochord changes into a backbone made up of units called vertebrae. The spinal cord runs through the backbone. Most vertebrates are bilaterally symmetrical; the body shape is roughly the same on each side of the backbone. Surrounding the brain, all vertebrates have a skull made of either bone or cartilage.

● **Mammals** Mammals have hair, a single lower jawbone that hinges directly onto the skull, and red blood cells that lack nuclei. Female mammals provide their young with milk. Mammals are able to create their own body heat (they are warm-blooded) and have a four-chamber heart.

● **Placental mammals** A placental mammal develops inside its mother's uterus, where it receives nourishment and oxygen from the mother through an organ called the placenta. This develops during pregnancy. The other two

▼ *The taxonomic relationships shown below represent the consensus of many biologists but are by no means universally accepted. Human taxonomy is fraught with difficulty and is constantly changing. While some biologists consider* Homo heidelbergensis, Homo erectus, *and* Homo neanderthalensis *to be separate species, others believe the last to be a subspecies of* Homo sapiens.

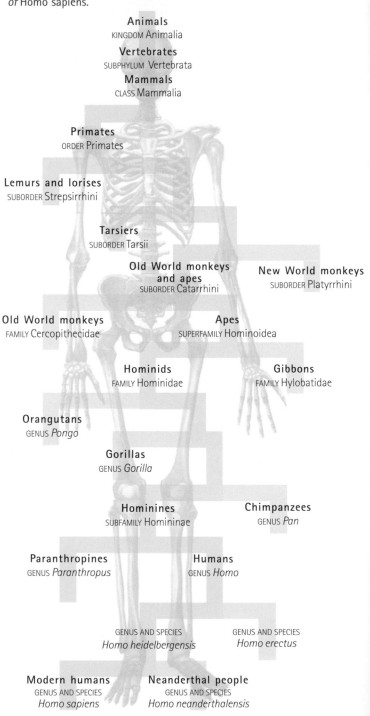

**Animals**
KINGDOM Animalia

**Vertebrates**
SUBPHYLUM Vertebrata

**Mammals**
CLASS Mammalia

**Primates**
ORDER Primates

**Lemurs and lorises**
SUBORDER Strepsirrhini

**Tarsiers**
SUBORDER Tarsii

**Old World monkeys and apes**
SUBORDER Catarrhini

**New World monkeys**
SUBORDER Platyrrhini

**Old World monkeys**
FAMILY Cercopithecidae

**Apes**
SUPERFAMILY Hominoidea

**Hominids**
FAMILY Hominidae

**Gibbons**
FAMILY Hylobatidae

**Orangutans**
GENUS *Pongo*

**Gorillas**
GENUS *Gorilla*

**Hominines**
SUBFAMILY Homininae

**Chimpanzees**
GENUS *Pan*

**Paranthropines**
GENUS *Paranthropus*

**Humans**
GENUS *Homo*

GENUS AND SPECIES
*Homo heidelbergensis*

GENUS AND SPECIES
*Homo erectus*

**Modern humans**
GENUS AND SPECIES
*Homo sapiens*

**Neanderthal people**
GENUS AND SPECIES
*Homo neanderthalensis*

mammal groups are the marsupials, which give birth to tiny young that complete their development in the mother's pouch; and monotremes, which lay eggs.

● **Primates** Primates form a large group of mammals that include prosimians, such as bush babies and lemurs, monkeys, and apes. There are around 279 species of primates; they have a well-developed cerebral hemisphere enclosed by a large globe-shaped cranium. Most primates have short jaws and flat faces, with short noses and large, forward-pointing eyes. For most primates the sense of smell is less important than vision, touch, and hearing.

● **Hominids** The family Hominidae traditionally consisted solely of humans and their immediate ancestors and relatives, but recently the great apes (the chimpanzees, gorillas, and orangutans) have been included. Hominids have a short spine with shoulder blades that provide an exceptionally wide range of movement for the arms.

▲ *Unlike many other mammals, humans have relatively little facial hair. Facial expressions are therefore easy to read.*

● **Hominines** This group includes all the non-ape hominids. Humans are the sole living representatives, though there are many fossil species. These include *Australopithecus*, the group from which true humans evolved. Hominines are bipedal. Unlike those of the great apes, the first two digits on humans' feet are not opposable.

● **Humans and very close relatives** The genus *Homo* includes modern humans, plus a number of extinct relatives such as Neanderthals and *Homo floresiensis*, a species of 3-foot (90-cm) people. *Homo* differs from earlier hominines such as *Australopithecus* in having a skeleton better adapted to standing upright, slighter jaws and chewing muscles, and a particularly large brain. Scientists may soon agree to re-classify hominids on the basis of new evidence. The new classification would place chimpanzees in the genus *Homo*.

**FEATURED SYSTEMS**

**EXTERNAL ANATOMY** Humans are bipedal with an upright posture, leaving the hands free to manipulate objects. *See pages 126–128.*

**SKELETAL SYSTEM** The human skeleton shows unique adaptations to cope with a massively increased brain, a softer diet, and an upright, bipedal stance. *See pages 129–132.*

**MUSCULAR SYSTEM** Some muscles are well-developed for maintaining an upright position and a well-balanced bipedal gait. *See pages 133–135.*

**NERVOUS SYSTEM** Humans have the most complex central nervous system in the animal kingdom, and have unique problem-solving and cognitive abilities. *See pages 136–139.*

**CIRCULATORY AND RESPIRATORY SYSTEMS** Humans have a four-chamber heart and a pair of lungs inflated by the action of the diaphragm. *See pages 140–141.*

**DIGESTIVE AND EXCRETORY SYSTEMS** Humans have a relatively simple digestive system with few unique adaptations. *See pages 142–143.*

**ENDOCRINE AND EXOCRINE SYSTEMS** These systems are groups of glands. One type, mammary glands, occurs only in mammals. *See pages 144–145.*

**REPRODUCTIVE SYSTEM** The female reproductive system allows for the efficient development of one or two offspring at a time. As in most mammals, the male's testes are held outside the body. *See pages 146–147.*

# External anatomy

**CONNECTIONS**

**COMPARE** humans' upright stance with the stances of other bipeds, such as *KANGAROOS* or *WOODPECKERS*.

**COMPARE** human feet with those of a *CHIMPANZEE*.

Biologically, humans are among the most unusual mammals. For example, humans have an erect posture and are bipedal. Almost all other mammals are quadrupedal, or four-legged. The only other truly bipedal mammals are kangaroos, and some rodents such as jerboas. Although monkeys and apes occasionally walk upright, they usually move around on four legs.

## Why walk on two legs?

Bipedalism leaves the front limbs free to carry and use tools; thus it may have kick-started humans' rapid increase in brain size. Despite its

▲ *Humans are able to balance on two legs with the aid of organs that form part of the inner ear.*

importance, however, biologists have little idea why human ancestors began to walk on two legs rather than four. Bipedality may have evolved after a change in habitat; climatic change around 4 million years ago brought a decline in tropical forests, so human ancestors were forced to switch to life on grasslands.

Biologists often suggest that bipedalism may have been advantageous for observing predators, or for reducing the surface area of body exposed to the hot sun. However, other grassland animals, such as baboons, do just fine walking on four legs. Perhaps the likeliest explanation involves the energetics of walking. Bipedal movement is more efficient than a

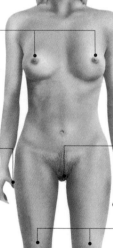

*Forward-facing eyes provide humans with stereoscopic vision. This enables people to accurately judge distances.*

*The head contains the most important sense organs: the eyes, nose, tongue, and ears.*

*Like all adult female mammals, human females have mammary glands, which provide nutrient-rich milk for newborn young.*

*Human thumbs are opposable; they can be placed against the other digits. This ability enables humans to handle objects with great dexterity.*

*Human genitals are similar to those of other mammals; the female has a vagina and the male a penis and testicles.*

▶ **Female human**
*Humans have very little body hair in comparison with most other mammals. They are also sexually dimorphic: males and females look noticeably different. Females have a broader pelvis, breasts, and less body hair than males.*

*Walking on two legs—bipedality—is an unusual trait shared by only a handful of other mammals such as kangaroos and jerboas.*

*Humans are plantigrade; they walk on the soles of their feet rather than on their toes.*

*Unlike other primates, humans do not have opposable toes.*

## The whites of the eyes

**Humans are one of the few mammals** in which the whites of the eyes are visible. This feature makes it easier to determine where a person is looking and might help humans communicate. The eye whites are visible in some other social animals such as wolves.

chimp's quadrupedal knuckle-walking. For a knuckle-walking ancestor living on the plains, switching to bipedality would have offered the best means of moving long distances in the absence of trees to swing from.

## Limb dimensions

Unlike other apes, humans have long, powerful legs and relatively short arms. Humans are plantigrade; that is, they walk on the soles of the feet with the heels on the ground. The arm span of some apes can be more than twice their height, whereas arm span and height are almost equal in humans. Although humans do not use their arms for locomotion, the arms are relatively powerful, reflecting their former use for swinging from branch to branch and their importance for tool manipulation. As in all apes, human hands have five fingers including an opposable thumb. It is the opposable thumb, an adaptation for grasping branches when climbing, that has allowed humans to make and manipulate tools and change the environment in which they live.

**▼ SKIN CROSS SECTION**

*This diagram shows the structures typically found in the epidermis (outer skin layer), the dermis (middle layer), and a portion of the thickest layer, the hypodermis (lower layer), of human skin. The outer layer of skin cells is constantly shed and replaced by new cells rising from the lower epidermis.*

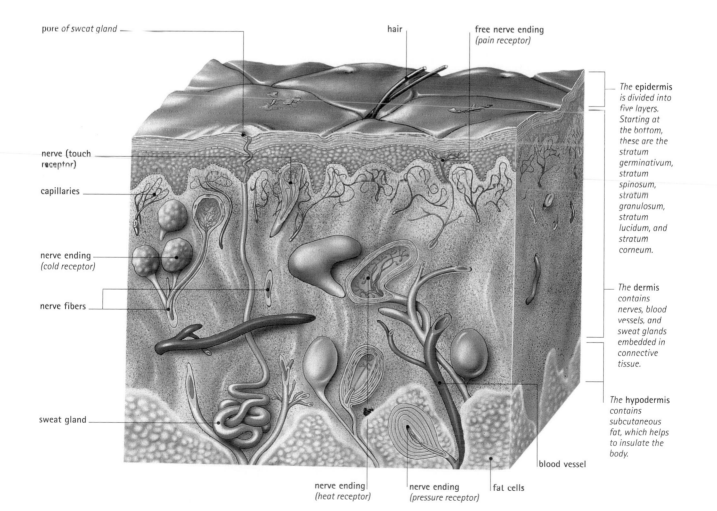

pore of sweat gland

hair

free nerve ending (pain receptor)

nerve (touch receptor)

capillaries

nerve ending (cold receptor)

nerve fibers

sweat gland

*The* **epidermis** *is divided into five layers. Starting at the bottom, these are the stratum germinativum, stratum spinosum, stratum granulosum, stratum lucidum, and stratum corneum.*

*The* **dermis** *contains nerves, blood vessels, and sweat glands embedded in connective tissue.*

*The* **hypodermis** *contains subcutaneous fat, which helps to insulate the body.*

blood vessel

nerve ending (heat receptor)

nerve ending (pressure receptor)

fat cells

▶ *The beard worn by this Confucian holy man has become white with age. A hair grows from a group of cells under the skin called a follicle. As people grow older, the cells in the follicle that produce pigment gradually die and the hairs grow white.*

### Where did all the hair go?

Another biological enigma is humans' relative lack of hair. Hairs are present all over the body (apart from on the lips, palms, and soles) in numbers similar to those of other primates. However, human hairs are short and very fine. Biologists struggle to explain this unusual feature. The reduction in hair occurred not less than 70,000 years ago, when people began to wear clothes, but may have evolved long before that. Biologists have suggested a variety of explanations for the reduction in hair: an aquatic human ancestry; a means of foiling parasitic insects; and a way of keeping cool in hot climates. None of these ideas stands up to close scrutiny, however. The most convincing theory suggests that hair reduction evolved for sexual display, perhaps to advertize the absence of parasites and therefore suitability for mating.

### Explaining the anomalies

How can the unusual distribution of the remaining human hair be explained? Women have hair on the top, sides, and back of the head, leaving the face and forehead only sparsely covered with tiny fine hairs, apart from conspicuous eyebrows. Most adult men have a dense covering of hair on their head and also on the lower face. This facial hair starts to develop in human males when they reach puberty at about 13 years old. Hair on top of the head probably helps protect the brain from the heat of the sun. The hairs of the eyebrows channel sweat and water away from the eyes.

A partially or wholly naked face may have allowed human ancestors to communicate visually with a wide range of facial expressions. It may also have indicated a person's level of health (and therefore sexual desirability). What about beards? Their presence in men but not women strongly suggests that evolution favored the retention of beards as an ornament of sexual display and status, either for display to other males or to attract females.

### Other external features

Compared with other primates, humans have a higher forehead and smaller jaws that do not project as far forward. Modern humans have a larger, more spherical head, accommodating a larger brain than that of their hominid ancestors, and they have smaller jaws.

Like other primates, humans have forward-facing eyes and good stereoscopic (three-dimensional) vision. This feature was important for human ancestors' tree-living lifestyle, when it was necessary to judge distances accurately while jumping from bough to branch. It also enables detailed close-up vision.

**CLOSE-UP**

### Explaining pubic hair

**As well as on the head,** the otherwise hairless human has retained hair in the armpits and pubic regions. In human ancestors, these hairs may have served as a large surface from which to broadcast chemicals called pheromones into the air. These chemicals served as a sexual attractant. Modern humans may still release attractant pheromones, although this possibility has been little studied by biologists.

# Skeletal system

At birth, a human's skeleton is made up of 270 bones. During development from baby to adult many of the bones fuse, so by the age of about 20 the total number of bones has reduced to 206. The human skeleton can be divided into two main sections: the axial skeleton consists of the skull, vertebral column, and ribs; and the appendicular skeleton is made up of the limbs and limb girdles. There are three main types of bones in the human skeleton: long bones, flat bones, and short bones. Long bones, such as leg and arm bones, are long and tubular, usually with joints for movement at each end. Flat bones have a flat cross section, and include the ribs and shoulder blades. Short bones have irregular shapes and include the vertebrae and the small block-shaped bones in the hands and feet.

## Skeletal functions

The skeleton provides support and structure for the whole body. The legs and back support the weight of the rest of the body. The skeleton allows movement by providing attachments for muscles to pull against. It also protects internal organs such as the heart, lungs, and brain. The marrow of the long bones is the source of white and red blood

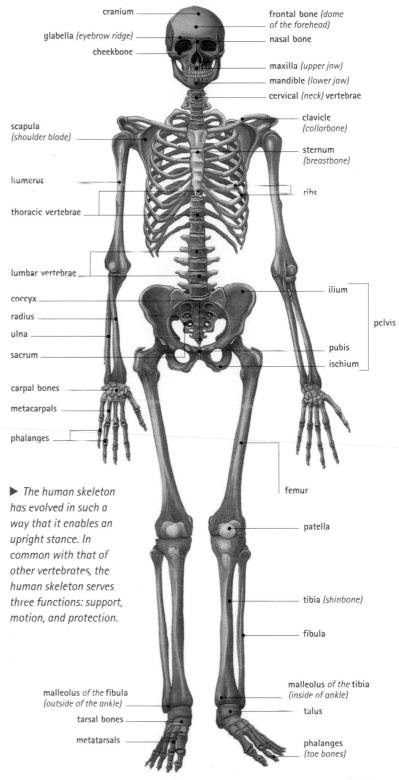

cranium

glabella *(eyebrow ridge)*

cheekbone

frontal bone *(dome of the forehead)*

nasal bone

maxilla *(upper jaw)*

mandible *(lower jaw)*

cervical *(neck)* vertebrae

clavicle *(collarbone)*

sternum *(breastbone)*

ribs

scapula *(shoulder blade)*

humerus

thoracic vertebrae

lumbar vertebrae

coccyx

radius

ulna

sacrum

ilium

pelvis

pubis

ischium

carpal bones

metacarpals

phalanges

femur

patella

tibia *(shinbone)*

fibula

malleolus *of the tibia (inside of ankle)*

malleolus *of the fibula (outside of the ankle)*

talus

tarsal bones

metatarsals

phalanges *(toe bones)*

▶ *The human skeleton has evolved in such a way that it enables an upright stance. In common with that of other vertebrates, the human skeleton serves three functions: support, motion, and protection.*

## CLOSE-UP

### The smallest bones

**The smallest bones in the human body** are the ossicles, a series of three tiny bones located in the middle ear. These bones are named the malleus, the incus, and the stapes. They transfer sound vibrations from the eardrum to the inner ear, where they are converted to nerve signals sent to the brain. The ossicles are unique to mammals. Reptiles and amphibians have a stapes, but the mammalian incus and malleus evolved from some of the bones that formed the lower jaw in mammals' reptilian ancestors.

## EVOLUTION

### Shifts of the foramen magnum

**The foramen magnum is an opening** at the base of the skull where nerves of the medulla oblongata connect the brain to the spinal cord. The position of the foramen magnum in ancient hominids gives a clue to how they moved. In hominids, unlike chimpanzees and other apes, the foramen magnum opens toward the front of the skull; its forward position is particularly pronounced in modern humans. This is the best arrangement for bipedality, since it allows the head to sit directly on top of the shoulders. The foramen magnum of a quadrupedal animal is located farther back toward the rear of the skull.

cells, crucial for oxygen transport and for immunity against diseases. Bones also provide a store of essential minerals such as calcium and phosphorous.

### The skull

The human skull is made up of at least 22 bones, eight of them in the top, back, and sides of the head (the cranial bones), and the rest in the facial area. In newborn babies, many of these bones are only loosely joined by fibrous elastic tissue; that allows the baby's large head easier passage through the mother's birth canal. Later, these joints, or sutures, in the skull fuse, providing a protective helmet for the brain.

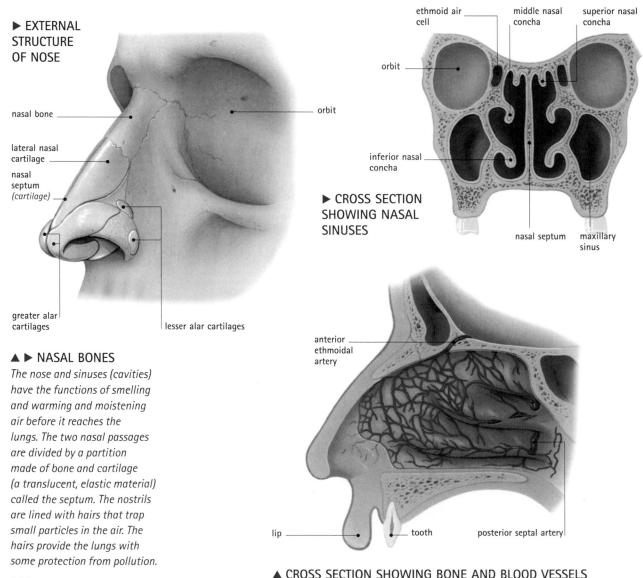

▶ EXTERNAL STRUCTURE OF NOSE

nasal bone

lateral nasal cartilage

nasal septum (cartilage)

orbit

greater alar cartilages

lesser alar cartilages

ethmoid air cell

middle nasal concha

superior nasal concha

orbit

inferior nasal concha

▶ CROSS SECTION SHOWING NASAL SINUSES

nasal septum

maxillary sinus

anterior ethmoidal artery

lip

tooth

posterior septal artery

▲ ▶ NASAL BONES
*The nose and sinuses (cavities) have the functions of smelling and warming and moistening air before it reaches the lungs. The two nasal passages are divided by a partition made of bone and cartilage (a translucent, elastic material) called the septum. The nostrils are lined with hairs that trap small particles in the air. The hairs provide the lungs with some protection from pollution.*

▲ CROSS SECTION SHOWING BONE AND BLOOD VESSELS

## The vertebral column and ribs

Humans have 33 vertebrae arranged in five groups. Flexible fibrous disks between the vertebrae allow bending movement in the spine and act as shock absorbers against the jolting forces that occur during running or jumping. The uppermost seven vertebrae are the cervical vertebrae; they give the neck flexibility. The top two of these bones are the atlas, which allows the head to nod up and down, and the axis, which allows the head to move from side to side.

Next come the 12 thoracic vertebrae, to which the rib cage attaches. The first seven

▼ The skeleton provides support for movements such as bending and lifting. Muscles attached to the bones provide mechanical force, while the bones provide a firm structure against which the muscles can move.

---

**EVOLUTION**

## Ancient diets

**Skull shape can tell scientists** a lot about the diets of extinct hominids. Early hominids such as *Paranthropus boisei* had large jaws and enlarged bony processes on the skull for the attachment of powerful chewing muscles. These structures, and the presence of large molar teeth, reveal that these creatures ate tough fibrous food that needed a lot of chewing. Other hominids such as *Homo habilis* had much smaller jaws and teeth. *Homo habilis* was omnivorous, feeding on plant and animal matter; it used tools to help it cut animal hide or break up bones to get at the marrow within. Even though modern humans have smaller jaws and jaw muscles than our predecessors, a human bite is still powerful and can inflict injuries comparable to a dog bite.

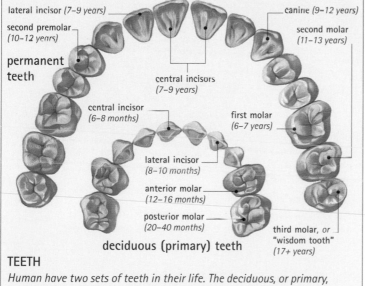

lateral incisor (7–9 years)

second premolar (10–12 years)

**permanent teeth**

central incisors (7–9 years)

canine (9–12 years)

second molar (11–13 years)

central incisor (6–8 months)

first molar (6–7 years)

lateral incisor (8–10 months)

anterior molar (12–16 months)

posterior molar (20–40 months)

third molar, or "wisdom tooth" (17+ years)

**deciduous (primary) teeth**

**TEETH**

*Human have two sets of teeth in their life. The deciduous, or primary, teeth develop in early childhood. These begin to fall out as the young person ages and are replaced by larger permanent teeth. This diagram shows the approximate ages at which different teeth first appear.*

---

As well as housing the brain, the skull also holds the most important human sense organs: the eyes, nose, ears, and tongue.

The human skull has a number of holes, or foramina, particularly around the base. These holes allow various blood vessels and nerves to pass through, going to or from the brain. The largest of these holes is the foramen magnum, through which pass various important arteries and the medulla oblongata, the lower part of the brain stem that continues downward to form the spinal cord.

## Skeletal changes for bipedality

**The structure and arrangement** of many human skeletal features enable bipedality. This is especially true of the pelvic girdle and legs. The human pelvis is shorter and wider than that of a chimp; also, the socket joints that accommodate the heads of the femurs (thighbones) point downward, so the weight of the body passes efficiently through the hip. The separated hipbones, or ilia, allow a wide stance, important for good balance on two legs. The hipbones also act as an attachment point for the gluteal muscles, which aid balance. The femurs point inward a little from the hips to the knees, making it easier for humans to remain balanced when shifting their weight from one foot to the other during walking. Human knee joints are broad to help keep a stable posture. The lack of an opposable toe and the development of a large heel bone (or talus) have made human feet efficient for walking.

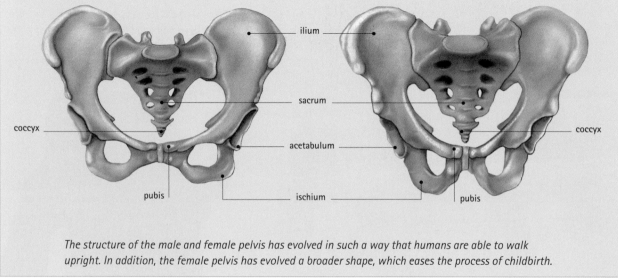

FEMALE PELVIS        MALE PELVIS

ilium

sacrum

coccyx

acetabulum

coccyx

pubis

ischium

pubis

*The structure of the male and female pelvis has evolved in such a way that humans are able to walk upright. In addition, the female pelvis has evolved a broader shape, which eases the process of childbirth.*

pairs of ribs connect via cartilage to a long, flat bone at the front of the chest called the breastbone, or sternum. The sternum is also joined at its top to the collarbones, or clavicles. The ribs form a cage that protects delicate internal organs such as the heart and lungs.

The next five vertebrae are the largest of the vertebral bones and support most of the body's weight. These are the lumbar vertebrae, which support the lower back. Below the lumbar region is the sacrum, a series of four or five sacral vertebrae that become fused in adults to provide sturdy support for the pelvis.

The final section of the vertebral column is the coccyx, or tailbone, which is made up of three to five vertebrae that fuse by adulthood. The coccyx curves under the pelvis and serves as a site for muscle attachment.

### The limbs

There is a total of 126 bones in the human appendicular skeleton, which includes the bones of the arms and legs, the pelvis, and the shoulder area. Like apes, humans have five-fingered hands with opposable thumbs. In humans and apes, a series of long finger bones, or phalanges, give the hands considerable dexterity and the ability to grasp objects. The upper arm bone, or humerus, is able to rotate freely in the shoulder joint, an adaptation that allows gibbons, apes, and humans' distant ancestors to move through trees by swinging from one hold to another.

Human leg bones, such as the femur (thighbone) and the fibia and tibia (shinbones), are much longer than those of apes. The femur is the largest bone in the human body.

# Muscular system

In common with all vertebrates, humans have three kinds of muscles: cardiac, or heart, muscle; smooth muscle, which is mostly involuntary (it operates without conscious thought); and skeletal muscle, which is under conscious control. Skeletal muscles enable humans to move around and account for around 40 percent of body weight in adult males, but only 23 percent in females. There are more than 600 skeletal muscles in the human body. Muscles of all shapes and sizes are made up of blocks of muscle fibers. These fibers contract when they receive signals from motor neurons (nerve cells). Since muscles can exert only a pulling force, they often work in antagonistic pairs, able to pull against each

▼ Muscles
*The main voluntary muscles on the front and back of a human. The voluntary muscles are those that are under conscious control and enable humans to move.*

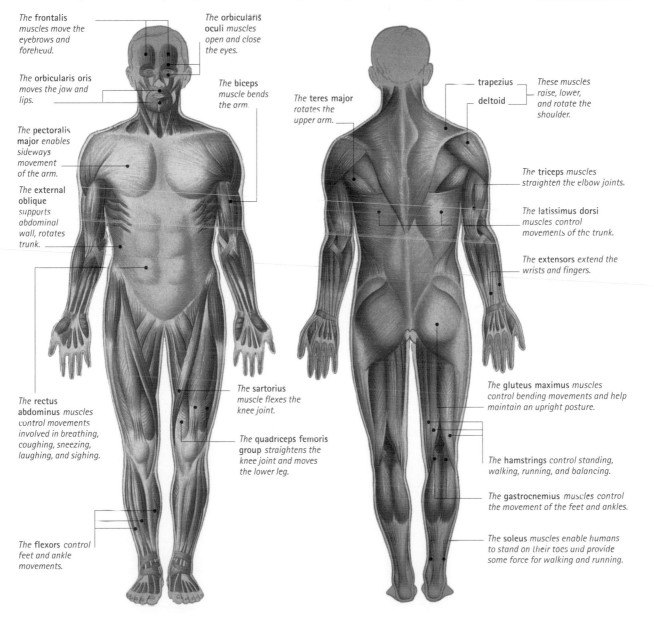

*The frontalis muscles move the eyebrows and forehead.*

*The orbicularis oris moves the jaw and lips.*

*The orbicularis oculi muscles open and close the eyes.*

*The biceps muscle bends the arm.*

*The pectoralis major enables sideways movement of the arm.*

*The external oblique supports abdominal wall, rotates trunk.*

*The rectus abdominus muscles control movements involved in breathing, coughing, sneezing, laughing, and sighing.*

*The flexors control feet and ankle movements.*

*The sartorius muscle flexes the knee joint.*

*The quadriceps femoris group straightens the knee joint and moves the lower leg.*

*The teres major rotates the upper arm.*

trapezius

deltoid

*These muscles raise, lower, and rotate the shoulder.*

*The triceps muscles straighten the elbow joints.*

*The latissimus dorsi muscles control movements of the trunk.*

*The extensors extend the wrists and fingers.*

*The gluteus maximus muscles control bending movements and help maintain an upright posture.*

*The hamstrings control standing, walking, running, and balancing.*

*The gastrocnemius muscles control the movement of the feet and ankles.*

*The soleus muscles enable humans to stand on their toes and provide some force for walking and running.*

133

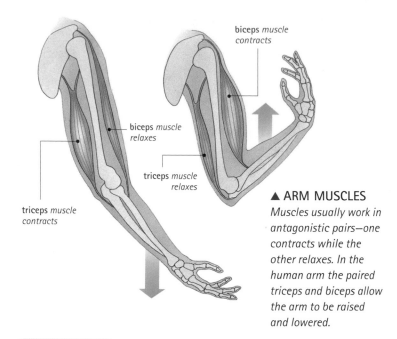

**▲ ARM MUSCLES**

*Muscles usually work in antagonistic pairs—one contracts while the other relaxes. In the human arm the paired triceps and biceps allow the arm to be raised and lowered.*

biceps *muscle contracts*

biceps *muscle relaxes*

triceps *muscle relaxes*

triceps *muscle contracts*

other. For example, the brachialis and biceps muscles in the upper arm, which make the arm flex, work against the triceps muscle, which extends the arm.

## Muscles in the head

There are 10 major muscle groups around the human head and neck. These are involved in supporting and moving the head, making facial expressions, moving the eyes, blinking, speaking, and eating. The facial musculature of chimps and gorillas is similar to that of humans but is not as complex. The strength and location of the muscles that move the lips allow for a uniquely human ability, speech.

A number of muscles in the front part of the neck move the hyoid bone and the voice box, or larynx. These muscles, along with those of the tongue, are used for speech. The principal muscles responsible for chewing are the

**CLOSE-UP**

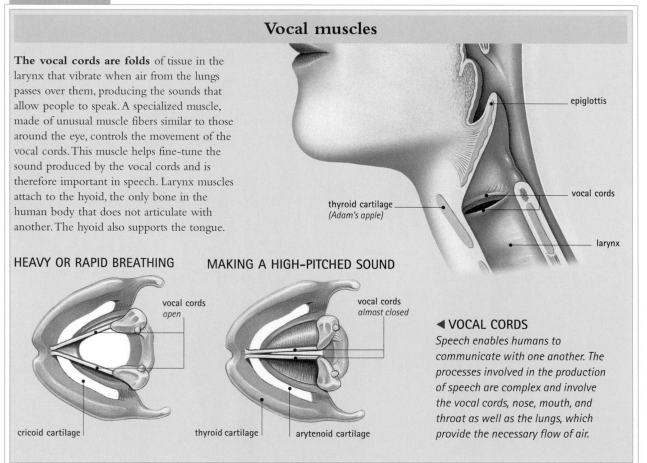

# Vocal muscles

**The vocal cords are folds** of tissue in the larynx that vibrate when air from the lungs passes over them, producing the sounds that allow people to speak. A specialized muscle, made of unusual muscle fibers similar to those around the eye, controls the movement of the vocal cords. This muscle helps fine-tune the sound produced by the vocal cords and is therefore important in speech. Larynx muscles attach to the hyoid, the only bone in the human body that does not articulate with another. The hyoid also supports the tongue.

epiglottis

thyroid cartilage *(Adam's apple)*

vocal cords

larynx

## HEAVY OR RAPID BREATHING

vocal cords *open*

cricoid cartilage

## MAKING A HIGH-PITCHED SOUND

vocal cords *almost closed*

thyroid cartilage

arytenoid cartilage

**◀ VOCAL CORDS**

*Speech enables humans to communicate with one another. The processes involved in the production of speech are complex and involve the vocal cords, nose, mouth, and throat as well as the lungs, which provide the necessary flow of air.*

134

## The tongue

**Relative to its size,** the tongue is the strongest muscle in the human body. It needs to be powerful to cope with the large amount of work it must do, including manipulating food and helping produce speech.

masseter muscles. In humans, they are less powerfully developed than those of apes but can still exert considerable pressure.

### Muscles of the back and chest

The superficial muscles of the back lie above other deeper muscle layers. There are two main superficial muscle groups: the trapezius in the upper back and the latissimus dorsii in the lower back. These muscles are important for moving the shoulder blades and upper arms, and extending the body from the waist. The arms are also moved by the pectoralis muscles, which extend across the chest.

Below the superficial muscles are the deep back muscles. One group of these muscles, the erector spinae, keeps the spine in an upright position and is important for stabilizing the spine in different positions. There are nine muscles in this group, and they attach to various parts of the dorsal (back) skeleton, including the ribs, the pelvis, and extensions of the vertebrae. The erector spinae muscles are larger in humans than in apes and are critical in maintaining an bipedal stance.

### Muscles of the legs

The musculature of human legs is complex; it needs to perform the tricky task of maintaining balance in a bipedal animal with a high center of gravity. Around the buttocks and hips are the gluteal muscles. This group is important for flexing, rotating, and extending the legs. It includes the largest muscle in the human body, the gluteus maximus. Another large member of this muscle group, the well-developed gluteus medius, is crucial for efficient bipedal walking. This muscle supports the side of the pelvis carrying the raised leg during the swing phase of the walking cycle,

when one leg is supporting and balancing the body while the other swings forward. The gluteus medius is poorly developed in chimpanzees; when chimps walk on two legs they must shift the position of their body to maintain balance during the walking cycle, giving them a side-to-side motion.

Toward the back of the thigh is the hamstring muscle group. There are three muscles in this group: the biceps femoris, the semimembranosus, and the semitendinosus. Each of the hamstring muscles is involved in flexing the knee and extending the leg. These muscles are especially active during running. The muscles of the calf in the lower leg, the soleus and gastrocnemius, are particularly large and strong in humans. These muscles give humans the ability to rise on their toes, and provide some of the driving force during walking and running.

## Muscle adaptation and training

**Human muscles can adapt** to the different stresses imposed on them. Athletes carry out different kinds of resistance training to increase muscle mass and improve strength and speed. When muscles are not used they atrophy (lose mass). Astronauts who spend extended periods in low-gravity or zero-gravity conditions lose muscle mass and strength in a matter of days and must exercise regularly to maintain their strength.

*Athletes follow rigorous training programs that strengthen the muscles necessary to excel at specific sporting events.*

# Nervous system

**CONNECTIONS**

**COMPARE** the structure of the human eye with that of an invertebrate such as an **OCTOPUS**, whose eyes have evolved independently of vertebrate eyes.

**COMPARE** the folds on the exterior of the human brain with those of a **MANATEE**. The greater number of folds on the human brain is an indication of the species' greater intelligence.

The nervous system controls and regulates essential and generally unconscious life-support systems, such as heartbeat, temperature regulation, and breathing, as well as coordinating the body's voluntary movements and interpreting the many signals from the sensory organs. The human nervous system is unique in its complexity and is responsible for consciousness, the mind, thought, and people's perception of the world. Like that of other vertebrates, the human nervous system can be divided into the central nervous system (CNS), which includes the brain and the spinal cord, and the peripheral nervous system (PNS), which includes all the nerves and sensory organs attached to the CNS.

## The neuron

Neurons are nerve cells. These cells bear long, thin projections called dendrites. Many neurons have one or more long, specialized dendrites called axons. Axons are able to transmit electrical signals rapidly along the length of the cell. These neurons make up some of the longest cells in the body. There are three main types of neurons: sensory neurons, motor neurons, and interneurons. Sensory neurons connect the sense organs to the CNS. Motor neurons carry signals from the CNS to the muscles to effect a response, and interneurons, which occur only in the CNS, connect the other types of neurons.

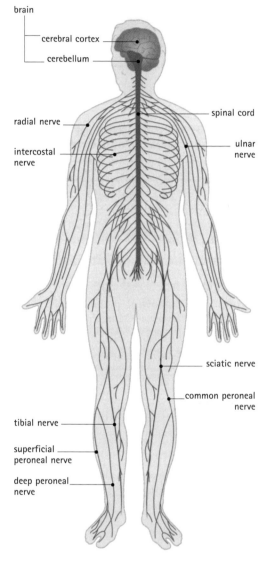

▲ **Human**
*A network of nerve fibers—the peripheral nervous system—conveys chemical and electrical messages between all parts of the body and the central nervous system, which is made up of the brain and spinal cord. The central nervous system processes information received from sensory organs and, in response, controls movement, via nerves that connect to muscles, and many other body processes in glands and organs.*

**IN FOCUS**

### Linking neurons

**Junctions between neurons** are called synapses. When an electrical signal reaches a synapse, chemicals called neurotransmitters are released into the synapse. The chemicals diffuse across the synapse and join with binding sites on the neighboring neuron. The binding triggers a new signal, allowing the message to pass on.

### Voluntary and involuntary

The PNS can be subdivided into two distinct systems: the somatic nervous system and the autonomic nervous system. The somatic system controls voluntary actions of the skeletal muscles; actions such as walking and talking depend on the somatic nervous system. The autonomic system controls involuntary body processes over which little or no conscious control can be exerted, such as the heartbeat. The autonomic nervous system also triggers the release of secretions from certain glands, such as production of epinephrine by the adrenal glands.

Autonomic nerves continuously regulate internal body conditions. There are two distinct subsystems within the autonomic nervous system: the sympathetic and parasympathetic systems. The sympathetic system governs responses associated with fear, escape, and aggression, such as the release of epinephrine from the adrenal glands and increases in heart rate. The parasympathetic system has the opposite effect; it stimulates tissues associated with digestion and relaxation.

### Peripheral organization

The cranial nerves, which include the optic nerves, exit the brain directly and form a major section of the PNS. There are also 31 pairs of spinal nerves that branch off from the spinal cord. Nerves are bundles of sensory and motor axons. The cell bodies of motor neurons, which contain the nucleus and other cellular machinery, lie in the spinal cord. Their axons pass out of the spinal cord on the front (ventral) side of the spinal column. Sensory neurons pass out of the back of the spinal cord. The cell bodies of sensory neurons occur in a cluster (or ganglion) outside the spinal

---

**CLOSE-UP**

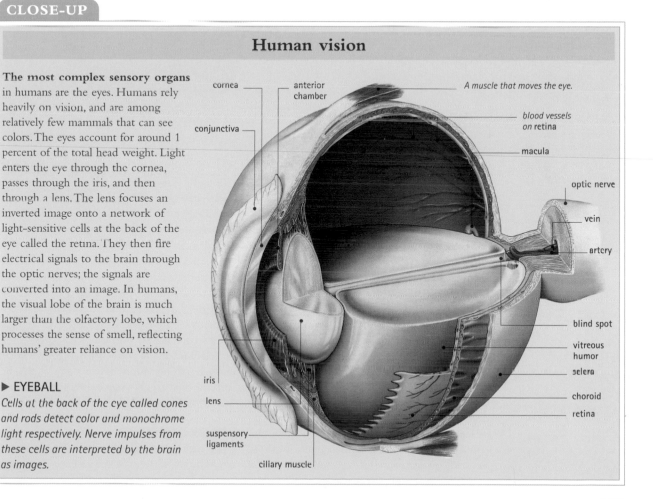

# Human vision

**The most complex sensory organs** in humans are the eyes. Humans rely heavily on vision, and are among relatively few mammals that can see colors. The eyes account for around 1 percent of the total head weight. Light enters the eye through the cornea, passes through the iris, and then through a lens. The lens focuses an inverted image onto a network of light-sensitive cells at the back of the eye called the retina. They then fire electrical signals to the brain through the optic nerves; the signals are converted into an image. In humans, the visual lobe of the brain is much larger than the olfactory lobe, which processes the sense of smell, reflecting humans' greater reliance on vision.

▶ **EYEBALL**
*Cells at the back of the eye called cones and rods detect color and monochrome light respectively. Nerve impulses from these cells are interpreted by the brain as images.*

cornea

anterior chamber

A muscle that moves the eye.

conjunctiva

blood vessels on retina

macula

optic nerve

vein

artery

blind spot

vitreous humor

sclera

choroid

retina

iris

lens

suspensory ligaments

ciliary muscle

# Brain size and smartness

**Various methods have been used** to attempt to measure the relative intelligence of animals. One method is the encephalization quotient (EQ). This is a number arrived at using a mathematical formula that involves comparing brain mass with body mass. A mammal with an EQ value of 1 represents a brain of expected size, and therefore average intelligence. Humans have by far the highest EQ (around 7.44). Neanderthals had an even larger brain relative to their size. Dolphins are second in the "smart list" of living animals (5.31), far ahead of chimpanzees (2.49). Mice, rats, and rabbits have the lowest EQ, with brains less than half the size expected for animals of their size.

Another method for assessing relative intelligence involves measuring the degree of folding in the cerebral cortex, the most recently evolved area of the brain and the one most often linked with the development of intelligence.

Such methods as these, however, are controversial and are not thought to provide entirely accurate results.

### The brain
*The human brain is divided into three main parts: the brain stem, the cerebellum, and the cerebrum.*

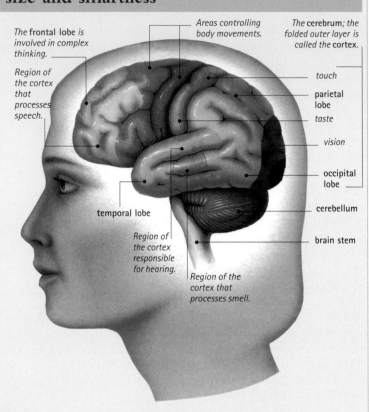

*The frontal lobe is involved in complex thinking.*

*Region of the cortex that processes speech.*

*Areas controlling body movements.*

*The cerebrum; the folded outer layer is called the cortex.*

touch

parietal lobe

taste

vision

occipital lobe

cerebellum

brain stem

temporal lobe

*Region of the cortex responsible for hearing.*

*Region of the cortex that processes smell.*

cord. The axons from the sensory and motor neurons join into a single nerve; they branch again farther along the nerve.

### The central nervous system
The spinal cord of adult humans measures around 18 inches (45 cm) long, and is about as thick as a person's thumb. The brain weighs around 3 pounds (1.4 kg) and is made up of at least 10 billion neurons. The entire CNS is surrounded by a liquid called the cerebrospinal fluid (CSF), which protects the delicate tissues and transports of oxygen and nutrients.

A single neuron in the brain can connect with 100,000 or more other neurons, with different rules governing the transmission of electrical signals between different neurons. The complexity of the human brain is crucial for the production of a unique level of consciousness and the capacity for abstract thought. Different parts of the brain are associated with different tasks, such as speech and body coordination. However, like all other vertebrate brains the human brain consists of three main parts: the forebrain, the midbrain, and the hindbrain. The hindbrain contains the medulla and pons, and the cerebellum and olfactory bulb are part of the midbrain. These regions are associated with life-support functions. The medulla regulates breathing and heart rates, blood pressure, and digestion. The cerebellum helps control balance, posture, and muscle coordination. These parts of the brain are the first to develop in fetal mammals and are collectively called the archipallium.

### The paleopallium
The next part of the brain to form during the growth of the fetus is the paleopallium, which mostly consists of the limbic system. This

includes the amygdala, which is responsible for emotions such as fear and anger; and the hippocampus, which is involved in memory and learning. Other parts of the limbic system also control emotions, moods, and motivations such as sexual drive.

The thalamus and hypothalamus are important paleopallium structures. The thalamus is involved in the coordination of movement and the processing of sensory information. It passes information to and from the most developed part of the human brain, the neocortex. The hypothalamus controls body temperature, the sensations of hunger and thirst, and the internal body clock; it also controls hormone output from the pituitary gland.

### The neocortex

The neocortex makes up much of the cerebral hemispheres. It is a relatively recently evolved structure and only occurs in mammal groups such as ungulates, cetaceans, carnivores, and

primates. The folding of the cortex creates a series of bumps and grooves called gyri and sulci. More gyri and sulci increase the brain's surface area. Particular regions of the neocortex are associated with advanced brain functions such as language, reasoning, perception, and voluntary movement. The neocortex is the seat of human consciousness.

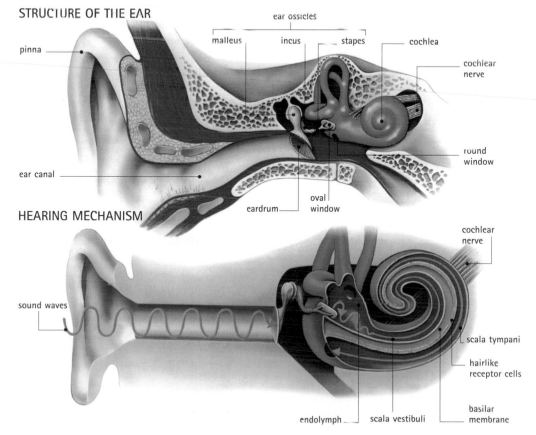

STRUCTURE OF THE EAR

ear ossicles

pinna — malleus — incus — stapes — cochlea

cochlear nerve

ear canal

round window

HEARING MECHANISM

eardrum — oval window

cochlear nerve

sound waves

scala tympani

hairlike receptor cells

basilar membrane

endolymph — scala vestibuli

◀ EAR

*Sound waves travel along the ear canal causing the eardrum to vibrate. These vibrations are transferred to the ear ossicles, which in turn cause a membranous structure called the oval window to vibrate. The sound pulses are transferred by the oval window to the endolymph in the scala vestibuli. They then pass across the basilar membrane, where hair-like receptor cells detect the pulses and produce nervous impulses, which are interpreted by the brain as sounds. The vibrations then pass to the scala tympani and on to the round window.*

# Circulatory and respiratory systems

Oxygen is required for cellular respiration, the series of chemical reactions that converts nutrients from food into usable energy. Small organisms such as amoebas and tiny worms can get enough oxygen by allowing it to diffuse through their outer membranes into the cell body. However, this diffusion becomes increasingly ineffective as animals get larger. Larger animals need dedicated organs to ensure that enough oxygen reaches all the cells in their body.

### Respiratory system

Like almost all other tetrapods (four-limbed vertebrates) humans use a pair of lungs for bringing oxygen into the bloodstream and removing carbon dioxide, the waste product of cellular respiration. Air enters the lungs through the nose or the mouth; passes down the windpipe, or trachea; and then passes into a pair of bronchi. The bronchi split into thousands of smaller tubes called bronchioles.

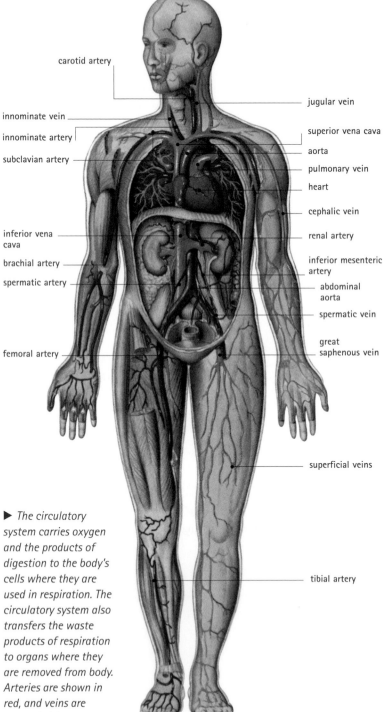

▶ The circulatory system carries oxygen and the products of digestion to the body's cells where they are used in respiration. The circulatory system also transfers the waste products of respiration to organs where they are removed from body. Arteries are shown in red, and veins are shown in blue.

carotid artery
jugular vein
innominate vein
superior vena cava
innominate artery
aorta
subclavian artery
pulmonary vein
heart
cephalic vein
inferior vena cava
renal artery
brachial artery
inferior mesenteric artery
spermatic artery
abdominal aorta
spermatic vein
great saphenous vein
femoral artery
superficial veins
tibial artery

---

**EVOLUTION**

## Life at high altitudes

**At altitudes above about 10,000 feet** (3,000 m) the air is thin and has little oxygen. Visitors to these high altitudes grow dizzy and feel sick owing to lack of oxygen. Their breathing rate rises, and if they stay longer than a few weeks they begin to make more hemoglobin, the protein that carries oxygen in the blood. However, people who live in mountain ranges such as the Andes and the Himalayas have adapted for life at high altitudes in apparently different ways. Scientists have discovered that people living in the Andes have higher concentrations of oxygen-carrying hemoglobin in their blood but breathe at the same rate as people living at low altitudes. People in the Himalayas of Tibet, however, breathe more quickly to obtain more oxygen. Both adaptations for life at high altitudes are successful.

All these respiratory tubes are reinforced with rings of cartilage to keep them from collapsing. At the end of the bronchioles are small air sacs called alveoli, where gas exchange occurs. There are millions of alveoli in human lungs; they give a total surface for respiration of more than 800 square feet (75 m²).

Unlike other tetrapods, humans and other mammals breathe using a large muscle called the diaphragm, which forms a muscular floor below the ribs. The diaphragm increases the volume of the chest cavity when it contracts, thus decreasing the pressure in this cavity and causing air from outside the body to inflate the lungs. Humans are one of the few terrestrial mammals that can voluntarily hold their breath. This ability is assisted by the unusually low position of the larynx in the trachea and probably evolved as an aid to speech.

## The circulatory system

Mammals and birds can control their body temperature internally, but this requires much more energy than a cold-blooded physiology, such as that of reptiles. Mammals and birds therefore need an efficient circulatory system to supply their oxygen-hungry tissues.

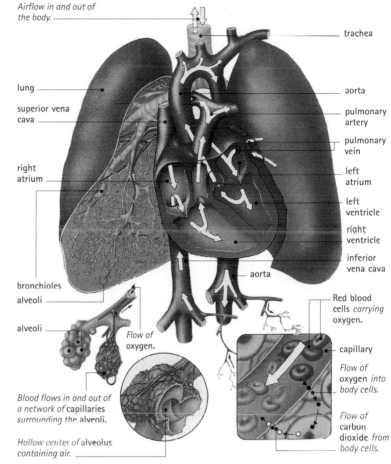

Airflow in and out of the body.

trachea

lung

superior vena cava

right atrium

aorta

pulmonary artery

pulmonary vein

left atrium

left ventricle

right ventricle

inferior vena cava

aorta

bronchioles

alveoli

alveoli

Flow of oxygen.

Red blood cells *carrying* oxygen.

capillary

Flow of oxygen *into* body cells.

Flow of carbon dioxide *from* body cells.

Blood flows in and out of a network of capillaries surrounding the alveoli.

Hollow center of alveolus containing air.

### IN FOCUS

## How heart attacks happen

**Heart attacks can occur** when the arteries supplying oxygenated blood to the muscles of the heart become blocked or inflexible. When this blocking or hardening happens, the oxygen supply to parts of the heart is cut down and the deprived sections can eventually fail, leading to the pain and problems of a heart attack. The changes to the artery walls that cause this are called arteriosclerosis, or hardening of the arteries. The damaging changes are partly a loss of elasticity in the artery wall and partly a laying down of fatty deposits inside the artery, blocking blood flow much as lime scale narrows a water pipe. These problems tend to accumulate with age, but can be made worse by smoking and a diet high in animal fats. High levels of cholesterol in the blood can lead to this kind of arterial blockage.

Birds and mammals pump blood around their body using a four-chamber heart, consisting of two atria and two ventricles. Blood loaded with carbon dioxide and depleted of oxygen first enters the right atrium, which squeezes blood through a set of valves into the right ventricle. Contraction of the right ventricle then pushes blood through one-way valves into the pulmonary artery, which leads to the lungs. The pulmonary artery branches into thousands of tiny capillaries that wrap around the alveoli; exchange of carbon dioxide and oxygen takes place across the surfaces of the capillaries and alveoli. Oxygen-rich blood returns to the left atrium of the heart via the pulmonary veins. Blood is squeezed through valves into the most powerfully built chamber of the heart, the left ventricle. Contractions from this chamber force blood into the body's main artery, the aorta, from which other arteries stem.

## ▲ HEART AND LUNGS

*Air passes along the trachea and into the bronchi of the lungs. It then passes into smaller tubes called bronchioles until it reaches tiny air sacs called alveoli. There oxygen in the air diffuses across the walls of the alveoli into tiny blood vessels called capillaries. Red blood cells pick up the oxygen and carry it to the body's cells. Carbon dioxide takes the reverse path out of the body.*

# Digestive and excretory systems

**CONNECTIONS**

**COMPARE** the human cecum and appendix with the cecum of a herbivore such as a *HARE*.

**COMPARE** the intestines of an omnivorous human with the intestines of a herbivore such as a *GIRAFFE* and a carnivore such as a *LION*.

Vertebrate digestive systems generally can be divided into four main parts. These are the buccal cavity (inside the mouth) and the associated food pipe (the esophagus); the stomach; the small intestine; and the large intestine, which leads to the anus. As in other vertebrates, humans possess a liver that secretes digestive chemicals and processes the nutrients absorbed through the intestine wall, and a pair of kidneys to extract and excrete superfluous or toxic substances from the blood.

## Food's journey

Food is swallowed and forced down the esophagus by muscular contractions until it reaches the stomach. The stomach is an elastic, muscular bag that can stretch greatly after a large meal. In the stomach lining, or epithelium, there are many gastric pits lined with cells that secrete hydrochloric acid and protein-digesting enzymes. Goblet cells in the lining of the stomach produce copious mucus secretions, which protect the stomach wall from the strong acid.

Compared with the large multichambered stomachs of ruminants like cattle, the human stomach is simple, like that of most carnivores. Semi-digested food leaves the stomach in small portions and moves into the duodenum, the first 10 inches (25 cm) of the small intestine. There, further protein and carbohydrate digestion takes place, a process driven by a cocktail of enzymes secreted from glands in the epithelium of the duodenum and the pancreas. Bile salts produced in the liver and stored in the gallbladder are added to the mixture to break up fats into small droplets to aid fat digestion. Movement of food is driven by waves of muscular action called peristalsis.

## Maximum area

The rest of the small intestine consists of sections called the jejunum and the ileum. These regions are devoted to food absorption,

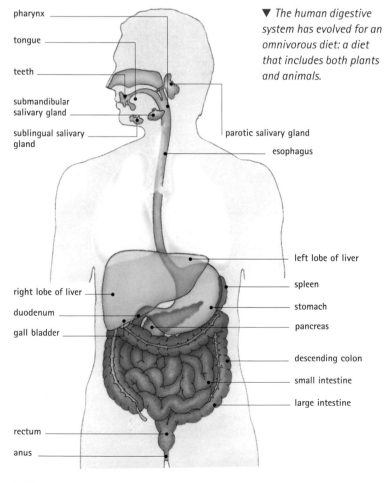

▼ *The human digestive system has evolved for an omnivorous diet: a diet that includes both plants and animals.*

pharynx

tongue

teeth

submandibular salivary gland

sublingual salivary gland

parotic salivary gland

esophagus

left lobe of liver

spleen

right lobe of liver

stomach

duodenum

pancreas

gall bladder

descending colon

small intestine

large intestine

rectum

anus

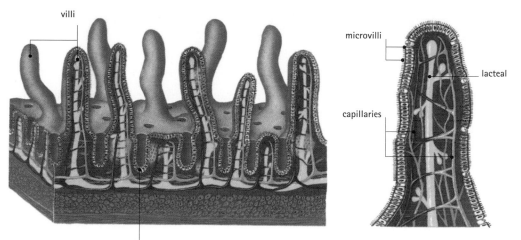

villi

crypt of Lieberkühn

microvilli

lacteal

capillaries

◄ **VILLI**

*In the duodenum, small projections called villi absorb the products of digestion. These projections dramatically increase the surface area of the intestine, allowing the rapid and efficient absorption of digested food. Small depressions between the villi, called crypts of Lieberkühn, secrete digestive juices.*

with no further enzyme secretion. Most meat eaters have relatively short small intestines, ranging from two to six times the body length. The human small intestine falls within this range. Herbivore small intestines are much longer; those of ungulates may be between 20 and 25 times longer than the body.

The surface area of the inside of the small intestine is very large; this area is important for maximizing the rate of absorption. The surface area is increased through folds called villi. These are covered by tiny fingerlike projections called microvilli. The average surface area of the small intestine of an adult human is around 3,350 square feet (310 m²).

### Into the large intestine

The small intestine opens into the cecum at the beginning of the large intestine. At only 5 to 6 feet (1.5–1.8 m) long, the large intestine is much shorter than the small intestine, but it is much thicker and bulkier. Some herbivorous animals such as horses and rabbits have an enlarged cecum where the bacterial fermentation of vegetation takes place. Humans have a small cecum, with an outgrowth called the appendix. This outgrowth serves no function in modern humans; it is a vestigial structure. Some bacterial fermentation does take place in the large intestine, especially after certain meals such as beans, resulting in gaseous emissions. In humans, the large intestine is primarily the site of water and vitamin absorption and a storage place for feces, the remaining undigested material, prior to release at the anus.

---

**COMPARATIVE ANATOMY**

### Teeth

**Adult humans have 32 teeth,** which include eight incisors, four canines, eight premolars, and 12 molars. The incisors have straight edges that are useful for nipping, and the molars and premolars are used for mashing food. Human teeth are not adapted for slicing meat like the carnassial teeth of carnivores, nor are they adapted for grinding a heavy fibrous vegetable diet, like the ridged molars of many ungulates. Gorillas are vegetarian and have the most powerfully built molars of the great apes. Gorillas and chimpanzees also have large canines, but these are adaptations for fighting and display rather than feeding.

◄ *Digestion begins in the mouth, where salivary amylase begins the process of breaking down starches to simple sugars.*

# Endocrine and exocrine systems

**CONNECTIONS**

**COMPARE** the mammary glands of a human with those of a monotreme mammal such as a *PLATYPUS* and a marsupial such as a *KANGAROO*.

Glands are tissues that secrete a variety of important substances, ranging from sweat to hormones. The glands of the exocrine system are connected to ducts that channel the secreted substance to a surface. These glands include the sweat and mammary glands, which secrete sweat and milk, respectively, to the surface of the skin; and the pancreas, liver, and glands in the wall of the gut, which secrete digestive enzymes and bile onto the inner surface of the digestive tract. Endocrine glands have no ducts; they secrete their products into the bloodstream. Endocrine glands produce chemical messengers, or hormones. Examples of endocrine glands include the ovaries, testes, adrenal glands, and pituitary gland.

## The exocrine system

Some exocrine glands such as the salivary glands, liver, and pancreas occur in all vertebrates, although they may take different forms. Humans have three pairs of salivary glands that secrete enzymes in a solution of mucus; the salivary glands lubricate food and begin the digestive process. Vertebrate liver tissue is organized into small lobes, consisting of strings of liver cells surrounding a central vein coming from the small intestine. Bile ducts surround each lobe to channel away bile and waste products excreted by the cells. All four-limbed vertebrates have a two-lobed pancreas.

## Uniquely mammalian

Some exocrine glands, such as the sweat and mammary glands, occur only in mammals. The sweat glands secrete liquids onto the surface of the skin. They help cool the animal; the sweat draws away heat as it evaporates. Not all mammals have sweat glands. Sweat glands are absent in some marine mammals, and in mammals such as dogs they are restricted to just a few places. That is why a hot dog pants; it loses body heat through its tongue.

▶ **FEMALE ENDOCRINE SYSTEM**

*The endocrine system consists of glands that secrete chemical messengers called hormones into the bloodstream. In contrast, exocrine glands secrete substances to a surface such as the surfaces of the stomach lining and the skin.*

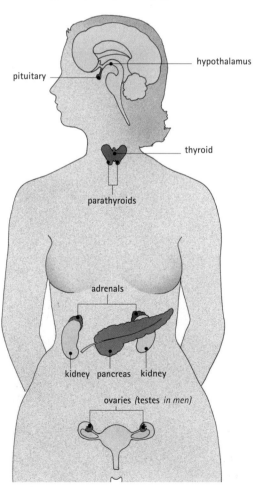

pituitary

hypothalamus

thyroid

parathyroids

adrenals

kidney  pancreas  kidney

ovaries (*testes in men*)

### IN FOCUS

## Fight or flight

**The adrenal glands,** situated above each kidney, are vital for the "fight or flight" response to danger in a human or another vertebrate. These orange glands contain a central area, the medulla, and a surrounding layer, called the cortex. When signals from the sympathetic nervous system reach the adrenal medulla two hormones are produced. These are epinephrine (adrenaline) and norepinephrine. These hormones stimulate a number of responses that assist immediate action, including increased heart rate, dilation of airways in the lungs to increase oxygen uptake, and restricted gut action so more energy can be focused on the muscles.

## Sugar levels

**The level of glucose,** a sugar, in the blood is kept under strict control and must be maintained within a very narrow range. Glucose is controlled by secretions from part of the pancreas called the islets of Langerhans, which produces the hormones insulin and glucagon. If there is too much sugar in the blood, the pancreas secretes insulin, which helps cells absorb the excess. If there is too little sugar, glucagon is released; this triggers the liver to release glucose from storage.

*Some people with diabetes control the disease with injections of insulin to regulate their blood sugar levels.*

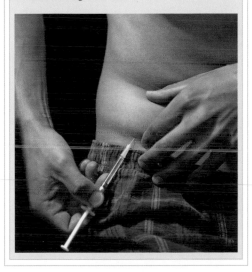

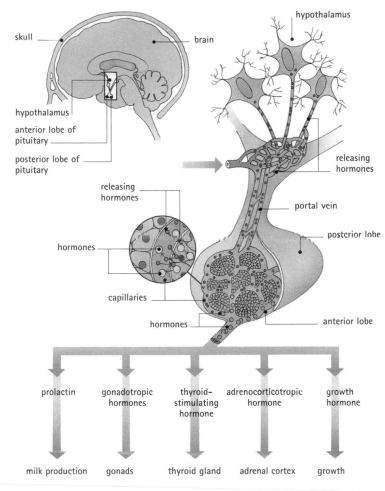

| prolactin | gonadotropic hormones | thyroid-stimulating hormone | adrenocorticotropic hormone | growth hormone |
| milk production | gonads | thyroid gland | adrenal cortex | growth |

Human females have two mammary glands that produce nourishing milk for newborn offspring. It is rare for a woman to give birth to more than two babies at once, so two mammary glands are generally sufficient. Mammals that produce larger numbers of young have many more mammary glands.

### The endocrine system

One of the most important endocrine glands is the pea-size pituitary gland located just under the hypothalamus of the brain. The pituitary controls the secretion of hormones by other endocrine glands. It has two distinct parts: the posterior pituitary, which derives from the hypothalamus; and the anterior pituitary, which is formed by tissues originating from the roof of the mouth. The posterior pituitary is connected to the hypothalamus by neurons and secretes two hormones: antidiuretic hormone (ADH), which regulates water balance; and oxytocin, which promotes muscular contractions in the mammary glands during lactation and in the uterus during childbirth.

The anterior pituitary produces more hormones. Most stimulate hormone secretion in other endocrine glands. For example, the anterior pituitary produces luteinizing hormone; this stimulates the testes to produce testosterone. Testosterone is a hormone that starts and maintains male characteristics such as body hair and large muscle size. In females, luteinizing hormone plays an important role in the menstrual cycle.

### ▲ HYPOTHALAMUS

*The hypothalamus secretes hormones that pass to the pituitary gland and cause the pituitary to release further hormones, which are secreted into the bloodstream. Most of the hormones released by the pituitary gland stimulate other glands to release still further hormones.*

# Reproductive system

CONNECTIONS

**COMPARE** human males' reproductive organs with those of a *HARE*, in which the position of the penis and testicles is reversed.

**COMPARE** the position of the human female's vagina with that of a female *ELEPHANT*. The elephant's vagina is positioned on the underside of the animal, nearer the stomach.

Men produce sperm in a pair of testes; a woman's eggs are produced in a pair of ovaries. When compared with many other mammals, humans have some unusual sexual strategies and structures that are a legacy of our species' evolutionary history.

### The male reproductive system

The body temperature of mammals is too warm for optimum sperm production, so the testes of men and most other mammals are held outside the body cavity in a sac called the scrotum. The temperature of the scrotum is usually around 7.2°F (4°C), cooler than inside the body. Muscles in the scrotum move the testes slightly in response to changing temperature. Inside each testis, sperm is stored in a coiled tube called the epididymis.

Male mammals and many other animals insert sperm into the female with an organ called the penis. Mammal penises develop around the urethra, the tube that transports urine from the bladder. The penis contains chambers filled with spongy material that become engorged with blood during sexual arousal. The blood-filled chambers provide the rigidity that allows copulation to take place.

### The female reproductive system

The ovaries are inside the body cavity of the female. Mammal oviducts (tubes that lead to the outside) form several discrete structures. The fallopian tubes lead from the ovaries to the uterus, where the fertilized egg develops into an embryo. The uterus connects through the cervix to the vagina, an elastic tube which receives the penis during copulation and through which young are born.

During ovulation, an egg is released from the ovary to the fallopian tube. The walls of the uterus thicken at this time. If the egg remains unfertilized, the uterus walls are shed in a process called menstruation.

### Copulation and fertilization

During copulation, the male releases up to 400 million sperm into the vagina. The sperm pass from the epididymis into tubes called the vasa

▶ MALE REPRODUCTIVE SYSTEM

*The male reproductive organs are able to produce sperm and deposit them in the female reproductive organs. Erectile tissue in the penis enables the penis to become stiff so that it may be inserted in the vagina. Sperm is made in the testes and stored in the epididymis.*

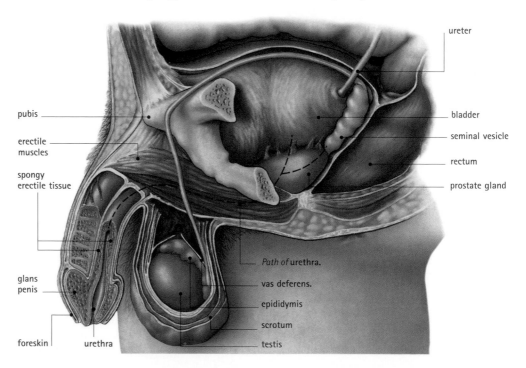

pubis

erectile muscles

spongy erectile tissue

glans penis

foreskin          urethra

ureter

bladder

seminal vesicle

rectum

prostate gland

*Path of* urethra.

vas deferens.

epididymis

scrotum

testis

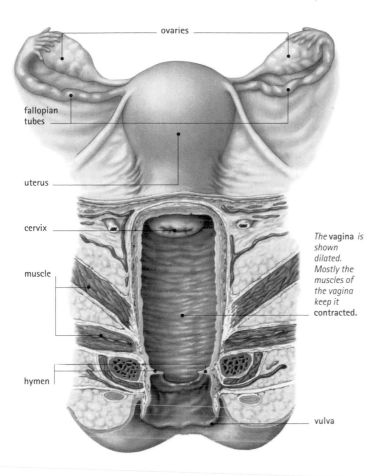

ovaries

fallopian
tubes

uterus

cervix

muscle

hymen

*The* vagina *is
shown
dilated.
Mostly the
muscles of
the vagina
keep it
contracted.*

vulva

▲ FEMALE
REPRODUCTIVE
SYSTEM

## The race for fertilization

Male mammals compete for females before copulation, and sperm also compete inside the female in the race for fertilization. This sperm competition can have a major effect on male reproductive anatomy. For example, the size of primate testes varies depending on the type of society that the animals live in. There is a neat correlation between testis size and levels of promiscuity, the number of sexual partners an animal has. Having many different partners implies more rivals' sperm for an individual male to compete with. Bigger testes produce more sperm with which to overwhelm the sperm of rivals. This is a vital advantage.

Promiscuity is almost unknown in gorillas, and they have correspondingly tiny testes. However, bonobo chimpanzees are extremely promiscuous. Female bonobos mate up to 1,000 times per fertilization; male bonobos have very large testes. Male humans' testes are an intermediate size.

These lines of evidence suggest that recent human ancestors lived in societies with moderate amounts of promiscuity. Humans remain, to an extent, promiscuous. Between 2 and 30 percent of all babies are the products of extra-pair paternity; they are fathered by a man from outside the parental couple.

## Development of the embryo

A fertilized egg moves from the fallopian tube to the uterus, carried by muscular contractions of the tube. Filaments called cilia on the inside of the tube also help transport the egg. The egg embeds into the thickened uterus wall, where it develops into an embryo. The embryo is nourished and provided with oxygen through an temporary organ called the placenta. This grows partly from the embryo and partly from the mother. Pregnancy ends after around nine months, when the baby is born through the vagina.

ADRIAN SEYMOUR

deferentia, which lead to the urethra. Glands, such as the prostate gland, secrete other components of the seminal fluid, or semen. These secretions carry the sperm and contain a sugar called fructose that nourishes them.

**FURTHER READING AND RESEARCH**
Baggaley, A., and J. Hamilton. 2001. *Human Body: An Illustrated Guide to Every Part of the Human Body and How It Works.* DK Publishing: NY.
Van der Graaf, K. 1997. *Schaum's Outline of Human Anatomy and Physiology.* McGraw-Hill: Columbus, OH.

### EVOLUTION

## Sexual dimorphism

**Like many mammals,** male and female humans are different shapes and sizes. This difference is called sexual dimorphism. Generally, men are larger and heavier; this may be an adaptation for fighting rivals. Females have wider hips that result from a differently shaped pelvis. Wider hips accommodate childbirth. Among the more striking sexually dimorphic traits are women's breasts. Female chimps and other primates suckle their young perfectly well without having breasts; if anything, breasts hinder the action of suckling by human babies. This suggests that human breasts evolved for display to males, perhaps as an indicator of health or to stimulate sexual activity.

# Kangaroo

ORDER: Diprotodontia  SUBORDER: Phalangerida
FAMILY: Macropodidae

Kangaroos are Earth's best-known marsupials and among the most easily recognized of all mammals. They are famous for their spectacular hopping gait and for rearing their young in a special pouch. They have become a symbol of their native country, Australia.

## Anatomy and taxonomy
Scientists group all organisms into taxonomic groups based largely on anatomical features. Kangaroos belong to a group of mammals called marsupials, which also includes wombats and possums.

● **Animals** Members of the animal kingdom are multicellular organisms. They are heterotrophic: they obtain energy and nutrition by eating other organisms. Animals are able to move about mostly by using their muscles, and they have a variety of senses through which they are able to respond rapidly to external stimuli.

● **Chordates** Chordates are animals in which the long axis of the body is supported by a stiff rod called the notochord at some stage in the life cycle.

● **Vertebrates** Vertebrates are animals with a bony or cartilagenous backbone consisting of several units called vertebrae. Vertebrate animals have bilateral (mirror) symmetry, a distinct head at the front, and muscles arranged in symmetrical pairs along the length of the body.

● **Mammals** All mammals are warm-blooded; most have fur. In mammals, the lower jaw hinges directly with the skull. Females feed their young on milk secreted by mammary glands. Mammalian red blood cells do not contain nuclei, unlike those of other vertebrate groups.

● **Marsupials** These mammals are an early offshoot within the mammalian family tree. Marsupial females give birth to underdeveloped young, and the offspring complete their development outside the womb, usually in a pouch on the female's abdomen. Marsupials have evolved an enormous diversity of forms, many of which parallel those of the more familiar placental mammals. They include the badgerlike wombat, catlike quolls, squirrel-like possums, and, of course, the kangaroos and their relatives. One of the most diverse orders of marsupials is the Diprotodontia. The name "diprotodont" refers to the characteristic of having only one pair of lower incisors. These animals are also syndactylous—that is, the second and third toes of the hind feet are always fused. Arboreal (tree-climbing) members of the group, such as possums and koalas, usually have an opposable big toe on the hind feet to grasp branches. Ground-dwelling species (kangaroos and wombats) do not have this toe.

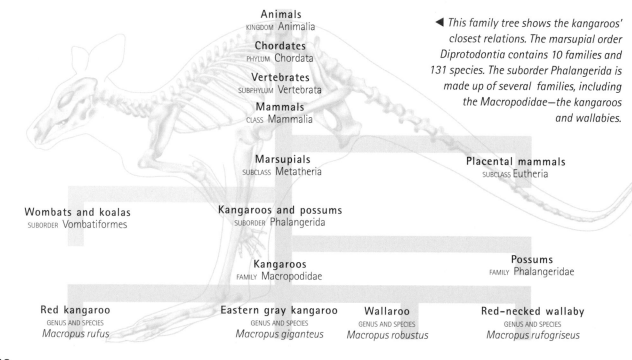

◀ This family tree shows the kangaroos' closest relations. The marsupial order Diprotodontia contains 10 families and 131 species. The suborder Phalangerida is made up of several families, including the Macropodidae—the kangaroos and wallabies.

**Animals**
KINGDOM Animalia

**Chordates**
PHYLUM Chordata

**Vertebrates**
SUBPHYLUM Vertebrata

**Mammals**
CLASS Mammalia

**Marsupials**
SUBCLASS Metatheria

**Placental mammals**
SUBCLASS Eutheria

**Wombats and koalas**
SUBORDER Vombatiformes

**Kangaroos and possums**
SUBORDER Phalangerida

**Kangaroos**
FAMILY Macropodidae

**Possums**
FAMILY Phalangeridae

**Red kangaroo**
GENUS AND SPECIES
*Macropus rufus*

**Eastern gray kangaroo**
GENUS AND SPECIES
*Macropus giganteus*

**Wallaroo**
GENUS AND SPECIES
*Macropus robustus*

**Red-necked wallaby**
GENUS AND SPECIES
*Macropus rufogriseus*

● **Phalangerida** This large group contains all the long-tailed members of the diprotodonts. It includes four groups of possums and the kangaroos.

● **Macropodoidea** The Macropodoidea superfamily unites the kangaroos and wallabies (Macropodidae) and their close cousins, the Potoroidae. These latter include the primitive rat-kangaroos, potoroos, and bettongs. The Potoroidae are all small, brown, jumping marsupials with a thin, ratlike tail, rather like a small rodent. Potoroids feed on fruits, nuts, insects, and other invertebrates.

● **Kangaroos and wallabies** The Macropodidae family is made up of 12 genera and 61 species of kangaroos and wallabies. They have long hind feet, in which the fourth and fifth toes bear the animals' weight. The fused third and second toes are smaller, and the first toe is absent. The hind legs are large, and the forelegs are small and armlike, each with five digits. Macropods live in both arid and temperate grasslands, and in rocky outcrops and tropical forest.

Among the Macropodidae, the rock wallabies (in the genus *Petrogale*) are the most agile of all the kangaroos, and they can travel fast over precarious boulder slopes and rocky outcrops. Several are very colorful, such as the yellow-footed rock wallaby, which has a banded tail and facial markings. Tree kangaroos (in the genus *Dendrolagus*) have returned to the arboreal lifestyle of their ancestors. Tree kangaroos' hind feet are shorter than those of ground-dwelling kangaroos and have soft, flexible pads that help them grip branches. The tail is long and furry, and acts as a counterbalance when the animal is climbing. The quokka is a secretive species of wallaby, little bigger than a hare. The quokka lives only in the extreme southwestern region of Western Australia.

● *Macropus* **kangaroos** There are four large and widespread species in the genus *Macropus*: red, eastern and western gray, and the wallaroo. The western gray kangaroo is generally

▲ *The red kangaroo is the largest of the kangaroo species. It has the hopping gait and marsupial pouch typical of all kangaroos.*

smaller and browner than its eastern cousin. The genus also includes several smaller species, called wallabies, two of which weigh only 7 pounds (3.5 kg) or less.

---

**FEATURED SYSTEMS**

**EXTERNAL ANATOMY** Kangaroos are medium to large mammals with massively developed hind legs and a long, muscular, tapering tail. *See pages 150–153.*

**SKELETAL SYSTEM** The skeleton has large bones in the hind feet and legs. The bones of the second and third hind toes are fused by skin. *See pages 154–155.*

**MUSCULAR SYSTEM** The muscular system of kangaroos is dominated by powerful hind leg muscles and long tendons. These allow kangaroos to hop at high speeds for long periods using very little energy. *See page 156.*

**NERVOUS SYSTEM** Kangaroos have acute senses of sight, smell, and hearing. *See page 157.*

**CIRCULATORY AND RESPIRATORY SYSTEMS** Although a kangaroo's heart is small, it is efficient. The peripheral circulation plays an important role in keeping the animal cool. *See page 158.*

**DIGESTIVE AND EXCRETORY SYSTEMS** The digestive system is highly efficient, with a large, chambered stomach and long intestines. *See pages 159–160.*

**REPRODUCTIVE SYSTEM** Female kangaroos have two wombs and two vaginas for mating. Young are born as embryos through a third, central vagina. Development is completed in a pouch, where the embryo attaches to a teat. *See pages 161–163.*

# External anatomy

**CONNECTIONS**

**COMPARE** a kangaroo's hare-lip with that of a **HARE**.

**COMPARE** the kangaroo's long neck and ears and sideways-facing eyes with those of a **RED DEER**. These animals have evolved similar forms for avoiding predation.

The kangaroos and large wallabies are unmistakable. Even someone who has never before seen one of these extraordinary Australian mammals would have no difficulty identifying the fleet, bounding form.

Australia has no native hoofed mammals, and kangaroos have evolved to fit similar types of environment as some nonmarsupial herbivores (plant-eating animals), such as cattle and deer, in other dry parts of the world. All these animals have a similar diet and digestive physiology. The evolution of both groups has also led to similar adaptations for avoiding predation. Both kangaroos and antelopes are tall and alert, with a long neck, large swiveling ears, and eyes located on the sides of the head that offer all-around vision. Kangaroos and antelopes both have long legs, and when alarmed take flight in leaps and bounds. Kangaroos that inhabit open grassland (such as

The **ears** are large and flexible. They are able to detect distant sounds—for example, the footsteps of an approaching predator.

In males the **fur** is russet to brick red on the back, and paler on the throat, belly, and limbs.

Large **eyes** provide good night vision.

▶ **Red kangaroo**
*The body shape of the kangaroo makes it one of the most recognizable of all mammals, with its upright (or hopping) stance, huge hind legs and tail, very short forelimbs, and large, pointed ears.*

The **nose** is very sensitive to odors. This sense is important for kangaroos, which are most active at night.

The **forelimbs** have five digits and are used to manipulate food and in slow locomotion.

The **hind limbs** are much larger than the forearms.

foot

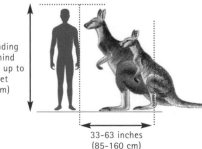

standing on hind legs up to 6 feet (1.8m)

33-63 inches (85-160 cm)

Wallaroo

Red kangaroo

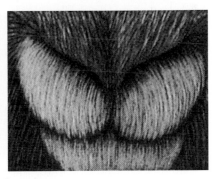

Gray kangaroo

## ▲ NOSES

*The nose area of these three species is very distinctive. The bare area of a wallaroo's snout is black and hairless. The gray kangaroo has the hairiest snout; and the red kangaroo's nose is intermediate.*

red kangaroos) live in groups that enhance their awareness of predators. Those species that live in forests, such as the forest wallabies, tend to be solitary.

In both wallabies and kangaroos, the neck is long and slender. The head is small, with large, erect ears and bulging eyes located on the side of the head. The muzzle is blunt and soft, with large nostrils and a harelip (divided upper lip). A small area at the tip of the nose of the red kangaroo is hairless, whereas that of the gray kangaroo is furry. In the wallaroo—a species superficially similar to the gray kangaroos—the snout is naked over a much larger area.

*The thick, muscular tail acts as a counterbalance when the kangaroo is bounding and as a stabilizer when the animal is feeding.*

*The hindquarters are large and strong.*

## ▼ FOOT, FROM BELOW
### Kangaroo

*The long, narrow shape of a kangaroo's foot helps give the animal stability when it stands upright and acts like a spring when it lands between bounds. The first digit is absent in the foot, and the small second and third digits are held together by skin. The fourth and fifth digits are strong.*

fourth digit

fifth digit

*There is a double claw at the end of the second and third digits.*

*▼ Male red kangaroos can be substantially larger than females. Their fur color is also very different: the male's fur is reddish brown and the female's is bluish gray.*

◀ *The kangaroo hop is a very efficient way of moving around. Red kangaroos can make bounds up to 30 feet (9 m) long or more and reach speeds of up to 30 miles per hour (50 km/h). The smaller gray kangaroo has been recorded jumping 44 feet (13.5 m).*

## IN FOCUS

### Time dwarfs

**Studies of the remains** of long-dead marsupials in Australia have revealed that the average size of bones and teeth in most large species has decreased quite dramatically over the last 40,000 years. This strange phenomenon is especially apparent in the large kangaroos, which now appear to be about 30 percent smaller than their ancestors. Why have they shrunk? Scientists believe the reason for this has a lot to do with humans, since the shrinkage began at around the time the first people arrived in Australia. Human hunters tend to target large individuals, so hunting may have exterminated the larger species but left the smaller kangaroos.

## Body and tail

A kangaroo's body is large, with a deep but narrow chest and pronounced collarbones. The rump tapers into an enormous tail, which is at least as long as the body. The body itself is covered in soft, slightly woolly fur, the color of which varies considerably within and between species. In the red kangaroo, most males (boomers) are reddish brown with a pale color on their underside, while females (blue fliers)

are a shade of bluish gray. Both the male and the female colors blend well with the arid scrub habitat, providing camouflage. The reddish fur of the males matches the color of the poor desert soils, and females can be very difficult to see among the blue-green foliage of shrubs such as saltbush.

## EVOLUTION

### Kangaroo ancestors

**The ancestors of all kangaroos and wallabies** were small, forest-dwelling marsupials that fed mostly on fruits, nuts, insects, and leaves, much as the smaller forest wallabies do today. As the grassland habitat opened up, grazing and browsing animals evolved, and some of them grew very large. An extinct species of the Pleistocene epoch (1.6 to 0.01 million years ago), *Procoptodon goliah,* was the largest species of kangaroo ever to have lived. It weighed up to 400 pounds (200 kg), had one well-developed toe on each hind foot, and had unusual front paws with two long and three short digits on each. The forearms were long, and the face was very short, with a deep, powerful-looking jaw.

▶ *This black-footed rock wallaby is a close cousin of the kangaroos. Although considerably smaller, it shares the same distinctive body shape. Its home is among rocky hills and cliffs, and it feeds mostly on grass, although sometimes on bark and roots.*

Male kangaroos are often considerably larger than females; a male red kangaroo can be up to four times larger than a female. Males continue to grow and change body shape throughout their life; old males may not get any taller, but the chest continues to broaden and the forearms become increasingly muscular. For a female, these features are probably indicators that a male has had a long life and would probably be a good choice of mate.

Female kangaroos have a large pouch on the lower part of their abdomen in which they carry their young. All pouched animals, or marsupials, are named for the scientific term for this pouch, the marsupium. The pouch of kangaroos opens toward the front, so there is little danger that the passenger will fall out as its mother stands upright or moves around. The opening of the pouch is very elastic. It closes to a narrow slit but stretches wide to allow older, larger joeys—or kangaroo infants—to clamber in and out.

## Kangaroo movement

Like humans, kangaroos are bipedal; they move on two legs. However, kangaroos do not walk (transfer their body weight from foot to foot) as we do, and they cannot move backward. Instead, they bounce on greatly enlarged hind legs. The genus name *Macropus* means "great-foot." The hind feet of the large kangaroo species are narrow, but up to 14 inches (36 cm) in length, with hairless soles covered in hard, calloused skin. The forelegs are small in comparison, especially those of females. The forepaws have five separate digits ("fingers"), each with a long, blunt claw.

Kangaroos are famous for bounding, but they also have another means of getting around. When moving slowly—for example, while grazing—they use a unique "five-legged" technique. In this method of movement, the tail acts as a fifth limb, supporting the back end of the animal while it leans on its forelegs. The hind legs are then swung forward together.

### Quokka climbers

**Kangaroos and wallabies** use their tail as a fifth leg when walking slowly. Their relative the quokka, however, uses only its legs. When moving quickly, the quokka hops in the same way as other kangaroos, but unlike most other macropodids it is also capable of climbing to 5 feet (1.5m) above ground to reach twigs.

## Careful chewing

**Kangaroos spend a very long time** chewing their food and turning it into a fine pulp before swallowing. Unlike cows, they do not regurgitate food to chew cud, so they get only one opportunity to reduce the plant fibers to an easily digested mush.

and converting it into sugars and other easily absorbed compounds. Like most herbivores, kangaroos have a very long intestine to allow plenty of time for full absorption of the products of digestion to take place.

Red kangaroos that have the chance to feed on lush, green grass do less well than those that eat dry, shriveled grass. Because of the large amount of water in fresh grass, weight for weight it contains less energy than dry grass and takes up more stomach space. A kangaroo that eats its fill of dry grass will benefit more than one that fills up on the fresh version.

Kangaroos living in arid habitats can go for weeks without drinking. Instead, they lick dew that forms on leaves or rocks and use all the available moisture in their food. They conserve water by producing concentrated urine, and they avoid the need to sweat by feeding at dawn and dusk and resting in the shade during the heat of the day.

humans, it is multichambered or "sacculated." Food passes slowly though the different stomach compartments, which are separated by bands of muscles that pucker the lining at intervals. The elongated middle section of the stomach acts as a fermentation chamber, where symbiotic cellulose-digesting bacteria get to work breaking down the tough plant material

▶ *Unlike ground-dwelling kangaroos, which live on grass, tree-dwelling kangaroos include plenty of leaves and fruit in their diet.*

# Reproductive system

The reproductive system of kangaroos and other marsupials is substantially different from that of placental mammals. Female kangaroos have not only two ovaries (as do placental mammals), but also two wombs—whereas in a placental mammal there is just one womb (uterus). The kangaroo also has two long, curved vaginas through which the male's sperm passes on its way to fertilize the eggs. As in all male marsupials, the male kangaroo's scrotum is positioned in front of the penis. When the female is ready to give birth, a third opening develops between the two side vaginas. This birth canal is similar to the single vagina of placental mammals and opens adjacent to the digestive tract in the cloaca. In most marsupials it seals over again after each litter is born, but in kangaroos it becomes a permanent structure after the first birth.

As with all marsupials, young kangaroos are born in an embryonic state. While in the womb, the embryo is surrounded by a thin membrane secreted by the uterus lining, in a manner similar to the eggshell in a reptile. Inside the membrane, the embryo is nourished by its own yolk. The beginnings of a placenta start to form as the yolk runs out, but this never develops fully, because the baby is born soon after, still at the embryo stage. The membrane and fluids in which the embryo develops are born with it and are usually eaten by the mother.

Unlike placental mammals, baby kangaroos complete most of their development outside the womb and do not benefit from a placental link with the mother. Instead, they attach to a teat within an hour or so of being born. The teat provides them with nourishing milk from a mammary gland. Once the baby has latched on, the teat swells inside its mouth so that it does not have to exert any energy to hold on. It will remain attached to the teat for weeks.

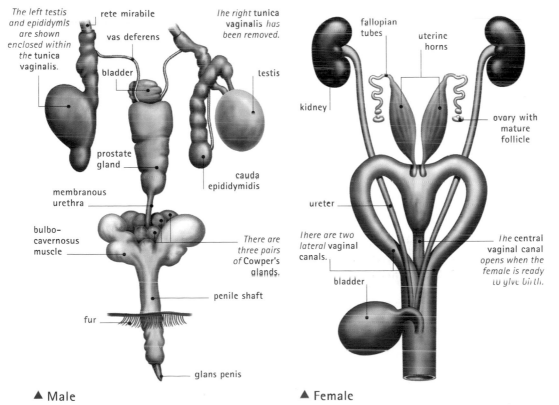

The left testis and epididymis are shown enclosed within the tunica vaginalis.

rete mirabile

The right tunica vaginalis has been removed.

vas deferens

bladder

testis

prostate gland

membranous urethra

cauda epididymidis

bulbo-cavernosus muscle

There are three pairs of Cowper's glands.

penile shaft

fur

glans penis

▲ Male

fallopian tubes

uterine horns

kidney

ovary with mature follicle

ureter

There are two lateral vaginal canals.

The central vaginal canal opens when the female is ready to give birth.

bladder

▲ Female

◄ REPRODUCTIVE ORGANS

*Female kangaroos are not unusual among mammals in having two ovaries. However, uniquely, kangaroos also have two uterine horns, or wombs, and two vaginas for mating.*

involuntary reflex helps a falling lion to right itself. In an automatic twisting reaction, the head rotates; then the spine and hindquarters align. At the same time, the lion arches its back to reduce the force of the impact when all four feet touch the ground.

### Territorial animals

Scientists believe that (unlike other carnivores) lions and other big cats rely less on their sense of smell, or olfaction, to locate prey. However, smell seems to be important when big cats communicate with other members of their own species.

Lions of both sexes mark the boundaries of their pride territories with scent, using urine, feces, and scented secretions from glands between their toes. The urine of females in estrus also contains a distinctively scented chemical called a pheromone. Male lions can identify this using an organ in the roof of the mouth called the vomeronasal or Jacobson's organ. When a male detects the scent he pulls his upper lip back with his teeth bared in a grimace called the Flehmen response. The response helps the sensory cells of the vomeronasal organ analyze the pheromone and assess the female's breeding condition.

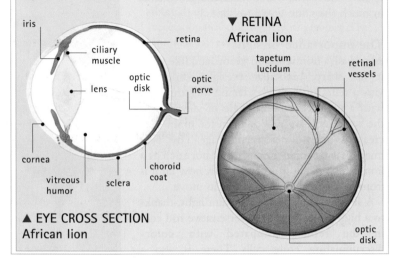

## CLOSE-UP

# Retina cells

**The mirrorlike membrane at the back of a lion's eyes** is called the tapetum lucidum. It is formed from specialized platelike cells that intercept any light that passes between the cells of the retina and reflect it back to the highly sensitive rod cells. The eyes of many night hunters have this type of structure, but it is particularly well developed in lions and other cats, which have as many as 15 layers of reflective cells. They reflect up to 90 percent of the light that enters the eye, causing the "eyeshine" of a cat illuminated by flashlight.

▼ RETINA
African lion

▲ EYE CROSS SECTION
African lion

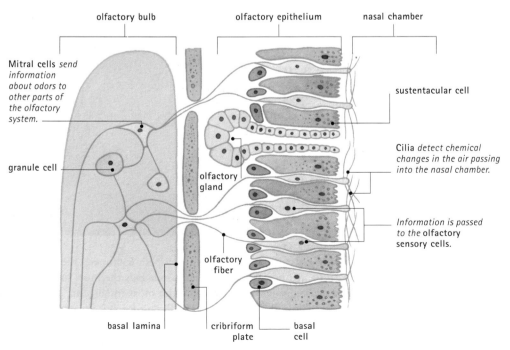

▶ OLFACTORY SYSTEM
Mammal

*Lions and other mammals detect odors with their olfactory system. Cilia extend into the nasal chamber from each olfactory sensory cell. The cilia detect chemical changes in the air that the animal breathes. Nerve fibers extend from each olfactory cell to mitral cells. Fibers of the mitral cells together make up the olfactory tract, which goes to the brain.*

Mitral cells *send information about odors to other parts of the olfactory system.*

granule cell

olfactory gland

olfactory fiber

olfactory bulb

olfactory epithelium

nasal chamber

sustentacular cell

Cilia *detect chemical changes in the air passing into the nasal chamber.*

*Information is passed to the* olfactory sensory cells.

basal lamina

cribriform plate

basal cell

# Circulatory and respiratory systems

Hunting large prey is strenuous work. When a lion pursues and struggles with its prey, its muscles are using a lot of energy. Ultimately this energy is derived from both its food and the air that it breathes.

Digested food is absorbed into the blood, where some of its ingredients are turned into a simple sugar called glucose. The bloodstream delivers this blood sugar to the lion's muscles and other organs, along with oxygen taken up via its lungs.

When it reaches the cells of the muscles and organs, the sugar is mixed with the oxygen to trigger a chemical reaction called oxidation. It is virtually the same as burning, and like burning it produces energy. The energy powers the muscles, and the oxidized sugar is turned into carbon dioxide and water. The whole process is known as aerobic respiration.

## Vital oxygen

If the lion is able to catch food, it usually has a good supply of blood sugar. Getting enough oxygen to oxidize the sugar is more difficult, so the lion has a very deep chest containing large lungs. Each lung is essentially a mass of small bubble-like sacs called alveoli, which are linked to a network of air tubes or bronchioles. These branch from larger tubes called bronchi, which are connected to the lion's windpipe, or trachea.

When the lion breathes in, it contracts the muscular diaphragm at the bottom of its rib cage. This makes its sealed lung cavity bigger, and expands its lungs so that they draw in air. The air passes into the alveoli, where oxygen passes through their thin walls and into a surrounding network of fine blood capillaries. At the same time, waste carbon dioxide and

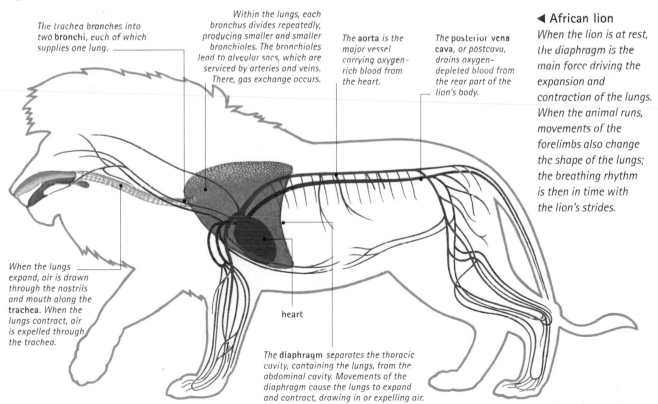

The trachea branches into two **bronchi**, each of which supplies one lung.

Within the lungs, each bronchus divides repeatedly, producing smaller and smaller bronchioles. The bronchioles lead to alveolar sacs, which are serviced by arteries and veins. There, gas exchange occurs.

The **aorta** is the major vessel carrying oxygen-rich blood from the heart.

The posterior **vena cava**, or postcava, drains oxygen-depleted blood from the rear part of the lion's body.

When the lungs expand, air is drawn through the nostrils and mouth along the **trachea**. When the lungs contract, air is expelled through the trachea.

heart

The **diaphragm** separates the thoracic cavity, containing the lungs, from the abdominal cavity. Movements of the diaphragm cause the lungs to expand and contract, drawing in or expelling air.

◄ **African lion**
*When the lion is at rest, the diaphragm is the main force driving the expansion and contraction of the lungs. When the animal runs, movements of the forelimbs also change the shape of the lungs; the breathing rhythm is then in time with the lion's strides.*

▶ *This male lion has just attacked and killed a zebra. When a lion mounts an explosive attack, it cannot deliver enough oxygen to its muscles. The lion then relies heavily on a process called anaerobic respiration.*

### Heavy breathers

**When a lion catches its prey**, it has to seize the prey with its teeth while breathing heavily through its nose to gather vital oxygen. Doing both at once is not easy, but the problem is far worse for the cheetah. At the end of its record-breaking sprint a cheetah needs much more oxygen to clear the buildup of lactic acid in its muscles. To make this possible, its nasal passages are proportionately larger than those of a lion. This leaves less room for the roots of its upper canine teeth, so its canines are proportionately shorter, limiting the size of prey that it can kill.

water pass out of the blood and into the air in the alveoli. When the lion relaxes its diaphragm, its lungs contract again, forcing the waste air out of its trachea.

### Clogging the system

The lion's blood is pumped through its lungs by the right-hand side of its heart. Newly oxygenated blood from the lungs returns to the left-hand side of the heart, which then pumps it to the muscles and other tissues. These use the oxygen and replace it with carbon dioxide and water. The blood then returns to the right-hand side of the heart, which pumps it back to the lungs for more oxygen. When a lion is working hard, its heart

pumps rapidly and it breathes very deeply. Yet it still cannot gather and deliver enough oxygen to its muscles. So when a lion mounts explosive attacks, it relies heavily on another process, called anaerobic respiration. This process releases energy without any immediate need for oxygen, by converting a sugary substance called glycogen into lactic acid. The lion can do this for only a short while, however; and if it sprints for more than about 1,000 feet (300 m), the lactic acid clogs its system and it must stop. The acid must then be cleared by using a lot of oxygen to change it to carbon dioxide, forcing the exhausted animal to breathe very heavily to recover.

### Lion's blood

**Mammalian blood** is colored by red blood cells, which contain a red pigment called hemoglobin. Hemoglobin has a strong affinity for oxygen and allows blood to carry far more oxygen than it would otherwise. Each hemoglobin molecule binds to four oxygen molecules to form oxyhemoglobin. When blood is delivered to oxygen-depleted tissues, the oxyhemoglobin breaks up to release oxygen.

# Digestive and excretory systems

Like all cats, lions are adapted for eating meat and nothing else. Most mammal carnivores—including bears, raccoons, dogs, and even weasels—eat vegetable foods regularly or occasionally and are equipped to chew and digest them. A lion may eat a little fruit to obtain water, but otherwise eats only flesh.

A lion has no chewing molar teeth, and its lower jaw can move only up and down, not from side to side in a chewing action. A lion can crush bones, although not with the same efficiency as a dog or hyena. A lion's lack of chewing ability is partly offset by sharp spikelets on its tongue that can shred meat and rasp it from the bone, but it swallows most of its food in big chunks sheared from the carcass by its scissorlike carnassial teeth.

A lion may also swallow a lot of meat very quickly because, like most hunters, it never knows when it will get its next meal. An adult male can eat up to 95 pounds (43 kg) at a sitting.

Meat is relatively easy to digest, so lions—and other cats—do not need a complex digestive system. A lion's stomach can hold a large amount of meat, but the animal's intestine is relatively short. Lions spend most of their time resting between infrequent hunting forays, and during these inactive periods the meat that they have eaten passes through the intestine, where it is digested.

## Digestive enzymes

Enzymes in the digestive juices break the bonds that bind complex protein molecules together, reducing them to the simpler molecules of amino acids. Since amino acids are the building blocks of all proteins, the lion's cells can use them to make the proteins that its body tissues need. The amino acids are absorbed through the wall of the intestine into the bloodstream, along with some proteins and the digestion products of fats and glycogen.

COMPARE the simple digestive system of the lion with the complex, multistage digestive system of a *GIRAFFE* or *WILDEBEEST*. Both these animals are ruminants that eat leaves or grass, which are much more difficult to digest than meat.

▼ African lion

*A lion's short intestine, which does not have to digest tough plant cell walls, is typical of that of carnivores. A lion may have to go a long time between meals, so its stomach is capable of holding a large amount of food.*

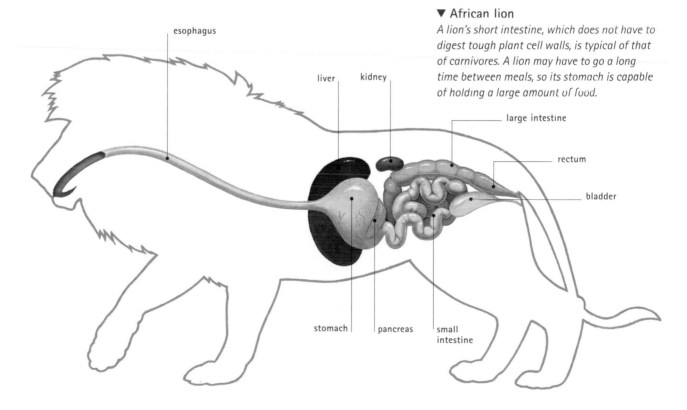

esophagus

liver  kidney

large intestine

rectum

bladder

stomach  pancreas  small intestine

179

female around, and if he is persistent enough the female will lie down on her belly and allow him to mate with her. Since all the females in a pride are often in heat at once, each typically mates with just one pride male that guards her while mating every 20 minutes or so.

The male's penis is covered with tiny backward-facing spines that probably make his withdrawal painful for the female, and after dismounting he leaps aside quickly to avoid her teeth and bared claws. The function of the spines is uncertain, but during early matings they may stimulate the female's ovaries into releasing eggs, which are then fertilized by the male's sperm after one of the later matings.

Once a single sperm has penetrated an egg, the fertilized egg becomes implanted into the thick wall of the female's uterus, or womb, and

▼ *This pair of African lions are mating. If the female (below) is fertilized, she will undergo a gestation period of just under four months before giving birth. Litters usually contain two, three, or four cubs.*

**GENETICS**

## Infanticide

**Since pride males are usually related** to each other, they are also related to most of the cubs born within the pride. This makes them attentive uncles as well as fathers. When other males take over a pride, however, they know that any cubs already born are not related to them, and do not share any of their genes. Their aim is to change this as soon as possible, so they kill any young cubs they find. This has the effect of making their mothers come into estrus much earlier than usual, so the males get to mate sooner and father cubs that carry their own genes.

## EVOLUTION

### Spotty cubs

**When lion cubs are born** their coat is spotted with dark brown rather than plain tawny yellow. The spots usually fade at the age of three months or so, but some lions stay faintly spotted throughout their life. The spots may help conceal the helpless cubs from marauding hyenas and eagles, but the plain adults seem equally well camouflaged on the dry, dusty savanna. Some zoologists believe that the spots survive from a distant time when lions of all ages were spotted like leopards; future evolution may discard the spots completely.

▼ *This lion cub is only a few weeks old. Very young lions have dark-spotted fur, but the spots usually fade long before maturity.*

starts to develop into an embryo. Each of two to four unborn young are connected to the mother by an umbilical cord. The cord is attached to a placenta, a temporary organ that allows nutrients to pass from mother to young.

### Helpless cubs

The cubs are born after a short pregnancy of just 110 days. They are very small at birth, having only 1 percent of their adult weight, and they are born blind, deaf, and virtually helpless. The mother feeds them milk from her four nipples, and pride females that produce cubs at the same time may suckle each other's cubs. By 10 days old the cubs are fully active, and at 2 to 3 months they are following their mother to kills to eat meat. Despite this, they are not fully weaned until they are 5 or 6 months old. Young females generally stay and breed within their parents' pride, but sometimes groups of sisters leave to establish a new pride, either with or without accompanying males. Young males always leave the pride when they reach sexual maturity at around three years old. Brother lions often team up with unrelated males to form "bachelor gangs," and if they are lucky they will take over a pride and have an opportunity to father their own cubs.

JOHN WOODWARD

**FURTHER READING AND RESEARCH**

Kitchener, A. 1991. *The Natural History of the Wild Cats*. Natural History of Mammals Series. Cornell University Press: Ithaca, NY.

Macdonald, David. 2006. *The Encyclopedia of Mammals*. Facts On File: New York.

Sunquist, M., and F. Sunquist. 2002. *Wild Cats of the World*. University of Chicago Press: Chicago.

# Manatee

ORDER: Sirenia  FAMILY: Trichechidae
GENUS: *Trichechus*

The three species of manatees live in separate geographical locations. The West Indian manatee inhabits the warm coastal waters and rivers of the southeastern United States, Central America, and the islands of the Caribbean; the Amazonian manatee lives in northern South America; and the West African manatee is found in western Africa. These large, sluggish, aquatic mammals are vegetarian and feed variously on water plants in freshwater, brackish (slightly salty) water, or salt water.

## Anatomy and taxonomy

Scientists categorize all organisms into taxonomic groups based partly on anatomy. The three species of manatees, together with the dugong, are sirenians—that is, members of the order Sirenia. A fifth sirenian, Steller's sea cow, became extinct in the 1760s as a result of intensive hunting.

● **Animals** Manatees, like other animals, gain their food by eating other life-forms. Animals differ from other multicellular organisms in their ability to move from one place to another (in most cases, using muscles). They generally react rapidly to touch, light, and other stimuli.

● **Chordates** At some time in its life cycle a chordate has a stiff, dorsal (along the back) supporting rod called the notochord that runs all or most of the length of the body.

● **Vertebrates** In vertebrates, the notochord develops into a backbone (the spine or vertebral column) made up of separate units called vertebrae. The vertebrate muscular system moves the head, trunk, and limbs. It consists primarily of muscles arranged in mirror-image symmetry on either side of the backbone.

● **Mammals** Mammals are warm-blooded vertebrates that have hair made of keratin. Females have mammary glands that produce milk to feed their young. In mammals, the lower jaw is a single bone (the dentary) hinged directly to the skull—a different arrangement from that found in other vertebrates. A mammal's inner ear contains three small bones (ear ossicles), two of which are derived from the jaw mechanism in mammalian ancestors. Mammalian red blood cells, when mature, lack a nucleus; all other vertebrates have red blood cells that contain nuclei.

● **Placental mammals** These mammals nourish their unborn young through a placenta, a temporary organ that forms in the mother's uterus (womb) during pregnancy.

● **Sirenians** Members of this group of mammals are well fitted for life in water, where they spend their entire life. Sirenians, also called sea cows (because of their docile nature and grazing habit), look superficially like a cross

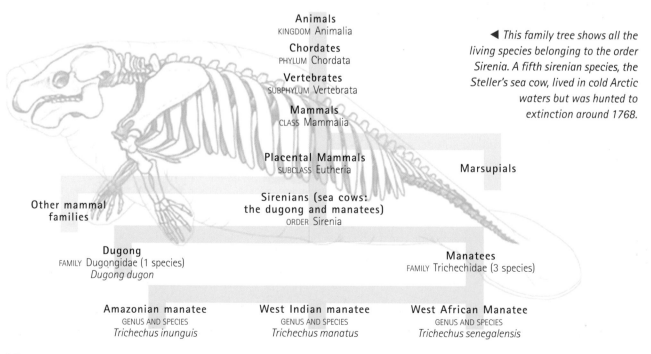

**Animals**
KINGDOM Animalia

**Chordates**
PHYLUM Chordata

**Vertebrates**
SUBPHYLUM Vertebrata

**Mammals**
CLASS Mammalia

**Placental Mammals**
SUBCLASS Eutheria

**Marsupials**

Other mammal families

**Sirenians (sea cows: the dugong and manatees)**
ORDER Sirenia

◀ *This family tree shows all the living species belonging to the order Sirenia. A fifth sirenian species, the Steller's sea cow, lived in cold Arctic waters but was hunted to extinction around 1768.*

**Dugong**
FAMILY Dugongidae (1 species)
*Dugong dugon*

**Manatees**
FAMILY Trichechidae (3 species)

**Amazonian manatee**
GENUS AND SPECIES
*Trichechus inunguis*

**West Indian manatee**
GENUS AND SPECIES
*Trichechus manatus*

**West African Manatee**
GENUS AND SPECIES
*Trichechus senegalensis*

between a walrus and a small whale, but they are not closely related to either. The name sirenian comes from the myth of sirens, or mermaids, because early sailors mistook these animals for creatures that were half woman, half fish.

Sirenians are slow-swimming and bulky, with a streamlined body shape that reduces drag as the animal swims. Sirenians have a paddlelike tail; flippers that are modified forelimbs with no visible digits (toes or fingers); no hind limbs; and no dorsal fin. Sirenians give birth underwater. They are the only mammals that have evolved to graze plants in coastal waters, and their dentition (teeth) evolved for this purpose.

● **Dugong** Dugongs, unlike manatees, live only in salt water. They are largely restricted to water warmer than 64°F (18°C). The sea grasses on which dugongs feed grow in shallow water, and dugongs rarely dive deeper than 65 feet (20 m). A dugong's tail is broad with a straight or slightly concave trailing edge. The snout hangs down to form a flexible, bristle-covered muzzle. Adult males have incisor teeth that point forward as very short tusks.

● **Manatees** West Indian and West African manatees range between salt water and freshwater, but the Amazonian manatee spends its entire life in freshwater. Some scientists recognize two subspecies of the West Indian manatee: the northerly Florida manatee and the southerly Antillean manatee. The subspecies have distinct geographic distributions and are distinguished largely on the basis of subtle features of the skull and biochemical differences. Manatees have a paddlelike tail, similar in shape to that of beavers. The manatee's muzzle is less downturned than that of dugongs, and manatees have many more teeth. Manatees' teeth form at the back of the mouth and move forward to replace worn teeth at the front.

▲ The West Indian manatee is the largest of the three living manatee species. It lives in the warm coastal waters of Central America, the southeastern United States, and the Caribbean.

**EXTERNAL ANATOMY** Manatees are sirenians (sea cows) with a relatively streamlined body, paddlelike flippers, and a horizontally flattened tail. *See pages 186–188.*

**SKELETAL SYSTEM** To provide ballast, the bones are particularly heavy, with the spine acting as an anchor for muscles that raise the tail up and down. *See pages 189–191.*

**MUSCULAR SYSTEM** A large sheet of muscle extending from head to tail along both sides of the body protects the contents of the chest and abdominal cavities and provides the power stroke in swimming. *See page 192.*

**NERVOUS SYSTEM** The sirenian brain is unusually small and simple in structure, compared with brains of other marine mammals. In manatees, touch, taste, and hearing are more important than vision and smell. *See pages 193–194.*

**CIRCULATORY AND RESPIRATORY SYSTEMS** Sirenians do not need high energy levels, so their circulatory and respiratory systems are relatively simple. Manatees have unusually elongated lungs. The lungs, together with a very large diaphragm, enable the animal to make fine adjustments to its buoyancy in the water. *See pages 195–196.*

**DIGESTIVE AND EXCRETORY SYSTEMS** Sirenians digest plant material using bacteria in their intestines, as elephants and horses do, rather than in their stomachs, as in cows and sheep. *See pages 197–198.*

**REPRODUCTIVE SYSTEM** The female's mammary glands are located under the flippers, and the male's sex organs are internal. These features aid streamlining. *See pages 199–201.*

# External anatomy

**COMPARE** the mammary glands of a female manatee with the similar arrangement of an *ELEPHANT*. Both animal's mammary glands are just inside the forelimbs.

**COMPARE** the flapless ears of a manatee with the ears of an *OTTER*, which have flaps.

Manatees and dugongs have a basically fusiform (torpedo-shape) body with a head that merges with the trunk and no visible neck. The body shape helps the animals move through the water with minimal drag but is less streamlined than that of a shark or dolpin. Sirenians rarely need to swim fast because they graze on plants rather than hunt fish and tend to rely on their bulk or their numbers to avoid attacks by predators. In addition, many large predators, such as sharks and toothed whales, do not hunt in the shallow waters where sirenians usually graze.

Adult West Indian and West African manatees can grow up to 15 feet (4.6 m) long and weigh 2,500 pounds (1,136 kg). The dugong is slightly smaller, up to about 13 feet (4 m) and 2,000 pounds (900 kg), and the Amazonian manatee smaller still, at 10 feet (3 m) and 1,100 pounds (500 kg). Steller's sea cow was a massive sirenian that grew to 25 feet (7.5 m) long and weighed up to 6.5 tons (5.9 metric tons). It became extinct around 1768.

## Accomplished swimmer

Manatees and dugongs swim using up-and-down movements of their flattened tail to drive them forward, in a manner similar to whales. Sirenians steer by flexing the body and tail and adjusting the angle of their forelimbs, which are flattened into paddlelike flippers. The flippers move at the elbow, with the upper

The **eye** *is small in relation to the size of the head.*

The **ear canal** *opens just behind the eye. There is no earflap.*

The skin has a sparse covering of pale **hairs.**

The manatee's **skin** *is rough and is often scarred from contact with ships' propellers. Naturally gray or brown, the skin may look greenish if it has extensive algal growth.*

The two **nostrils** *can be closed by valves when the manatee dives.*

► **West Indian manatee**
*This is the largest living species of sirenian. Its streamlined shape enables it to swim through water with ease.*

*There are whiskers on the upper lip of the* **snout,** *which is deeply cleft.*

12–15 feet
(3.5–4.5 m)

*The relatively short* **flippers** *are used to push food into the mouth. In the West Indian and West African manatee each flipper has four nails, which are absent in the Amazonian manatee.*

nails

*Sirenians have no hind limbs.*

arm enclosed in the animal's flank. The flippers serve a number of other uses. Manatees use their flippers to "walk" in shallow water along a seabed or riverbed. They also scratch themselves with their flippers, embrace other individuals, and direct food into the mouth. The flippers of West Indian and West African manatees have rudimentary nails at the tips of the concealed second, third, and fourth digits ("fingers"); the Amazonian manatee and the dugong do not have this feature. The flippers of dugongs are less flexible than those of manatees. As in whales, there are no hind limbs.

Manatee skin is wrinkled and tough, and it is up to 2 inches (5 cm) thick. Over most of the body it is only very sparsely haired. Around the lips are touch-sensitive, bristly hairs (vibrissae), which probably help the manatee to navigate in murky water and investigate the texture of

its food quickly. Skin color ranges from slate gray to brown, often with an overgrowth of patches of green algae. Dugong skin is also gray or gray-brown, but it is less wrinkled than the manatee's and has shorter, more rigid hairs.

The sirenian head ends in a blunt muzzle with the pendulous upper lip hanging down over the mouth. The nostrils, located on the upper side of the muzzle, have valves that close when the animal dives.

Sirenian eyes are relatively small and lack well-defined eyelids, but they have a third, inner eyelid, called a nictitating membrane. This, along with heavy secretions of tears, cleans and protects the surface of the eyes. Sirenians see well underwater, but they rarely (if ever) use their eyes above the water. There are no external earflaps, and the ear canal opens onto the skin surface behind the eye.

▼ TAILS
**Sirenians**
*Sirenians move their tail up and down to swim. Manatee tails are large, broad, and paddle-shaped. Dugongs have a characteristic fluke-shape tail, like that of a whale.*

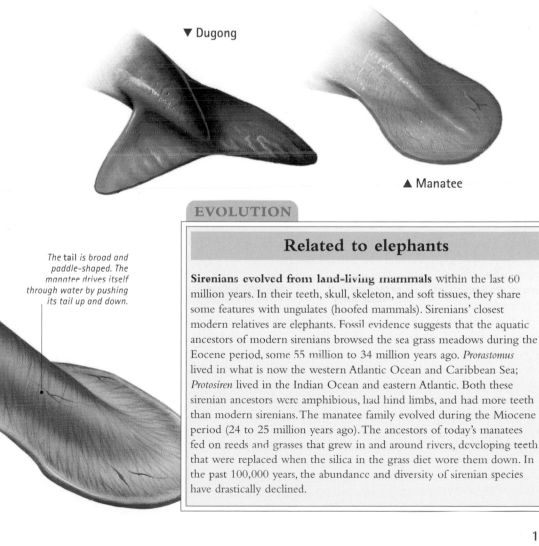

▼ Dugong

▲ Manatee

*The **tail** is broad and paddle-shaped. The manatee drives itself through water by pushing its tail up and down.*

## EVOLUTION

### Related to elephants

**Sirenians evolved from land-living mammals** within the last 60 million years. In their teeth, skull, skeleton, and soft tissues, they share some features with ungulates (hoofed mammals). Sirenians' closest modern relatives are elephants. Fossil evidence suggests that the aquatic ancestors of modern sirenians browsed the sea grass meadows during the Eocene period, some 55 million to 34 million years ago. *Prorastomus* lived in what is now the western Atlantic Ocean and Caribbean Sea; *Protosiren* lived in the Indian Ocean and eastern Atlantic. Both these sirenian ancestors were amphibious, had hind limbs, and had more teeth than modern sirenians. The manatee family evolved during the Miocene period (24 to 25 million years ago). The ancestors of today's manatees fed on reeds and grasses that grew in and around rivers, developing teeth that were replaced when the silica in the grass diet wore them down. In the past 100,000 years, the abundance and diversity of sirenian species have drastically declined.

▲ *Manatees (this is a West Indian manatee) and whales are only distantly related vertebrates, but in their use of forelimbs as flippers or fins, the loss of hind limbs, and the use of the tail as a paddle that moves up and down, they show convergent evolution. Manatees and whales have evolved similar anatomical solutions to the demands of moving in the same environment—water.*

Females have a pair of mammary glands, each with a nipple, in the "armpit" under the flipper. (Elephants' mammary glands are in a similar location, just inside the forelimb.) In males, the testes (sperm-producing organs) are contained within the abdomen, allowing greater streamlining—a feature found in other marine mammals, such as whales and seals.

In marine mammals, the fatty layer of blubber that lies beneath the skin is the main form of insulation that reduces loss of body heat into cold water. In living sirenians the blubber is relatively thin, compared with that of seals and whales of equivalent size. This, combined with their slow rate of metabolism and low heat output compared with more active marine mammals, probably restricts sirenians to warmer waters. Many sirenians live all year in tropical or subtropical waters. In temperate (mid-temperature) seas and rivers, sirenians migrate to warmer latitudes when water and air temperatures drop in the autumn.

## COMPARATIVE ANATOMY

### Snout and mouth

**The profile of the snout** and the position of the mouth in sirenian species vary according to their diet. The Amazonian and West African manatees eat mostly floating water plants, because the waters in which they feed are usually too murky for plants to grow beneath the surface. The snouts of these manatees do not slope down as markedly as those of other sirenian species. The dugong, whose diet consists largely of sea grasses that grow rooted in the seabed, has an underslung mouth. The West Indian manatee, with its varied diet of plants from the surface, middle, and bottom of the water, has a snout and mouth position between that of the dugong and the other manatees.

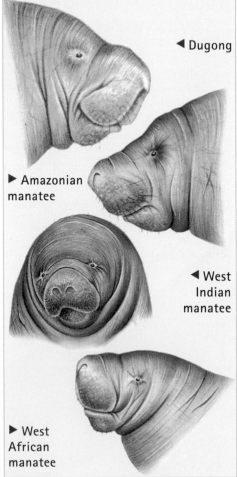

◀ Dugong

▶ Amazonian manatee

◀ West Indian manatee

▶ West African manatee

# Skeletal system

In all species of vertebrates, the skeleton has several functions: it shapes and supports the animal's body; protects vital internal organs; and allows movement of body parts, thus enabling the animal to move around.

The skeleton of a sirenian is similar to that of a whale, but with some differences. Like whales, sirenians spend their entire life in water, which provides plentiful support, so they do not need strong limbs to support their body. Sirenians' use their forelimbs for steering through water rather than for support. Over millions of years of evolution, their hind limbs have shrunk and disappeared. Only the vestiges of a pelvis—which once connected the hind limbs and the spine—remain.

## Skull and jaw

The skull and jaw of sirenians are heavily built, in part because of the need for firm attachment of the large muscles involved in grinding the large volumes of plant food they consume each day. In all sirenians, the forward part of the palate and the corresponding surface in the lower jaw are covered with rough, horny plates. These plates help in grasping and processing plant material before it is passed to molar teeth at the back for chewing.

In both manatees and dugongs, the nasal openings are set at or near the tip of the snout so that the animal does not have to raise much of its head above water to breathe. Manatees have nasal bones, but dugongs do not.

**COMPARE** the teeth of a manatee with those of an *ELEPHANT*. These animals share a common ancestor within the last 100 million years, and both consume silica-rich grasses.

## COMPARATIVE ANATOMY

### Skulls of manatees and the dugong

**The skull of an adult** West Indian manatee averages 26 inches (66 cm) long. These animals typically have four to seven molar teeth at the back of each half jaw. New teeth erupt and move forward from the back to replace teeth toward the front that wear down and eventually fall out. The manatee is likely to lose 30 to 50 teeth in its lifetime.

The skull of an adult dugong averages 24 inches (61 cm) long. Its profile is more angular than that of the manatee, with the mouth more downward-pointing for feeding on bottom-living plants. There are only two or three molar teeth at the back of each half jaw. Adult male dugongs have forward-pointing incisor teeth that serve as tusks for ritualized fights with other males

and for guiding or stimulating a mating partner. Growth rings form in cheek teeth enamel, and scientists use these to calculate the age of dugong specimens.

Dugong

molar teeth

incisor tooth

molar teeth

West Indian manatee

▲ SKULLS
*The skull of a dugong is slightly smaller and much more angular than that of a West Indian manatee. This shape helps dugongs feed on plants on the seabed; West Indian manatees generally feed on plants near the surface.*

## COMPARATIVE ANATOMY

### Sirenian skeletons

**The three species of manatees** have longer and thicker ribs, larger shoulder blades, and a broader spine than a dugong. These differences can be explained partly by the different types of water in which the animals live.

Dugongs live in seawater, and manatees spend some or all of their time in freshwater or brackish water. Freshwater and brackish water provide less buoyancy than seawater, so dugongs can rely more on the water to support their body.

▼ *The bones of all sirenians are very dense, but those of manatees are generally thicker and heavier than those of dugongs. The ancestors of sirenians were four-legged terrestrial animals, but none now has hind limbs.*

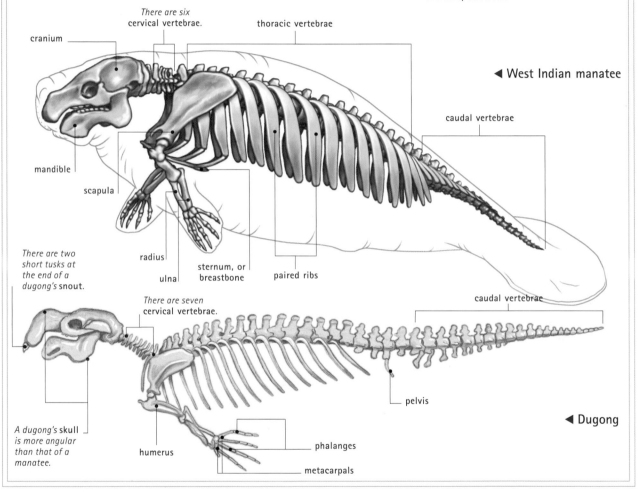

There are six cervical vertebrae.

cranium

thoracic vertebrae

◄ West Indian manatee

caudal vertebrae

mandible

scapula

There are two short tusks at the end of a dugong's snout.

radius

ulna

sternum, or breastbone

paired ribs

caudal vertebrae

There are seven cervical vertebrae.

pelvis

◄ Dugong

A dugong's skull is more angular than that of a manatee.

humerus

phalanges

metacarpals

The vertebrae are separate and distinct throughout the sirenian spinal column. Manatees, in contrast to dugongs and almost all other mammals, have six cervical (neck) vertebrae instead of seven. In land mammals, the spine acts as a firm girder to support the animals' weight in air. Water helps support a sirenian's weight so the backbone is relatively more important for locomotion than it is for support. The number of vertebrae varies between individual manatees, but typically there are 56: 6 cervical (neck), 17 to 19 thoracic (chest), 3 sacral (originally concerned with attachment to the pelvis), and 23 to 29 caudal (tail). The neck is short, and the 6 cervical vertebrae are flattened along the axis of the spine. The neck moves little, so it does not increase drag or instability of the front end of the body during swimming.

The 17 to 19 ribs that attach to the thoracic vertebrae are very dense and probably serve as ballast: they help weigh the animal down in water. Behind the ribs, the vertebrae, especially those involved in moving the tail, have large transverse processes, or projections. Muscles attach to the processes. Beneath seven, eight, or nine of the tail vertebrae lie chevron-shape bones that help protect blood vessels from damage when the tail flexes. Strong, elastic ligaments running between the tail vertebrae allow the tail to bend and cushion and support the vertebrae, minimizing wear on the bones.

The last few caudal vertebrae are simple, flattened bones that support the tail at the center. The tail's paddle blades are supported by fibrous material in an arrangement similar to that found in the tail flukes of whales.

## Limbs and their supports

In the terrestrial mammals from which sirenians evolved, the limbs were connected to the spine through limb girdles. The front girdle of land mammals typically contains two scapulae (shoulder blades) and clavicles (collarbones). Over millions of years, the front limbs of the ancestors of today's sirenians evolved to become flippers.

Compared with a human arm, the skeleton of a sirenian's forelimb is similar but with the upper and lower arm bones shortened and the digits lengthened. The "fingers" are enclosed in skin and connective tissue that makes the

outline of the flipper relatively smooth. The five digits characteristic of most land vertebrates are present but are not visible through the body surface. The presence of nails on the second, third, and fourth digits of West Indian and West African manatees hints at the pentadactyl (five-finger) structure that lies beneath. The flipper has the standard mammalian complement of phalanges, or finger bones, with the digits increasing in length from first to fifth to create the long, blunt-ended paddle shape.

In land mammals, the rear girdle (the pelvic girdle) is anchored to the backbone by sacral vertebrae that are fused together. During the sirenians' evolutionary transition over millions of years from a terrestrial to an aquatic mammal, the hind limbs have disappeared, along with most parts of the pelvis. Only small fragments of pelvic bone remain, and they provide points of attachment for muscles.

◄ Although manatees are relatively slow-moving animals, their flippers, body shape, and buoyancy mechanisms make maneuvering in water easy. Here, a manatee enjoys an underwater back scratch.

# Muscular system

**COMPARE** the muscles of a manatee's tail with those of another marine mammal, such as a *DOLPHIN* or a *GRAY WHALE*. All have strong muscles, unlike the tail muscles of an *ELEPHANT* or a *GRIZZLY BEAR*.

The manatee's muscle arrangement is suited for relatively slow movement, especially in brackish or freshwater. However, the dugong's tail muscles and whalelike tail blades enable rapid acceleration and fast swimming over short distances in coastal waters.

In manatees, a sheet of muscle extends from the pelvic region to the head. Over most of this area the muscle is more than 1 inch (2.5 cm) thick. Some muscle fibers and tendons extend into the forelimb; others pass beneath the neck. This massive muscle helps protect the organs inside the abdomen, substituting for the protective cartilage that extends from the sternum in other animals. When the muscle sheet on both sides of the tail contracts, together with abdominal muscles, this causes the tail to bend downward, producing the power stroke in forward propulsion. Contraction of muscle groups on the upper part of one side of the tail and relaxation of muscle groups on the opposite side cause the tail to tilt so that it acts as a rudder for steering.

The manatee uses its flippers in a variety of ways. They can be drawn forward to guide strands of weed toward the mouth. When the manatee is swimming fast, as when a male pursues a receptive female or escapes a predator, the flippers are held against the side of the body to minimize drag. The flippers can be extended slightly to help guide turns. When turned broadside against the direction of travel, the flippers act as brakes.

The flippers come into their own when the manatee is moving slowly or is stationary. On a seabed or riverbed, the flippers can be moved forward alternately so that the manatee "walks" along the bottom. When alarmed, the manatee pushes itself along the bottom using both flippers in unison. For slow swimming, the flippers are used like the oars or paddles of a rowboat. To turn to the right, the manatee pushes backward with its right flipper while pulling forward with its left. In "sculling" at low speed, the flippers are swung forward together and positioned to minimize resistance as they cut through the water. They are turned broadside for the backstroke, and are then tucked against the body before the next stroke. Manatees swim backward by moving the flippers in the reverse direction, without employing the tail.

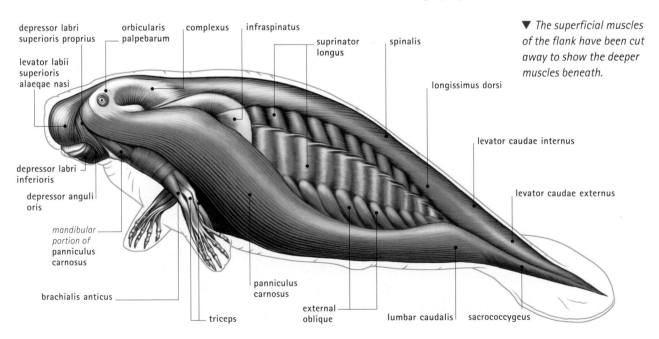

▼ *The superficial muscles of the flank have been cut away to show the deeper muscles beneath.*

depressor labri superioris proprius

orbicularis palpebarum

complexus

infraspinatus

suprinator longus

spinalis

levator labii superioris alaeqae nasi

longissimus dorsi

depressor labri inferioris

levator caudae internus

depressor anguli oris

levator caudae externus

*mandibular portion of* panniculus carnosus

brachialis anticus

panniculus carnosus

triceps

external oblique

lumbar caudalis

sacrococcygeus

# Nervous system

As with other vertebrates, there are two main parts to a manatee's nervous system: the central nervous system, including the brain, and the peripheral nervous system. Compared to other marine mammals of similar size, sirenians have a small brain. The surface of their brain is also surprisingly smooth, with few of the surface folds normally associated with mammals of relatively high intelligence. The brain of an adult West Indian manatee weighs about 13 ounces (370 grams) on average, and that of a dugong about 11 ounces (300 grams). These weights are considerably less than the brain weights for a dolphin or sea lion of equivalent body size. Trainers are unable to teach captive sirenians to perform tasks, whereas they have had considerable success with sea lions, dolphins, and killer whales.

### Brain structure

Recent studies of the manatee brain have shed light on aspects of manatee behavior and the relative importance of different sensory systems. The structures found in a manatee's brain are the same as those in most other mammals, but in manatees the relative importance of different regions is distinctive. The various parts of the midbrain and forebrain that relay and process sensory information from the mouth region, the flippers, and the tail are enlarged. The sense of touch (and possibly the detection of vibrations and water movement) is thus probably particularly significant in those parts of the body. In the hindbrain, the parts of the medulla concerned with moving the snout, lips, and sensory hairs around the mouth are also large. In the brainstem, relay centers concerned with contracting muscles of the tail and the diaphragm are large. The cerebellum, the part of the hindbrain that coordinates movement and balance, is large in sirenians, as would be expected for animals that spend their lives swimming.

The parts of the brain that are linked with social and emotional expression (such as the amygdala, the basal forebrain nuclei, and the hypothalamus) are not particularly large or elaborate in the manatee. This correlates well with the docile disposition of sirenians, with their apparent lack of complex social behavior, and with the absence of tight-knit social groups among them.

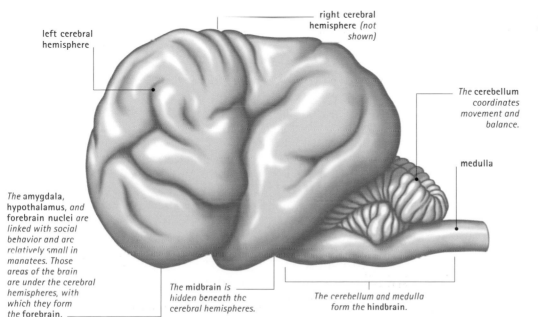

left cerebral hemisphere

right cerebral hemisphere *(not shown)*

The cerebellum coordinates movement and balance.

medulla

The amygdala, hypothalamus, and forebrain nuclei *are linked with social behavior and are relatively small in manatees. Those areas of the brain are under the cerebral hemispheres, with which they form* the forebrain.

The midbrain *is hidden beneath the cerebral hemispheres.*

The cerebellum and medulla form the hindbrain.

◀ BRAIN
**West Indian manatee**
*The surface of the cerebral hemispheres is relatively smooth, lacking the folds usually associated with high intelligence.*

▲ *Despite having small eyes and no external earflaps, manatees see and hear well underwater.*

Manatees and dugongs have relatively good hearing from low to high frequencies (that is, pitches). This is borne out by the relatively large size of the parts of the hindbrain and midbrain that relay auditory, or sound, information, and of those parts of the cerebral cortex that interpret it.

## Means of communication

Manatees produce sounds with the larynx (voice box), and they communicate with each other with middle- and low-frequency chirps and squeaks, and higher-frequency whistles, screams, and squeals. The precise meaning of these vocalizations is unclear, although they change according to whether or not the individuals are sexually aroused, frightened, or playing. Mothers and calves exchange chirps with one another and utter screams of alarm at times of danger.

Manatees also generate infrasonic sounds (frequencies too low for human hearing). These signals may be used by sexually active females to attract males. Some scientists speculate that manatees "echolocate" using sound—that is, produce sound beams or pulses that bounce off objects in their surroundings and are reflected back to them. This ability to "see with sound," which is well demonstrated in toothed whales, would be a valuable asset in the often murky waters where manatees live. However, sirenians do not appear to produce the pulsed and directed beams of sound that would be necessary for echolocation.

Manatees can probably smell only moderately well in water and perhaps in air. The olfactory nerves running from the organs of smell, and the parts of the brain that relay and interpret messages from these nerves, are only of modest size. The sense of taste is relatively well developed, as indicated by taste buds at the back of the tongue and prominent gustatory (taste) nerves running between them and the brain.

In manatees and dugongs, hairs scattered over the body sense water movement and direct contact with other objects, including other individuals. At certain times, such as when resting after feeding, manatees will interact with other members of the species and may act "playfully," rubbing against each other, gently grasping each other with their flippers, and even "kissing" snout to snout.

## Sirenian senses

Sirenian eyes are quite small, but their behavior in the wild and in captivity suggests that they can see for long distances underwater. Manatee eyes see in color and have a reflective layer—the tapetum lucidum—behind the light-sensitive retina. This bounces light back through the retina, to maximize the light sensitivity of the eye. The tapetum lucidum is a feature of many birds and mammals that hunt at night or in poor light. It allows the manatee to see in murky water. At night, the tapetum lucidum gives manatee eyes a pinkish reflective shine like cats' eyes. Dugong eyes lack the tapetum lucidum and presumably can see less well in poor light.

Analysis of the structure of the parts of the brain and the nerve pathways concerned with vision suggests that in manatees this sense is not as highly developed as hearing and touch. The optic nerve and those parts of the brain that relay and process visual information are relatively small. The brain areas that control eye movement are also relatively small.

# Circulatory and respiratory systems

As is typical for mammals, a sirenian has a four-chamber heart that pumps blood through a double circulation (the main and pulmonary circulations). Arteries with thick, muscular walls carry blood under high pressure away from the heart to supply other organs. Thin-walled veins carry blood back to the heart under low pressure. In the pulmonary (lung) circulation, carbon dioxide is expelled, and the blood is recharged with oxygen.

Like other mammals, sirenians inhale air through nasal passages, warming it before it travels down the trachea to the lungs. In the lungs, oxygen is exchanged for carbon dioxide, and the breath is exhaled when the animal surfaces. The respiratory system of a sirenian is more efficient than that of most terrestrial mammals, including humans.

Manatee and dugong lungs are unique in being positioned alongside the stomach and intestines, rather than in front of them. The manatee's chest cavity extends almost the entire length of the trunk, and this probably produces great benefits in terms of buoyancy control. The manatee's lungs are also unusual in having fewer bronchi (primary air passages) and fewer major blood vessels than are found in the lungs of other mammals. The dugong

too has simple lungs, each with a main bronchus that runs almost the entire length of the lung with only a few side branches. Manatee lungs contain large amounts of smooth muscle and elastic fibers, which enable the animal to fine-tune lung volume to adjust buoyancy during a dive.

The **trachea** leads from the mouth to the lungs.

The **nasal passage** connects to the trachea (connection not shown here), allowing the manatee to breathe with only its nose at the surface of the water.

The **lungs** are very large, extending the length of the body. By adjusting the volume of the lungs, a manatee can control its buoyancy and thus its position in the water.

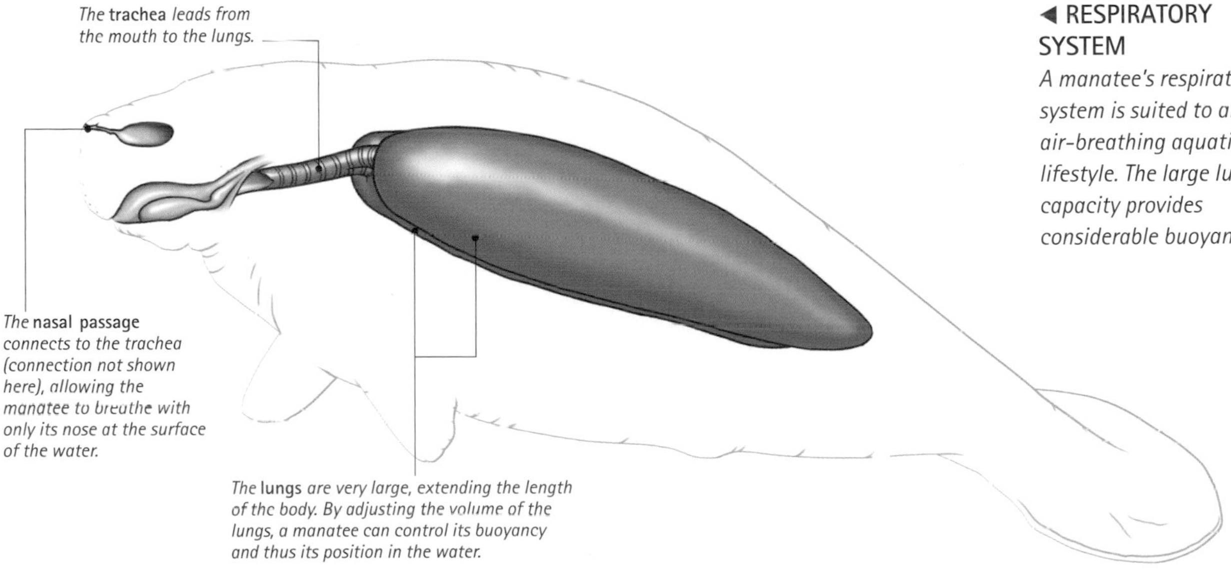

◀ RESPIRATORY SYSTEM
*A manatee's respiratory system is suited to an air-breathing aquatic lifestyle. The large lung capacity provides considerable buoyancy.*

▲ *Although they do not dive deep, manatees are well adapted for plunging underwater. Their lungs inflate with inhaled air very rapidly, and their nostrils have valves that close when the animal dives.*

Unlike whales and seals, sirenians do not dramatically slow their heart rate when they dive. The Amazonian manatee's heart, for example, beats about 50 times a minute when the animal is at the water surface and slows slightly to about 30 to 40 beats a minute during normal dives. Only when a manatee is threatened does its heart rate plummet to as low as five or six beats a minute—a change as dramatic as that found in deep-diving whales and seals—allowing it to remain safely submerged for a longer period.

Manatees, like other marine mammals, cannot breathe underwater, so they store the air they require for the dive in their respiratory system. Oxygen is also stored temporarily in hemoglobin and myoglobin, the oxygen-carrying pigments in blood and muscle. Manatee blood does not have the high levels of hemoglobin that is found in active, deep-diving marine mammals such as most whales and seals. This is understandable, as manatees do not usually dive as deep or for as long, and are much less active, and so do not require large amounts of oxygen to provide the energy for muscle contraction. This lower demand for

## IN FOCUS

### Lungs for diving

**Sirenians dive** with their lungs inflated. In this regard they are similar to whales but different from seals, which hold minimal air in their lungs during a deep dive. Manatees can stay submerged for 20 minutes when resting or swimming slowly, and dugongs can stay underwater for about half this time. Manatee lungs are efficient, and—like the lungs of whales—can exchange nearly 90 percent of the air in them with each breath; the figure for humans is typically only 15 to 20 percent.

oxygen relative to other sea mammals is also indicated by the low levels of myoglobin. In whales and seals, this substance is present at high levels in the muscles and gradually releases oxygen during dives. In manatees, myoglobin (as well as hemoglobin) levels are similar to those found in land mammals.

# Digestive and excretory systems

Sirenians feed on water plants, and exclude most of the water when they swallow. The West Indian manatee eats up to about 40 species of aquatic plants, including floating water hyacinth and rooted sea grasses, as well as 10 kinds of algae. The dugong, with its more downturned snout, prefers sea grasses. Sirenians will also eat attached or slow-moving marine invertebrates such as sea squirts and sea cucumbers. Manatees have been found eating fish caught in gill nets, but for these animals fish is not a usual part of the diet.

Most mammals are "diphyodont"—that is, they have milk teeth when juvenile, which are later replaced with one set of permanent teeth. In contrast, tooth replacement in manatees is almost continuous (polyphyodont) throughout their lives. Replacement of the first teeth is triggered when the young calf begins to add vegetable matter to its milk diet.

The dugong has an unusual arrangement of lips and mouthparts for consuming marine grasses and their rootlike rhizomes. The upper lip is extended to form a heavily bristled muscular pad with a deep cleft, which overhangs the downward-pointing mouth. The dugong grasps the base of a sea grass plant with one or both sides of the muscular pad. Horny pads toward the front of the dugong's jaws help pull the plant out of the sediment along with its roots or rhizomes (which are rich in carbohydrates) or, in the case of larger sea grasses, break off the stem. This feeding action is similar to the way in which cattle use their tongue and lips to grasp grass stems. The sea grass material is passed to the back of the mouth to be ground up by molar teeth. The dugong is so efficient at grazing small sea grasses that it leaves bare seabed.

The West Indian manatee has an even more adaptable upper lip arrangement than the dugong. The upper lip is less deeply divided than the dugong's, and is used in feeding at the surface. The lower lip is used for taking food that is growing lower in the water. Like the dugong, this manatee can wrap its top lip around objects and pluck them up, with an action almost like big soft tweezers.

Sirenians, like land-living plant-eaters, produce saliva from glands in the mouth to lubricate their food and begin the process of digestion. Once ingested, food passes down a muscular esophagus into a two-part stomach through a strong ring of muscle, the cardiac sphincter, which acts as a valve. The first chamber, or main stomach, has thick, muscular

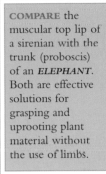

COMPARE the muscular top lip of a sirenian with the trunk (proboscis) of an ELEPHANT. Both are effective solutions for grasping and uprooting plant material without the use of limbs.

CONNECTIONS

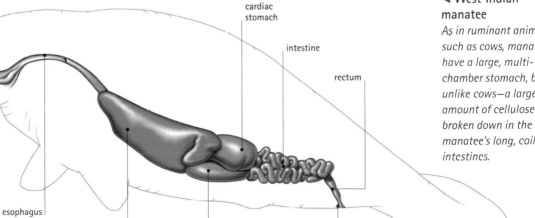

◄ West Indian manatee
*As in ruminant animals such as cows, manatees have a large, multichamber stomach, but—unlike cows—a large amount of cellulose is broken down in the manatee's long, coiled intestines.*

*◄ Manatees mate throughout the year, but mating occurs most commonly at a season when the water is warmest. This warmth allows the calf to be born, one year later, when food supplies for the suckling mother are at their peak.*

disperse to find other females, and the potential fathers play no further role in the life of mother or calf.

Dugong mating behavior is broadly similar to that of manatees, but competition between males is even more intense. Mature males will fight with each other to establish a territory and gain access to one or more females in the vicinity. These ritual fights, in which one male uses his tusks and body weight to gain advantage over the other, can leave males with deep scars and even more serious injuries. Before mating, a male also uses his tusks to help turn the female onto her back.

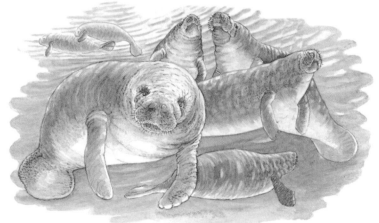

**▲ Mating behavior**
*A dozen or more male manatees will pursue a receptive female, with one eventually mating with her.*

**▼ Social bond**
*Mother and calf form a strong social bond. They greet each other snout to snout, and communicate using a variety of calls.*

## IN FOCUS

### Scent messages

**Observers often see manatees** rubbing their genitalia, armpits, and head—regions where glandular secretions are released— against particular objects in the water, such as rocks or logs. An individual will use the same "rubbing post" year after year. In all likelihood, the animal is scent-marking. Leaving scent can provide a variety of informative messages about the individual's condition, including its readiness to mate.

## The cradling myth and mermaids

**The presence of the sirenian's two mammary glands** in the chest region close to her flippers has given rise to fanciful tales. One describes the mother cradling the calf "in her arms" while it suckles. In fact, the calf usually suckles while the mother swims upright—although the mother does sometimes swim on her back with the calf on top when they play together. The arrangement of the mother's flippers and mammary glands has led to sailors to imagine the upper half of the sirenian's body as that of a woman, with the lower half having a tail like that of a fish (although it is more like that of a whale or giant otter). This is probably how the mermaid legend began.

▲ **Birth**
*Female manatees almost always give birth to just one calf per pregnancy. The calf is able to swim as soon as it is born.*

▼ **Suckling**
*A manatee calf swims alongside its mother to suckle from the nipple behind the base of the flipper.*

### Pregnancy and birth

Manatees do not become mature until they are six to eight years old, and dugongs not until their teens. Females typically produce only one calf at a time, and they often have intervals of several years between calves. In sirenians, the gestation period (the time from copulation to birth) is 12 to 13 months, similar to that of many whales. Often breeding is timed to occur in the warmer months, so that the calf is born the following year in the season when vegetation is abundant and provides plenty of nutrition for the suckling mother.

Manatees and the dugong usually give birth to one calf, which is often born tail first, like most toothed whales. This may be an adaptation to delay the time when the calf has to take its first breath, until the last possible moment. As a fetus, the manatee is covered in fine downy hair, but at birth it is more or less hairless. A newborn West African or West Indian averages about 4 feet (1.2 m) long and weighs 65 pounds (about 30 kg). Dugong and Amazonian manatee calves are slightly smaller. A newborn calf can usually swim unaided, but its mother will often help it to the surface to breathe.

### Suckling and weaning

The manatee calf suckles its mother's milk for 12 to 18 months; the dugong for up to 24 months. In both cases, however, the calves also graze vegetation when only a few months old. The mother's mammary glands are in the axillary, or armpit, position close to the base of the flipper. The calf swims slightly below and to one side of her to take her milk, which is rich in fats, proteins, and salts. The mammary glands lack storage sacs, as found in cattle and goats, and so the calf suckles for a short time at regular intervals. Mother and calf have a strong social bond and often greet each other with snout-to-snout nuzzling that looks like kissing.

TREVOR DAY

**FURTHER READING AND RESEARCH**
Perrin, W. F., B. Würsig, and J. G. M. Thewissen (eds.). 2002. *Encyclopedia of Marine Mammals.* Academic: San Diego, CA.
Reynolds, John E., III, and S. A. Rommel (eds.). 1999. *Biology of Marine Mammals.* Smithsonian Institution Press: Washington, D.C.

# Seal

ORDER: Carnivora FAMILIES: Phocidae, Otariidae, and Odobenidae SPECIES: 33

Centuries ago, sailors called seals "sea bears," and bears are indeed seals' closest living relatives on land. Both bears and seals are members of a group of mammals called the carnivores, or meat eaters. The anatomy of seals reflects the fact that they spend most of their life in water, so their eyesight, hearing, body shape, and method of movement all work better in water. However, seals' anatomy is also affected by their ancestry as air-breathing land mammals, and they do not live all their life in water. Seals must leave water and stay on solid surfaces to rest, breed, and molt their skin. Therefore, they must be able to move about, see, and hear adequately in air as well as water.

● **Animals** Animals are many-celled organisms that actively eat other organisms to obtain energy and nutrients. Most are responsive to external stimuli and have cells that are organized into tissues and organs.

▼ *There are three families of seals: true, or earless, seals form the largest family, which includes the harbor seal and the ringed seal; there are 14 species of fur seals and sea lions; and the walrus is in a family of its own.*

● **Chordates** Chordates are animals that, in at least one stage in their life cycle, have both a dorsal nerve cord and a notochord running along their back. The nerve cord is a bundle of nerve fibers, and the notochord is a stiff rod that in most chordates develops into a backbone.

● **Vertebrates** Chordates that have a notochord that changes into a backbone during the development of the embryo are called vertebrates. They include fish, reptiles, amphibians, birds, and mammals. A backbone, or vertebral column, comprises a chain of small units called vertebrae, which are made of cartilage or bone. Vertebrates also have a braincase, or cranium, which gives the group the alternative name Craniata.

● **Mammals** Mammals are vertebrates in which females have mammary glands that secrete milk to feed the growing young. Most mammals have fur. They all have a jaw that hinges farther forward than that of their reptilian ancestors, and the lower jaw comprises a single bone, the dentary. The teeth have diverse forms and functions within the mouth, and the teeth mesh together precisely and can grind food. Mammals' mature red blood cells lack a nucleus, unlike those of reptiles and birds.

● **Carnivores** Mammals that are usually meat eaters, such as cats, dogs, badgers, weasels, bears, raccoons, and seals, make up the order Carnivora. Most members of the order have bladelike cheek teeth called carnassials, which slice the food before swallowing. Not all meat-eating mammals

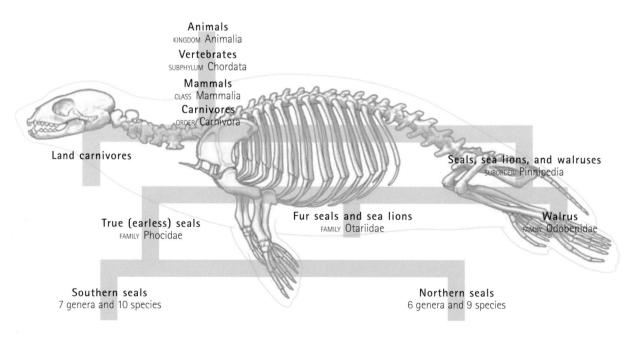

**Animals**
KINGDOM Animalia
**Vertebrates**
SUBPHYLUM Chordata
**Mammals**
CLASS Mammalia
**Carnivores**
ORDER Carnivora

Land carnivores

Seals, sea lions, and walruses
SUBORDER Pinnipedia

**True (earless) seals**
FAMILY Phocidae

**Fur seals and sea lions**
FAMILY Otariidae

**Walrus**
FAMILY Odobenidae

**Southern seals**
7 genera and 10 species

**Northern seals**
6 genera and 9 species

are in this order, and not all members of this order eat meat. Bears and raccoons eat both plants and animals, and the panda eats only plants. Seals do not have the carnassial teeth characteristic of most animals in the order Carnivora.

● **Pinnipeds** Seals, sea lions, fur seals, and walruses are marine carnivores with paddle-shape flippers that are used for propulsion in water. The pinnipeds, whose name means "finned foot," include the eared seals (sea lions and fur seals); earless, or "true," seals (such as the ringed seal); and walruses. Pinnipeds have a body that is covered with a thick layer of fat, giving the body a neat, streamlined shape and insulating the internal organs from cold water.

● **Eared seals** Sea lions and fur seals are pinnipeds with small external ears. They look different from the true seals because they are more mobile on land and are able to hold their body more erect, sometimes raising it clear of the ground using both foreflippers and hind flippers.

● **Walrus** There is only one living species of walrus. This huge pinniped lives in the Arctic and has very sparse fur and enormous tusks.

● **True seals** These pinnipeds have no external ears. True seals are more fully suited to life in water than the eared seals. On land, true seals cannot bring their hind flippers forward beneath their body to raise it above the ground. Their forelimbs are buried in their thick fat layer up to the wrist, so the limbs appear very short. True seals move on land by an undulating movement, but in water they are much more accomplished divers than eared seals.

● **Northern true seals** The northern true seals differ from the southern branch of the family (the monk, elephant,

▲ *This Weddell seal is searching for prey. Like all seals, it has a body shape perfectly suited to rapid movement underwater.*

and Antarctic seals). The northern seals' flippers have long, thick claws, but southern seals' claws are small and do not extend beyond the end of the flipper. Southern seals' hind flippers are thickened and stiffened with fibrous tissue and look a little like the tail flukes of dolphins. Northern seals' hind flippers are more flexible and can bend to scratch each other.

● **White-coated true seals** The harbor seal belongs to a small grouping of northern true seals whose young are born with a dense, white fur coat called lanugo. This group also includes the ringed seal, harp seal, and gray seal.

**FEATURED SYSTEMS**

**EXTERNAL ANATOMY** Although some seals look clumsy on land, their body is streamlined and cuts easily through water, propelled by flipper-shape limbs. *See pages 204–207.*

**SKELETAL SYSTEM** The skeleton of seals does not offer much support to the body. The limb bones are short, sturdy appendages with long digits forming paddles. The flexible spine allows underwater maneuverability. *See page 208.*

**MUSCULAR SYSTEM** A seal's muscles act as an important oxygen store. They are packed with myoglobin, a protein that binds spare oxygen and releases it as required when the seal is diving. *See page 209.*

**NERVOUS SYSTEM** Seals must hunt in dark polar winters and find food deep in the ocean beyond the reach of the sun. Their vision is excellent, and hearing, touch, and taste are all highly developed, too. *See pages 210–211.*

**CIRCULATORY AND RESPIRATORY SYSTEMS** Seals are champion divers, equaled in duration and depth only by the largest species of whales. Their circulatory and respiratory systems are suitable for operating under high pressure and for long periods of time without inhalation of air. *See pages 212–213.*

**DIGESTIVE AND EXCRETORY SYSTEMS** A seal's diet consists exclusively of fish and shrimp, and thus lacks both carbohydrate and freshwater. The seal is able to process the fat and protein in its food to release all the water and carbohydrate it needs. *See pages 214–215.*

**REPRODUCTIVE SYSTEM** By producing rich, fatty milk for their young, female seals transfer their protective blubber to their offspring; as a result, seal pups have a very fast growth rate. *See pages 216–217.*

# External anatomy

**CONNECTIONS**

**COMPARE** the sleek body shape of a seal with that of another warm-blooded diver in cold seas such as a *PENGUIN*.

**COMPARE** the touch-sensitive hands of a *MANDRILL* with the touch-sensitive whiskers of a seal.

Most seals are mammals of cold oceans. Seals live farther north and south than any other group of mammals. In the far north, ringed seals live under the permanently frozen surface of the Arctic Ocean and carve snow lairs where they find weak points in the ice. Ringed seals swim between breathing holes 0.6 mile (1 km) apart with ease. In the far south, the Weddell seal gnaws the sea ice to maintain breathing holes that allow it to live far under the permanent ice around Antarctica. It can swim 3 miles (5 km) away from its breathing hole before returning. The water in its habitat has a temperature around 29°F (−1.8°C), but on the ice shelf the air temperature can drop to −58°F (−50°C) and howling gales produce an intense wind-chill factor. Since they are mammals, all seals nevertheless maintain a core body temperature of 99°F (37°C).

Not all species of seals live in extremely cold environments. Most seals prefer water below 68°F (20°C), but some, such as the Hawaiian monk seal, live in tropical seas. Even so, the body form of seals is dominated by the need to swim well and stay warm. Therefore, all seals have a smooth, streamlined shape that slips through the water with minimal turbulence and drag. Seals' large size and simple shape minimize body surface area relative to mass

▶ **Harbor seal**
*The harbor seal has a broad, rounded, doglike head, no visible ears, large eyes, a streamlined body, and short flippers. The fur of adults and pups is pale to dark gray.*

*The adult coat of **fur** is relatively thin, but the body is insulated against the cold by a layer of blubber beneath the skin.*

*The **ears** have no external flap and are very sound-sensitive. In diving, the air space in the inner ear is pressurized by a blood-filled sinus to match the increasing water pressure at greater depth.*

*Forward-looking **eyes** provide good binocular vision, which is essential for judging distances in hunting.*

*The **muzzle** is broad. A seal is able to open its mouth very wide to swallow prey.*

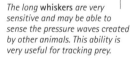

*The long **whiskers** are very sensitive and may be able to sense the pressure waves created by other animals. This ability is very useful for tracking prey.*

*There are five **claws** on each forelimb.*

*The **forelimbs** form flippers. They are held close to the flanks during fast swimming and are used to help the animal maneuver during slow swimming. The flippers support the front part of a seal's body when it is hauling itself onto land, and they are also used to hold large prey while the animal tears off chunks of meat with its teeth.*

▲ *Two Weddell seals have swum up to a hole in the ice to breathe air. Individuals of this species sometimes spend more than 80 minutes underwater, but they have to breathe air periodically. The seal in the foreground is a pup.*

and volume; this arrangement serves to minimize heat loss. The ringed seal is the lightest pinniped, at about 110 to 210 pounds (50–95 kg). Many pinnipeds are much larger. The elephant seal, for example, grows to a massive 8,000 pounds (3,600 kg).

Seals have curved contours because they are covered by a thick layer of fat called blubber, which smooths all their sharp corners. Any features that would spoil a smooth outline, such as nipples and genitals, are tucked away in neat grooves. Fur seals and sea lions (together called eared seals) have small external ears, which cause a little water resistance. The more aquatic true, or "earless," seals, such as the harbor seal, have no external ears at all.

### Blanket of fat

The blubber layer of seals serves several purposes; one of the most important is the conservation of heat. Blubber forms a blanket

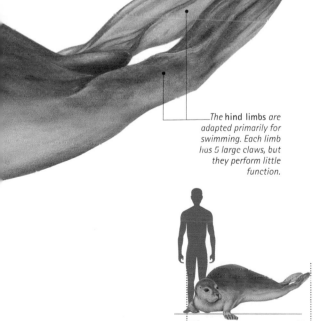

*The* **hind limbs** *are adapted primarily for swimming. Each limb has 5 large claws, but they perform little function.*

6 feet
(2 m)

## EVOLUTION

### Pinniped origins

**Scientists still argue about pinnipeds,** but most now agree that all pinnipeds descend from the same land-based, bearlike ancestor, which took to the seas. A fossil animal from California sheds some light on pinniped evolution. Named *Enaliarctos mealsi,* it lived 23 million years ago. Some scientists believe it represents a snapshot of the evolutionary change from bearlike carnivore to a seal-like animal. *Enaliarctos* swam with undulations of its body, like a seal, but it also propelled itself with thrusts from its fore flippers, like a sea lion, and strokes from its hind limbs. The combination was not unlike the swimming of today's otters, and the artist's impression below reconstructs the animal as otterlike in appearance.

▼ *Enaliarctos mealsi*
*The ancestor of seals was related to bears but probably had an appearance more like that of an otter.*

# Skeletal system

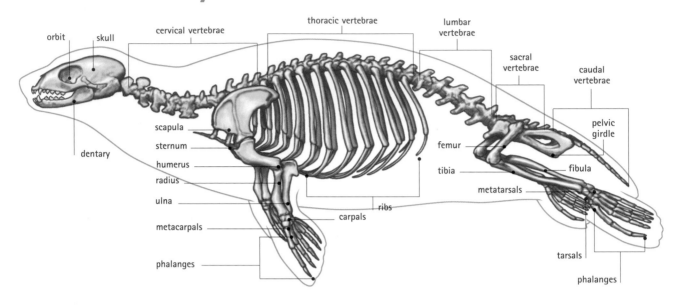

orbit
skull
cervical vertebrae
thoracic vertebrae
lumbar vertebrae
sacral vertebrae
caudal vertebrae
pelvic girdle
dentary
scapula
sternum
humerus
radius
ulna
metacarpals
phalanges
carpals
ribs
femur
tibia
fibula
metatarsals
tarsals
phalanges

Under a seal's skin and soft tissue are most of the familiar bony elements of a typical mammalian skeleton. The parts that differ most from that of its land-based relatives, such as bears and dogs, are the limbs. The bones of the seal's forelimb—the humerus, radius, and ulna—are short, stout, and heavy, and are buried in the seal's blubber. Only the wrist bones and long digits are free. The limbs are not connected by a clavicle (collarbone), so they are free to move in all directions. Seals can scratch their chin, then reverse and rotate their flipper to scratch the top of their head. The phalanges (bones of the digits) are extremely long, none more so than the pollex (thumb), which forms the long leading edge of the flipper. The major bones of the hind limbs (femurs, tibiae, and fibulae) are short, broad, and flattened. A seal's femurs (thighbones) stick out sideways from the pelvic girdle (hipbone), so that although the seal's rear is narrow and tapered, its hind flippers are set wide apart.

Seal skulls are generally short, with huge orbits (the recesses that accommodate their large eyes). In the smallest species, the ringed seal, only 0.1 inch (3 mm) of bone separates the two orbits, and the bone is delicate and almost transparent. As in the skulls of other seals, the shortness of the ringed seal's snout is acheived by overlapping supraoccipital and

▲ Harbor seal

*The lumbar vertebrae are large and strong. They provide anchorage for the powerful muscles that drive the seal through the water. The limb bones are short and powerful.*

parietal bones. A short snout increases the biting power of the jaws.

In the backbone of the ringed seal and other true seals, the lumbar vertebrae (those between the ribs and the pelvis) are the most heavily built bones. They bear sturdy spines that point sideways and serve as attachments for the swimming muscles. The spines on the tops of all the vertebrae (the neural spines) are very short, however, as are the zygapophyses (the interlocking knobs where the vertebrae link together). This gives the backbone great upward flexibility, so that, amazingly, a seal can bend backward and touch its tail with its nose.

## COMPARATIVE ANATOMY

### Fur seal skeleton

**There are major differences in skeletal structure** between true seals and eared seals (fur seals and sea lions). The most important differences are in the shoulders and forelimbs. Eared seals, unlike true seals, power themselves through water with their forelimbs, and it is the neck region of the spine that is heavily built, not the lumbar region as in true seals. All the forelimb bones are bigger and longer than those of true seals. The ridges on the huge shoulder blades and the long, broad neural spines on the neck (thoracic) vertebrae all act as attachments for powerful muscles associated with swimming.

# Muscular system

The locomotion of seals, particularly true seals, is controlled by muscles very different from those that power the movement of land mammals. True seals, such as the ringed seal and harbor seal, swim by undulating the hind body from side to side. Their hind flippers face inward. They alternate in making inward-moving power strokes with the digits spread, followed by outward-moving recovery strokes with the digits curved and closed.

The main swimming power comes from long muscles in the lumbar region of the spine: the iliocostalis and the longissimus. When these muscles contract, they flex the spine to and fro. The muscles are aided by long tendons running to the flippers and by sets of muscles on each side of the limb bones: the gracilis, biceps femoris, and semitendinosus. These muscles firmly secure the hind limbs close to the pelvis and nearly parallel to the spine. With the limbs in this restricted position, the power from the lumbar muscles is effectively transmitted down to the flippers. Because of this arrangement, true seals cannot rotate their flippers forward under their body as eared seals and land mammals can.

▼ *A true seal's neck muscles are so thick and powerful that no narrowing of the neck is visible on the exterior of the seal's body.*

## Neck muscles

The neck muscles keep the seal's neck flexed in a shallow U-shape. A short, stiff neck is necessary because the seal must maintain a strong, hydrodynamic profile into the flow of water as it is powered along from behind. However, the neck muscles also permit a sudden extension of the neck to change direction or to lunge for prey.

▼ FORELEG MUSCLES
**Sea lion**
*The foreleg muscles power the paddlelike forelimbs, which are all-important for propelling seals and other pinnipeds through water.*

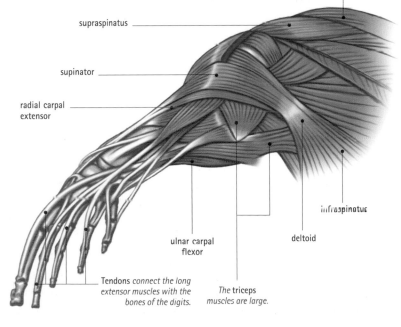

subscapularis

supraspinatus

supinator

radial carpal extensor

ulnar carpal flexor

infraspinatus

deltoid

Tendons *connect the long extensor muscles with the bones of the digits.*

*The* triceps *muscles are large.*

# Nervous system

Like the nervous system of any vertebrate, a seal's nervous system is centered on its brain. The brain receives messages from the network of nerves branching through every part of its body. Many of the nerves receive messages from sense organs, such as the eyes and ears. The brain processes the messages and sends instructions for action to muscles.

A seal's brain is much like the brain of other carnivores, such as bears and dogs. It is more or less spherical and has a folded surface. It has a particularly large cerebellum, which is the region responsible for coordinating precise movements of the body. This gives the seal the fine control it needs to pursue fast-moving prey that move both horizontally and vertically.

### Eyes, ears, and whiskers

The seal's sense organs have been principally shaped by the need to catch prey in demanding environments. The eyes, ears, whiskers, and taste buds all work well in water and in air. They guide seals in the darkness of the deep sea and in the long, dark polar winter. Seals' vision is therefore excellent and similar to that of nocturnal mammals. Seals' eyes are very large, capable of maximizing brightness and sharpness of vision in low light. Also, just behind the retina (the layer of light-sensitive cells on the back of the eyeball) is a reflective layer called a tapetum lucidum, which bounces light back toward the retina, thus making the most of whatever light is available. Many nocturnal animals have a tapetum lucidum.

Seawater scatters and absorbs light and does not allow it to penetrate to great depth. Red light is absorbed first, leaving only green and blue light, and at greater depths, blue only. Deep-diving seals, such as the elephant seal, have eyes that are most sensitive to the wavelengths of blue light, whereas seals that remain in the shallows, such as the spotted (larga) seal, are most sensitive to green light. Seals do not truly see in color, but they do have two different types of visual pigment (pigments are the light-sensitive chemicals in the cells of the retina), which are sensitive to different colors. Experts think seals use these different sensitivities to see color contrast and are thus able to see objects against a colored background.

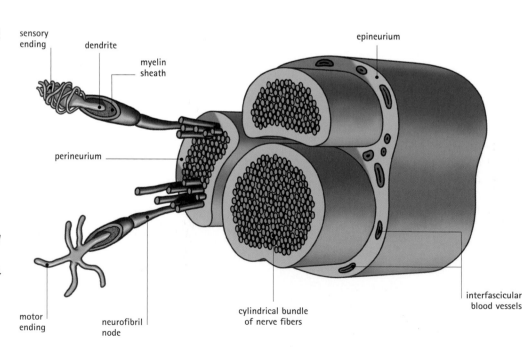

▶ **PERIPHERAL NERVE**
*Like other mammals, seals depend on an extensive network of peripheral nerves to supply the brain with sensory information and to carry motor signals back to organs such as muscles. The nerves are insulated by a sheath of fatty tissue called myelin, which prevents their electrical signals stimulating inappropriate reactions.*

sensory ending

dendrite

myelin sheath

epineurium

perineurium

motor ending

neurofibril node

cylindrical bundle of nerve fibers

interfascicular blood vessels

## A refined palate

**A seal's sense of taste** was once thought to be unrefined and unimportant. However, it is now know to be finely tuned to differences in the saltiness of seawater. By tasting the water, a seal gets clues about its location and thus can home in on areas where prey are likely to be (fish often congregate in certain places relative to freshwater runoff from land). Seals can discriminate the difference between 3 percent salt in seawater and 3.1 percent or 2.9 percent salt. That sensitivity is 4.5 times better than in humans, and better than in any other mammal.

### Whisker stimulation

Blind seals have been known to survive perfectly well in the wild, so eyesight is apparently not vital to their survival. Other senses must compensate, and one of them might be the touch sense of the seal's whiskers, or vibrissae. Each whisker sits in a hair follicle served with a dense mesh of 1,000 to 1,600 nerves—10 times the number associated with the whiskers of cats or rats. When the whisker is deflected by an object or by water movement, it bows within the follicle and stimulates tiny sense organs that detect pressure and stretch. They send impulses to the brain along the trigeminal (facial) nerve, which is particularly large in seals. The sense of touch could help seals find their way—and even find their prey—in the dark.

### Underwater hearing

Seals hear a little better underwater than they do in air, but it is not clear exactly how. In water, an external ear is transparent to sound—sound waves pass straight through because a seal's body tissues are about the same density as water. That is the reason why true seals do not need external ears. However, the sound waves also pass straight through the seal's head, striking only the bones in its skull, which are less dense. The sound is conducted through the skull bones to the middle ear, reaching and stimulating both inner ears at about the same

time. It is not clear how the seal can then tell which direction the sound comes from. Nonetheless, seals have good directional underwater hearing. It may be that the route of sound into their ears is restricted. For example, in dolphins, this restriction is achieved by the isolation of the ear bones from the skull, and the channeling of incoming sound through a conductive fat channel in the jaw. A seal's ear bones—its periotic bones and tympanic bulla—are not isolated.

▲ A seal has many whiskers around the mouth and nose. Each whisker sits in a hair follicle with a dense mesh of nerves. Each time a whisker moves— even slightly—nerve impulses are sent to the brain.

## Vision in air and water

**In air, the eyes of mammals** focus incoming light with the power of two lenses: the cornea (the curved protective front covering of the eye) and the lens itself, behind the cornea. In water, the cornea effectively disappears, because it has roughly the same refractive index as water, so it cannot bend light. The lens is still effective, though, and that of seals is large and almost spherical to compensate for the lack of corneal focusing. In air, seals should be nearsighted because the focusing power of the cornea should come into effect. However, seals have a flat cornea that may actually have negative refractive power, correcting the overpowerful spherical lens. Even so, seals' eyesight is not as good in air as it is in water.

# Circulatory and respiratory systems

An animal's circulatory and respiratory systems work together to obtain oxygen and to pass it around its tissues. For an air-breathing animal such as a seal, the respiratory system comprises a pair of lungs, a diaphragm, and airways in the nose and throat. The circulatory system (the heart and blood vessels) transports the oxygen dissolved in blood, carries other substances around the body, and regulates the animal's temperature.

## Cut off from air

The circulatory and respiratory systems of seals face an unusual challenge. A seal is working hardest, and its body is creating the greatest demand for oxygen, when it is hunting underwater. At these times, it cannot take fresh oxygen because it must hold its breath until it surfaces. Seals, therefore, have onboard oxygen stores in their tissues, mostly in their blood. Some of the oxygen is dissolved in the blood, but most is chemically bound to hemoglobin—the protein molecule packed into red blood cells. A Weddell seal's blood has five times the oxygen storage capacity of human blood. Weight for weight, the seal has twice as much blood as a human, and the hemoglobin in its blood is 1.6 times more concentrated. Even its red blood cells are larger than those of humans, giving this seal's blood a thicker consistency.

A seal's circulatory system has many other features suited to diving. Underwater, the circulation concentrates on supplying the heart, lungs, and brain—those organs that will not tolerate a drop in oxygen level. The arteries supplying the other body parts constrict to limit blood flow. Blood going to the digestive system, muscles, skin, and flippers is reduced by 90 percent. The seal's heart now has to work less hard, and the heart rate drops from 50 and 60 beats per minute on the surface to about 15 beats per minute, greatly reducing the overall demand for oxygen.

## Baggy veins

A seal's veins are wide and baggy with thin walls. They act as a reservoir for blood diverted from the seal's tissues. Instead of coursing through the seal's body, losing oxygen on the way, the blood pools in these large veins, acting as an oxygen store for the heart, lungs, and brain. The hepatic sinus, a network of baggy veins between the lobes of the liver, is huge and holds six pints (three liters) of blood in the Weddell seal. The largest vein is the Y-shape vena cava: that of

**▼ RESPIRATORY SYSTEM AND HEART
Harbor seal**
*The seal's respiratory and circulatory systems can operate under pressure and for long periods without a fresh supply of air. The diaphragm is unusual because it runs at an oblique angle.*

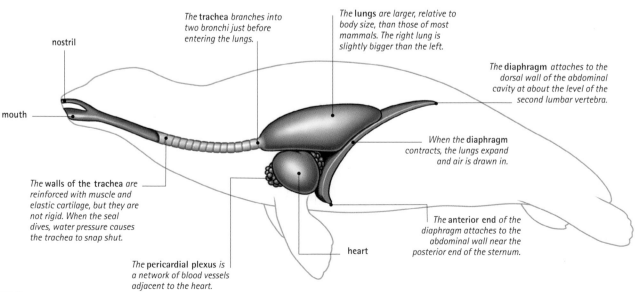

The **trachea** *branches into two bronchi just before entering the lungs.*

The **lungs** *are larger, relative to body size, than those of most mammals. The right lung is slightly bigger than the left.*

The **diaphragm** *attaches to the dorsal wall of the abdominal cavity at about the level of the second lumbar vertebra.*

*When the* **diaphragm** *contracts, the lungs expand and air is drawn in.*

nostril

mouth

The **walls of the trachea** *are reinforced with muscle and elastic cartilage, but they are not rigid. When the seal dives, water pressure causes the trachea to snap shut.*

The **anterior end** *of the diaphragm attaches to the abdominal wall near the posterior end of the sternum.*

heart

The **pericardial plexus** *is a network of blood vessels adjacent to the heart.*

**CLOSE-UP**

## Noisy noses

**In a seal's throat** is the usual mammalian larynx (voice box). It consists of a tubular skeleton of cartilage supporting a folded membrane (the vocal cords), which is vibrated to produce sound. However, seals possess a range of other sound-producing structures. Male hooded seals have an enlarged nose that produces not one but two bizarre visual and audible displays. A hood of skin on the snout can be inflated with air from the nostrils until it is twice the size of a soccer ball and covers the head. Alternatively, the male can close one nostril and inflate the stretchy, membranous nasal septum (the wall that divides the two nostrils). The septum pushes out of the other nostril and expands to form a bright red balloon. These bizarre displays are accompanied by a variety of equally odd blooping, pinging, and whooshing noises.

▲ **Hooded seal**
*Males make a variety of loud noises when they are competing for the right to mate with a female, and when they are threatening an adversary.*

the walrus is big enough for a person to pull it on like a pair of pants. The blood is held back in the veins by a muscular ring around the vena cava called the caval sphincter, which controls the return of blood to the heart.

The oxygen-starved cells and tissues continue to function using their own oxygen stores, but eventually they may begin to respire without oxygen (anaerobically). This process produces lactic acid as a by-product, which causes pain and fatigue when it builds up. Seals can tolerate a higher level of lactic acid than humans, but eventually they must return to the surface to breathe in air. Still, seals can hold their breath for very long periods. For example, a Weddell seal can last more than one hour between breaths and an elephant seal for over two hours. When the seal reaches the air, its massive veins return blood quickly to the heart, which starts pumping very quickly. Together with rapid breathing, the heart replenishes oxygen stores, and lactic acid in the tissues is broken down. Normal dives tend not to involve much anaerobic work, and the seal can usually dive again very soon.

In diving to 300 feet (90 m), the pressure on a ringed seal multiplies by 10, owing to the weight of the water above. The water pressure compresses air in the lungs, which decrease to 1/10 their surface volume. The lungs of deeper-diving seals collapse completely. The construction of a seal's respiratory system copes with these pressure changes. All the airways in the lungs are reinforced with muscle and rings of elastic cartilage, but they are neither thick nor rigid and will not break. They collapse safely, then pop open again when the seal ascends.

The tiny alveoli (the chambers at the end of every airway that exchange gases with the bloodstream) are the first structures to squash flat. Next, the smallest bronchioles (narrowest airways) collapse, followed by the bronchi, and finally the trachea. This sequence ensures that air is forced from the lungs and out of the body, away from contact with the bloodstream, thus preventing gas exchange. Exchange of gas at depth is dangerous, because nitrogen in the air dissolves in the blood and can cause "the bends" when the seal ascends to the surface.

# Digestive and excretory systems

**COMPARE** the intestines of a seal with those of a plant-eating *ELEPHANT*. Meat is easier to digest than plant matter, so meat-eating animals usually have shorter intestines than plant-eaters. However, seals are exceptional: like plant-eating animals, they have long intestines.

The digestive system of most mammals in the order Carnivora is fairly simple and forms a path from the mouth, through the stomach and short intestine, to the rectum. The animal matter that they eat is easy to digest—it has little of the indigestible fibrous tissue of plants. Seals are members of the Carnivora, but their digestive system differs in some significant ways.

First, seals lack the characteristic slicing carnassial teeth of other carnivores. Their teeth act only to grab and hold their prey, whether these are fish, shrimplike crustaceans, squid, or penguins. The front teeth are therefore large and pointed, and the cheek teeth are usually simple and conical, without the complex cusps and range of forms and functions seen in most mammals. There are, however, exceptions to this rule. The crabeater seal, for instance, feeds almost entirely on krill—a swarming, shrimplike crustacean. Its cheek teeth are finely divided into many lobes. It feeds by sucking krill into its mouth and then squeezing all the water out through its teeth, trapping the krill inside. The ringed seal also feeds on shrimplike animals (mysids and amphipods), but it eats many fish, such as polar cod, as well. Its teeth are not specialized in shape or function.

Seals do not slice or chew their food—they swallow it whole. The throat, or esophagus, is therefore pleated with folds that can expand to allow large food items to slip down easily. The stomach is a simple sack, similar to that of most carnivores. Unlike other carnivores, however, seals may have an enormously long small intestine. In the small intestine, digestion is completed and absorption of the liberated nutrients takes place. This is a quick and relatively simple process in the case of meat eaters, so it is unclear why elephant seals, for instance, have small intestines up to 660 feet (202 m) long. It is normal for a carnivorous mammal to have a small intestine only five or

▼ **Harbor seal**
*The most notable feature of the seal's digestive tract is the very long small intestine—reaching a staggering 660 feet (202 m) long in elephant seals. Seals have a high-protein diet, and the kidneys filter out urea—a toxic by-product of protein breakdown—and excrete it in the urine.*

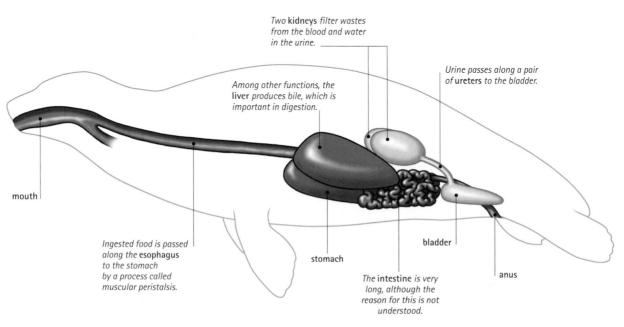

*Two **kidneys** filter wastes from the blood and water in the urine.*

*Among other functions, the **liver** produces bile, which is important in digestion.*

*Urine passes along a pair of **ureters** to the bladder.*

mouth

*Ingested food is passed along the **esophagus** to the stomach by a process called muscular peristalsis.*

stomach

bladder

*The **intestine** is very long, although the reason for this is not understood.*

anus

six times its body length. Also unusual is the large intestine, which has no specific adaptation for absorbing water. Most mammals recover as much water as they can from the remains of their food by absorption across the wall of the large intestine. Seals, however, do not reabsorb much water, and they pass frequent, watery feces.

## Diet

The diet of seals contains plenty of fat and protein, but almost no carbohydrate. They do not receive sugars by direct breakdown of dietary carbohydrate. Their metabolism (cell chemistry) must be based on the breakdown of lipids (fats) and proteins, both of which can yield glucose. Glucose is the most common blood sugar and a vital energy source for organs such as the brain.

Another element lacking in seals' diet is freshwater. Seals have no access to freshwater, although some polar species may chew ice and snow to obtain it. However, seals get all the water they need from their prey. The breakdown of both proteins and fats in food releases "metabolic" water as a by-product. Fat yields more than twice as much water as protein does, so a thirsty seal would do well to choose to eat oily fish.

▲ *This gray seal is eating a fish. Seals eat a large range of aquatic prey, mostly fish and aquatic invertebrates. Some Antarctic species hunt and eat penguins, and sea lions sometimes eat fur seal pups.*

## IN FOCUS

### Fasting

**Each year, during breeding and molting,** seals remain out of water. During this time they cannot eat or drink. This fast can last 90 days in the case of dominant male elephant seals in a breeding colony. Newly weaned elephant seal pups that have become fat on their mothers' milk may fast for 12 weeks before they learn to feed themselves. During these periods, seals live off their blubber. As is the case with fat in their food, breaking down the fat in their own body releases energy, the sugar glucose, and a lot of metabolic water. Even so, water must be conserved, and an elephant seal pup's urine volume reduces by 84 percent over 10 weeks of fasting, becoming extremely concentrated as the animal strives to save water.

## Water balance

The breakdown of dietary protein also produces the toxic, nitrogen-containing by-product urea. Seals must expel urea in solution in water, as urine. Owing to the loss of water in urine, seals experience a net loss of water from breaking down protein, but water from the breakdown of fat more than compensates for this. Even so, seals must constantly conserve water, especially during periods of fasting.

Production of urine is the principal role of the kidneys. They regulate levels of dissolved substances in the blood and filter out unwanted substances, to be expelled in the urine. Seals' kidneys must work intensively, because they have to remove the large quantities of salt that build up in the blood. The kidneys must also eliminate unwanted substances in concentrated form to avoid losing too much water. The kidneys are therefore large and made up of many lobes, sometimes more than 200. Each lobe functions as a miniature kidney with its own blood supply. Seals' veins branch into a complex mesh around the kidneys to keep them supplied quickly with new, salty blood to filter. Among mammals, only whales and seals have such "lobular," or "reniculate," kidneys.

# Reproductive system

The external sex organs of seals are all tucked away in neat crevices to maintain optimum streamlining. In most male mammals, the testes hang outside the body in the scrotum, so as to keep cool. In seals, they are inside the body, underneath the skin and blubber, but not embedded in deeper tissue. It is critical for sperm manufacture, which occurs inside the testes, that the temperature is kept lower that the normal mammalian body temperature of around 99°F (37°C). The testes of seals are therefore cooled by blood flowing in from the cold hind flippers. The blood is diverted into a mesh surrounding the testes and can cool the testes by up to 7°F (4°C). This arrangement is an example of countercurrent heat exchange.

Another striking feature of a male seal's reproductive system is the large baculum, or penis bone. It is formed from the mineralized spongy tissue of the penis itself. Its function is unclear, but when the penis is not fully erect, a male seal can successfully mate with a female by using the penis bone.

The female reproductive system is of the standard Y-shape form of mammals. Each of the two ovaries is enveloped in a sac called the ovarian bursa. Eggs released from an ovary pass into a fallopian tube and down into the uterus (womb). The uterus is bicornate, and its two horns join near the cervix. Pregnancies therefore usually occur in one of the two arms of the Y-shape uterus.

Courtship and mating occur on land in the same places the females use to give birth and nurse their pups. The males and females mate, and next season's egg is fertilized as soon as the females have finished nursing this season's pup. The egg develops into a blastocyst (a hollow ball of cells), but does not implant in the uterus or develop any further for several months. The eventual implantation and development of the embryo are timed so that the pup is born almost a year later. Seals are vulnerable on land, and extending the gestation period in this way enables the seals to make just one trip to the breeding grounds a year, rather than two.

▼ **Harbor seal**
*The female has two ovaries, and the uterus is bicornuate (two-horned). The male seal has internal testes, in which sperm is made, and a baculum (penis bone).*

ovary

uterine tube

bicornuate uterus

ovarian bursa

opening of uterine tube

fimbriae

opening of uterine horn

cervix

vagina (cut open)

bladder

urethra

urethral opening

clitoris

**Female**

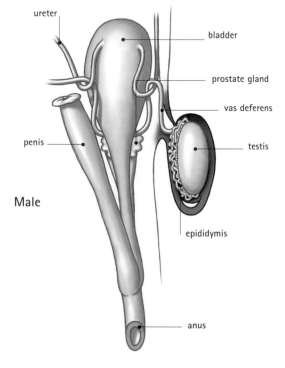

ureter

bladder

prostate gland

vas deferens

testis

penis

epididymis

**Male**

anus

CLOSE-UP

## Sexual display

**Different species of seal use** various parts of their anatomy to attract mates or intimidate sexual rivals. The most important function of walrus tusks, for instance is thought to be sexual display. Likewise, the male elephant seal's proboscis signals his fitness as a mate. It begins growing at age two years, but it is not fully developed until the male is eight years old. When the seal is excited, the proboscis is enlarged by muscle action, by engorgement with blood, and by inflation using the lungs.

## Growth spurt

Newborn pups lack thick blubber and are thus less well insulated than adults. Pups of most species have a fluffy, often white, coat (called laguno) that helps them keep warm while they work on building up a layer of fat. However, unlike the sleek adult coat, laguno is not waterproof so these fluffy pups must stay on land or on the ice until after their first molt. The precocious young of harbor and hooded seals molt before they are born, and they are able to swim almost from birth.

Seal mothers feed their young intensively on milk, in a process called lactation, from either two or four mammary glands (nipples). The nipples are positioned on either side of, and a little above and below, the mother's navel. The milk is rich and creamy, with the consistency of melted vanilla ice cream and a bland, waxy taste. In elephant seals, the milk's fat content rises from 15 to 55 percent in the first 21 days, while the water content falls from 75 to 35 percent. These changes suit the metabolic needs of the pup. At first, it needs plenty of water, but later it can make its own water by breaking down some of its newly formed blubber. Its priority then is to pile on as many pounds of blubber as it can, as quickly as possible.

Lactation is very demanding on the mother, because she is effectively transferring her blubber to her pup while taking on no food or water herself. She is expending energy six times as quickly as in resting (elephant seal

▲ *These two gray seals are mating in shallow water off the English coast. The male seal is above the female.*

mothers lose some 40 percent of their body weight during this period). The effort translates into incredible growth rate in pups. The elephant seal pup doubles its birth weight in 11 days, gaining 13 pounds (6 kg) a day. The harp seal pup puts on 5.5 pounds (2.5 kg) a day and triples its birth weight in a lactation period of only 9 days.

## Snow lair

Suckling of young takes place either on land, on solid "fast" sea ice, or on pack ice. The female ringed seal uses her strong, clawed front flippers to dig a snow lair, from below, at a weak point in the fast ice. She remains close to her pup, feeding it milk for some weeks. Species that use less stable pack ice, such as the harp seal, have an extremely short, rapid form of lactation. The hooded seal is the most extreme species in this respect. It has the shortest suckling period of any mammal, completing it in an astonishing 3 to 5 days, during which the pup almost doubles in weight from 48 to 94 pounds (22–42.6 kg). Most of the weight gain is as blubber rather than growth of muscles or skeleton.

ROB HOUSTON

**FURTHER READING AND RESEARCH**

Bonner, Nigel W. 1989. *The Natural History of Seals.* Christopher Helm: London.

Vaughan, T. A., J. M. Ryan, and N. J. Czaplewski. 2000. *Mammalogy.* 4th edition. Saunders College Publishing: Philadelphia, PA.

# Squirrel

ORDER: Rodentia  FAMILY: Sciuridae
SUBFAMILY: Sciurinae  GENERA: 50

Squirrels are among the most widespread of mammals and live in a diverse range of habitats. From tropical rain forests and semiarid deserts to coniferous forests and even temperate city gardens, squirrels have been able to exploit many ecological niches. Many species of squirrels have an arboreal (tree-living) lifestyle, but there are also ground-living species that live in burrows.

## Anatomy and taxonomy

Scientists group all organisms into taxonomic groups based largely on anatomical features. Scientists place squirrels in the order Rodentia—the rodents—which are among the most numerous and successful of all animal groups. Squirrels belong to a group of rodents that also includes chipmunks, marmots, and prairie dogs.

● **Animals**  All animals are multicellular. They get the energy and materials they need to survive by consuming other organisms. Unlike plants, fungi, and the members of other kingdoms, animals are able to move around for at least one phase of their life.

● **Chordates**  At some time in its life cycle, a chordate has a stiff dorsal (back) supporting rod called a notochord. Most, although not all, chordates are vertebrates. The notochord of vertebrates becomes part of the spine, or backbone. The spine is made up of units called vertebrae, which are generally made of bone.

● **Mammals**  One of the eight classes of vertebrates, mammals are warm-blooded animals with four limbs and, in most cases, a tail. They have body hair, which generally covers nearly all of the body surface, making a thick fur. All mammals nourish their newborns with milk secreted from

▼ There are three main types of squirrels: tree squirrels, ground squirrels, and flying squirrels. This family tree shows that the gray and red squirrels are members of the family Sciuridae, which are mammals in the order Rodentia.

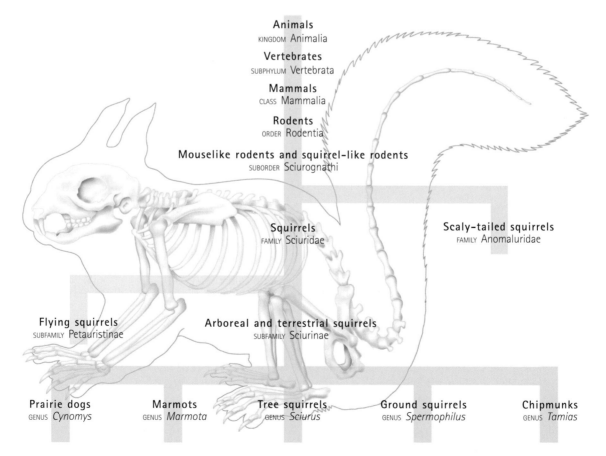

**Animals**
KINGDOM Animalia

**Vertebrates**
SUBPHYLUM Vertebrata

**Mammals**
CLASS Mammalia

**Rodents**
ORDER Rodentia

**Mouselike rodents and squirrel-like rodents**
SUBORDER Sciurognathi

**Squirrels**
FAMILY Sciuridae

**Scaly-tailed squirrels**
FAMILY Anomaluridae

**Flying squirrels**
SUBFAMILY Petauristinae

**Arboreal and terrestrial squirrels**
SUBFAMILY Sciurinae

**Prairie dogs**
GENUS Cynomys

**Marmots**
GENUS Marmota

**Tree squirrels**
GENUS Sciurus

**Ground squirrels**
GENUS Spermophilus

**Chipmunks**
GENUS Tamias

mammary glands on the female's underside or front. Three species of mammals lay eggs, and some others suckle their young in pouches on the underside of the body. Most mammals, including squirrels, nourish their unborn young through a temporary organ called the placenta. This organ allows the young to develop while still inside the mother. Mammalian red blood cells lack a nucleus.

● **Rodents** This group is a very large order of placental mammals. Compared with other mammals, most of the 2,000 species of rodents are small. They are equipped with large chisel-like incisors, which make these mammals expert gnawers. This ability has allowed rodents to exploit a huge variety of foods and live in a wide array of habitats.

● **Sciurognathi** This suborder of rodents includes the squirrels, prairie dogs, beavers, and mouselike rodents, such as rats. Sciurognaths are distinguished from other rodents, which include guinea pigs (or cavies), chinchillas, capybaras, and porcupines. Members of this second group— the cavylike rodents—have a larger head and a more robust body than sciurognaths. The sciurognaths are thought to resemble more the primitive rodent form from which all modern rodents evolved.

● **Sciuridae** This family includes the arboreal and terrestrial squirrels but does not include the scaly-tailed squirrels, which belong to the family Anomaluridae. The family Sciuridae contains more than 270 species and is divided into two subfamilies: the Sciurinae and the Pteromyinae. The Pteromyinae includes the flying squirrels.

● **Sciurinae** This subfamily of rodents contains the tree squirrels, ground squirrels, chipmunks, and marmots. Their

▲ *The coloration of the red squirrel varies from bright reddish brown to dark grayish brown or almost black.*

range covers most continents except Australia, southern South America, and some desert regions.

● *Sciurus* The American tree squirrels and the Eurasian tree squirrels that are found north of the tropics belong to the genus *Sciurus*. This geographically widespread genus has a total of 28 species, including the Eurasian red squirrel, Arizona gray squirrel, Japanese squirrel, and yellow-throated squirrel.

**EXTERNAL ANATOMY** Squirrels are medium-size rodents with a small, rounded head and a long, bushy tail. Squirrels have dexterous front paws that they use to manipulate food and, in the case of tree squirrels, use for climbing. *See pages 220–223.*

**SKELETAL SYSTEM** The skeleton of a squirrel is relatively light, allowing the squirrel to climb and leap easily from tree to tree. Squirrels walk on the soles of the feet and have long toes terminating in claws. *See pages 224–225.*

**MUSCULAR SYSTEM** The tail muscles enable a squirrel to move its tail in any direction. Flying squirrels have a muscular gliding membrane called a patagium. *See pages 226–227.*

**NERVOUS SYSTEM** Squirrels have an excellent sense of smell and use scent to communicate with other squirrels.

They also have very good eyesight, which tree squirrels use to navigate accurately from branch to branch. *See page 228.*

**CIRCULATORY AND RESPIRATORY SYSTEMS** Like all other mammals, squirrels have a four-chamber heart and a closed circulatory system consisting of arteries and veins. Respiratory gases are transferred in and out of the body across the surfaces of a pair of lungs. *See page 229.*

**DIGESTIVE AND EXCRETORY SYSTEMS** The digestive system is suited to a diet made up mostly of plant matter and has a large cecum containing bacteria that break down cellulose. *See pages 230–231.*

**REPRODUCTIVE SYSTEM** Squirrels have one or two litters each year, depending on the species. There are usually one to six pups in each litter. *See pages 232–233.*

FEATURED SYSTEMS

# External anatomy

**CONNECTIONS**

**COMPARE** the hind feet of a squirrel with those of a *HARE*, which has hind feet that are suited to leaping rather than climbing and cannot be rotated at the ankle.

**COMPARE** the tail of a squirrel with that of a *JACKSON'S CHAMELEON.* The reptile's tail is fully prehensile (able to grip), whereas that of the squirrel is used only for balance.

Squirrels are expert climbers and diggers. They are also among the most successful mammalian groups in terms of the number of species: there are more than 270 species worldwide. They have evolved to suit life in a wide variety of habitats. Many species live in forests, from the tropics to the cool temperate zone. Other species inhabit deserts, plains, or tundra. A few species, particularly the eastern gray squirrel, have even adapted to life in city parks and backyards. The smallest species is the mouse-size African pygmy squirrel, with a head and body length of just 2.6 to 3.9 inches (6.6–10 cm). The largest species is the heavyweight alpine marmot, which is 20.8 to 28.7 inches (53–73 cm) long. The biggest tree squirrel is the black giant squirrel of southeastern Asia, which has a head and body length of up to 18 inches (46 cm) and a tail almost as long again.

11 inches
(28 cm)

▶ **Eurasian red squirrel**
*This species of squirrel is easily recognized by its reddish brown fur, large, dark eyes, prominent ear tufts, rounded head, bushy tail, and long facial whiskers. Adults of this species weigh 9 to 11.3 ounces (250–320 g).*

*Prominent tufts of fur give the **ears** a pointed appearance.*

*The **eyes** are large and dark, set high and slightly to the sides of the head. They give a wide field of view without impairing the vision needed to see in stereo.*

*The **whiskers** are long and sensitive, helping squirrels "feel" their way as they move rapidly along branches.*

*The **nose** provides an excellent sense of smell, which helps the squirrel detect even food that is buried underground.*

*The **claws** are robust and sharp, anchoring the squirrel as it scales or descends steep angles on tree trunks and branches.*

*The **forelimbs** are stout and used for grasping food and climbing.*

The **tail** *is a versatile appendage providing balance, warmth, or shade and is essential in communicating with other squirrels.*

The **fur** *is soft, is richly colored, and grows much thicker during winter to provide better insulation from cold weather.*

Flexible **ankle joints** *enable the hind feet to rotate backward, allowing the squirrel to dangle from its hind feet or descend a tree trunk headfirst.*

## Footpads

**All squirrels have hard pads of skin** on the soles of their feet that provide a better grip for holding food and extra traction when the animal is in motion. The long footpads of the long-clawed ground squirrel are covered by fur, which protects the feet from burning when the animal is running over hot desert sand. The outer edges of the hind feet also have fringes of stiff hair that help push the sand away in burrowing.

### Body shapes

Typical tree squirrels, such as the Eurasian red squirrel, have a mainly arboreal lifestyle, spending much of their time high in the trees. Tree squirrels have a long, supple, cylindrical body, a rounded head with prominent ears, and a large bushy tail. Squirrels have short forelegs and longer hind legs. They can descend trees headfirst and rotate their double-jointed hind feet backward while their claws dig into the bark for support.

Ground-dwelling squirrels, such as the arctic ground squirrel, are heavier-bodied with shorter legs, ears, and hair and a less bushy tail than tree squirrels. These features help squirrels pass in and out of their burrows with ease. Their strong forelimbs have large claws for scratching and digging in the soil. Both tree and ground

▲ SIZE COMPARISON

*The black giant squirrel (right) of southeastern Asia is much larger than the Eurasian red squirrel and can reach 18 inches (46 cm) from nose to rump, with a tail as long as its body or even longer.*

▲ **Ground squirrel**
*Ground squirrels in the genus* Spermophilus *inhabit open country in North America, eastern Europe, and central Asia. The name* Spermophilus *means "seed-lover," reflecting the animal's preferred diet.*

## COMPARATIVE ANATOMY

### Head shapes

**Most squirrels typically have a rounded head** with large eyes, a short snout, and prominent front teeth, which are used for gnawing food. Some ground squirrels have cheek pouches for storing food. Nocturnal flying squirrels have larger eyes and ears; well-developed senses help these squirrels live in darkness. Unusually, the aptly named shrew-faced ground squirrel from southeastern Asia has a long, pointed muzzle similar to that of the tree shrews, but its short, bushy tail helps distinguish it from these rodents.

▶ EAR SHAPES
*Good hearing is vital for flying squirrels because they are active at night and thus less able to rely on sight. The ears of the gray squirrel lack the tufts of the red squirrel, but gray squirrels are equally sensitive to sounds of danger and the calls of other squirrels.*

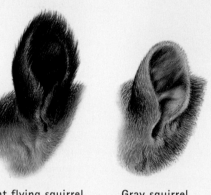

**Giant flying squirrel**          **Gray squirrel**

squirrels have a small thumb and four toes on the forelegs and five toes on the hind legs, with the exception of the woodchuck of North America, which has just four hind toes.

### Ears and eyes
Chipmunks, tree squirrels, and flying squirrels all have large ears that are highly sensitive to sound. The Eurasian red squirrel also has distinctive tufts of fur that give its ears a pointed appearance, a feature shared by several other species, including its North American relative, Abert's squirrel; and the groove-toothed squirrel, which lives only in Borneo. All squirrels have large eyes circled by a ring of pale fur. The eyes are positioned high on the sides of the head. They give a wide field of view and binocular vision, which enables squirrels to judge distances with great accuracy.

### Multipurpose tail and sensitive hair
A squirrel's bushy tail has several important functions. It acts as a rudder when the squirrel leaps, provides essential balance during climbing and running, and serves as a signaling device to other squirrels, particularly when danger threatens. A squirrel's tail is 80 to 90 percent the length of its head and body and can thus provide vital warmth when curled around the body during sleep. Similarly, when draped across the back it shades the animal from the sun during hot weather.

Like other squirrels, the Eurasian red squirrel has highly touch-sensitive hairs called vibrissae on its head, feet, and outer legs, and at the base of its tail. The extra sensitivity these hairs give helps the squirrel navigate quickly and efficiently as it moves through the trees. The Eurasian red squirrel molts its body fur twice each year, in spring and fall; but the tail and ear tufts are molted only once, during the summer. Its fur is usually rich chestnut on most of the body with pale cream fur on the underside, but there is much regional variation, and color may vary from light brown to almost black. The fur of a typical Eurasian red squirrel becomes thicker and darker during the winter, and in Russia this species is still hunted for its attractive pelt during the cold months.

patagium (gliding membrane)

▲ **Giant flying squirrel**
*The gliding membranes on the flanks of the giant flying squirrel are tucked away when the animal climbs along branches.*

▲ *Although a flying squirrel, such as this small Japanese flying squirrel, does not have the advantage of powered flight, it can glide through the forest air with grace and precision. The fur-covered gliding membrane is called a patagium.*

## Leapers and gliders

Although bats are the only mammals that can truly fly, flying squirrels have evolved over millions of years the ability to glide from tree to tree using a parachute-like membrane of furry skin stretched between their long forelegs and hind legs. This gliding is a very efficient form of locomotion: giant flying squirrels in Asia can travel as far as 1,500 feet (460 m) in a single glide. Flying squirrels have large, dark eyes, dense, soft fur, and a long, flattened tail, which they use to steer as they glide. They are highly arboreal: they spend most of their time in trees and rarely descend to the ground. One of the best-known species, the southern flying squirrel, is found across much of the eastern United States. Like most flying squirrels, however, it is strictly nocturnal and therefore difficult to observe. Biologists believe the gliding membranes make these squirrels more vulnerable to predators during daylight, so nocturnal habits enable them to avoid danger.

The scaly-tailed flying squirrels of Africa are not considered true squirrels. The anatomy of their head differs significantly from that of other flying squirrels, and their gliding membranes are attached at the elbow rather than at the wrist. They also have a shorter, tufted tail. The underside of the tail has twin rows of raised scales that are used for gaining extra purchase during climbing, and the tail serves as a rapidly deployed anchor when the squirrel lands.

◄ *Sharp hind claws, flexible ankle joints, and a balancing tail enable tree squirrels, such as this Eurasian red squirrel, to perch on branches with poise and climb with extraordinary agility.*

# Skeletal system

**COMPARE** the plantigrade feet of a squirrel with the digitigrade feet of a **PUMA**. Locomotion in plantigrade animals involves walking or bounding with the soles of the feet touching the ground, whereas digitigrade animals use just the tips of their toes for walking or running.

In common with all other mammalian skeletons, a squirrel's skeleton can be divided into two parts: the axial skeleton, which is the skull and spine from neck to tail; and the appendicular skeleton, which consists of the limbs, pectoral girdle, and pelvic girdle. A tree squirrel's skeleton typically has lightweight bones with flexibility that allows the squirrel to leap and climb easily. Caudal vertebrae form a long, slender, and very flexible tailbone, giving the tail greater mobility for balancing, signaling, and providing protection from the elements.

The hind limb bones are longer, denser, and heavier than those of the forelimbs, giving the squirrel extra strength and support as it moves. The toes are long. Squirrels are plantigrade

mammals: they bound with the soles of their feet touching the ground. The thumb bones on the forefeet are much smaller, but all digits are equipped with strong, curved claws. A squirrel's wrist bones are strong but flexible, enabling the forelimbs to be used constantly during foraging and eating. Ground squirrels also use their forelimbs to assist in digging; tree squirrels use them for climbing; and flying squirrels use them for adjusting the shape and size of the gliding membrane during glides.

## A rounded skull

A Eurasian red squirrel's skull is rounded and has deep eye sockets, which accommodate large eyes. Like other squirrels, the red squirrel has a

▼ **Eurasian red squirrel**
*The red squirrel's skeleton is a light, flexible frame that enables the animal to move easily in the trees. The hind limbs are longer than the forelimbs and propel the animal during running or climbing. The long tail helps balance the squirrel.*

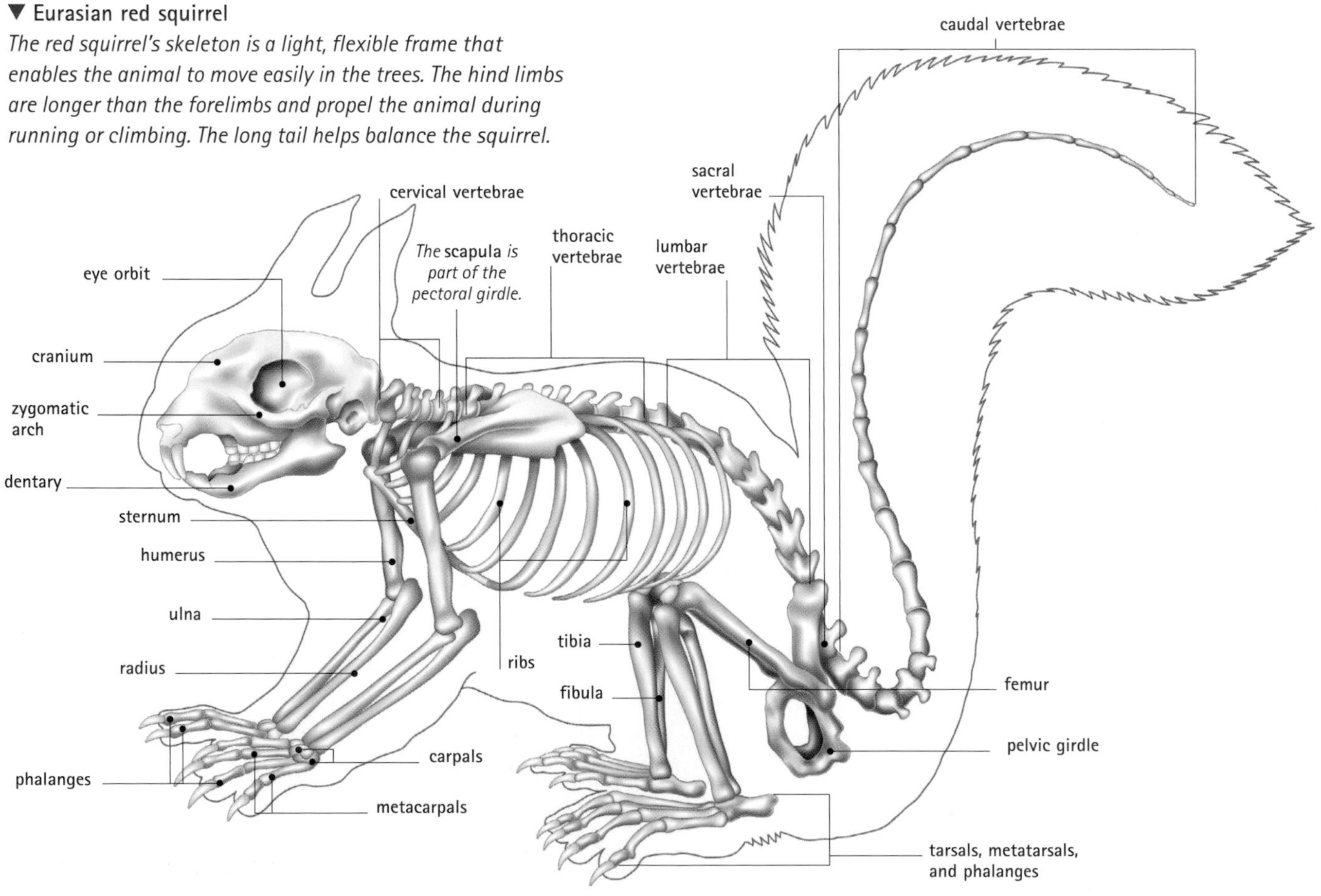

eye orbit

cranium

zygomatic arch

dentary

sternum

humerus

ulna

radius

phalanges

carpals

metacarpals

cervical vertebrae

*The **scapula** is part of the pectoral girdle.*

thoracic vertebrae

lumbar vertebrae

sacral vertebrae

caudal vertebrae

tibia

ribs

fibula

femur

pelvic girdle

tarsals, metatarsals, and phalanges

lower jaw structure that is relatively primitive but is also strong and mobile. The lower jaw juts forward when the squirrel gnaws.

## Gnawing teeth

Squirrels' teeth are typical of rodents in their adaptation for gnawing. Squirrels have a single pair of rootless, chisel-like incisors in each jaw, and one or two premolars and three molars on each side of each jaw. Squirrels do not have canines, teeth that are highly developed in carnivores for tearing meat.

There is a large gap between the incisors and premolars, which is called the diastema. Squirrels can suck their lips into this space to prevent nutshells and other inedible debris from being swallowed as the squirrel gnaws. Unlike the incisors, the cheek teeth have roots, and their crowns are low and covered by a rough ridged surface that helps the squirrel grind up hard food such as nuts.

**EVOLUTION**

## Determining relationships

**Scientific examination of fossil and modern skeletons** has shown that squirrels have changed little in millions of years. The pattern of evolution has made the determination of their family tree difficult. The earliest known squirrel, called *Protosciurus*, appeared in the late Oligocene epoch about 34 million years ago, and the fossil remains of its skeleton suggest that it was a tree climber.

Some scientists believe that flying squirrels evolved separately from other squirrels, and their ancestors were the paramyid rodents of the early Eocene period, about 54 million years ago. These large, primitive rodents had squirrel-like features, such as a long tail and clawed feet. This theory is based on studies of fossilized teeth, but increasingly other biologists argue that the evidence is incomplete and look instead to modern genetic studies to trace the origins and relationships within the squirrel family tree. Consequently, many experts now believe that flying squirrels are a subfamily of the family Sciuridae, having evolved from the same common ancestor as modern tree squirrels.

**CLOSE-UP**

## Incisors

**Like the incisors of all other rodents,** a squirrel's incisors have no roots and a high crown (such high-crowned teeth are termed hypsodont). They grow constantly throughout the animal's life and must therefore be worn down by constant use to prevent them from growing too long. The rear surface of the incisors has no enamel coating, so as the teeth grind against each other when the squirrel gnaws, the softer dentine layer on the rear surface is eroded. The enamel is then exposed as the chisel-like cutting edge of the tooth, which is highly effective at cutting open the hard outer shells of nuts and seeds.

▶ *Typical of squirrels and rodents in general, this arctic ground squirrel has large chisel-like incisors. The beveled edge of the teeth results from the erosion of dentine on the incisors' rear surface.*

# Muscular system

**CONNECTIONS**

**COMPARE** the structure of the patagium of a flying squirrel with that of a *FRUIT BAT*. The flying squirrel's patagium is a fur-covered muscular membrane used for gliding, whereas that of the fruit bat is thinner, with fine hairs, and is used for true flight.

A squirrel's musculature can be divided into three types: the cardiac muscles of the heart; the smooth muscles that enclose the blood vessels and the digestive and excretory systems; and the skeletal, or striated, muscles that are attached to the bones and enable the squirrel to move. Skeletal muscles are arranged in opposite, or antagonistic, pairs. When one muscle (the extensor) contracts, it causes a movement in one direction. The contraction of the opposing muscle (the flexor) results in movement in the opposite direction. The action of skeletal muscles is essential for all the squirrel's movements, from climbing, leaping, and gnawing to digging and blinking.

## Jaw muscles

Squirrels have a distinctive arrangement of jaw muscles that enables them to gnaw their food. The principle jaw muscle is the masseter, which has several branches and is responsible for moving a squirrel's lower jaw as it gnaws and chews. The lateral branch stretches in front of the eye to the snout and is anchored by way of a broad plate on the skull. It is responsible for directing the movement of the incisor teeth by pushing the lower jaw forward when the squirrel gnaws. The superficial branch is much shorter and is used only for closing the jaws. The lateral branch of the masseter is attached to the skull by way of a

▼ BODY MUSCLES
**Eurasian red squirrel**
*Squirrels, like other rodents, have well-developed jaw muscles for gnawing and strong hind limb muscles for bounding between branches in trees.*

zygomatic arch

*The* temporalis muscle *is relatively large.*

lateral masseter

*The* point of attachment *of the lateral masseter.*

superficial masseter

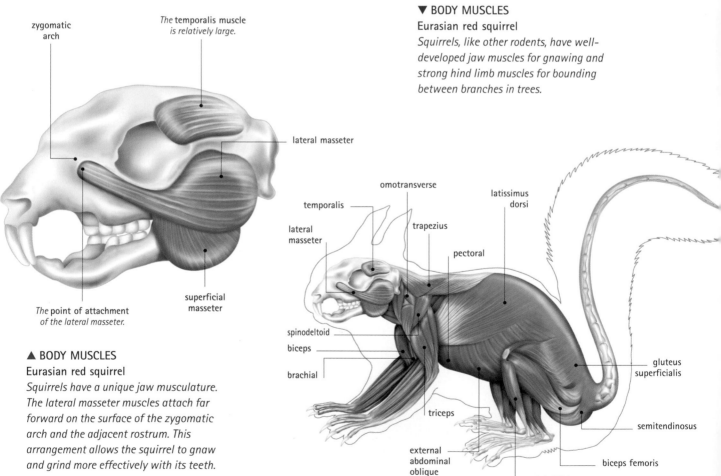

▲ BODY MUSCLES
**Eurasian red squirrel**
*Squirrels have a unique jaw musculature. The lateral masseter muscles attach far forward on the surface of the zygomatic arch and the adjacent rostrum. This arrangement allows the squirrel to gnaw and grind more effectively with its teeth.*

omotransverse

temporalis

lateral masseter

trapezius

latissimus dorsi

pectoral

spinodeltoid

biceps

brachial

triceps

external abdominal oblique

cranial tibial

gluteus superficialis

semitendinosus

biceps femoris

knob of bone on the rostrum (front of the skull) called the masseteric tubercle.

As the squirrel chews and gnaws, the masseter is assisted by two additional sets of jaw muscles: the pterygoid and temporal muscles. The pterygoid muscles generate horizontal movement, and the temporal muscles create vertical movement. The pterygoid's flexibility helps the squirrel grind its food effectively. The arrangement and structure of jaw muscles are remarkably similar in most species of squirrels, but scientists have discovered that pygmy tree squirrels have unusually small temporal muscles and a superficial masseter muscle positioned in such a way that it allows the jaw to retract.

## Muscles for gliding

Flying squirrels have a fur-covered muscular gliding membrane called a patagium, which acts like a parachute. The patagium looks like a flap of loose skin running continuously from the front legs to the hind legs—in some species it is also attached to the neck and tail. The patagium is made up of thin sheets of muscle that can be tensed or relaxed at will. At the front it is supported by a thin rod of cartilage on each side, attached to the wrists. When

### IN FOCUS

## The muscular tail

**Squirrels have superb muscular control over their tail** and are able to maneuver it in any direction for balance, communication, and protection. When threatened, a squirrel will rapidly flex its tail muscles to flick the tail from side to side and erect the long brush hairs, perhaps to distract the enemy and warn other squirrels of danger. If the tail is held by a predator, it can break off, allowing the squirrel to escape. Any exposed muscle and vertebrae soon dry up and are then shed. The animal can usually survive despite the loss of its tail.

A flying squirrel uses its tail as an effective brake just before landing, by suddenly flexing the muscles: the tail curves upward at the end of a glide, and the squirrel's body immediately follows suit. The velocity of the glide is then considerably reduced just before contact with a tree trunk. The place from which the squirrel launches its glide is always higher than the place at which it lands. The tail is also used for balance as the squirrel then climbs the tree.

airborne, the squirrel steers with great accuracy by varying tension in the patagial muscles and changing the position of its limbs and tail. A flying squirrel is even able to maneuver abruptly at a right angle to a branch at the last moment before landing.

◀ Just before contact with a tree trunk, the southern flying squirrel raises its tail by flexing muscles at the base. In this position, the tail acts as a brake, lessening the impact on landing.

# Nervous system

Within the nervous system, there are two branches working together: the central nervous system (CNS; brain and spinal cord) and the peripheral nervous system (PNS; nerve fibers branching from the CNS). The CNS controls the voluntary actions of the body, such as skeletal-muscle movement. The PNS controls the involuntary movements and regulates heartbeat, the movement of smooth muscles in the digestive system, and the glandular release of hormones. The last is the trigger for the rapid responses of "fight or flight," flight being particularly important when the squirrel needs to escape from a predator.

### Dichromatic eyesight

The visual sensitivity of most mammals is concentrated in a small area of the retina called the fovea. However, squirrels have the advantage of equal sensitivity across their entire retina, which gives them excellent eyesight for seeing food and predators, such as hawks and martens. Densely packed cones in the retina also provide very good dichromatic color perception: squirrels can distinguish most colors except red and green.

### The endocrine system

The nervous and endocrine systems work together to control and regulate a squirrel's body activities and senses. The endocrine system affects growth, development, tissue function, and metabolic and reproductive processes. It is a network of glands that produce hormones, which are secreted directly into the squirrel's bloodstream and reach all regions of its body. Exocrine glands play an important role, as they produce scent secretions. Squirrels have an excellent sense of smell and use scent as a means of communication. The exocrine glands are located on the feet and are used to mark territory or leave other chemical messages, such as when a female comes into estrus and is ready to mate. Some species also scent-mark branches by wiping them with secretions from inside the mouth.

▶ **Eurasian red squirrel**
*Squirrels have four sets of sensitive whiskers, or vibrissae, on the head. They are located above and below their eyes, in front of the throat, and alongside the nose and act as touch receptors that help relay information about the squirrel's immediate surroundings to the brain. There are also touch-sensitive whiskers on the wrist, at the base of the tail, and around the feet.*

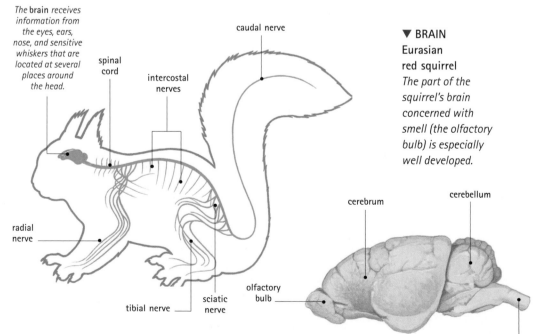

*The brain receives information from the eyes, ears, nose, and sensitive whiskers that are located at several places around the head.*

spinal cord

intercostal nerves

caudal nerve

radial nerve

tibial nerve

sciatic nerve

olfactory bulb

▼ **BRAIN Eurasian red squirrel**
*The part of the squirrel's brain concerned with smell (the olfactory bulb) is especially well developed.*

cerebrum

cerebellum

spinal cord

# Circulatory and respiratory systems

The squirrel's circulatory system is essential for survival. It sends oxygen from the lungs to cells throughout the body and sends soluble nutrients from the small intestine to the cells. The circulatory system also transports important antibodies and hormones, pumps water from the cells to the kidneys, and takes carbon dioxide to the lungs, where it is released from the body as the squirrel exhales.

## The heart and arteries

The driving force of the circulatory system is the heart. The squirrel's heart is a typically mammalian four-chamber structure and is made of cardiac muscle. Blood is pumped from the heart to the lungs, where oxygen is collected, and carbon dioxide is expelled. The blood then returns to the heart to be pumped around a larger circuit taking in the organs and other parts of the body. It travels in large arteries, which are long, robust tubes with strengthened walls to cope with the pressure of blood being pumped around the body. The arteries are connected to a network of ultrafine tubes called capillaries, which have thin walls and are in direct contact with the body's cells. Capillaries facilitate the exchange of both beneficial materials and waste. The blood is then drained back through veins to the heart, where the cycle begins again.

## Respiration

Squirrels share a very similar respiratory structure with other rodents, such as rats, mice, and jerboas. A squirrel's respiratory system consists of lungs with alveoli and air passages—bronchioles, bronchi, the trachea (windpipe), and the nasal passages. The lungs, combined with the heart, fill most of the space in the squirrel's upper body, called the thoracic cavity. The highly muscular diaphragm controls the movement and volume of air that passes to and from the lungs. As the diaphragm contracts and forces the rib cage to rise, negative pressure is created in the thoracic cavity, which makes the lungs expand, drawing in air.

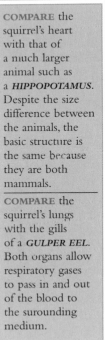

CONNECTIONS

COMPARE the squirrel's heart with that of a much larger animal such as a *HIPPOPOTAMUS*. Despite the size difference between the animals, the basic structure is the same because they are both mammals.

COMPARE the squirrel's lungs with the gills of a *GULPER EEL*. Both organs allow respiratory gases to pass in and out of the blood to the surounding medium.

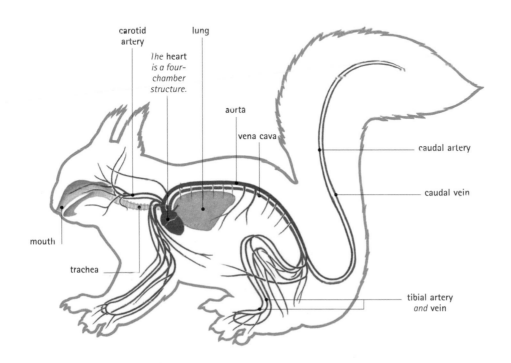

carotid artery

lung

The heart is a four-chamber structure.

aorta

vena cava

mouth

trachea

caudal artery

caudal vein

tibial artery *and* vein

◀ Eurasian red squirrel
*The muscular heart pumps blood to the lungs, where it picks up oxygen from inhaled air. The oxygenated blood returns to the heart, where it is then pumped around the rest of the body to supply cells with oxygen for respiration.*

229

# Digestive and excretory systems

CONNECTIONS

**COMPARE** the function of a squirrel's large cecum with the short vestigial appendix of a *HUMAN*. They evolved from the same structure.

**COMPARE** the structure of a squirrel's digestive system with that of a carnivore such as a *WEASEL*. Meat is easier to digest than plant matter, and so a weasel's digestive tract is much shorter than that of a squirrel.

Squirrels are mainly herbivorous, so their digestive system is equipped to break down the tough cellulose found in plant matter. In the mouth, food is chewed and ground into a soft lump called a bolus and then swallowed. The bolus passes along the esophagus, which is lined with mucous membranes that allow the food to pass smoothly down into the stomach. The food is broken up and softened in the stomach by muscular action and enzymes, including pepsin. This enzyme requires an acidic environment to be effective and is activated by hydrochloric acid produced by cells in the stomach wall. The food is prevented from leaving the stomach during this process by two circular muscles, called sphincters, which are located at either end of the stomach.

From the stomach, the food passes through the pyloric sphincter and into the small intestine. Most absorption (movement of food molecules from the intestine into the blood) occurs when the food enters the large intestine. A pouch connected to the large intestine, called

the cecum, contains a multitude of bacteria. These microorganisms specialize in breaking down large cellulose molecules into simple sugars and starches. The squirrel is therefore far more efficient at digesting plant carbohydrates than animal proteins. The cecum also absorbs most of the water produced by digestive secretions, enabling it to be used elsewhere within the body. There is some variation in digestive abilities among species. For example, the robust digestive tract of eastern gray squirrels can cope with large quantities of chemicals called tannins, which occur in acorns, far more effectively than the digestive tract of red squirrels.

## Food and feeding behaviors

Tree squirrels eat a wide variety of foods, including nuts, fruits, seeds, buds, catkins, sap, and even fungi and lichens. Ground squirrels forage mainly on grasses, roots, flowers, and bulbs. Many squirrels are opportunistic feeders and will supplement their diet with protein

▶ **Eurasian red squirrel**
*An important feature of the squirrel's digestive system is the cecum. This pouch in the large intestine contains bacteria that break down the tough plant protein cellulose.*

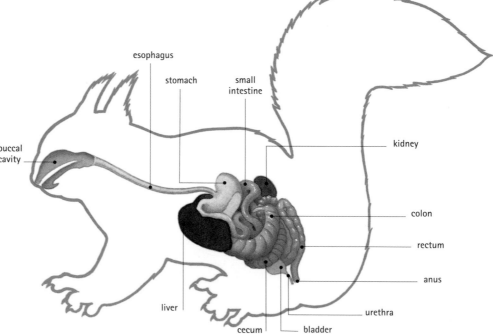

when available, from sources such as insects; small vertebrates, including frogs; and birds' eggs and nestlings. Both red and gray squirrels have often been observed chewing on animal bones, antlers, and even turtle shells—perhaps to supplement their calcium-poor diet with calcium and other essential minerals. Squirrels usually gain sufficient water from their regular food, but they may sometimes need to drink from puddles or pools during hot summer weather or in winter when food is scarce.

### Storing food

Foraging and feeding may take up to 80 percent of a squirrel's active time, and in northern species this time increases markedly during the fall because the animal increases food intake to build up body fat and thicken its fur for winter. Many species store food in caches by burying nuts just below the topsoil and hiding pinecones or seeds in burrows.

Fungi are stored as single pieces higher in trees. Caches usually contain one to four items of food, and buried seeds are often not found again and so may germinate. That is why—despite their reputation as a forest pest—squirrels play a key role in the dispersal and regeneration of trees such as oak and beech.

▲ *An Arizona gray squirrel gnaws fruit. Squirrels eat a variety of foods, including nuts, fruits, buds, and fungi.*

### Feeding on fungus

**Squirrels are able to eat certain fungi** that contain highly poisonous amanita toxins. Their stomachs are lined with a layer of mucus made up of glycoproteins that neutralize the toxins and allow the squirrel to digest the fungi. The glycoproteins bond with the toxic element and make it indigestible, so instead of entering the bloodstream the toxins are excreted harmlessly. In this way, squirrels are able to feast on mushrooms that would poison or even kill other animals.

# Reproductive system

**CONNECTIONS**

**COMPARE** the developmental stages of a newborn squirrel with a newborn *GIRAFFE*. Squirrels are born virtually helpless. A newborn giraffe, however, is highly developed.

**COMPARE** the large litter size of a squirrel with the small litters of an ape such as a *CHIMPANZEE* or a *HUMAN*. Ape babies are born large so there is not enough room in the uterus for several young.

The reproductive anatomy of squirrels is very similar to that of other mammals. There is little external difference between the sexes, although males have a wider space—about 0.4 inch (1 cm)—between their genital and anal openings. A male's testes become swollen in the breeding season, and their color may darken, possibly owing to staining by urine. Females have a Y-shape reproductive tract and six pairs of nipples, which deliver the milk from mammary glands for suckling young. The milk is rich in proteins and fats, and nourishes the newborn pups throughout their early stages of development. Lactation usually lasts for up to nine weeks after the young are born.

## Breeding and birth

Most Eurasian red squirrels become sexually mature at about 11 months old, and both sexes may be polygamous (they have numerous mates), particularly males. The female is in estrus for just one day of her cycle, and at this time her urine and vaginal secretions contain

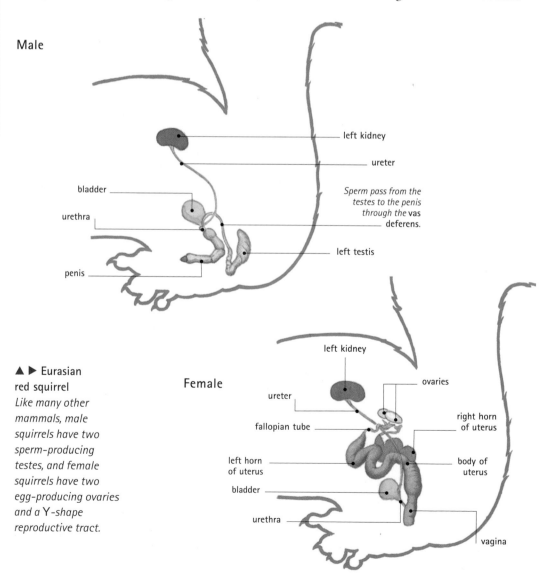

Male

left kidney

ureter

bladder

urethra

*Sperm pass from the testes to the penis through the* **vas deferens.**

left testis

penis

▲ ▶ Eurasian red squirrel
*Like many other mammals, male squirrels have two sperm-producing testes, and female squirrels have two egg-producing ovaries and a Y-shape reproductive tract.*

Female

left kidney

ovaries

ureter

right horn of uterus

fallopian tube

left horn of uterus

body of uterus

bladder

urethra

vagina

## The development of young squirrels

**Like all squirrels, Eurasian red squirrels** are born blind, deaf, and hairless and are completely dependent on their mother for the first seven weeks of life. After eight or nine days, their skin darkens with pigmentation and the first hairs begin to sprout. By 21 days, the entire body is covered with fur and the lower incisor teeth have appeared. The upper incisors follow at 31 to 42 days. The pups' eyes open by the time they are 30 days old, and they are able to hear at between 28 to 35 days. The mother uses her tongue to stimulate the pups to urinate and defecate until about the seventh week, when they begin to eat solid foods. By this time, they are able to begin leaving the nest for short periods; by the eighth week they are fully weaned, although the female may continue to protect them for a few extra weeks. They finally gain a full coat of adult fur at three to four months old and then disperse.

◀ *Like red squirrels, gray squirrels spend the first few weeks of life in the dray blind, deaf, and entirely dependent on their mother.*

chemical messages that signal to males that she is ready to mate. The female is often pursued relentlessly by several suitors, who may fight for the chance to mate with her. Courtship is extremely brief: the male mounts the female, and immediately after mating is completed the pair separate. Fertilization occurs internally, and the fertilized eggs (zygotes) become implanted in the wall of the uterus. Each fetus, like those of most mammals, attaches to a placenta and has fetal membranes through which it receives nutrition and expels waste. The female gives birth at about 38 days and tends the young alone, often remaining in the nest, or dray, for long periods when the pups are very young. She may sometimes transport the pups in her mouth to a new dray and usually covers them with nesting material if she leaves to forage.

Many species of squirrels, such as rock squirrels and the northern flying squirrels, have a single litter each year in spring. However, several species, such as chipmunks and eastern gray and Eurasian red squirrels, have two litters annually. They usually breed from mid-January to April and again from July to September, although this may depend on availability of food and other environmental conditions. The first breeding in spring may be delayed or avoided if there are insufficient food stocks available, but equally the breeding season may be prolonged if there is a good crop of seeds and mild weather. Litter size is usually one to six pups, but up to 11 have been recorded, although the larger species usually have smaller litters.

STEVEN SWABY

**FURTHER READING AND RESEARCH**

Macdonald, David. 2006. *The Encyclopedia of Mammals.* Facts On File: New York.

Nowak, Ronald M. 1999. *Walker's Mammals of the World.* Johns Hopkins University Press: Baltimore, MD.

# Wolf

ORDER: Carnivora  FAMILY: Canidae  GENUS: *Canis*

There are two species of true wolves in the genus *Canis*: the gray, or timber, wolf; and the red wolf. Some biologists consider the red wolf to be a hybrid and not a species in its own right. With a natural range taking in most terrestrial regions of the Northern Hemisphere, the gray wolf is one of the world's most widespread mammals. It is a superb predator, built for athleticism and endurance. Wolves have sharp vision and a phenomenally acute sense of smell. The biggest secret of their success, however, is teamwork—wolves are among the most social of all mammals.

## Anatomy and taxonomy
Scientists categorize all organisms into taxonomic groups based on anatomical, biochemical, and genetic similarities and differences.

● **Animals** Wolves, like other animals, are multicellular and fuel their body by eating organic material (food) from other organisms. Animals differ from other multicellular life-forms in their ability to move from one place to another (in most cases, using muscles). Animals are sensitive to stimuli such as touch, light, and various chemicals.

● **Chordates** At some time in its life cycle, a chordate has a stiff, dorsal (back) supporting rod called the notochord that runs all or most of the length of the body.

● **Vertebrates** In vertebrates, the notochord develops into a backbone (spine or vertebral column) made up of units called vertebrae. The vertebrate muscular system that moves the head, trunk, and limbs consists primarily of muscles arranged like a mirror image on either side of the backbone (bilateral symmetry about the skeletal axis).

● **Mammals** These vertebrate animals are warm-blooded and have hair made of keratin. Females have mammary glands that produce milk to feed their offspring. In mammals, the lower jaw is a single bone, the dentary, whereas in other vertebrates it is several fused bones. A mammal's inner ear contains three small bones (ear ossicles). Mature mammalian red blood cells lack a nucleus;

▼ *Wolves are mammals in the order Carnivora and family Canidae. There are two species of true wolves—gray and red wolves—both in the genus* Canis. *This genus also includes the dingo, domestic dog, coyote, Ethiopian wolf, and jackals. The maned wolf is placed in a different genus,* Chrysocyon.

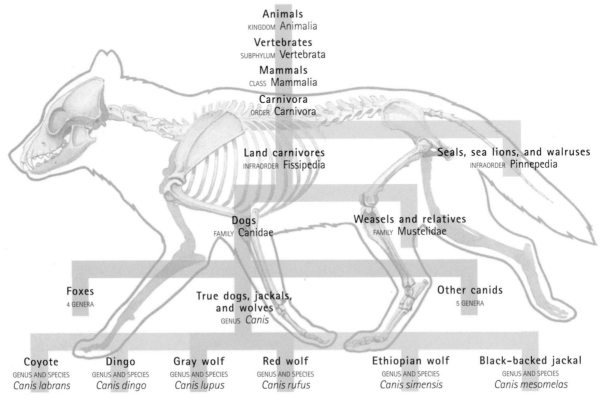

**Animals**
KINGDOM Animalia

**Vertebrates**
SUBPHYLUM Vertebrata

**Mammals**
CLASS Mammalia

**Carnivora**
ORDER Carnivora

**Land carnivores**
INFRAORDER Fissipedia

**Seals, sea lions, and walruses**
INFRAORDER Pinnepedia

**Dogs**
FAMILY Canidae

**Weasels and relatives**
FAMILY Mustelidae

**Foxes**
4 GENERA

**True dogs, jackals, and wolves**
GENUS *Canis*

**Other canids**
5 GENERA

**Coyote**
GENUS AND SPECIES
*Canis labrans*

**Dingo**
GENUS AND SPECIES
*Canis dingo*

**Gray wolf**
GENUS AND SPECIES
*Canis lupus*

**Red wolf**
GENUS AND SPECIES
*Canis rufus*

**Ethiopian wolf**
GENUS AND SPECIES
*Canis simensis*

**Black-backed jackal**
GENUS AND SPECIES
*Canis mesomelas*

all other vertebrates have red blood cells that contain a nucleus. Placental mammals nourish their unborn young through a placenta, a temporary organ that forms in the mother's uterus during pregnancy.

• **Carnivores** The word *carnivore* can be used to describe any animal that eats meat, but it applies more specifically to members of the mammalian order Carnivora. Members of this group include dogs, cats, bears, raccoons, mustelids, civets, hyenas, and their close relatives. Most members of

▲ *These gray wolves are howling—a form of communication that helps regroup a dispersed pack, signifies the beginning of a hunt, or tells other packs of wolves to keep off their territory.*

the group eat meat almost exclusively, but some have a mixed diet. One member of the group, the giant panda, eats only plants. Carnivores have cheek teeth called carnassials, which are specialized for slicing flesh. Another characteristic is that males have a penis bone, or baculum, which supports the penis and prolongs mating.

**FEATURED SYSTEMS**

**EXTERNAL ANATOMY** Wolves are quadrupeds with a narrow body, deep chest, and long bushy tail. The head is large with a slender pointed snout and large ears. The fur is shaggy. *See pages 237–241.*

**SKELETAL SYSTEM** Wolves have long legs with separate bones in the forelimbs and no collarbone. The skull bears a ridge called the sagittal crest for the attachment of the powerful jaw muscles. *See pages 242–243.*

**MUSCULAR SYSTEM** Wolves are lithe, athletic animals. The neck, shoulders, and hips are muscular. Smaller muscles in the face and tail allow the fine movements that are important in visual communication. *See pages 244–245.*

**NERVOUS SYSTEM** Wolves are intelligent, with excellent vision and hearing and a phenomenally acute sense of smell. The vomeronasal organ in the roof of the mouth

provides wolves with an additional olfactory sense. *See pages 246–248.*

**CIRCULATORY AND RESPIRATORY SYSTEMS** Wolves are warm blooded with a typical mammalian circulation. The lungs are large, and the larynx and vocal cords can produce a range of vocalizations. *See page 249.*

**DIGESTIVE AND EXCRETORY SYSTEMS** Wolves are committed carnivores with carnassial teeth suited to slicing up meat. The intestine is relatively short and simple. Metabolic waste is removed from the blood by a pair of efficient kidneys. *See pages 250–251.*

**REPRODUCTIVE SYSTEM** Female wolves bear litters of young and nourish them with milk from 8 or 10 nipples. Males have a baculum (penis bone). Wolves are social and live in cooperative family groups. *See pages 252–255.*

▲ Despite their name, gray wolves have coats varying in color from near white to black with a yellow, red, or brown tinge. Only a small percentage of gray wolves—less than 5 percent—are black.

▲ Compared with the gray wolf, the red wolf is smaller in stature and has relatively longer legs, a narrower body, and larger ears. In addition, its coat is shorter and redder than that of a gray wolf.

● **Dogs** Members of the family Canidae are generally easy to recognize. They are fully quadrupedal (unlike bears or mongooses, which often stand on their two hind legs). They have a narrow body and a deep chest, and most are long-legged with a bushy tail. All except one species have four digits on each hind foot and five on each front foot. One of the front digits is a vestigial (evolutionary leftover, or remnant) that does not reach the ground, called a dewclaw. The African wild dog lacks dewclaws. All dogs have blunt claws that are used for traction when running. The main weapons for hunting and combat are the teeth. The snout is characteristically long, and in wild species the ears are usually large and erect. There are 34 species of wild canids and several hundred breeds of domestic dogs,

which far outstrip their wild relatives in variety of forms. However, all types of domestic dogs are considered a single species. Most dogs are social and use vocal communication, which includes barks, howls, growls, and whines.

● **True dogs, jackals, and wolves** Members of the genus *Canis* are distinguished by long legs and a bushy tail, which is not as thick or rounded as that of the foxes (genus *Vulpes*). The pupils of the eyes remain round in bright light, whereas those of foxes tend to look oval. Members of the genus *Canis* are all social, living in family groups that may coalesce into packs of 30 or more usually related animals. Apart from gray and red wolves, other members of the genus include the coyote, dingo, and jackals.

# External anatomy

The gray wolf is the archetypal wolf—a long-legged, shaggy-coated, rangy-looking dog, with a large head, a pointed snout, a deep chest, a narrow trunk, and a long, bushy tail. As in many animals with a very widespread distribution, there are geographical variations in appearance among wolves from different parts of a species' range. Local circumstances have created these differences. For example, the most obvious difference between a Canadian timber wolf and a Mexican gray wolf is size. The northern variety is suited to the crushing cold of subarctic winters, when large size is a definite advantage. Canadian and Alaskan gray wolves are the biggest in the world, with a large male weighing up to 180 pounds (80 kg).

Compare wolves of this size with the gray wolves from Mexico or Egypt—still the same species—where full-grown adults may weigh less than 44 pounds (20 kg). Not surprisingly, tundra-dwelling wolves also grow a much heavier winter coat (pelage) than gray wolves living in warmer climates, and this pelage makes them look even move impressive.

As their name suggests, gray wolves are generally a shade of gray, though coat color varies from off-white to black and may be tinged with red, brown, or yellow. The fur is thickest on the back and shoulders, where it forms a rough mane in some animals. The fur is thinnest on the belly.

The coat has two types of hairs. Primary hairs, or guard hairs, are long and pigmented, with a long cylindrical shaft that tapers to a point at the tip. Guard hairs grow from follicles in the outer layer of the skin. These follicles are usually arranged in tight rows all over the wolf's body, except on the pads of the feet and the tip of the nose. The guard hairs are coarse and give a wolf its shaggy appearance. The surface of each hair is made of many slightly overlapping scales. These give the shaft a distinct feel: if you were to slide your fingers along a wolf's hair, it would feel much smoother from base to tip than the other way. This "nap" is significant because when a wolf gets wet, water tends run out of the coat, away from the skin, rather than soaking in.

**COMPARE** the pelage (fur coat) of a wolf with **HUMAN** body hair. Human "fur" consists almost entirely of primary hairs, with no downy underlayer. In both species, the individual primary hairs have a "nap."

CONNECTIONS

◄ The maned wolf is the largest canid in South America, with a shoulder height of almost 39 inches (1 m). This cousin of the true wolves has a long, golden-red coat with a black mane of hairs that stand erect.

237

The second type of hairs, called secondary hairs, or awns, form a dense underlayer of fur. Awns are very fine, soft hairs, and there are up to several dozen for every guard hair. Awns provide insulation—by trapping a layer of air close to the skin, they help the wolf keep warm. Wolves in warm climates have much thinner underfur than those in the far north. Both types of hairs are kept slightly greasy by secretions from tiny glands in the skin. The grease helps condition the fur and makes it resistant to water.

As well as the primary and secondary hairs of the coat, wolves have two additional types of hairs. The upper lid of each eye bears a row of eyelashes, or cilia, which protect the surface of the eye from particles of dust or debris and from drops of water. There are no lashes on the lower eyelid. Wolves also have many long, sensory hairs or whiskers (also called

▲ *Depending on the region, adult gray wolves weigh between 44 to 180 pounds (20–80 kg). In general, they are larger than red wolves and considerably larger than most types of domestic dogs.*

▶ Gray wolf
*The coat is most commonly gray or yellowish brown but may also be other shades or have a red tinge. The body shape is streamlined with long legs and a bushy tail. The head has a narrow snout, or muzzle, and pointed ears.*

*The **eyes** are large and round and face forward. Eye color varies but is usually a shade of gold, brown, or even blue. The whites of the eye are often visible.*

*The **ears** are large and pointed. Hearing is excellent—wolves can hear very faint sounds made by prey from a considerable distance. Wolves rely more on hearing than vision for hunting.*

*The **canine teeth**—from which canids take their name—are used for tearing flesh.*

*The **nose** is hairless and black, brown, or sometimes pink. The surface of the nose has tiny fissures. The nostrils open under curving flaps. Smell is a wolf's most important sense for tracking prey and recognizing other wolves.*

*The **legs** are long and slim. Wolves walk with a trotting pace and leave a single line of paw prints. Both forepaws and hind paws have four functional toes with claws. The forepaws also have a fifth nonfunctional claw (dewclaw).*

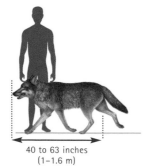

40 to 63 inches
(1–1.6 m)

vibrissae). Whiskers are deeper-rooted than normal hairs and their follicles are richly supplied with blood and nerves. They are located strategically around the wolf's body, mostly on the head. The whiskers are located in rows on the upper lip and in tufts on the lower lip, chin, throat, and cheeks, and above the eyes. Whiskers provide the wolf with excellent spatial awareness when it is moving about in the dark. However, canids are generally less reliant on their whiskers than cats are. Canids spend less time moving about in cluttered environments (such as among the branches of trees) and are often active during the day when it is light enough to see.

## COMPARATIVE ANATOMY

### Red fox and gray wolf

**There are 10 species of foxes**, and one, the red fox (*Vulpes vulpes*), rivals the gray wolf as the world's most widespread carnivore. Foxlike dogs are referred to as "vulpine" species. The differences between foxes and wolves generally have to do with scale and proportion. Foxes are smaller and have shorter legs. The tail is relatively large in fox species and often very bushy (and called a brush). Foxes also usually have very large ears relative to the size of the head, and the pupils of their eyes contract to ovals in bright light. Foxes produce a particularly strong musky scent from the caudal (tail) glands.

*The tail is long, bushy, and drooping. It varies in length from 12 to 20 inches (30–50 cm). Wolves and dogs wag their tail to communicate mood.*

*The body is streamlined and built for speed. The head is narrow and pointed, the body is slender with smooth fur, and the tail is long and pointed.*

*The fur has two types of hairs. Soft, thick underfur keeps a wolf warm and dry. Long guard hairs keep snow and water out. The blotchy markings of the coat match the habitat, camouflaging the wolf as it stalks prey.*

*The claws cannot be retracted, unlike those of most species of cats.*

GENETICS

## Red wolf

**The North American red wolf**, *Canis rufus*, was once thought to be the world's rarest species of dog. In 1975, when its numbers had shrunk to an all-time low of just a few dozen, conservationists took the drastic step of taking the entire population into captivity so that a captive-breeding program could be started. This program was very successful and red wolves have since been reintroduced into the wild on a number of refuges in the United States. However, wolf introductions are always controversial, and in the early 1990s the antiwolf lobby seized on the piece of genetic research that suggested the red wolf may in fact be a hybrid between the gray wolf and the coyote and not a species in its own right at all. Opinion remains divided, and meanwhile the future of the red wolf hangs in the balance.

The wolf's head is large relative to the size of its body. The domed section accommodates a relatively large brain, and the long, tapering snout contains phenomenally sensitive olfactory (smelling) equipment. The hair on the face is shorter and sleeker than elsewhere on the body. Not only does this make it easier to keep the face free of dirt during feeding; it also makes changes in facial expression more obvious. The external part of the ear (the auricle) consists of a large, triangular flap, usually held erect, though in some wolves it may be slightly floppy or torn. The ear can be rotated slightly, allowing the wolf to focus directly on the source of a sound. Movement of the ears also adds to the wolf's repertoire of facial expressions.

The eyes are large, round, and predominantly forward-facing. However, they also bulge slightly to the sides of the head, giving some peripheral vision. The color of the eyes varies but is usually some shade of gold or brown. Blue-eyed wolves are not uncommon. Wolves are among relatively few animals in which the whites of the eye are often visible. This is thought to be a feature that enhances communication in social species—making it easier for other members of the group to see where an individual is looking. (One reason human eyes are so expressive is that they show a lot of white around the iris, the colored part of the eyes.) The wolf's nose is hairless and usually black or brown—or occasionally pink. Its surface is covered in tiny fissures, and the nostrils open under curving flaps to either side.

COMPARATIVE ANATOMY

## Domestic varieties

**Domestic dogs are direct descendants** of wolves. They belong to the same species and share the same scientific name, *Canis lupus*; domestic dogs are *Canis lupus familiaris*. The connection is obvious in some breeds —the husky is effectively a tame wolf—and less so in others. It is difficult to imagine how a Pekingese or toy poodle can be first cousin to a wolf. Wolves were probably first tamed over 100,000 years ago, and some biologists think that different gray wolf subspecies gave rise to the main groups of modern domestic stock. So working dogs like spaniels and setters have an ancestry different from terriers, whereas yet another wolf subspecies was the starting point for the bulldog–boxer group.

▶ *All domestic dogs, including this standard poodle, are descendants of wild wolves. There are about 400 breeds of dogs, ranging in size from the tiny Chihuahua to the tall Irish wolfhound and Great Dane.*

Beneath the fur, the wolf's skin is usually pink with an extensive and variable mottling of dark brown to bluish black pigment, similar to that seen on domestic dogs. In addition to the glands that produce oils to condition the fur, there are a number of other glands than open directly onto the skin. Like all mammals, wolves have mammary glands on their underside, which in adult females produce milk to nourish the young. Most canids have five pairs of nipples, each of which contains the openings of about a dozen tiny ducts leading from the mammary glands. Another concentration of glands occurs on the top of the base of the tail. These caudal glands produce a scent unique to each wolf, but the scent of wolves is nowhere near as powerful as that of foxes.

Sweat-producing glands are notable by their absence over most of the body surface. Dogs do not sweat. Their thick coat prevents moving air from making contact with the skin, so sweating would be a much less effective means of cooling than it is for humans. Thus the animals must find alternative means of cooling. The long, lolling, pink tongue is an excellent cooling surface. It is permanently moist and

▼ MAKING TRACKS
*Wolves have fives toes on their forefeet and four toes on their hind feet. One of the toes of the forefeet—the dewclaw—is vestigial and does not make contact with the ground. The claws of the toes cannot retract and are visible in footprints.*

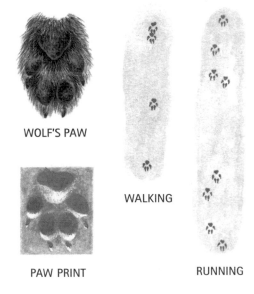

WOLF'S PAW

PAW PRINT

WALKING

RUNNING

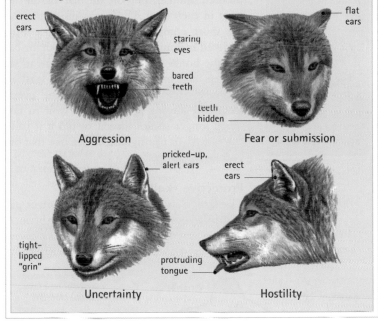

**CLOSE-UP**

## Express yourself

**A large part of the teamwork** that allows wolves to hunt successfully in packs is due to communication. It is no coincidence that the face of an average dog is considerably more mobile than that of a cat—cats are mostly solitary, whereas dogs are inherently social. Wolves and dogs can raise their eyebrows to show interest or alertness; gape in a happy, relaxed "laughing" face; or wrinkle the nose and curl the lip to bare the teeth to signal a threat or fear. This limited range of expression serves to emphasize other body language such as posture, tail position, and the raising and lowering of hair on the hackles (back of the neck).

Aggression — erect ears, staring eyes, bared teeth

Fear or submission — flat ears, teeth hidden

Uncertainty — pricked-up, alert ears, tight-lipped "grin"

Hostility — erect ears, protruding tongue

well supplied with blood vessels, and the animal's breathing generates a continuous flow of air over its surface. A panting dog is not necessarily tired or out of breath; it may be cooling itself.

Wolves have four functional toes on each foot, and the front feet have a vestigial hallux (first digit) that forms the dewclaw. Each toe has a well-developed pad, with very thick callused skin covered by small bumps, or papillae, which help provide a grip like the tread of a shoe or car tire. Each pad has a wad of fatty tissue inside it to provide cushioning, and the whole structure has a rich supply of blood vessels. This helps prevent frostbite in the cold. In warm conditions, the foot pads are the only place from which the wolf can sweat.

# Muscular system

Canine musculature is similar to that of most other carnivores and follows the same basic plan as that of most mammals. There are three types of muscles. Smooth muscle lines the walls of internal organs such as the intestine, bladder, uterus, and large blood vessels. It usually provides slow, low-energy contractions, and it does not tire. Smooth-muscle contraction is controlled by the autonomic nervous system (part of the peripheral nervous system), and the contractions are involuntary.

The second type, cardiac muscle, is closely related to smooth muscle. Its contractions are involuntary and tireless, keeping a wolf's heart beating at an average 120 beats per minute throughout its life.

The third type of muscle is skeletal muscle, which is also called striated muscle because under magnification, rows of microscopic fibers can be seen lining up to form striations, or stripes, in the tissue. Skeletal muscle is under voluntary control.

Under the skin, the first layer of muscle is cutaneous muscle. This allows the skin to quiver and twitch, and controls the lie of the fur—for example, raising the hackles when a wolf feels aggressive. The cutaneous layer is also able to accumulate fat when a wolf is well fed. Beneath the cutaneous muscle, the next layer, containing muscles such as the abdominal obliques, forms a taut sheath around the trunk and limbs. This helps keep the vital organs in place and prevents blood and lymph from pooling in the legs under the effects of gravity.

Deeper still lie the muscles that control posture and locomotion. They are arranged symmetrically within the body, and they act in

**▼ Gray wolf**
*Wolves are sleek but also very muscular. Large trunk muscles drive the slender legs, allowing the animal to run fast and leap far. Strong neck muscles hold up the head, and powerful jaw muscles give wolves their ferocious bite.*

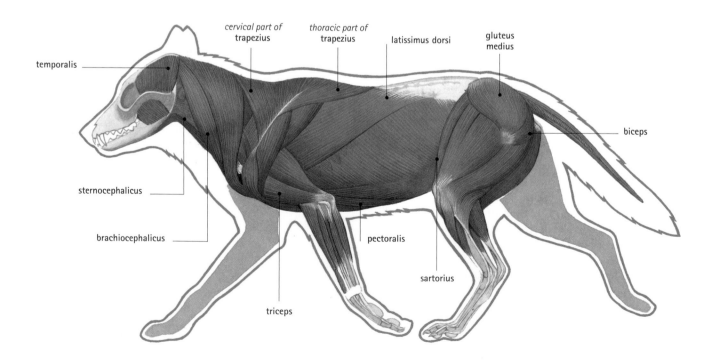

temporalis

cervical part of trapezius

thoracic part of trapezius

latissimus dorsi

gluteus medius

biceps

sternocephalicus

brachiocephalicus

pectoralis

sartorius

triceps

antagonistic pairs to move parts of the skeleton to and fro: for every muscle that pulls a bone in one direction, there is another to move it back to its original position.

## Powerful runner

The gray wolf can run at up to 43 miles per hour (70 km) over a short distance, and maintain a slightly slower pace for extended periods. It can travel continually for hours or days at a time and leap up to 16 feet (5 m) in a single bound. When hunting, wolves chase down their prey (usually deer) over a distance of a few hundred feet to several miles. Once overtaken, the prey is leaped at from the side and knocked to the ground. It usually takes the strength of several wolves to subdue a large deer.

**IN FOCUS**

### Why do dogs wag their tail?

**The muscles of the longissimus system** continue into a wolf's tail and can raise the tail, lower it, and wag it from side to side. As every dog owner knows, the tail signals mood. It is carried high when a dog feels confident or aggressive and is tucked in when a dog is submissive or afraid. Loose, airy wagging is usually interpreted as a sign of happiness. However, behavioral scientists think that tail wagging begins as a sign of conflict, reflecting an issue—"Should I stay or should I go?"—in the dog's mind. Dogs are smart, communicative animals. They learn that wagging the tail often elicits a favorable response from other dogs and humans—like a human smile, which is also thought to have evolved from a sign of anxiety.

◀ As well as being able to sprint at great speed, wolves can jump high, leaping up to 16 feet (5 m). Their speed and agility make wolves supreme predators.

▲ Gray wolves have good vision; forward-facing eyes are a common characteristic of predators. In addition, wolves have acute hearing and a phenomenal sense of smell.

## Sniffer dogs

**A dog's sense of smell is directional**—small changes in the concentration of scent molecules can tell the animal where a scent is coming from and which way prey was heading. This skill is put to good use by humans—trained sniffer dogs can be used to find chemical substances such as drugs or explosives, to find people lost or trapped in disaster areas, or to track missing persons. Dogs can distinguish the smell of clothes worn by different people (as long as the people are not identical twins, whose scent is identical). A trained bloodhound can follow the scent trail made by a particular person even after 24 hours, when other trails have been laid over the top.

Unlike taste, the sense of smell—also called olfaction—works over a long distance. Scent molecules are microscopic—they must be small enough to be carried in the air as vapor. An average human possesses about 5 million olfactory receptor cells in his or her nose, whereas a wolf has about 200 million. The surface area of the olfactory region inside the nose is increased by a convoluted membranous lining. If this lining were spread out flat, it would be larger than the surface area of the rest of the wolf's body.

The cells lining the olfactory region include mucus-secreting cells, pigment cells, and millions of olfactory receptor cells. These receptors trail long, hairlike cilia, which contain the scent-molecule receptors in the mucous lining of the nose. The base of each receptor cell tapers into a long narrow axon (fiberlike extension), which leads all the way to one of the two olfactory bulbs—parts of the forebrain that are located at the back of the nasal cavity.

Wolves also have excellent eyesight. The eyes face forward, with a total field of view of about 180 degrees. This range is more limited than in many prey animals, which have eyes located more to the sides of the head. But stereoscopic forward vision is advantageous to the hunter, because it aids in the perception of distance, allowing the wolf to judge leaps and pounces and move nimbly in cluttered environments, such as a forest. The peripheral vision is especially sensitive to movement—thus a wolf may spot a fleeing prey animal or another wolf out of the corner of its eye. The images gathered through the lens of the eyes are focused on the retina, on which they are sensed by specialized receptor cells called rods and cones. Rods detect monochrome light, whereas cones detect color. Wolves have good day and night vision.

# Circulatory and respiratory systems

All the cells in a wolf's body require oxygen and the sugar glucose for respiration. These are delivered by the bloodstream. In vertebrates, the blood circulates in a closed system and is pumped around the body under pressure by the heart, near the center of the thorax, or chest. Like all mammals, wolves have a four-chamber heart. The left atrium (plural, atria) receives blood from the lungs. The blood then passes into the left ventricle, which pumps the oxygenated blood out through the large aorta, from which smaller arteries branch off and carry blood to the rest of the body.

Having completed a circuit, blood drains back to the heart, entering the right atrium and then the right ventricle. This ventricle pumps the blood to the lungs, where carbon dioxide is released and oxygen is absorbed. Valves located between the atria and ventricles and in the two main veins leading into the heart prevent blood from flowing in the wrong direction.

Air is drawn into the lungs through the mouth and nose. The wolf has a deep chest and large lungs. Thus it is able to breathe deeply and sustain strenuous activity such as running. However, exercise is not the only reason a wolf might breath deeply or rapidly. Because wolves do not sweat, panting is a cooling mechanism. Also, each intake of breath brings a fresh sample of air into contact with the olfactory cells in the nose and vomeronasal organ. A wolf following a trail or investigating a scent will take sharp but shallow snuffling breaths.

▼ Gray wolf
*A four-chamber heart pumps blood around the body. Inhaled oxygen reaches red blood cells by way of the large lungs.*

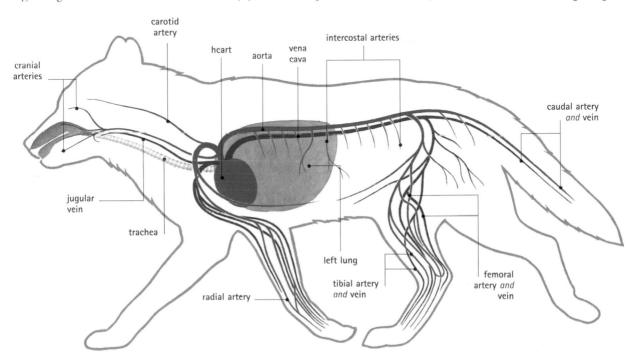

# Reproductive system

**COMPARE** the nipples of a wolf with those of the **GRIZZLY BEAR.** Female bears generally have smaller litters than wolves, so for them four nipples are more than enough. Female wolves lie down or stand to nurse their cubs, whereas bears generally sit down.

Among adult wolves, males are generally about 20 percent bigger than females. Males differ anatomically in having a penis supported by a special bone, the baculum. The penis is normally tucked away inside a fold of furry skin, the prepuce. In sexually mature males, the testes hang between the back legs in a scrotal sac, which is also lightly furred. Both males and females bear eight nipples, located in pairs on the chest and belly, but only the females produce milk.

Wolves' courtship and breeding are inextricably bound up with their complex social life. The gray wolf is highly gregarious—individuals that live alone are at a serious disadvantage. Wolf packs are extended family groups and usually contain five to eight members, though sometimes several groups combine to form a large pack of 30 or more.

**IN FOCUS**

## Stuck on you

**Mating is a fairly long-drawn-out affair.** The male wolf's penis, supported by the baculum bone, swells inside the female, making it virtually impossible for him to withdraw quickly. The pair usually remain locked together for at least half an hour. This looks uncomfortable, but it has a distinct advantage for the male, because as long as he remains locked in the female no other male can mate with her surreptitiously. By the time the pair disengage, the male's sperm have a head start, and there is a good chance they will fertilize the female's eggs.

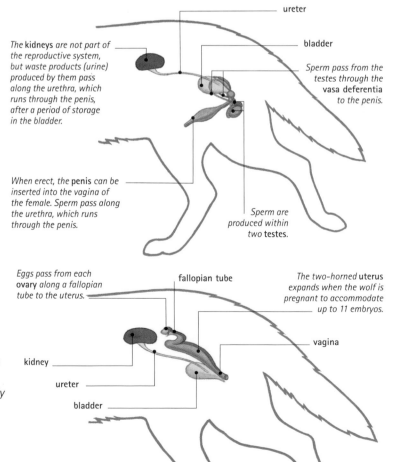

The **kidneys** are not part of the reproductive system, but waste products (urine) produced by them pass along the urethra, which runs through the penis, after a period of storage in the bladder.

ureter

bladder

Sperm pass from the testes through the vasa deferentia to the penis.

When erect, the **penis** can be inserted into the vagina of the female. Sperm pass along the urethra, which runs through the penis.

Sperm are produced within two **testes**.

◀ **Male gray wolf**
*Male wolves have two sperm-producing testes located in an external scrotal sac that hangs between the back legs. The penis, through which sperm is ejaculated during sex, has a supporting bone called the baculum.*

▶ **Female gray wolf**
*Female wolves have two egg-producing ovaries. From each ovary, a fallopian tube leads to the uterus, which has two horns (it is bicornuate). The uterus expands greatly during pregnancy and can hold up to 11 cubs.*

Eggs pass from each ovary along a fallopian tube to the uterus.

fallopian tube

The two-horned **uterus** expands when the wolf is pregnant to accommodate up to 11 embryos.

vagina

kidney

ureter

bladder

▲ *All the adults in a pack of gray wolves take care of the cubs. By about four months old, the cubs accompany the adults on hunting excursions.*

There are separate dominance hierarchies for males and females, and usually only the dominant, or alpha, animals breed. Subordinates are usually offspring or siblings of the dominant pair. Subordinates help with the rearing of young, gaining experience that may help them become better parents themselves one day. All adults help with hunting and defend the pack territory. Though old or infirm individuals may not be much use, they are often looked after by the pack nonetheless.

Communication is vitally important in maintaining order within a pack of wolves.

## GENETICS

### Genes and altruism

**Altruistic behavior occurs** when an animal helps another animal despite the cost to itself. Wolves in a pack perform altruistic acts, such as sharing food, daily. On the face of it, this kind of behavior appears to contradict the laws of natural selection, which suggest that all animals are in competition with one another and should therefore behave selfishly. So why are wolves so good to one another? The simple answer is that all the animals in a pack are usually closely related. They share a high proportion of the same genes. Thus if an individual wolf does something to boost a relative's chances of survival and successful reproduction, it may increase the number of copies of its own genes that pass into future generations.

## PREDATOR AND PREY

### Lessons in life and death

**Wolf cubs begin to be weaned** onto regurgitated meat at five weeks, but their diet is supplemented with milk for several more weeks. Gradually they move on to more solid food, and at about four months they attempt to join in hunting. This is about the same time as they begin to shed their baby teeth. During their first hunts, cubs are clumsy and excitable and more a hindrance than a help. By seven or eight months old they have a full set of adult teeth and have gained enough experience to begin making a useful contribution to hunting excursions.

Wolves can communicate both vocally and posturally, with body language and facial expressions playing a large part. Howls and scent allow wolves to communicate over long distances, and scent messages can last a long time, so two wolves do not have to meet to exchange information.

Wolves reach sexual maturity at about two years of age, by which time they will usually have left their original pack. When a wolf has found a mate, courtship may last many weeks. Females are seasonally monoestrous—they come into breeding condition just once a year, for one to two weeks in early spring. A female may mate several times but usually with just one male, who guards her jealously. The alpha pair suppresses breeding activity in subordinate animals and constantly reassert their dominance. They will disrupt anything that resembles courtship between other wolves in the pack.

The female reproductive tract is typical for a carnivore that gives birth to a large litter. Eggs are released from the two ovaries and pass

▼ *Gray wolf cubs are totally reliant on their mother's milk for up to the first five weeks of life, a period the cubs spend almost exclusively in a den. After that time, the cubs are weaned onto regurgitated meat.*

*▲ An Ethiopian wolf, also called a simian jackal, regurgitates meat for her cub.*

along the ovarian ducts to the uterus. Fertilization can take place at any time after the eggs are released. The uterus is bicornuate—that is, it is a two-horn structure and can expand greatly during pregnancy to accommodate litters of up to 11 cubs, though 6 are more normal. Gestation lasts about two

*◄ During adolescence, wolf cubs play-fight, laying the foundations for their future role in the group or pack.*

months, and newborn wolf cubs weigh about 1 pound (0.45 kg). The cubs are born deaf and blind and have only a sparse covering of downy fur. Their bones are still soft (helping to avoid damage to the mother during birth), and their muscles are very weak.

To begin with, cubs move about only by crawling. They remain snuggled together for warmth in a den (usually an underground burrow) for about three weeks and are entirely reliant on milk for the first month. Each of the female wolf's nipples has about a dozen tiny pores—the openings of ducts that bring milk from the mammary glands. Lactation (milk production) is controlled by hormones and is stimulated by the cubs sucking on the nipples.

AMY-JANE BEER

**FURTHER READING AND RESEARCH**

Macdonald, David W. 2006. *The Encyclopedia of Mammals*. Facts On File: New York.

Macdonald, David W., and C. Sillero-Zubiri (eds.). 2004. *The Biology and Conservation of Wild Canids*. Oxford University Press: Oxford, UK.

Nowak, R. M. 1999. *Walker's Mammals of the World* (6th ed.). Johns Hopkins University Press: Baltimore, MD.

Virtual Canine Anatomy: www.cvmbs.colostate.edu/vetneuro/dissection

# Zebra

ORDER: Perissodactyla   FAMILY: Equidae   GENUS: *Equus*

The three species of zebras live in sub-Saharan Africa and have adapted to life in a variety of arid and semiarid environments. Zebras are well equipped for speeding away from predators such as lions.

## Anatomy and taxonomy

Scientists group all organisms into taxonomic groups based largely on anatomical features. Zebras belong to the horse, or equid, family. Along with horses, tapirs, and rhinos, equids are part of a large group of mammals called Perissodactyla, the odd-toed ungulates. Mammals are among the most familiar of animal groups.

● **Animals**   All animals are multicellular and feed off other organisms. They differ from other multicellular life-forms in their ability to move around independently (generally using muscles) and respond rapidly to stimuli.

● **Chordates**   At some time in its life cycle a chordate has a stiff, dorsal (back) supporting rod called the notochord.

● **Vertebrates**   In vertebrates, the notochord develops into a backbone made up of units called vertebrae. Vertebrates have a muscular system consisting primarily of bilaterally paired masses (on each side of one line of symmetry).

● **Mammals**   Mammals are warm-blooded vertebrates. Fur is a unique feature of mammals, as are milk glands in the females. Also, the lower jaw is hinged directly to the skull; in this regard, too, mammals are different from all other vertebrates. Mature red blood cells in all mammals lack a nucleus; all other vertebrates have nucleated red blood cells.

● **Placental mammals**   These mammals nourish their unborn young through a placenta, a temporary organ that forms in the mother's uterus during pregnancy.

● **Perissodactyls**   The ungulates are a diverse group of mammals with four legs and hooves, and they are generally herbivores (plant eaters). Perissodactyls are ungulates with an odd number of toes on the hind feet at least; they have either one or three digits. The anatomical feature considered most

▼ *There are three species of living zebras, odd-toed ungulates in the genus* Equus. *The other four species in* Equus *are horses and asses. Only living species of perissodactyls are shown on this family tree.*

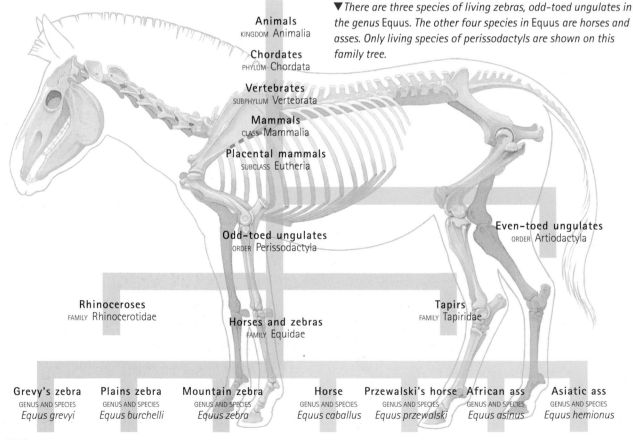

**Animals**
KINGDOM Animalia

**Chordates**
PHYLUM Chordata

**Vertebrates**
SUBPHYLUM Vertebrata

**Mammals**
CLASS Mammalia

**Placental mammals**
SUBCLASS Eutheria

**Odd-toed ungulates**
ORDER Perissodactyla

**Even-toed ungulates**
ORDER Artiodactyla

**Rhinoceroses**
FAMILY Rhinocerotidae

**Horses and zebras**
FAMILY Equidae

**Tapirs**
FAMILY Tapiridae

**Grevy's zebra**
GENUS AND SPECIES
*Equus grevyi*

**Plains zebra**
GENUS AND SPECIES
*Equus burchelli*

**Mountain zebra**
GENUS AND SPECIES
*Equus zebra*

**Horse**
GENUS AND SPECIES
*Equus caballus*

**Przewalski's horse**
GENUS AND SPECIES
*Equus przewalski*

**African ass**
GENUS AND SPECIES
*Equus asinus*

**Asiatic ass**
GENUS AND SPECIES
*Equus hemionus*

significant is that the axis of symmetry of the limbs passes through the third or middle toe. That toe is the strongest and the one on which most of the weight is borne. The 15 species of living perissodactyls are of medium or large size. They balance largely on the forelegs, and the hind legs are the main propellants. Their skeletal structure, including the firm girder of the backbone, permits fast running, and in the rhinoceroses it enables great weight to be borne. The stomach of perissodactyls is small, simple, and not divided into several chambers as in deer and antelope.

● **Rhinoceroses** The five species of living rhinoceroses are massive animals with a thick and nearly hairless hide, except in one species. They have three digits on each foot and hornlike structures on the head made of fused epidermal (skin) cells impregnated with the tough, fibrous protein keratin. The skin of rhinoceroses is very thick. The Indian and Javan rhinoceroses are covered with large, practically immovable plates, separated by joints of thinner skin to permit movement.

● **Tapirs** The four species of living tapirs are the smallest perissodactyls, along with the asses in the horse family. Tapirs are rounded, piglike, semiamphibious animals with a small proboscis (trunklike snout) and a coat of short, bristly hairs. Tapirs have primitive features, such as four hoofed toes in the forefoot and three in the hind foot, and they have relatively simple molar teeth.

● **Equids** The horses, asses, and zebras are long-legged, running perissodactyls with one functional digit in each foot. Limbs have long lower bones and digits and reduced or fused bones in the upper leg. The skull is long, with long, narrow nasal cavities. Equids have high-crowned cheek teeth for grinding plant matter.

● **Horses** The domesticated horse (*Equus caballus*) varies in appearance according to its breed. Breeds range from small

▲ *A herd of plains zebras chewing mouthfuls of grass. Each zebra's stripes are unique, with the differences being especially marked on the face and rump.*

Shetland ponies to hulking cart horses. Przewalski's horse is a descendant of the original wild horse from which domestic horses were bred.

● **Zebras** The three species of zebras are basically striped wild horses. They are easily distinguished by the pattern of stripes. The mountain zebra is the smallest species. Zebras can be further subdivided into subspecies, or local forms. The mountain zebra, for example, has two subspecies: Hartmann's zebra and the Cape mountain zebra. Subspecies are restricted to particular regions.

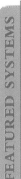

**FEATURED SYSTEMS**

**EXTERNAL ANATOMY** Zebras are four-legged hoofed mammals with a compact, sleek body; long legs; a flexible tail; and stripes. *See pages 258–261.*

**SKELETAL SYSTEM** A zebra's skeleton is suited to fast running, with long lower-limb bones and one very long single toe encased in a hoof. *See pages 262–264.*

**MUSCULAR SYSTEM** Muscles deliver great power to the rear legs for propulsion. *See pages 265–266.*

**NERVOUS SYSTEM** Zebras have a relatively complex brain, with an enlarged cerebellum for coordinating running with little conscious effort. *See pages 267–269.*

**CIRCULATORY AND RESPIRATORY SYSTEMS** The lungs are supplied with air through the nostrils, not from the mouth. Extra-long, dense leg arteries ensure that oxygen reaches all running muscles. *See pages 270–271.*

**DIGESTIVE AND EXCRETORY SYSTEMS** Zebras can digest a range of tough grasses and plant matter. They have a simple stomach. *See pages 272–273.*

**REPRODUCTIVE SYSTEM** A male zebra can tell when a female zebra is ready to mate by sniffing her urine. Male zebras that control female harems are more fertile than lone males. *See pages 274–275.*

single toe. The single hoof of the equids—the only mammals to walk on the tips of single digits—is the most highly developed structure of this kind among mammals.

Like all horses, zebras have facial muscles that allow them to make a variety of expressions.

Some facial expressions are functional—for example, flaring the nostrils to smell the air—whereas others serve in communication, such as pulling back the lips to show the teeth. The ears add to the range of expressions. Usually they are pricked forward, but they can flatten

## COMPARATIVE ANATOMY

### Stripe patterns

**Grevy's zebra**
Stripes take on a concentric pattern on the rump.

▲ The even and narrow stripes of the Grevy's zebra made it popular with furriers. The belly is white, and there is a black stripe running along the back.

**Mountain zebra**
Horizontal stripes form a gridiron on the rump.

▲ The stripes on the front half of the mountain zebra are usually narrower than those on the rear. The belly is generally white except for a black stripe on the chest.

**Plains zebra**
Broad stripes taper on the rump, where shadow stripes appear.

▲ Lighter shadow stripes on the rump and hindquarters distinguish plains zebras from mountain zebras. The broad body stripes extend beneath the belly.

## Domestication and selective breeding

**Horses were first domesticated** 3,000 to 4,000 years ago, and the true horse *Equus caballus* now exists only in a domesticated or feral (returned to the wild) condition. Even Przewalski's horse, often referred to as the last wild horse, persists only in its native range of Mongolia, owing to an intensive conservation effort that has included the release of captive-bred individuals back to the wild. Selective breeding has resulted in several hundred breeds of domestic horses, such as elegant Arabs, thoroughbreds and quarterhorses, immensely powerful cart horses, sturdy ponies, and novelty breeds such as the tiny Falabella. The diversity of form and appearance is extraordinary within what is technically a single species.

backward to indicate aggression. A zebra's tail is long, with a tuft of long hairs starting about one-third of the way down its length. It is mobile and makes an excellent fly whisk. Zebras and other horses are social animals, and pairs often stand nose to tail alongside each other, so each animal benefits from the flicking of its partner's tail, whisking annoying insects from around the face.

▼ *These zebras have congregated to drink at a pool. Each animal has a slightly different pattern of stripes on the head. The mane is short and erect, unlike that of most domestic horses.*

▲ *There are many theories about the function of a zebra's stripes. The combined effect of a herd of stripy animals, like this plains zebra herd, might confuse predators. A lion seeing a herd might find it difficult to target an individual, especially if the herd is already on the run.*

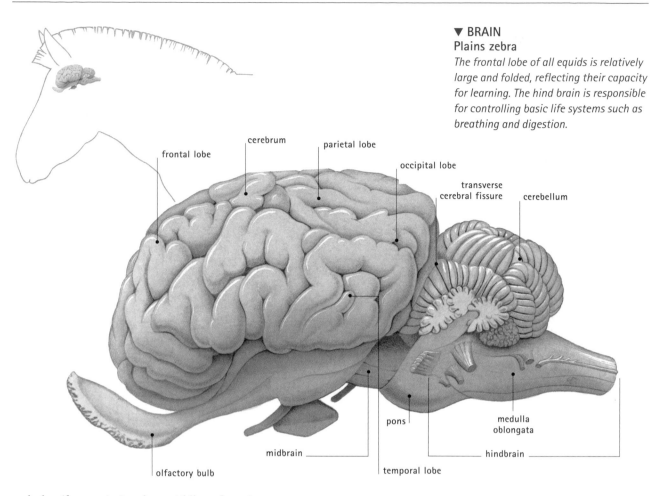

*The frontal lobe of all equids is relatively large and folded, reflecting their capacity for learning. The hind brain is responsible for controlling basic life systems such as breathing and digestion.*

frontal lobe

cerebrum

parietal lobe

occipital lobe

transverse cerebral fissure

cerebellum

olfactory bulb

midbrain

pons

temporal lobe

hindbrain

medulla oblongata

a hole (foramen) in the middle of each vertebra. Paired lateral (side) nerves branch off from the spinal cord at every joint between the vertebrae, and give rise to the efferent PNS. The PNS is made up mostly of motor or effector neurons that are responsible for stimulating tissues such as muscles into activity. Meanwhile, a multitude of sensory, or afferent, nerves converge at the same junctions and feed sensory information gathered all over the body back into the CNS. The branching pattern of lateral nerves is one of the few remaining clues to the segmented body plan of the simple, fishlike ancestor from which all vertebrates evolved many millions of years ago.

## Functions of the brain

The equid brain is relatively well developed. It is not particularly large and occupies only the very top part of the head in the dome of the skull above the level of the eyes and extending no farther back than the back of the ears. The

### IN FOCUS

## Scent sensing: The flehmen response

**Male zebras, horses, and several other grazing mammals** sniff a female's urine to detect hormones produced when the female is in estrus (releasing eggs that can be fertilized). On the roof of the male's mouth is a pad of tissue called Jacobson's organ, or the vomeronasal organ. To detect estrus hormones, the male raises his upper lip and snorts air over this pad in an action called the flehmen response.

Flehmen response

Jacobson's organ

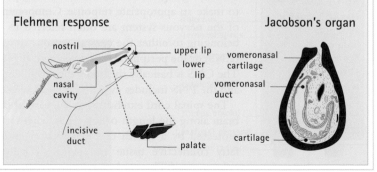

nostril

upper lip

lower lip

nasal cavity

vomeronasal cartilage

vomeronasal duct

incisive duct

palate

cartilage

brain can be divided into several regions, each with different functions. In evolutionary terms, the parts of the brain nearest the spinal cord (the hindbrain) are the oldest; they are responsible for controlling some of the most basic life-supporting functions, such as breathing and digestion. Farther forward are newer regions of the brain, which control some of the processes that set so-called "higher" animals apart from simple ones. These regions include various instinctive behaviors and some sensory processes. The forebrain, consisting of the walnut-like cerebrum, is a center for further sensory integration and higher thought processes such as memory and learning.

▼ *A noise has alerted these plains zebras, and they have turned their eyes and ears toward it. If the zebras see a predator they will turn and flee.*

## IN FOCUS

### Clever Hans

**A hundred years ago in Germany**, people were amazed by the apparent intelligence of a horse called Clever Hans. It seemed that Hans could answer arithmetic questions written on a chalkboard for him to read. Hans would respond to each question by tapping out the answer with a front foot, and he was never wrong. Scientists were astounded, and for a long time the horse had them baffled. Eventually a psychologist, Oskar Pfungst, worked out that Hans could answer questions only when the people in the room with him (in particular his trainer) could also see the board. Hans had no mathematical skills at all, but, like all horses, he was very sensitive to his surroundings. He picked up on the tiny unconscious nod given by his trainer as he approached the right answer. Hans may also have sensed other signs of tension such as an increase in the heart rates of onlookers as he got closer to a right answer. Horses are very perceptive.

# Circulatory and respiratory systems

**COMPARE** the systemic arch of the zebra with that of the **OSTRICH** and **BULLFROG**. Like all mammals, the zebra pumps blood around the body from the left side of its heart. In birds, the systemic circulation comes from the right side, and in the frog both sides of the heart contribute to systemic circulation.

**CONNECTIONS**

The zebra's heart is a large, powerful pump. It weighs about 10 pounds (4.5 kg) and is located low in the chest, between and just behind the front legs. The lungs are very large, filling most of the available space within the chest. The muscular diaphragm that separates the chest cavity from the abdominal cavity is also responsible for inflating the lungs. When the diaphragm contracts, the lungs expand and air is drawn in through the mouth and nose. When the diaphragm relaxes, tension in the springy tissues (the intercostal muscles and cartilage that hold the rib cage together) of the chest cavity squeezes the lungs back down and forces air back out the way it came in.

The large nostrils allow the zebra to breathe rapidly when necessary, and following prolonged exertion it is possible to see the sides of the zebra's chest pumping like bellows as the animal tries to compensate for the oxygen debt it has built up.

## Arteries and veins

Oxygen-rich blood leaves the left side of the heart via a massive artery called the aorta, which curves upward and backward and runs along the top of the abdominal cavity. In a large horse, the aorta is almost the thickness of a backyard hose, with an internal diameter up to 0.4 inch (1 cm). The walls are thick, with two layers of muscle and a sheath of rubbery connective tissue. The walls are able to withstand the repeated stress of blood forced along under high pressure. Major arteries that arise directly from the aorta include the cardiac arteries supplying the heart muscle, the carotid

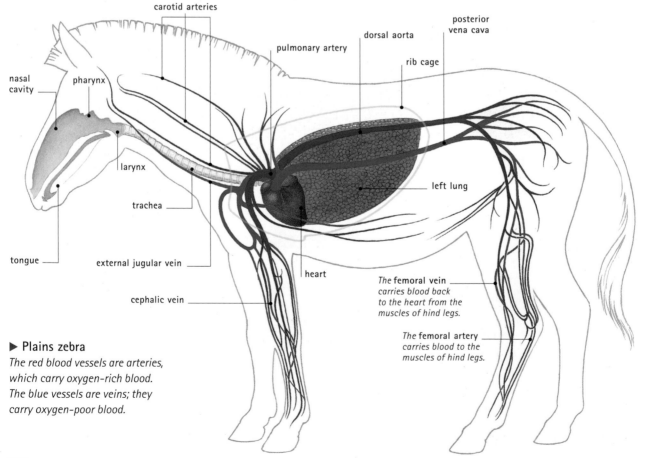

**▶ Plains zebra**
*The red blood vessels are arteries, which carry oxygen-rich blood. The blue vessels are veins; they carry oxygen-poor blood.*

arteries that carry blood directly to the brain, and the celiac artery that leaves the aorta in the middle of the abdomen and then splits to form the arteries bearing the rich blood supply required by the liver, stomach, and spleen. The renal artery directs blood to the kidneys, and the femoral artery supplies the powerful muscles of the hind legs.

Alongside most of the major arteries lie large veins that drain blood from the tissues and carry it back to the heart. In highly trained horses, blood vessels can often be seen standing out from the skin, in particular on the neck and legs. The same often happens in human athletes: where the vessels lie above well developed blocks of muscle they show up because there is very little fat in the overlying skin. Blood from the right side of the heart is pumped more gently around a smaller circuit that takes in the lungs, where waste carbon dioxide is exchanged for oxygen.

## IN FOCUS

### Horse talk

**Horses and their relatives** use exhalant breaths to produce a wide range of vocalizations, including snorts, squeals, roars, and gentle huffing sounds. These sounds are more or less similar for all species of zebras. However, the sounds produced as main contact calls are distinctive. Horses use a whinny, or nickering, call, whereas asses bray. The plains zebra utters a short, harsh bark, and the mountain zebra whistles. The call of Grevy's zebra is similar to a donkey's bray and is called belling.

▼ When zebras groom one another, as these two plains zebras are doing, their heart rate falls and they become less stressed.

# Digestive and excretory systems

**CONNECTIONS**

**COMPARE** the digestive system of a zebra with that of a ruminant such as a **RED DEER**. The zebra has a small stomach and a large cecum, where bacteria break down cellulose, whereas in the red deer cellulose is broken down in the large multichamber stomach, and the intestine is relatively simple.

Like other horses, zebras are vegetarian. Grass forms about 90 percent of the diet, with the remainder made up of herbs and other vegetation (mainly leaves) browsed from trees and shrubs. Zebras spend more time eating than doing anything else (roughly half their life) and consume about 3 percent of their body weight in forage every day.

The processing of plant material begins the moment it is cropped from the sward. The zebra uses its broad, blade-edged incisor teeth to pluck grass and other vegetation. Each mouthful is chewed well between large, millstonelike cheek teeth. The large muscular tongue keeps the food mass churning and helps blend in saliva, which contains digestive enzymes that immediately start the process of digestion. Food is then swallowed and passes

**IN FOCUS**

## Salts of the earth

**Zebras and other horses** often lick rocks and soil or even swallow chunks of earth. They do this to supplement their intake of dietary minerals. Zebras' natural diet is often lacking in certain essential minerals, in particular salt and iron, and so the minerals must be found elsewhere. Geophagia, or soil-eating, is common among zebras, and horse owners usually provide their animals with an artificial salt lick.

▼ Plains zebra
*Zebras have a simple stomach and very long intestines with a saclike cecum, which houses bacteria that break down tough plant matter.*

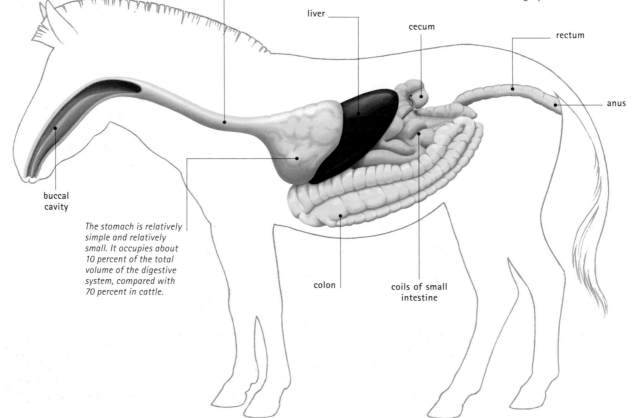

esophagus

liver

cecum

rectum

anus

buccal cavity

*The stomach is relatively simple and relatively small. It occupies about 10 percent of the total volume of the digestive system, compared with 70 percent in cattle.*

colon

coils of small intestine

via the esophagus to a simple stomach. The stomach is relatively small: it makes up about 10 percent of the total volume of the digestive system compared with 70 percent for the complex stomach of a cow. It is important that the zebra eats slowly but continually. Large meals cannot be accommodated in the stomach, and long periods without eating can cause the stomach to swell with gas. A zebra's intestines are extremely long, with a large saclike cecum where large numbers of bacteria aid the breakdown of plant matter such as cellulose.

A zebra's digestive system is well suited to processing large quantities of nutritionally low-grade fodder. Zebras eat long grasses with little nutritional value, but they make up for a lack of quality with quantity. These animals are able to survive on a diet that most other herbivores would find intolerable. The ability of zebras to consume very rough vegetation has important ecological effects. Areas of overgrown grassland are of little use to more refined grazers such as gazelles, whose digestive system cannot cope with rough grasses. However, once a herd of zebras has moved though an area of grassland, effectively mowing away the longer grass, other grazers can follow along behind, plucking at the fresh, tender shoots that soon begin to sprout in the zebras'

### CLOSE-UP

## In the horse's mouth

**Adult zebras have three pairs of bladelike incisors** in each jaw, used for cropping grass. The canines are small in females but large and chisel-shape in males, which use them for fighting. There are six pairs of cheek teeth (three pairs of premolars and three pairs of molars) in the lower jaw, and seven pairs in the upper jaw, which has an extra set of premolars. The cheek teeth are large, with distinctive cusps and folds in the enamel that make them very effective at grinding up plant material. The teeth appear in a predictable order in young equids. That, and an unusually consistent pattern of wear on the cheek teeth, allows zoologists to make relatively accurate estimates of a equid's age by looking inside the mouth. The expression "to look a gift horse in the mouth" is used to describe ungrateful or cynical behavior. If someone was given a horse as a gift, it would be rude to look immediately into its mouth to see if it was too old to be valuable.

wake. Plains zebras need to drink regularly and are rarely found more that 20 miles (32 km) from a water hole. Sometimes they dig for water with their front hooves, creating shallow wells. Grevy's zebras are better than plains zebras at withstanding drought and can tolerate brackish drinking water, something plains zebras and horses cannot do.

▼ Zebras eat about 3 percent of their body weight in plant matter (mostly grass) every day.

# Reproductive system

Zebras live in herds made up of a single dominant male (stallion), a harem of mares (females), and their recent offspring. Surplus males live in smaller bachelor herds, awaiting the opportunity to set up a breeding herd of their own. Few males develop the status and experience needed to maintain a herd before the age of four years, though they are physically capable of breeding much earlier.

Female zebras reach sexual maturity when they are between 16 and 22 months old, and under ideal circumstances they are capable of producing young every year. However, because gestation lasts almost exactly 12 months, a female must mate almost immediately after giving birth, to sustain a regular annual cycle.

## Precocious development

**Life on the open savanna is dangerous.** There is nowhere to hide, and the only real safety comes from remaining part of a herd. As an adaptation for life in these challenging circumstances, zebra foals are born in a very advanced state. The foal gets to its feet within 20 minutes of birth and can walk within an hour. Within its first few hours, it will discover the source of sustaining milk at its mother teats and attempt a skittering run. After 24 hours, it is strong and steady enough to follow its mother wherever she goes.

New mothers often come into estrus (the fertile period where females can mate and become pregnant) after giving birth. However, only those that are in exceptionally good condition will become pregnant. Females usually skip breeding for a year or even two years while rearing one youngster. Estrus lasts about a week. During this time, the soft labial tissues around the vagina swell up, and the female urinates often. The urine looks cloudy and contains pheromones, chemicals that attract the male and tell him the female will soon be ready to mate.

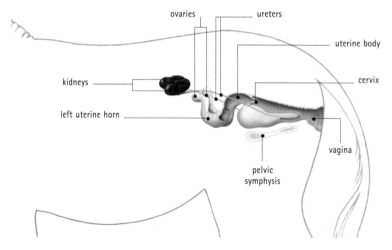

▲ FEMALE REPRODUCTIVE ORGANS
Plains zebra
*Female zebras have two egg-producing ovaries and a bipartite uterus.*

▶ MALE REPRODUCTIVE ORGANS
Plains zebra
*Male zebras have two sperm-producing testes, suspended in the external scrotum; and a penis, through which sperm are discharged during mating.*

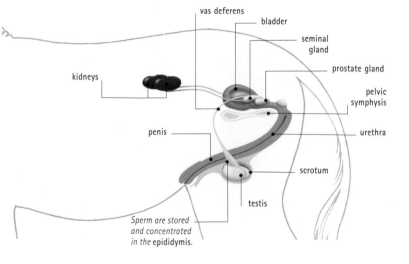

Foals are born singly, weighing about 70 pounds (33 kg). Twins are very rare: newborn zebras are so advanced that it is virtually impossible for mares to carry two to term. Giving birth is one of the few times a female zebra will distance herself from the rest of the herd. This behavior sounds risky, but it is vital that the mother and foal spend their first few days together, away from distractions, and the mother will aggressively repel any other animal that comes too close to her foal. Young zebras are born with a powerful instinct to follow any large moving object. Usually the first thing they see is the mother, and she needs to ensure that nothing else gets in the way. The foal's life may depend on the bond it forms with its mother.

AMY-JANE BEER

FURTHER READING AND RESEARCH

Etses, R. D. 1991. *The Behavior Guide to African Mammals.* University of California Press: Berkeley, CA.

Nowak, R. 1999. *Walker's Mammals of the World* (6th ed.). Johns Hopkins Press: Baltimore, MD.

▲ *A very young zebra foal suckles from one of its mother's teats. In zebras, the bond between a mother and her newborn is very strong.*

GENETICS

## Hybridization

**The horse family is anatomically and physiologically conservative**: it exhibits nothing like the variation seen in many other mammal families such the Bovidae (sheep, cattle, antelope, and goats). The basic similarities between different species of equids permit the creation of hybrids, or crossbreeds. The most familiar of these is the mule. Mules are the result of a cross between an ass or donkey and a horse—specifically between a male ass and a female horse. The hybrid offspring of a female ass and a male horse is called a hinny. Horse–ass hybrids are always sterile because the parent species have different numbers of chromosomes. A mule receives 31 chromosomes from its father and 32 from its mother, resulting in 63 chromosomes in every mule cell. The process of meiosis, by which gametes (eggs or sperm) are produced, requires chromosomes to pair up before they replicate and divide. In a mule, the spare horse chromosome has nothing to pair up with and so the process fails every time. The same is true of various zebra–horse or zebra–ass hybrids, which are sometimes bred in captivity and are collectively called zebroids.

# Glossary

**Abductor**
A muscle that moves a limb away from the body of an animal. Abductor muscles work antagonistically with adductor muscles.

**Acid**
Any substance that gives up hydrogen ions ($H^+$) in solution, increasing the overall hydrogen ion concentration of the solution.

**Actin**
Protein that is present in microfilaments, such as those that enable muscles to contract.

**Action potential**
A change in the voltage across the membrane of a nerve cell when an impulse passes along it. This results from a change in the permeability of the membrane, which causes sodium ions to pass into the cell and potassium ions to move out.

**Adaptation**
Accumulation of inherited characters or a certain genetically based character or behavior that makes an organism suited to its environment.

**Adaptive radiation**
Evolutionary diversification of a single species, with production of many different species adapted to different environments.

**Adductor**
A muscle that moves a limb toward the body of an animal. Adductor muscles work antagonistically with abductors.

**Adenine**
Nitrogen-containing base that is present in nucleic acids such as DNA and RNA.

**Adrenal gland**
Endocrine gland located close to the kidneys, consisting of an inner medulla and an outer cortex that produce steroids and hormones.

**Aerobic**
Describes a process that takes place, or an organism that grows or metabolizes, in the presence of gaseous or dissolved oxygen.

**Alimentary canal**
A roughly tubular organ where food is ingested, digested, and absorbed. In most mammals there are two openings: the mouth and the anus. The esophagus, stomach, small intestine, and large intestine are all component sections.

**Alkali**
Soluble base or a solution made up from a base.

**Alveolus**
One of the many tiny air sacs at the end of each bronchiole in the lungs of mammals. Alveoli increase the surface area available for gas exchange.

**Antibody**
Protein compound produced by vertebrate plasma cells that binds to foreign bodies (antigens), which then clump together and can be destroyed by white blood cells.

**Antigen**
Any molecule that can stimulate an immune response, inducing the production of a specific antibody.

**Aorta**
Largest artery of the mammalian body, leaving the heart from the left ventricle and supplying all parts of the body with oxygenated blood.

**Arboreal**
A term that describes animals that live in trees.

**Artery**
Vessel that carries blood from the heart to the rest of the body. Most carry oxygen-rich blood, but the pulmonary arteries carry oxygen-poor blood from the heart to the lungs.

**Axon**
Extension of neuron that transmits nerve impulses away from the cell body.

**Binocular vision**
Vision through two eyes pointed in the same direction. It restricts the area of view but allows accurate judging of distance. Many predators have binocular vision. When the eyes are positioned on the side of the head they give nonbinocular vision.

**Biodiversity**
Diversity of plant and animal species in an environment.

**Biomass**
Total quantity of organic matter in a region or habitat.

**Bipedal**
Walking on two limbs. Humans are bipedal, but most mammals are quadrupedal.

**Bladder**
An elastic-walled organ in the urinary systems of all mammals that acts as a receptacle for urine before excretion.

**Blood-brain barrier**
The protective membrane that controls the passage of substances from the blood to the fluid bathing the brain and spinal cord.

**Bronchi**
The tube that branches from the trachea and passes to the lung in vertebrates.

**Buccal cavity**
The mouth cavity.

**Camouflage**
Coloring, shape, or texture of the exterior of an organism that makes it hard to see. A camouflaged animal may match its surroundings (cryptic camouflage) or have patterns that break up its outline (disruptive camouflage).

**Canine tooth**
A sharp, pointed tooth found mainly in carnivores that is suited to tearing meat. There are two canines in each jaw, situated between the incisors and premolars. Some herbivorous mammals do not have canines.

**Capillary**
The narrowest type of blood vessel. Capillary walls consist of a single layer of cells, so nutrients, dissolved gases, and waste products can pass through them.

**Carbohydrate**
Compound that contains carbon, hydrogen, and oxygen in the ratio 1:2:1. Most are produced by green plants and provide an important food source for animals.

**Carbon dioxide**
A gas formed as a by-product of respiration in animals and plants, and when fuel such as oil is burned. This gas is thought to be a main cause of the greenhouse effect, a process by which energy from sunlight is trapped within Earth's atmosphere.

**Cardiac muscle**
A type of muscle that is unique to the vertebrate heart.

**Carnassial teeth**
A powerful scissorlike pair of teeth possessed by most carnivores apart from seals.

**Carnivore**
An animal or plant that feeds on animals. Also, members of the order Carnivora, such as bears, cats, and dogs.

**Cartilage**
A tough, elastic, gristly, and somewhat translucent tissue that holds together the skeleton of most vertebrates. In sharks and rays, the skeleton is made of cartilage.

**Cecum**
Blind-ending structure present in the digestive system of some animals; it may house cellulose-digesting bacteria.

**Cell**
The basic structural and functional unit of all living organisms except viruses. Organisms may consist of a single cell or — as with complex vertebrates — billions of cells.

**Central nervous system**
That part of the nervous system that coordinates nerve functions. In vertebrates it is made up of the brain and spinal cord, and in invertebrates it comprises nerve cords and ganglia.

**Cervical vertebrae**
The individual bones (vertebrae) of the neck.

**Chemical defense**
A chemical that is secreted by an animal to protect it from a predator. The chemical may be foul-smelling or foul-tasting, so repelling the predator; the chemical may disguise the animal's own smell, thus confusing the predator; or it may be a toxin that poisons the predator.

**Chemoreceptor**
A sense organ, such as a taste bud, that responds to chemical stimuli.

**Chromosome**
Long strand of coiled DNA composed of genes, the genetic information for most organisms.

**Cladistics**
A method of classifying organisms in which animals and plants are placed in taxonomic groups, or clades, strictly according to their evolutionary relationships.

**Coelom**
The fluid-filled body cavity of vertebrate and most invertebrate animals.

**Colloid**
Substance, such as gelatin or starch, that will not pass through a membrane.

**Convergent evolution**
Similar behavior or appearance of two organisms with similar lifestyles that are not closely related.

**Cytoplasm**
The material surrounding the nucleus of a cell, including the inner endoplasm and the outer ectoplasm.

**Diffusion**
The movement of particles, such as a gas, from a region of high concentration to a region of lower concentration.

**Digestion**
The process of breaking down food into easily absorbed substances.

**Digitigrade**
The gait of most fast-running mammals, in which only the toes make contact with the ground; the rest of the foot is raised off the ground.

**Diurnal**
A term meaning active during the day; the opposite of nocturnal, active during the night.

**Divergent evolution**
Evolution over time of a number of different species from one species of living organism.

**DNA (deoxyribonucleic acid)**
A molecule inside cells that carries genetic information and directs many of the cell's activities.

**Domain**
A taxonomic category above the level of kingdom in some classifications of organisms. The three domains are Archaea, Bacteria, and Eukarya.

**Dormancy**
A condition in which an animal or plant's metabolism slows down; often used by organisms to better survive periods of harsh environmental conditions.

**Echolocation**
Use of sound waves to find the way and detect prey in the dark. Bats, dolphins, and some birds use echolocation.

**Ecosystem**
Community of organisms and their interactions with one another, together with the environment in which they live and with which they interact.

**Embryo**
The first stage of an animal's or a plant's life cycle after fertilization of the egg.

**Enzyme**
Protein that catalyzes chemical reactions in organisms.

**Epidermis**
The outer layer of cells that covers the body of plants and animals.

**Esophagus**
The muscular tube by which food travels from the mouth to the stomach in vertebrates and many invertebrates.

**Estrus**
Period of sexual receptivity occurring in female mammals around the time of ovulation.

**Eukaryotic cell**
Cell in which the chromosomal genetic material is contained within one or more nuclei and is separated from the cytoplasm by two nuclear membranes.

**Evolution**
Any cumulative genetic change that occurs in a population of organisms from one generation to the next. Over many generations, evolution can change the structure of an animal or plant.

**Gene**
Discrete unit of hereditary information present in a chromosome.

**Genus**
Taxonomic grouping of very similar organisms thought to be closely related species.

**Graviportal**
A type of skeletal structure in which the limbs are straight and very sturdy and bear a large body mass. An elephant has a graviportal skeleton in contrast with a rhinoceros's mediportal structure and a cheetah's cursorial structure.

**Hallux**
Innermost digit on the hind limb of a vertebrate. For example, it is the big toe in humans.

**Haploid**
A type of cell containing only one copy of each chromosomes. Gametes are haploid cells.

**Hemoglobin**
An iron-containing red pigment that transports oxygen; found in vertebrate red blood cells and in some invertebrates.

**Herbivore**
An animal that eats only plants.

**Hormone**
A chemical messenger transported around the body by the blood or hemolymph. Hormones are secreted in small quantities by glands or nerve cells and can affect tissues in a distant part of the body.

**Jacobson's organ**
Either one of a pair of small pits or sacs situated in the roof of the mouth and developed as chemoreceptors in amphibians, reptiles, and some mammals.

**Larynx**
Voice box containing vocal cords. The larynx is situated at the anterior end of the trachea.

**Leukocyte**
White blood cell.

**Ligament**
Vertebrate connective tissue that joins bones.

**Lymph**
Clear fluid consisting mostly of water and dissolved salts and proteins that flows in vessels of the lymphatic system.

**Lymphocyte**
White blood cell that is responsible for immune responses.

**Marsupium**
The abdominal pouch of marsupial mammals, such as kangaroos and koala bears, in which young are reared.

**Mediportal**
A type of skeleton with many adaptations for bearing heavy loads, including thick limb bones and thick ankle and wrist bones. A hippopotamus has a mediportal skeleton.

**Meiosis**
A form of nuclear division in which, after chromosome duplication in a reproductive cell, the diploid parent nucleus divides twice, forming four haploid offspring cells.

**Metabolism**
The chemical changes in living cells by which energy is produced for vital processes in the body.

**Mitosis**
A type of nuclear division that results in two offspring cells, each having a nucleus containing the same number and kind of chromosomes as the parent cell.

**Molars**
Large teeth at the back of the mammalian mouth.

**Molt**
The shedding of the exoskeleton by an arthropod or the skin of a reptile as it grows; the seasonal loss of feathers in birds, or of fur or hair in mammals.

**Mucus**
A viscous, slimy fluid that is produced by, and protects, mucous membranes.

**Mutualism**
A relationship between unrelated organisms from which each benefits.

**Myoglobin**
A protein of vertebrate muscle fibers that binds to molecular oxygen.

**Natural selection**
Most widely accepted theory concerning the main mechanism of evolutionary change. The genetic composition of evolutionary lineage changes over time by a nonrandom transmission of genes from one parental generation to the next. Selection of gene combinations will favor those that are best suited to a particular environment.

**Neuron**
An elongated cell forming part of the nervous system through which electrical and chemical signals pass around the body. When neurons are collected in large numbers—for example, to form a brain—they process as well as transfer information.

**Nocturnal**
An organism that is active at night; the opposite of diurnal. Most bats and owls, and many invertebrates, are nocturnal.

**Notochord**
Flexible, longitudinal rod that acts as an internal skeleton in the embryos of all chordates and is retained in the adults of some.

**Nucleus**
The central, membrane-enclosed part of a cell, containing the chromosomes and acting as the cell's control center.

**Nutrient**
Any material taken in by a living organism that allows it to grow or replace lost or damaged tissue, and provides energy for metabolism.

**Omnivore**
An animal that feeds on both animals and plants.

**Opposable**
Capable of being placed opposite and against another digit. Humans, for example, have opposable thumbs.

**Ossicles**
The small bones in the middle ear of vertebrates. Also, the skin plates of many echinoderms.

**Ovary**
The organ in female animals in which eggs are produced. In most vertebrates there are two ovaries.

**Ovule**
The female gamete, or sex cell, of a seed plant. An ovule has a small opening called a micropyle through which pollen grains enter to fertilize the ovule. The fertilized ovule develops into a seed.

**Parasite**
An organism that feeds on another living organism, or host. The host may be damaged but is not killed by the parasite.

**Pathogen**
Disease-causing organism.

**Peristalsis**
Contractions of muscle that occur in the walls of hollow organs, such as parts of the digestive tract, that move the contents of the organ through the tube.

**Pheromone**
A chemical released by an animal, often to attract mates.

**Placenta**
The temporary organ that forms inside a female animal that nourishes the young.

**Plantigrade**
The gait of many mammals, including humans, in which the whole lower surface of the foot is on the ground.

**Plasma**
The fluid part of blood, excluding the blood cells. Plasma consists of water and many dissolved substances, including salts, proteins, fats, amino acids, hormones, vitamins, and excretory materials.

**Pollex**
Innermost digit on the forelimb of a vertebrate. In humans, for example, the thumb.

**Receptor**
A cell or group of cells that detects specific stimuli such as heat and pressure.

**Ribosome**
A particle within a cell that acts as the site of protein synthesis. Ribosomes "translate" messenger RNA (mRNA) into protein by using its chemically coded instructions to link amino acids in a specific order and thus make a strand of a particular protein.

**RNA**
Ribonucleic acid, an organic compound in living cells that is concerned with protein synthesis.

**Ruminant**
A hoofed herbivorous mammal, such as a deer or a goat, that chews cud. Ruminants have a multichamber stomach.

**Scent marking**
A behavior in which some animals leave strong-smelling secretions on the ground or vegetation to warn off rivals.

**Sensor**
A receptor cell or group of cells that reacts to a stimulus such as light or the presence of certain chemicals.

**Septum**
A dividing wall such as that between the different chambers of a heart.

**Sexual dimorphism**
Difference in appearance of males and females in a species—for example, difference in color or size.

**Speciation**
The development of a new type of species from an existing species. It occurs when different populations diverge so much from the parent populations that interbreeding can no longer take place between them.

**Sperm**
A male sex cell that can fuse with a female egg cell to form a new individual.

**Symbiosis**
A biological relationship between two species.

**Synapse**
The junction between two nerve cells or between a nerve cell and a muscle; the latter is also called a neuromuscular junction.

**Tendon**
Connective tissue that joins two muscles together or joins a muscle to bone.

**Testosterone**
Vertebrate steroid male sex hormone that is produced by the testes.

**Thermoregulation**
The general mechanism by which a life-form controls its body temperature. Mammals and birds (endotherms) have internal mechanisms for maintaining their body temperature at a level that is usually warmer than their environment.

**Thorax**
The body region of a vertebrate containing the lungs and heart and enclosed by the rib cage; the midbody section of an insect to which the legs and wings are attached.

**Toxin**
A poisonous substance produced by a plant or animal, which is often used as a means of defense. A toxin-producing animal secretes toxins from its own body.

**Trachea**
A tube in vertebrates that conducts air between the throat and bronchi; one of the tubes that forms a system through which air travels to the cells of the body in insects and other land-living vertebrates.

**Urea**
A waste product formed when proteins are broken down in the liver. Urea is excreted in the urine.

**Urine**
The watery fluid produced in the kidneys that carries ammonia, uric acid, urea, amino acids, and other waste products from the body through the urethra or cloaca after being stored in the bladder.

**Uterus**
Hollow, muscular organ in which an embryo develops after implantation in the endometrium, or lining.

**Vein**
A vessel that carries blood from the body to the heart. Veins almost always carry oxygen-poor blood, the exception being the pulmonary veins through which oxygenated blood from the lungs is pumped to the heart.

**Vertebrate**
An animal with a backbone. The five classes of vertebrates are amphibians, birds, fish, mammals, and reptiles.

**Vestigial organ**
Organ that has become reduced in size and structure over time because it is no longer required.

# Resources for further study

## Bibliography

Alberts, B., A. Johnson, J. Lewis, M. Raff, K. Roberts, and P. Walter. 2002. *Molecular Biology of the Cell.* Garland: New York.

Ankel-Simons, Friderun. 2007. *Primate Anatomy: An Introduction* (3rd ed.) Elsevier Academic: Boston, MA.

Arnold, Nick. 1999. *Horrible Science: Disgusting Digestion.* Scholastic Library: Danbury, CT.

Baggaley, A., and J. Hamilton. 2001. *Human Body: An Illustrated Guide to Every Part of the Human Body and How It Works.* DK: New York.

Ballard, C. 2005. *Lungs and Breathing.* KidHaven Press: Detroit, MI.

Bastian, G. 1997. *An Illustrated Review of the Skeletal and Muscular Systems.* Addison-Wesley: Boston, MA.

Beckingham, I. J. 2001. *ABC of Liver, Pancreas, and Gallbladder.* BMJ: Philadelphia, PA.

Bonner, W. Nigel. 1990. *The Natural History of Seals.* Facts on File: New York.

Callaghan, C. A., and B. M. Brenner. 2000. *The Kidney at a Glance.* Blackwell Science: Boston, MA.

Chivers, D. J., and P. Langer (eds.). 2005. *The Digestive System in Mammals: Food, Form, and Function.* Cambridge University Press: New York.

Eckert, R. 1997. *Animal Physiology.* Freeman: New York.

Etses, R. D. 1991. *The Behavior Guide to African Mammals.* University of California Press: Berkeley, CA.

Evans, P. J. H. 2001. *Marine Mammals: Biology and Conservation.* Plenum: New York.

Friedlander, Mark, and Terry M. Phillips. 1998. *The Immune System: Your Body's Disease-Fighting Army.* Lerner: Minneapolis, MN.

Futuyma, D. 1998. *Evolutionary Biology.* Sinauer: Sunderland, MA.

Geist, V. 1998. *Deer of the World: Their Evolution, Behavior, and Ecology.* Stackpole: Mechanicsburg, PA.

Goodall, Jane. 1996. *My Life with the Chimpanzees.* Aladdin Paperbacks: New York.

Gould, Stephen J. (ed.) 2001. *The Book of Life: An Illustrated History of the Evolution of Life on Earth.* Norton: New York.

Griffin, J. E., and S. R. Ojeda. 2004. *Textbook of Endocrine Physiology.* (5th ed.) Oxford University Press: Oxford, UK.

Hare, T., and M. Lambert. 1997. *The Encyclopedia of Mammals.* Marshall Cavendish: New York.

Harold, Franklin. 2001. *The Way of the Cell: Molecules, Organisms, and the Order of Life.* Oxford University Press: Oxford, UK.

Hickman, B. F. 2001. *Perception: The Amazing Brain.* Blackbirch: New York.

Kitchener, A. 1991. *The Natural History of the Wild Cats.* Natural History of Mammals Series. Cornell University Press: Ithaca, NY.

Lazaroff, M. 2004. *The Complete Idiot's Guide to Anatomy and Physiology.* Penguin: New York.

Macdonald, David W. 2006. *The Encyclopedia of Mammals.* Facts On File: New York.

Macdonald, David W., and C. Sillero-Zubiri (eds.). 2004. *The Biology and Conservation of Wild Canids.* Oxford University Press: Oxford, UK.

Marshall Graves, Jenny. 2004. *Sex, Genes, and Chromosomes.* Cambridge University Press: Cambridge, UK.

McGowan, Christopher. 1999. *A Practical Guide to Vertebrate Mechanics.* Cambridge University Press: Cambridge, UK.

Mead, James G., and Joy P. Gold. 2002. *Whales and Dolphins in Question: The Smithsonian Answer Book.* Smithsonian Books: Washington, DC.

Nowak, Ronald M. 2005. *Walker's Marsupials of the World*. Johns Hopkins University Press: Baltimore, MD.

Nowell, K., and P. Jackson (eds.). 1996. *Wild Cats*. IUCN: Gland, Switzerland.

Perrin, W. F., B. Würsig, and J. G. M. Thewissen (eds.). 2002. *Encyclopedia of Marine Mammals*. Academic: San Diego, CA.

Purves, W. K., G. H. Orians, D. Sadava, and H. C. Heller. 2003. *Life: The Science of Biology*. Freeman: New York.

Raven, Peter H., George B. Johnson, Susan R. Singer, and Jonathan B. Losos. 2004. *Biology*. McGraw-Hill Science: New York.

Restak, R. M. 2001. *The Secret Life of the Brain*. National Academy Press: Washington, DC.

Reynolds, John E., III, and S. A. Rommel (eds.). 1999. *Biology of Marine Mammals*. Smithsonian Institution Press: Washington, DC.

Seibel, M. J., *et al.* (eds.) 1999. *Dynamics of Bone and Cartilage Metabolism*. Academic: New York.

Siegal, I. S. 1998. *All about Bone: An Owner's Manual*. Demos Medical: New York.

Silverthorn, Dee. 1998. *Human Physiology: An Integrated Approach*. Prentice Hall: Upper Saddle River, NJ.

Snedden, R. 2008. *Cell Division and Genetics*. Heinemann Library: Chicago, IL.

Sompayrac, Lauren. 2008. *How the Immune System Works*. Blackwell: Malden, MA.

Sunquist, M., and F. Sunquist. 2002. *Wild Cats of the World*. University of Chicago Press: Chicago, IL.

Swindler, Danis Ray. 2002. *Primate Dentition: An Introduction to the Teeth of Non-Human Primates*. Cambridge University Press: Cambridge, UK.

Teaford, M. F., M. M. Smith, and M. W. J. Ferguson. 2000. *Development, Function, and Evolution of Teeth*. Cambridge University Press, Cambridge, UK.

Tortora, G. J., S. R. Grabowski, and B. Roesch. 2000. *Principles of Anatomy and Physiology*. (9th ed.) John Wiley: New York.

Unglaub Silverthorn, Dee. 2003. *Human Physiology*. Benjamin Cummings: San Francisco, CA.

Van der Graaf, K. 1997. *Schaum's Outline of Human Anatomy and Physiology*. McGraw-Hill: Columbus, OH.

Vaughan, Terry A. 1999. *Mammalogy*. Brooks/Cole: Belmont, CA.

Vogel, Steven. 2003. *Comparative Biomechanics: Life's Physical World*. Princeton University Press: Princeton, NJ.

# Internet resources

**American Museum of Natural History**
Resource that includes a virtual tour of the museum.
**http://www.amnh.org**

**Animal Diversity Web**
Information about the characteristics of animals.
**http://animaldiversity.ummz.umich.edu**

**Cells Alive**
Resource on cell biology microbiology, immunology, and microscopy.
**http://www.cellsalive.com**

**Comparative Mammalian Brain Collections**
Pictures of brains and brain slices from more than 100 species of mammals.
**http://www.brainmuseum.org**

**ENature**
Database of more than 5,500 species of animals and plants.
**http://www.enature.com**

**Evolution**
Information about all aspects of evolution.
**http://www.pbs.org/wgbh/evolution**

**Hall of Mammals**
Information and links to many mammal sites.
**www.ucmp.berkeley.edu/mammal/mammal.html**

**How Animals Work**
Animation showing how birds' lungs function.
**www.sci.sdsu.edu/multimedia/birdlungs**

**How Your Immune System Works**
Information on the human immune system.
**http://health.howstuffworks.com/immune-system.htm**

**Human Anatomy Online**
Resource showing anatomy of human body systems.
**http://www.innerbody.com**

**Immune system**
Information on the immune system and infectious diseases.
**www.niaid.nih.gov/final/immun/immun.htm**

**JGI Center for Primate Studies**
Information on the immune system of chimpanzees.
**www.discoverchimpanzees.org**

**Museum of Vertebrate Zoology, University of California**
Resource showing collections of the museum.
**http://mvz.berkeley.edu**

**National Geographic**
The Web site of the National Geographic Society.
**http://www.nationalgeographic.com**

**Natural History Museums**
Web links to natural history museums and collections around the world.
**http://www.lib.washington.edu/sla/natmus.html**

**Natural Perspective**
A collection of images of four of the kingdoms: protists, fungi, plants, and animals.
**http://perspective.com/nature**

**Neuroscience for Kids**
Information about the nervous system, with activities and experiments.
**http://faculty.washington.edu/chudler/neurok.html**

**Smithsonian National Museum of Natural History**
Online information about the natural history museum.
**http://www.mnh.si.edu**

**Tree of Life**
Over 1,350 Web pages on the diversity of life.
**http://tolweb.org**

**Vertebrate Zoology**
Web links to information about vertebrate animals.
**http://www.lions.odu.edu/~kkilburn/vzhome.htm**

**Virtual Canine Anatomy**
Information about dog anatomy.
**www.cvmbs.colostate.edu/vetneuro**

**World Wildlife Fund**
Information about endangered wildlife.
**http://www.worldwildlife.org**

# Index